LABORATORY TECHNIQUES IN BIOCHEMISTRY AND MOLECULAR BIOLOGY

Volume 1

Edited by

T. S. WORK – *N.I.M.R., Mill Hill*
E. WORK – *Imperial College, London*

NORTH-HOLLAND PUBLISHING COMPANY – AMSTERDAM • OXFORD
AMERICAN ELSEVIER PUBLISHING COMPANY, INC. – NEW YORK

Part I   A. H. Gordon

ELECTROPHORESIS OF PROTEINS
IN POLYACRYLAMIDE AND
STARCH GELS

Part II   L. Fischer

AN INTRODUCTION TO
GEL CHROMATOGRAPHY

Part III   J. Clausen

IMMUNOCHEMICAL TECHNIQUES
FOR THE IDENTIFICATION AND
ESTIMATION OF MACROMOLECULES

NORTH-HOLLAND PUBLISHING COMPANY – AMSTERDAM • OXFORD
AMERICAN ELSEVIER PUBLISHING COMPANY, INC. – NEW YORK

© *1969 North-Holland Publishing Company – Amsterdam*

No parts of this book may be reproduced in any form by print, photoprint, microfilm or any other means without written permission from the publishers

Library of Congress Catalog Card Number 68-54514
North-Holland ISBN 7204 4201
American Elsevier ISBN 0444 10036 9

Publishers:

NORTH-HOLLAND PUBLISHING COMPANY – AMSTERDAM
NORTH-HOLLAND PUBLISHING COMPANY, LTD. – OXFORD

Sole Distributors for the U.S.A. and Canada:

AMERICAN ELSEVIER PUBLISHING COMPANY, INC.
52 VANDERBILT AVENUE, NEW YORK, N.Y. 10017

1st edition:	1969
2nd printing:	1970
3rd printing:	1972
4th printing:	1974

Printed in The Netherlands

Editors' preface

Progress in research depends upon development of technique. No matter how important the cerebral element may be in the planning of experiments, a tentative hypothesis cannot be converted into an accepted fact unless there is adequate consciousness of the scope and limitation of existing techniques; moreover, the results may be meaningless or even positively misleading if the technical 'know how' is inadequate.

During the past ten or fifteen years, biochemical methods have become specialized and sophisticated to such a degree that it is now difficult for the beginner, whether undergraduate, graduate or specialist in another field, to grasp all the minor but important details which divide the successful from the unsuccessful experiment. In order to cope with this problem, we have initiated a new series of Laboratory Manuals on technique. Each manual is written by an expert and is designed as a laboratory handbook to be used at the bench.

It is hoped that use of these manuals will substantially reduce or perhaps even remove that period of frustration which so often precedes the successful transplant of a specialized technique into a new environment. In furtherance of this aim, we have asked authors to place special emphasis on application rather than on theory; nevertheless, each manual carries sufficient history and theory to give perspective. The publication of *library volumes* followed by *pocket paperbacks* is an innovation in scientific publishing which should assist in bringing these manuals into the laboratory as well as into the library. In undertaking the editing of such a diverse series, we have become painfully conscious of our own ignorance but have been encouraged by our board of advisers to whom we owe many valuable suggestions and, of course, by our authors who have co-operated so willingly and have so patiently tolerated our editoral intervention.

T. S. & E. Work

Editors

Contents of parts I–III

PART I

PART II

PART III

ELECTROPHORESIS OF PROTEINS IN POLYACRYLAMIDE AND STARCH GELS

A. H. Gordon

National Institute for Medical Research
Mill Hill

Contents

The following abbreviations are used:
EDTA – Ethylenediaminetetraacetic acid
SDS – Sodium dodecyl sulphate
Tris – Tris-(hydroxy-methyl)-amino-methane

CHAPTER 1

Applicability of starch and acrylamide zone electrophoresis

Introduction

The proliferation in the number of techniques which are claimed to be suitable for the separation of proteins makes the choice of the most appropriate method for any particular purpose a matter of very great difficulty. This is especially true if the mixture to be separated is not one which has already been subjected to intensive study. However, experience of those methods previously found to be suitable for mixtures of substances of a similar type, together with close attention to the relevant properties of the substances actually present, will generally indicate which of the multifarious methods should be tried.

When attempting to make a choice of this kind, practical questions, such as the complexity of the required apparatus, the degree of 'know how' needed for its successful operation, and the scale on which the separation is to be carried out, all have to be taken into account. As a basis for such choice an indication of the range of problems for which electrophoresis in starch and acrylamide gels may offer the best chance of success will now be given.

Analytical applications

The most convenient methods of analysis are those in which all the apparatus and materials are readily available and can be used without any kind of pretreatment. Electrophoresis in gels such as those of starch and acrylamide does not come in this category. This is because,

 Subject index p. 145

unlike for instance the method of electrophoresis on filter paper, the media in which the electrophoresis is to be conducted must be prepared before the analysis can be started. However, a single gel once prepared can be used for the analysis in parallel of a number of samples. The analysis itself, up to the stage in which the pattern of separated and then stained bands becomes visible, can be carried out in less than three hours. Both with starch and acrylamide gels extremely small amounts of proteins (10–50 μg) can be separated and clearly visualised. In summary, these methods are reasonably rapid and can be carried out on microquantities of material. The apparatus required is of a medium degree of complexity. Previous experience of such methods is not usually necessary although optimum results can be achieved with less delay if experience is available. Fortunately, at least with proteins, interactions, such as adsorption in the gel, are rare so that mixtures of all kinds of proteins including histones and nucleoproteins can be successfully separated.

Preparative applications

When recovery of separated material from the gel is required the scale of working becomes all important. If samples of no more than a few μg of purified material are required the simplest apparatus will suffice. Thus, for instance, Disc electrophoresis (cf. pp. 23, 46 and 50) which can handle up to 0.1–0.2 mg of protein per tube can be used preparatively by slicing the gel cylinder longitudinally cf. fig. 3.5 and using one half after staining to aid location in the other. For this purpose the apparatus is the same short glass tube, jar and electrode holder as is used when the aim is purely an analytical one. Although other methods in which larger gels are used can also be similarly adapted recovery of more than very small amounts of separated material from the gel is a major difficulty and sets a limit to the usefulness of simple electrophoretic apparatus. For work on a larger scale the position is different. Many problems, some of which will be discussed below, prevent direct scaling up of the short vertical tubes which are used for 'disc electrophoresis'. Even when a separation has been successfully achieved in larger slabs or cylinders of gel the final separation of each protein from the gel is often difficult. Furthermore especially with starch gel it is difficult to free separated proteins from traces of soluble starch. These considerations strongly indicate that electrophoresis in starch or acrylamide gel is not as yet a suitable method for the first stage of fractionation of a mixture of proteins. On the other hand for the separation of a mixture which is itself the product of other methods of fractionation one of these methods of electrophoresis, used preparatively, may well be of great value. Unfortunately, however, relatively complex apparatus is needed for such purposes. A realistic appraisal of the difficulties involved should be made before the construction of any one of these types is decided upon. As indicated by the numerous apparatuses which have been described optimum conditions for large scale preparative electrophoresis in gel have yet to be found. Nevertheless useful separation can be achieved.

Properties of starch and acrylamide gels

The refined separations of mixtures of proteins obtainable by electrophoresis in starch and acrylamide gels has led to the very wide use of both of these materials now recorded in an inconveniently wide range of journals. The most useful reviews of this literature include Whipple (1964), Morris and Morris (1964) and Porter (1966). Since 1955 when starch gel was introduced by Smithies a considerable body of information has accumulated about the properties of both types of gel. In particular the size of the pores in gels of different composition and concentration has been studied in the hope of relating this parameter to the size of molecules able to pass through each gel.

The ability of molecules to pass through a sieve evidently depends on the size and shape of the holes in the gel, the size and shape of the molecules being sieved and interactions such as adsorption or ion exchange which may occur between the molecules and the matrix of the gel. For any detailed analysis of the sieving process which occurs in starch and acrylamide gels to be possible a knowledge of the range of

Subject index p. 145

sizes of the holes present in gels of different concentration and composition is necessary. Unfortunately no information regarding absolute pore size in starch gel is yet available (see p. 98 for a relative estimate). On the other hand, in respect to acrylamide gels a considerable body of information has already been accumulated. This data will be considered below, but before making such an attempt, a description of the structure of both starch and acrylamide gels seems necessary. Such gels consist of long chain molecules with, in the case of acrylamide, a varying proportion of cross linkages resulting from the addition of a proportion of bisacrylamide before polymerisation. Both acrylamide and bisacrylamide must be handled cautiously because of their toxic properties (Fullerton and Barnes 1966). Fortunately after polymerisation the gel is harmless.

Starch gel as used in electrophoresis is a gel rather than a viscous liquid because the carbohydrate chains branch and intertwine sufficiently to form a semi-rigid solid of the gel type. Although gels and especially those of starch and acrylamide have been almost universally used as media in which molecular sieving can take place, it is important to note that molecules are retarded according to their molecular size and shape during passage through concentrated solutions where the solute consists of any long chain molecule. Thus as Laurent and Persson (1963) have shown with concentrated solutions of hyaluronic acid, molecular sieving effects can be observed in the ultracentrifuge. These findings of molecular sieving effects in viscous solutions make especially important a consideration of the role of cross links in acrylamide gels. A most important point is whether an alteration in the proportion of cross links, as is easily achieved with acrylamide by varying the proportion of bisacrylamide, can be expected to give gels of particularly useful properties as compared to starch gels in which cross links in the strict sense are absent. The work of Fawcett and Morris (1966) on the effects of varying concentration of bisacrylamide in gels from 6.5–20% total acrylamide concentration provides considerable data on this question. On the basis of chromatographic experiments with granulated gels made with an increasing percentage of bisacrylamide the following changes can be distinguished.

Addition of as little as 2 %* of bisacrylamide allows gel formation to occur. In such gels the polyacrylamide molecules exist as a system of random strands each consisting of some 2–5 parallel chains. With increasing proportions of bisacrylamide the extra cross links lead to an increase in chain thickness up to a value of approximately 60 Å. Chains of this diameter are obtained by the use of 15% of bisacrylamide. Pore diameter in all these gels is greatly dependent on total acrylamide concentration. Surprisingly, however, at any given total acrylamide concentration the pore diameter shows a minimum at approximately 5% of bisacrylamide. Thus a gel of greater total acrylamide concentration may have larger pores than one of lower concentration if the bisacrylamide proportion is either above or below the optimum value of 5%. By a combination of the theory of Ogston (1958), Laurent and Killander (1964) and on the basis of numerous chromatographic experiments using a series of test proteins of known molecular size Fawcett and Morris (1966) have been able to provide a set of values for the average pore size of acrylamide gels from 6.5–20% total acrylamide with six different proportions of bisacrylamide. As shown in fig. 1.1 these contain pores of average diameters from 0.6–4 mμ. The usefulness of this range of pore sizes is immediately apparent as the molecular diameters of protein likely to require separation range from 1.6–8 mμ.

Comparison of the sharpness of the bands formed by proteins in starch and acrylamide gels shows clearly that the bands formed by the larger proteins in certain acrylamide gels are considerably sharper than those of the same proteins in starch gel. In the absence of adequate information regarding the pore size in starch gels any explanation of this difference in behaviour must be tentative. Possibly the explanation for the sharp separations of many sizes of protein molecule in acrylamide gels is the existence of a very wide range of pore sizes in any given acrylamide gel. However this may be, the question raised above as to whether the presence of cross linkages in acrylamide gels permits

---

* As a percentage of the total acrylamide present. % Bisacrylamide is used in this sense throughout.

Subject index p. 145

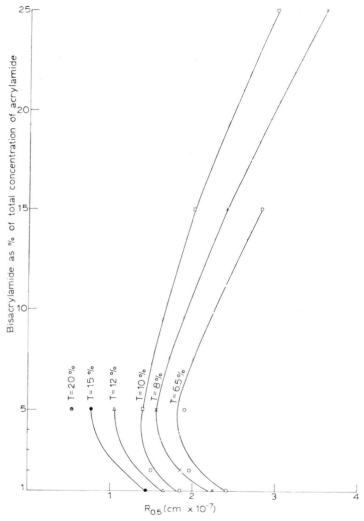

Fig. 1.1. Relationship of $R_{0.5}$ to the percentage of bisacrylamide in gels of total acrylamide concentration 6.5–20%. $R_{0.5}$: radius of molecules for which 50% of the total gel volume is available. T: total concentration of acrylamide plus bisacrylamide. The information was obtained by chromatography using the various gels in granular form. (From Fawcett and Morris 1966.)

the formation of gels of more useful properties than can be obtained with starch gels may be answered positively. A much wider range of pore sizes is available in acrylamide gels partly because the content of bisacrylamide can be varied very widely.

As normally prepared acrylamide gels are entirely without charged groups. Starch gel on the other hand contains a small proportion of carboxyl groups which at neutral pH values each carry a negative charge. As a consequence of this property a slow rate of electro-endosmosis toward the cathode occurs in these gels. The excellent separation of the α-globulins which has been claimed by Pert and Pinteric (1964) to be better than that obtainable in acrylamide may also be connected with the presence of charged groups.

This claim is mentioned here to emphasize that pore size is not the only parameter of a gel which should be taken into account when considering its suitability for separation of a particular mixture. Acrylamide gels have the great advantage of providing an uncharged matrix in which separations based on molecular sieving and mobility differences can be conducted. However, more complicated gels of synthetic or natural origin which may become available in the future may make possible separations which are based in part on additional parameters. The importance of the effects of charged groups on the separation of haemoglobins during electrophoresis in agar gel is an example which shows that effects of this kind are sometimes of great practical value (Gratzer and Beaven 1961).

Movement of fluid through gels

The passage of fluids through the pores of a gel may be due to hydrostatic pressure, electroendosmosis or a combination of both these effects. In relation to electrophoretic separation of proteins in a gel a knowledge of the rate of fluid flow through the gel may be of importance in order to correct for this factor when measuring mobilities of the substances being investigated. Such measurements are simple enough to make by observation of the movement of a suitable unchanged substance, such as dextran or a dinitrophenylated amino acid for the pH range above pH 5. Fortunately, however, with acrylamide gels electroendosmosis does not occur or is so slow compared with the mobility of proteins that it can be ignored. In starch gel, the rate of electroendosmosis is appreciable and γ-globulins move towards the cathode at pH 8.6, despite the fact that at this pH the γ-globulin carries a negative charge. In addition the pore size of the gel is of some importance. In gels of large pore size electroendosmotic flow may be stopped or reversed by application of a contrary hydrostatic pressure. In gels with smaller pores electroendosmotic flow rates are somewhat lower but as mentioned by McDougall and Synge (1966) the pressure required to oppose this flow becomes impracticably large. With synthetic gels such as acrylamide, the possibility exists of introducing a proportion of chemical groupings differing from those of the original monomer. For instance, the introduction of acrylic acid causes an electroendosmotic flow towards the cathode easily sufficient to balance the mobility of haemoglobin (Raymond and Nakamichi 1962).

The movement of fluid through a porous medium can lead to transport of uncharged molecules through the medium and thus separations based on molecular sieving effects. This process under the name of electrokinetic ultrafiltration has been investigated by Synge and Tiselius (1950). Under such circumstances in addition to sieving and as a result of the charged groups in the gel some degree of adsorption is sure to take place. However, as Synge himself has pointed out optimum electrophoretic separation can be expected in gels which do not appreciably absorb the substances undergoing separation. Thus the negligible rate of electroendosmosis characteristic of acrylamide gels is a most useful property and attempts at gel modification such as that mentioned above must be approached with considerable caution.

Adsorption effects – band shapes

As already mentioned gels prepared from pure acrylamide and bisacrylamide monomers do not themselves contain ionised groups. Thus retardation due to ion exchange effects or to adsorption processes involving ionic bonds are not to be expected with these gels. On the other hand adsorption of molecules containing aromatic rings has been demonstrated by Fawcett and Morris (1966) who carried out chromatographic experiments with dinitrophenylethanolamine. Apart from effects of this kind which may be important for a protein rich in aromatic amino acids little or no protein gel interaction except of course for the retardations due to molecular sieving seems to take place. This fact explains the highly symmetrical band shapes obtained with most proteins after electrophoresis through acrylamide gels. The unsymmetrical shape of the albumin band in starch gel provides an interesting contrast. A useful consequence of the symmetrical band shapes always obtained with homogeneous proteins is that the occurrence of an unsymmetrical band at once suggests the presence of a heterogenous population of protein molecules. If the pore size of the gel is large compared with the size of the molecules undergoing separation the heterogeneity may be in respect to charge only. If, however, the pore size is small enough for retardation by sieving to be appreciable unsymmetrical or even multiple bands may result either from a combination of charge and molecular size differences or simply from the existence of molecular size differences within a population of molecules of uniform charge.

One further type of gel protein interaction must be mentioned although it has not yet been systematically studied. This concerns the observed extremely low rates of diffusion of some proteins in acrylamide gels through which the same protein molecules have been transported relatively rapidly by electrophoresis. A possible explanation for this phenomenon may be that the bundles of polyacrylamide molecules of which the gel consists are sufficiently flexible for some bending to take place induced by protein molecules moving in an electric field. If this is true it follows that when diffusion alone is occurring the pore size through which a given molecule can pass is smaller than under the conditions of electrophoresis. A practical consequence of the observed slow diffusion of proteins in both starch and acrylamide gels is that the efficiency of elution from the gel is greatly improved by electrophoretic or other procedures (cf. p. 129).

Subject index p. 145

Mechanical properties

For successful separation in gels the properties of the gel itself, e.g. pore size, and chemical nature of the matrix material are of primary importance. Since, however, the slab or cylinder of gel must be supported by a suitable solid, non-conducting container or alternatively be in contact with a non-conducting liquid the mechanical properties of the gel are also of some importance.

One of the problems in the design of suitable apparatus for electrophoresis in gels is the possible presence of a film of electrolyte between the surface of the gel and the supporting surface on which it rests. Such films lead to poor separations and must if possible be avoided. Their existence is less likely if the gel is allowed to set in the same holder in which it is to remain while in use. The existence of such films can easily be demonstrated with dyes which do not adhere appreciably to glass. This phenomenon has been observed most clearly with buffers of low ionic strength in agar gels. Its importance for starch gel is, however, suggested by the practice which is common with these gels of slicing to remove the surface layer before staining. Fortunately with acrylamide gels except in rather exceptional circumstances (cf. p. 17) the adherence to glass is such that difficulties from behaviour of this kind are not met with. In fact the stickiness of acrylamide gel is a valuable property of which great advantage can be taken in properly designed apparatus. When acrylamide gels are set in a separate mould and transferred before use the existence of a film of electrolyte at the gel surface is probable. Fortunately apparatus (Lorber 1964) is available in which slabs of such gel can be squeezed before use so that very close contact with the container can be achieved.

For convenient handling, gels should be firm enough not to fracture or tear even when present as thin sheets. Starch and acrylamide gels both have these properties to a considerable degree. Because starch gel is the weaker, at least in thin sheets as obtained by slicing (cf. p. 120) it is best handled when in contact with a sheet of plastic such as parafilm. This precaution is not necessary with acrylamide gels because their rubber-like texture makes them very easy to handle both in the form of sheets and as cylinders. Unfortunately this elasticity has the disadvantage that cutting either with a taught wire or a blade is difficult. For this reason the method of sample insertion in which a piece of stiff filter paper, wetted with a small volume of the solution to be analysed, is pushed into a slot in the gel is difficult to carry out and is not recommended for optimum results. The degree of stickiness and in the more concentrated acrylamide gels, the rigidity and resistance to fracture, are determined to a considerable extent by the proportion of bisacrylamide present. Because this can be varied at will, gels with specified mechanical properties can easily be prepared. The ability to obtain gels with appropriate mechanical properties is of particular importance in apparatuses designed for preparative electrophoresis. An acrylamide gel which has been allowed to form in contact with a glass surface will adhere to that surface to a degree dependent both on the cleanliness of the glass surface and the concentration and composition of the acrylamide. This adherence will gradually decrease with time until at the end of an experiment it may be possible to slide the gel over the glass. For this reason while acrylamide gels can be credited with better adherence to glass than starch gel (which itself adheres better than does agar) this adherence is easily disrupted and in any experiment where avoidance of detachment of the gel from its container is of importance the conditions leading to changes in gel shape and total volume must be controlled. Such changes can be expected if conditions are such that the gel can act in the manner of an osmometer. Because water diffuses from gel into a region of higher osmolarity faster than for instance sucrose can diffuse in the opposite direction the effect of a solution of high osmolarity in contact with a gel is to cause contraction. With acrylamide gels such contractions are often fully reversible but if the gel has been partially detached from the walls of its containing apparatus during the stage of sample insertion (cf. p. 83) seriously irregular patterns may result. Irreversible swelling of acrylamide gels may sometimes occur. Although further study is needed before the conditions which lead to reversible and irreversible swelling of these gels can be fully defined, it is already clear that very concentrated gels and gels set in the presence of urea are subject to irreversible swelling. Such effects may cause difficulty in some types of preparative apparatus.

Subject index p. 145

Transparency

Acrylamide gels except for those where the proportion of bisacrylamide and the total concentration leads to strands of maximum (60 Å) or nearly maximum diameter are almost water clear. Starch gels are opalescent unless prepared in the presence of concentrated urea or after treatment with glycerol.

Gels suitable for separation on the basis of charge difference alone

Zone electrophoretic separations on the basis of charge differences can be conducted in any media capable of stabilising against convection. Because most mixtures of proteins contain molecules of quite different sizes it is rare for an electrophoretic separation in an acrylamide gel to take place purely as a result of charge differences between the molecular species present. However, examples of such separations have been investigated. Probably best known are the excellent separations of γ-globulin light chains, all with molecular weights just over 20,000 which have been achieved in acrylamide gels of 4% concentration. By electrophoresis in such gels both at pH 8 and at pH 4 regular patterns of equally spaced bands have been obtained. That these have separated on the basis of charge rather than by sieving has been clearly demonstrated (Feinstein 1966). Thus treatment of an individual band with iodoacetate which reacts only with the single SH group present and thus adds a single charge to each light chain molecule increases the mobility of the band thus treated just sufficiently for it to be the same as that of the next fastest band. Since these separations are the result of mobility rather than molecular size differences it is not surprising that similar results have been obtained in other gels. In fact, separations of light chains of γ-globulin have been reported both in agar gel (Feinstein 1966) and in starch gel containing 8 M urea. In the latter system at least ten bands have been demonstrated (Cohen and Porter 1964). As is mentioned on p. 27 the presence of concentrated urea is not required for the formation of multiple bands in acrylamide gel. On the other hand in starch gel multiple band formation from γ-globulin light chains has not been reported except in the presence of concentrated urea. An explanation for this requirement of urea in starch gel would be of interest. Possibly, unless urea is present, adsorption in this gel prevents the formation of separate bands. The restricted rates of diffusion shown in large pore gels by molecules much smaller than the average size of the pore in these gels may also be relevant. The importance of this factor for chromatography in Sephadex G 200 has been shown by Ackers (1964). Low rates of diffusion in acrylamide gels may perhaps aid separation of some classes of proteins if some pores in these gels are able to distort sufficiently to permit passage of oversize molecules when these are subject to electrophoretic transport. In this regard it may be noted that the presence of concentrated urea renders starch gel much more flexible. In concentrated solutions of urea the rates of diffusion of proteins are considerably reduced (Craig et al. 1965).

However, this effect alone cannot be expected to lead to the production of sharper bands because as a result of the increased viscosity of the medium, a longer time or a higher voltage gradient is required to achieve the same degree of separation.

Evidently some further experiments are necessary to explain the different behaviour of γ-globulin light chains when subjected to electrophoresis in starch and acrylamide gels. For most other proteins, differences of this kind have not been reported so that either gel may be used with some confidence that at least the smaller proteins will separate mainly on the basis of their charge differences. In low concentration acrylamide gels the pore sizes can reach 3–4 mμ so that the separation of the larger proteins will still be mainly the result of their charge differences.

Buffers suitable for electrophoresis in gels

For the successful conduct of electrophoretic separations of the zone type in which the individual constituents move further and further apart from one another the presence throughout the system of charged molecules other than those undergoing separation is essential. Because of the importance of a uniform pH, at least in the part of the apparatus in which the separations occur, a suitable buffer consisting either of a metallic salt of a weak acid or a weak acid partially neutralised with a base is employed. If a sufficient concentration of an appropriate buffer is present the characteristics of the system should be as follows.

The same buffer in the gel and in the electrode vessels

(1) The pH in the region of the gel in which separation occurs should be such that the maximum difference of mobility exists between the different molecular species undergoing separation. See fig. 1.2 for the mobilities found during free electrophoresis of certain plasma proteins at different values of pH. It is well known that the electrophoretic mobility of proteins varies with change of pH primarily as a result

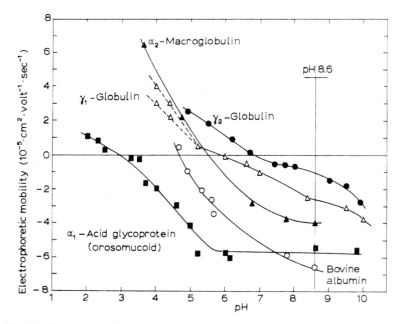

Fig. 1.2. Electrophoretic mobility curves of purified human serum proteins and of bovine serum albumin. (Phelps and Putnam 1960.)

of the ionisation of COOH to COO$^-$ and NH$_2$ to NH$_3^+$. Data for the net charge of a given protein at any pH can be obtained by titration. However, the relationship between the charge thus determined and the charge found to be effective during electrophoresis is complex. Electrophoresis charge is considerably smaller than titration charge for ovalbumin at values of pH suitable for electrophoresis as shown in fig. 1.3.

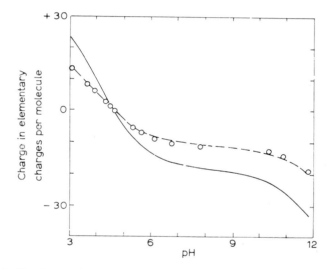

Fig. 1.3. The charge of ovalbumin as a function of pH as determined from electrophoretic mobilities. The charge is compared with the charge due to acid–base equilibria as determined from the titration curve. Part of the discrepancy can be explained by the fact that charges due to acidic and basic groups on the molecule do not constitute the total charge on the protein ion. The ionic strength in these experiments was 0.10. Solid line: titration charge; broken line: electrophoresis charge. (Data of Longsworth (1941). The figure is taken from Overbeek (1950).)

(2) The ionic strength and thus the conductivity of the buffer must be as low as possible because at low conductivity higher mobilities can be achieved with minimum production of heat. The relationship of conductivity to potential gradient is shown in fig. 1.4. As indicated,

for any given heat output the relationship of the conductivity to potential gradient is curvilinear. If in a particular apparatus no more than a given rate of heat evolution can be allowed, a less than proportional decrease in potential gradient need be introduced when a more concentrated buffer is used. Thus the disadvantage in terms of evolution of heat involved in working with more concentrated buffers is somewhat compensated for by the properties of buffers of higher conductivity.

Although buffers of low conductivity have advantages due to the high potential gradients which can be employed and thus the rapidity of the separations which can be achieved, the degree to which the various buffers can be diluted is strictly limited. This is because on dilution of the buffer in which proteins are dissolved the probability of molecular association increases. In sufficiently dilute buffer, adsorption

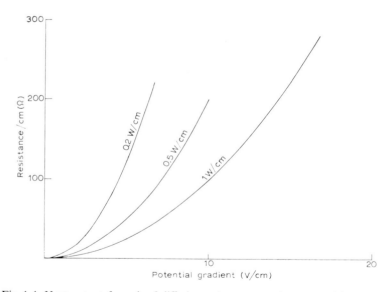

Fig. 1.4. Heat output for gels of differing resistance at various potential gradients. Each line gives the heat which will be evolved in watts per cm heigh of gell, based on the applied potential gradient and the resistance of the gel, calculated from $H = RC^2$, where R = resistance/cm (Ω); C = current (A); and H = heat (W).

effects, although minimal for the two gels at present under consideration are a possibility.

(3) The buffer should be such that the possibility of interactions between proteins is minimised. As already mentioned this is less likely in stronger buffers. In this respect the presence of a low concentration of substances with specific effects may be important. An example is the presence of EDTA in the borate Tris buffer of Aronsson and Grönwall (1957). The very considerable effects of different buffer solutions on the pattern obtained with serum in a standard acrylamide gel has been demonstrated by Ferris et al. (1964). Although the properties of a number of buffer systems have been examined no general rules in relation to the effect of the various ions on the mobilities of protein have so far emerged.

(4) The buffer should be such that interaction with the proteins undergoing separation does not lead to the formation of more than a single band from each protein. That such an interaction can lead to this result has been proved in at least one case. Thus as shown by Cann (1966) a 5% solution of bovine serum albumin when subjected to electrophoresis on cellulose acetate in 0.4 M H_3BO_3, 0.0081 M NaH_2PO_4, 0.012 M Na_2HPO_4 at pH 6.15 forms two bands. Each of these, if eluted and re-run under identical conditions, itself forms two bands. Although this behaviour is believed to be a result of interaction between molecules of albumin and borate ions or H_3BO_4 molecules the effect is not understood so that predictions concerning the likelihood of similar interactions in other systems cannot be made.

Different buffers in the gel and in the electrode chambers

Under this heading will be considered systems in which there are changes in buffer concentration along the length of the gel as well as those in which different buffer ions move as fronts through the gel.

As employed by Davis (1964) and Ornstein (1964) the contents of each tube consisted of three layers of acrylamide gel with different buffers present at the various levels. The system thus constituted was named by its originators 'disc electrophoresis', because of the very narrow bands or discs of the separated proteins. Since equally sharp zones of protein are obtainable more simply (cf. p. 50) without the use of the rather complex system of buffers employed by Davis and Ornstein, in the present book the words 'disc electrophoresis' will be used to describe all those systems in which the separations take place in narrow vertical tubes. A rather simple way by which a layer of protein solution which has just been added to an electrophoresis column can be narrowed has been known for some time. Thus the advantages of applying the mixture to be separated in dilute buffer and/or following the sample with a layer of water or diluted buffer were thoroughly studied by Porath (1956) in relation to electrophoresis in columns packed with cellulose powder. By such means very useful band sharpening was obtained as a result of the higher potential gradient produced in the region of the column occupied by the sample. That this effect is equally applicable as a means of band sharpening in acrylamide gels has been shown more recently by Hjerten et al. (1965). These authors obtained at least as many stained bands from human serum electrophoresed in 0.37 M Tris glycine at pH 9.5 as were obtained from the same serum by a discontinuous buffer system of Ornstein (1964) and Davis (1964). In the single buffer system the sample was not dialysed but was diluted with water to 29% of its original concentration.

Although a considerable degree of band sharpening (concentration) of the sample can be achieved in this very simple way the possibility of band sharpening by means of a buffer front consisting of ions of a different mobility has also been exploited. The system introduced by Poulik (1957) in which borate (a slower ion) follows citrate (faster) leading to a considerable increase in potential gradient has been found to give sharp bands with the plasma proteins. The behaviour of proteins in systems of this kind is primarily based on the Kohlrausch regulating function (see below). Because this effect has been fully exploited by Ornstein and Davis in order to provide starting zones of almost ideal sharpness some consideration of the mechanisms involved will now be given. Before this is done, however, certain characteristics of the Ornstein–Davis system need to be distinguished from the discontinuous buffer system of Poulik. In the latter system band sharpening occurs after all the constituents of the protein mixture have left the origin, i.e. after some degree of separation has already taken place. Only a single gel of uniform pore size throughout is used. Thus for good results to be obtained the sample must be applied as a concentrated solution. The Ornstein–Davis system employs gels of two porosities, these are set in the tube with the large pore or spacer gel on top of the small pore gel. The sample is introduced in a third gel again of the large pore variety which is placed on top of the spacer gel. Because of the presence of different buffers in the small and large pore gels the sample is caused to concentrate sharply at the gel interface. Only after this process is complete does separation of the constituents begin as they migrate through the small pore gel. The greatest advantage of this system is that it permits the concentration of the sample from a relatively large volume. This is done at the expense of relatively complex system of gels and buffers which inevitably require considerable time to prepare and set in the tubes. As mentioned above the behaviour of slower and faster ions in separate zones is determined by the so called Kohlrausch regulating function. As originally described (Kohlrausch 1897) these ions were layered over one another in a vertical tube. If such a system is present in a gel and if the current is passed so that both ions move downwards a sharp boundary will be maintained between the so called 'leading' and 'trailing' ions. In addition an increased voltage gradient will come into existence where the faster ion has been replaced by the slower. Under these circumstances a protein with a mobility intermediate between those of the leading and trailing ions, if present in the upper part of the system will migrate rapidly downwards and form a concentrated disc at the upper surface of the small pore gel. Subsequently the proteins enter and separate from one another in the small pore gel which is maintained at a somewhat higher pH. Details of the buffers used for separation of plasma proteins in this way are given in table 2.2. Also given in table 2.2 are the details of the simpler system of Hjerten et al. (1965) using a single gel and a single buffer with which an equal degree of resolution can be obtained assuming only that the sample is available as a concentrated solution.

Subject index p. 145

Exchange of buffer after gel has been set

The properties of acrylamide gels are such that the buffer originally in the gel may be allowed to exchange with another by simple diffusion or by electrophoresis without any deterioration of physical properties. In these ways also a volatile buffer can be introduced. At the same time the persulphate and other ions required for polymerisation and traces of UV-adsorbing material always present in the gel after setting can be almost completely removed. Approximately 5 days are required for complete exchange of buffer in a gel 1.0 cm thick. This may be reduced to a few hours by electrophoretic exchange.

Gels containing solubilisers

Urea

The use of starch and acrylamide gels containing substances capable of solubilising certain classes of proteins has permitted a number of separations not yet achieved by any other method. In each case the mixture to be separated has been dissolved in presence of the appropriate solubiliser and because the same substance has been present in the gel electrophoresis has been carried through successfully without loss by precipitation. As may be seen in tables 2.1 and 5.2 urea at concentration from 3–12 M has been used in this way to render soluble certain classes of proteins. Since H bonds no longer exist in solutions containing urea at high concentration, protein complexes or aggregates, the structure of which is maintained solely by bonds of this kind, are readily disassociated in concentrated urea. Behaviour of this kind is shown by α-crystallin (Bloemendal et al. 1962). In such systems removal of urea may be expected to lead to reaggregation. Thus the presence of urea in the gel in which electrophoresis is conducted is essential. The tertiary structure of some other protein molecules of which γ-globulin is an example, is maintained not only by H bonds but also by s–s linkages. When dissolved in concentrated urea these molecules retain sufficient of their structure to prevent separation by electrophoresis of their constituent sub-units. However, after addition of reducing agents such as mercaptoethanol followed by an alkylating agent (iodoacetamide or iodoacetic acid) to prevent reformation of interchain s–s bridges electrophoretic separation of the sub-units is possible. A particularly valuable new reducing agent is now available in the form of dithiothreitol. This substance is odourless, has little tendency to autoxidation, is freely soluble in water and will maintain monothiols in the reduced state as well as reducing disulphides quantitatively (Cleland 1964). Separations were first achieved in starch gels containing 8 M urea (Cohen and Porter 1964). However, when carried out in acrylamide gels in absence of urea equally good resolution at least of the light chains can be obtained (Small et al. 1965). Evidently once the s–s bridges have been broken these sub-units do not reaggregate due to the reformation of interchain H bonds in absence of urea.

Sodium dodecyl sulphate

Solubilisation of certain proteins and protein aggregates by addition of sodium dodecyl sulphate (SDS) is brought about because the treated protein is thus rendered more hydrophylic. Fortunately in such cases although no reduction in size of the protein has occurred the molecules or aggregates thus formed may still be successfully separated in acrylamide gels. Doubtless this is possible because gels are available with average pore size of sufficient magnitude to accommodate the rather large molecules thus formed. Preliminary treatment with 0.1 % SDS and 0.5 M urea together with reduction by mercaptoethanol or preferably dithiothreitol have also been successfully used to obtain the heavy and light chains from γ-globulin (Schapiro et al. 1966). A similar system has been used for solubilisation of virus proteins in poliovirus infected Hela cells by Summers et al. (1965). The cell cytoplasm was acidified with 0.1 vol. glacial acetic acid and then made 0.5 M with urea and 1 % with SDS. After reduction with mercaptoethanol and dialysis against 0.01 M sodium phosphate buffer at pH 7.1 containing 0.1 % SDS, 0.5 M urea and 0.1 % mercaptoethanol the samples were subjected to electrophoresis in gels containing the same concentrations of SDS and urea. Presumably to assist band sharpening at the gel surface the concentration of the buffer in the gel was higher (0.1 M) than in the sample solutions.

Phenol and acetic acid

When proteins are insoluble in a concentrated aqueous solution of urea, electrophoresis may be possible in solvent systems of a different type. Such a system, with phenol, acetic acid and water (2:1:1) in an acrylamide gel has been used by Work (1964) to separate the proteins of ribosome sub-units. The gel was prepared from 6% acrylamide as described by Hermans et al. 1960. After setting the gel was soaked in the phenol:acetic acid:water solution (which was replaced three times) for 24 hr. The protein and/or the nucleoprotein solutions were dissolved in the same solvent and applied at the origin soaked into pieces of filter paper. The slots were then sealed with a paste consisting of homogenised gel and the whole surface of the gel was covered with a thin sheet of glass. The conditions under which electrophoresis was carried out were the same as used by Hermans et al. except that an upper cooling plate was not employed. After the electrophoresis as many as 16 bands were revealed by staining with amido black dissolved in methanol:water:acetic acid (8:12:1) and destaining in 5% acetic acid. A preliminary wash in acetone–water (6:4) for 10 min. before staining gave the best results.

Evolution of heat and permissible thickness of gels

The mobility of ions is inversely proportional to the viscosity of the medium in which they are moving. It follows that because viscosity is temperature dependent mobility is also similarly affected. An approximate figure of 2.4% increase in mobility per degree rise in temperature is given by Morris and Morris (1964). Since in practice in zone electrophoresis experiments, increases in temperature of 10 °C or more may occur unless special precautions are taken to cool the gel, it follows that large changes in mobility are to be expected. In these circumstances seriously distorted bands will occur as a result of the temperature difference existing between the inner and outer layers of the gel. The use of gels not more than 1 cm thick which are well cooled by the circulation of a refrigerant through channels in the gel retaining plates (figs. 1.5, 1.6 and 1.7) is recommended. For analytical purposes still thinner gels are desirable because, if they are efficiently cooled, higher voltage gradients can be employed. With starch gel cooling by liquid passing through channels in the plates has not often been used. Despite lack of efficient cooling and because interface effects are liable to occur with this gel, slabs as thick as 0.6 cm from which the outer surfaces can be removed by slicing have usually been used. It is of interest, however, that Bloemendal (1963, p. 63)

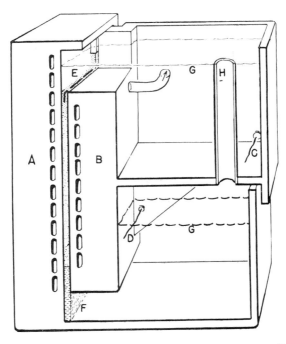

Fig. 1.5. Vertical plate apparatus of Raymond (1964). A: outer cooling plate; B: inner cooling plate; C: upper electrode; D: lower electrode; E: slots for samples; F: sponge strips supporting gel slab; G: levels of buffer in electrode compartments; H: buffer overflow tube.

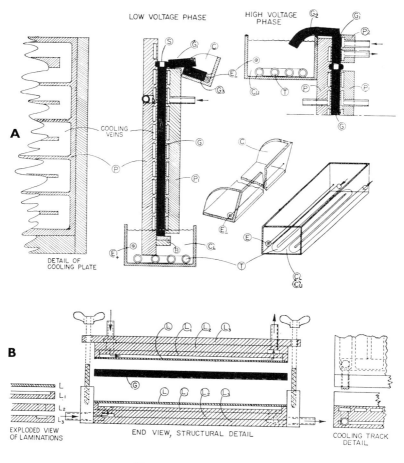

LOW VOLTAGE PHASE

HIGH VOLTAGE PHASE

A

COOLING VEINS

DETAIL OF COOLING PLATE

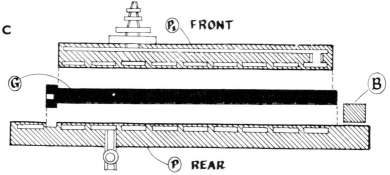

B

EXPLODED VIEW OF LAMINATIONS

END VIEW, STRUCTURAL DETAIL

COOLING TRACK DETAIL

C

FRONT

REAR

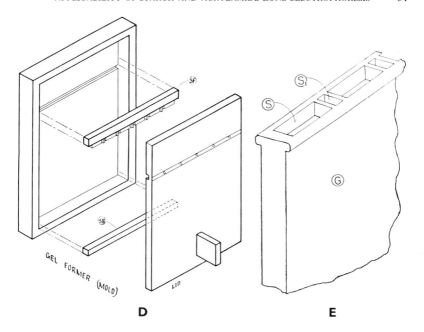

Fig. 1.6. Vertical plate apparatus of Lorber (1964). (A) B: supporting bar; C, C_L, C_U: buffer compartments; E, E_-, E_+: electrodes; G, G_1, G_2, G_3: gel; P, P_1, P_2: cooling plates; S: sample trough; T: cooling tube. (B) Detailed view of front and rear cooling plates. (C) Horizontal positioning of gel between front and rear cooling plates. Note the position of the anterior and posterior gel lips relative to the front and rear cooling plates. (D) Three-dimensional exploded view of the gel mold and lid. (E) Detailed view of gel cartridge in vertical position. Sample troughs are fully opened and ready to receive protein specimens.

recommends the use of gels no more than 0.9 mm thick. When such gels are efficiently cooled by means of an organic solvent a considerable separation of serum proteins can be achieved in no more than 15 min (Daams 1963).

For preparative purposes, very thin gels are inadequate, so that special attention to cooling must be given. In these circumstances the very much higher conductivity for heat of glass as compared with that

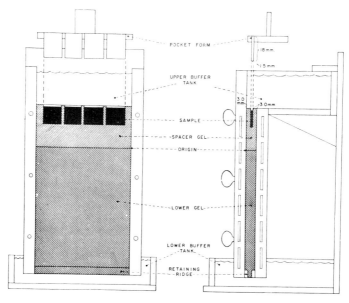

Fig. 1.7. Vertical plate apparatus of Ritchie et al. (1966) suitable for use with a large-pore gel for sample concentration. Note presence of retaining ridges at bottom of the chamber.

of plastics becomes important. Thus apparatus in which the gel is retained between two cooled glass cylinders such as that designed by Jovin et al. (1964) can be cooled efficiently and is relatively simple to construct (see p. 81). For this system a power output of not more than 0.5 W/cm of gel is recommended by its originators.

The permissible temperature rise in any apparatus of course depends on the nature of the separations being undertaken. Strictest control must be exercised when measurements of absolute mobilities are to be made. More commonly complete or partial separation of components and/or measurement of relative mobilities is all that is required. In such experiments, especially if some irregularity of band shape can be tolerated a temperature rise in the gel of a few degrees is unimportant. If such an increase is allowed to occur extreme care should be exercised that irregular band shapes do not lead to misinterpretation of the nature of the separations which have taken place. Particular danger of misinterpretation exists if unsymmetric cooling is employed as for instance if a gel is placed on a horizontal cooling plate and no provision is made for cooling of the upper surface. As shown in fig. 1.8 if

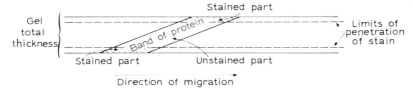

Fig. 1.8. Side view of gel after staining for too short a time. Viewed from on top two bands of stain are visible. They correspond to the front and rear portions of a single band of protein which has been incompletely stained.

incomplete staining has also occurred a tipped band can give the impression of two well separated bands. Although cooling by means of circulating water or other liquid is much more effective than air cooling much useful work including the original experiments of Smithies (1955) with starch gels has been done without benefit of cooling arrangements of any kind. As might be expected such apparatus will perform better if kept in a room at 0 °C.

Since the rate of heat loss which will occur in any given apparatus is a fixed feature of that apparatus it is specially important to avoid unnecessary heat production by the use of unnecessarily concentrated buffer solutions. The relationship of buffer resistance to potential gradient and heat production have already been considered (fig. 1.4).

CHAPTER 2

Acrylamide gel

Choice of gel

Complex mixtures of proteins when subjected to electrophoresis in acrylamide gels usually divide up into numbers of well defined zones or bands. As is evident from the wide range of gel concentrations which have been used for this purpose some separation can be expected with gels containing pores of very different sizes. However, the ease with which some degree of separation can be obtained should not deter attempts to obtain a gel with optimum properties for any given separation. If the mixture requiring separation consists of molecules having the same or almost the same free solution mobilities the choice of gel is specially critical. In practice good results have been obtained with gels in which the average pore size is roughly half of the average size of the protein molecules undergoing separation. This very approximate relationship extends from particles as large as ribosome sub-units (radii approx. 8 mμ) for which gels with average pore size 4.0 mμ have been used, down to proteins such as myoglobin and cytochrome of radius 2 mμ for which gels with average pores of only 1 mμ have proved satisfactory. The concentrations of acrylamide and bisacrylamide necessary for the production of gels of these pore sizes is shown in fig. 1.1.

Since the average pore size in those acrylamide gels which have been found to be of most value as sieves for fractionation of proteins during electrophoresis, is much smaller than the average size of the molecules being separated two possibilities must be considered: (1) That sieving takes place by passage of the protein molecules exclusively through the small proportion of pores in the gel of much more than average size. Evidently the range of pore sizes present and the proportion of blind pores are also parameters which are likely to be of great importance in determining mobility differences under conditions such as those existing during electrophoresis in acrylamide gels. Unfortunately no relevant experimental data have yet been reported. (2) Alternatively pores of average size or even smaller are able to open up and permit passage of molecules of which the Stokes radius is larger than the radii of the pores. If such effects are possible estimates of pore size derived from measurements of diffusion made in the absence of superimposed electrophoretic transport and the actual pore sizes existing during electrophoresis may be very different. Full consideration of these alternatives would involve discussion of the methods used for calculation of average pore size in gels. For the present purpose it is sufficient to note that in absence of electrophoresis very similar values for gel pore size have been arrived at by two methods. These are calculation from the acrylamide concentration using the theory of Ogston (1958) (see p. 11) and more directly by measurements of retention volumes for proteins of known molecular size when these are subjected to chromatography on columns of granulated acrylamide gel (Fawcett and Morris 1966). Assuming that the average pore sizes thus obtained provides an accurate estimate of those existing under conditions of electrophoresis the separation of different sized molecules with equal charges must result mainly from differences in numbers of pores large enough for passage of each size of molecule. It is of some interest that a mechanism of this kind is different from that postulated by Ackers (1964) to explain retardation of protein molecules during chromatography on gels such as Sephadex G 200. The pores in these latter, but not in the lower members of the Sephadex series, are believed to have average diameters some ten times larger than those of the proteins for which they provide a suitable chromatographic matrix. In these large pore gels used in chromatography, retardation is believed to be due to 'restricted diffusion' in a part of the gel internal volume rather than the existence of regions which are unavailable to the proteins in question

Subject index p. 145

due to the pore geometry. The behaviour of Sephadex is discussed in detail by L. Fischer in a companion volume in this series of laboratory manuals. Although as yet unproven, the suggestion that some of the smaller pores in acrylamide gels may be able to expand sufficiently during electrophoresis to permit the passage of 'oversize' molecules may well be correct. If so an explanation will be available for the very low yields of proteins such as γ-globulin when attempts are made at recovery from acrylamide gel by simple diffusion.

To make possible optimum fractionation of mixtures containing molecules of different mobilities as well as of different sizes, the choice of gel is again important. No general rule can be suggested because of the almost infinite combination of properties which may be in question. However, examination of fig. 2.1 may be of assistance especially for mixtures of proteins with properties similar to those which are shown. As first demonstrated by Morris (1966), if both the free solution mobility of a given protein and its retardation on a column of granulated acrylamide gel of known average pore size, have been measured, the mobility which will occur in the same gel under electrophoretic conditions can be calculated. In practice, however, in respect to a given protein sufficient data of this kind are unlikely to be available. Even so a gel of suitable pore size may be selected by consideration of the relative mobilities of the components of the mixture and the range of sizes of the molecules present. Reference to fig. 2.1 shows that two cases must be distinguished. These are exemplified on the one hand by γ-globulin and myoglobulin which can be expected to separate to a greater degree in gels with smaller average pore size. In this case the protein with the higher mobility is the smaller. On the other hand the dimer of bovine serum albumin and myoglobin will show decreased separation with decrease in pore size down to a pore size of 1.3 mμ due to the protein with the higher mobility being the larger. The use of gels with pore sizes which can be expected to bring about super-imposition of bands as a result of this effect must of course be avoided. This example serves also to demonstrate the falsity of the concept of an optimum pore size which at a given pH value will give optimum separation of all components. A safer approach when studying complex

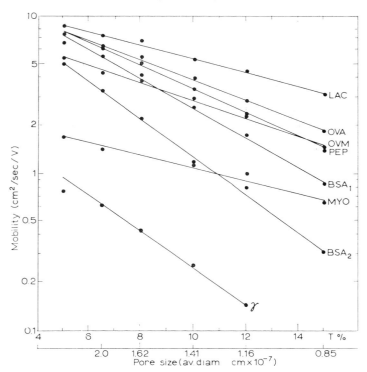

Fig. 2.1. Relationship of gel concentration and mobility for a number of different proteins. With increased total concentration of acrylamide plus bisacrylamide (T) the pore size decreases as shown. For all the proteins examined log mobility is found to be proportional to pore size. All mobilities have been measured in gels with 5% of bisacrylamide at pH 8.83 (Morris 1966). LAC: β-lactoglobulin; OVA: ovalbumin; OVM: ovomucoid; PEP: pepsin; MYO: myoglobin; γ: bovine γ-globulin; BSA1, BSA2: bovine serum albumin monomer and dimer.

mixtures is to assume that single bands obtained by electrophoresis in a gel of a particular pore size and a single pH value may be heterogeneous. If this assumption is made then when the material which appeared as a single band in the first gel is refractionated in a gel with a different porosity and/or at a different pH a set of at least two more nearly homogenous bands will probably be obtained. For such an experiment the pore size should not be reduced to such a degree that

Subject index p. 145

the larger molecules are unable to enter the gel. In fact this occurs with proteins of average size in gels of 20–25% acrylamide concentration. Gels with larger pores will also be useful at least up to a pore size at which some retardation of the molecules undergoing separation still takes place. Unfortunately relative retardation in large pore gels has been little studied so that a maximum useful pore size cannot be given. See however Loening (1967) for the use of gels consisting of 2.1 and 2.4% acrylamide.

Choice of buffer solutions

Because the mobilities of proteins are usually considerably greater at pH values removed some distance from the isoelectric point of the protein in question electrophoretic separations, including those in gels able to cause retardation by molecular sieving, are generally more successful at such pH values. Indeed in conditions of free electrophoresis including separations in gels with pores too large to cause appreciable retardation of the molecules undergoing separation the choice of a pH value which will maximise mobility differences is of primary importance. In gels such as acrylamide, however, where sieving can take place, a wider range of pH values is available. In other words an optimum separation may be achieved at a pH other than that at which there is the greatest charge difference between the molecules undergoing separation. In order to take advantage of sieving it is quite sufficient if all the proteins present have a considerable mobility towards either of the electrodes. The case where one protein has a very low mobility is of course not excluded so long as the proteins from which separation is required themselves have usefully high mobility values. As in all experiments with proteins the limits of pH which can be employed are those which are just short of the values at which denaturation begins to occur. While these limitations are fully applicable in experiments with acrylamide gel the fact that separation is not only dependent on the free solution mobilities of the substances undergoing separation allows more freedom of choice of pH within the range of stability of the molecules in question.

As a first approximation, most protein molecules are stable in aqueous solution, at pH values from 3 to 10 if the temperature is below 50 °C. This statement is true at least in the sense that irreversible denaturation cannot be demonstrated. As is shown in fig. 1.4 a greater amount of heat is produced for a given mobility in more concentrated buffer solutions. However, in most small scale apparatuses dissipation of heat is not a difficult problem so that buffers at concentrations up to 0.5 M are not disadvantageous. Indeed as shown by Hjerten et al. (1965) bands entering a gel containing a concentrated buffer can be caused to sharpen if applied in a dilute buffer (see p. 24 for explanation of this behaviour). Of the very large number of weak acids and bases capable of acting as buffers within this range a restricted number have been used for this purpose in electrophoresis in acrylamide gels. Some of those which have been most commonly used are shown in tables 2.1 and 2.2. As is apparent from the tables separations have been conducted over a wide range of pH and in buffer solution of molarities from 0.03 to 0.4.

References to tables 2.1 and 2.2

[1] FERRIS, T. G., R. E. EASTERLING and R. E. BUDD (1964) Anal. Biochem. 8, 477

[2] PUN, J. Y. and L. LOMBROZO (1964) Anal. Biochem. 9, 9

[3] JENSEN, K. (1965) Scand. J. Clin. Lab. Invest. 17, 192

[4] SMALL, P. A., W. F. HARRINGTON and W. W. KEILLEY (1961) Biochim. Biophys. Acta 49, 462

[5] WORK, T. S. (1964) J. Mol. Biol. 10, 544

[6] MATSON, C. F. (1965) Anal. Biochem. 13, 294

[7] LORBER, A. (1964) J. Lab. Clin. Med. 64, 133

[8] SHEPHERD, G. R. and L. R. GURLEY (1966) Anal. Biochem. 14, 356

[9] DAVIES, B. J. (1964) Ann. N.Y. Acad. Sci. 121, 404

[10] PASTEWKA, J. V., A. T. NESS and A. C. PEACOCK (1966) Clin. Chim. Acta 14, 219

[11] RITCHIE, R. F., J. G. HARTER and T. B. BAYLES (1966) J. Lab. Clin. Med. 68, 842

[12] HJERTEN, S., S. JERSTEDT and A. TISELIUS (1965) Anal. Biochem. 11, 219

[13] REISFELD, R. A., U. J. LEWIS and D. E. WILLIAMS (1962) Nature 195, 281

[14] BLOEMENDAL, H., W. S. BOUT, J. F. JONGKIND and J. H. WISSE (1962) Exptl. Eye Res. 1, 300

[15] GORDON, A. H. and L. N. LOUIS (1967) Anal. Biochem. 21, 190

Subject index p. 145

TABLE 2.1

Buffers for acrylamide gels (single-gel systems)

Buffer solutions						Characteristics of system	Apparatus type*	Examples of materials investigated
In gel			In electrode vessels					
Buffer ions	M	pH	Buffer ions	M	pH			
Veronal	0.09	8.6	Same as in gel			—	VP	Serum[1]
{ Tris	0.070	8.7				Albumin band too narrow for accurate quantation	VP	Serum[1]
EDTA	0.007							
Borate†	0.010							
Tris	0.070							
{ Tris	0.007	8.65				Mobilities are low in this buffer	VP	Serum[1]
EDTA	0.0016							
Ca lactate	0.006							
{ Tris	0.022	8.5				—	VP	Serum[1]
Veronal	0.017							
Na lactate								
Acetate	0.05	5.7				Rapid. Cooled in petroleum ether	FP	Lactic dehydrogenase isoenzymes[3]
{ Tris	0.068	7.2	Borate†	0.05	8.6	12 M urea in gel	VP	Myosin sub-units[4]
Citrate	0.025							
Phenol:acetic acid:water 2:1:1			Same as in gel			—	FP	Ribosomal proteins[5]
{ Tris	0.010	9.2	Tris	0.04	9.2	Sample unstabilised	D	Serum[6]
Glycine	0.005		Glycine	0.022				
Tris borate	0.1	8.7	Same as in gel			Preliminary soaking of gel possible	VP	Serum[7]
Potassium acetate	0.02	2.9	Valine (anode) / Glycine (cathode)	0.3 / 0.3	{ 4.0 (acetic)	Sucrose used to stabilise sample	D	Histones[8]
Tris glycine	0.37	9.5	Tris glycine	0.37	9.5	Sucrose used to stabilise sample	D	Serum[12]
Veronal	0.05	8.4	—			7 M urea in gel	FP	Lactic dehydrogenase isoenzymes[3]
Tris	0.083	8.9	Same as in gel			Sample concentrates as it enters gel	D	α-Crystallin[14]
Tris	0.37	8.8	Borate†	0.05	9.2		D	Serum[15]

For footnotes see table 2.2

TABLE 2.2

Buffers for acrylamide gels with more than one layer

	In gel			In electrode vessels			Characteristics of system	Apparatus type*	Ref.
Gel layer	Buffer ions	M	pH	Buffer ions	M	pH			
Sample (large pore)	Tris Chloride	0.062 0.06	6.7	Tris Glycine	0.005 0.038	8.3	The sample is set in the upper-most gel and concentrates in the spacer gel. The actual separation occurs in the bottom gel	D	9
Spacer (large pore)	Tris Chloride	0.062 0.06	6.7						
Small-pore gel	Tris Chloride	0.37 0.06	8.9						
Same gel layers and buffers as above				Tris Glycine	0.05 0.38	8.3	Same as 9 except that improved resolution is obtained if carried out at 4-5 °C	D	10
Spacer (large pore)	Tris Chloride	0.075 0.075	6.7	Tris Glycine	0.05 0.38	8.3	Same as 9 except that sample gel is omitted. The sample is stabilised with sucrose	D	2
Small-pore gel	Tris Chloride	0.046 0.075	8.7						
Spacer (large pore)	Tris H₃PO₄	0.049 0.026	6.7	Tris Glycine	0.025 0.19	8.4	Same as 9 except that sample gel is omitted. The sample is stabilised with acrylamide monomer	VP	11
Small-pore gel	Tris Chloride	0.37 0.06	8.9						
Sample (large pore)	Acetic acid KOH	0.062 0.06	6.8	Acetic acid β-Alanine	0.14 0.35	4.5	An acid gel suitable for separation of bases	D	13
Spacer (large pore)	Acetic acid KOH	0.062 0.06	6.8						
Small-pore gel	Acetic acid KOH	0.75 0.12	4.3						

* D: disc; FP: flat plate (in the horizontal); VP: vertical plate.

† Molarity based on weight of orthoboric acid (H₃BO₃) taken.

For additional buffers see tables 5.1 and 5.2. All buffers recommended for starch gel can be used in acrylamide gels.

For refs. see p. 39.

The presence of EDTA and Ca lactate at low concentration in certain buffers will be noted. Although both of these substances are themselves capable of buffer action they are not added as buffers but rather because of their ability to form complexes with certain ions. A buffer containing EDTA, boric acid and Tris was introduced for electrophoresis on paper by Aronsson and Grönwall (1957) because of the increased resolution of both α- and β-globulins that was thus obtained. More recent work indicates that the effects of both the EDTA and the boric acid in this buffer are due to the ability of these substances to form complexes with certain plasma proteins. Aronsson and Grönwall themselves noted that a buffer containing Tris only did not lead to any increased resolution of the plasma proteins.

Acrylamide gel rendered soluble after use

By treatment with a 30% solution of H_2O_2 at 50 °C acrylamide gel can be rendered completely soluble in water (Young and Fulhorst 1965). Since however, substantial chemical changes in proteins will be caused by this rather severe treatment the method is only likely to be useful for the detection and estimation of proteins. Sections of gel containing ^{14}C-labelled proteins can be treated in this way as a preparation for estimation of radioactivity when mixed with an appropriate scintillation fluid. However cf. p. 69 for an alternative procedure.

If ethylene diacrylate is used instead of bisacrylamide as cross linking agent gels are formed which are completely soluble when treated with piperidine (Choules and Zimm 1965). The use of this cross linking agent permits dissolution of sections of gel which have been cut out after the electrophoresis has been completed. Thus if radio-active substances are present in the gel, this treatment provides solutions suitable for estimation of radioactivity. Alternative methods by which the normal type of acrylamide can be dispersed sufficiently for admixture with scintillation fluids have been more extensively used and are in practice simpler to apply (cf. p. 69).

Catalysts

The formation of polyacrylamide gel by polymerisation of monomer acrylamide and bisacrylamide occurs only in the presence of free radicals. In practice these have been provided by several different reactions of which the simplest is the photodecomposition of riboflavin in presence of traces of O_2. Riboflavin has the unusual property that its ribose groups can act as reducing agents with the result that partial conversion of the flavin to the leuco-form is brought about. In the complete absence of O_2, however, no free radicals are produced, and polymerisation does not take place. In the presence of traces of O_2 photodecomposition of riboflavin is followed by reoxidation of the leuco form and production of free radicals. If acrylamide is present polymerisation starts and then continues as a result of free radicals derived from the acrylamide itself. Meanwhile the traces of O_2 originally present are used up. It is important to note that the continued presence of O_2 during polymerisation limits chain growth. The reactions occurring during the photodecomposition of riboflavin are as yet incompletely understood. However, investigations by Oster et al. (1957) have shown that if the initial formation of free radicals is of brief duration, as for instance when a solution of acrylamide and riboflavin is illuminated by an intense flash lasting less than a millisecond, then after a lag period of an hour the viscosity of the solution will begin to rise and not until many hours later will gelation be complete.

The use of riboflavin and a source of UV light to bring about gel formation has the following two advantages. Firstly, riboflavin is effective at very low concentrations (1 mg per 100 ml) so that even if it remains in the gel in which proteins are undergoing separation it is unlikely to lead to any adverse effects. Secondly, gelation can be brought about at a predetermined time by application of light. Although gelation occurs when solutions containing only acrylamide and riboflavin are irradiated addition of tetramethylethylenediamine (TEMED) has sometimes been found to be advantageous. Thus Davis

Subject index p. 145

TABLE 2.3

Catalysts used to promote setting of acrylamide gels

Gel layer	Urea molarity	pH	Riboflavin* (mg/100 ml)	Final concentration in gel			Ref.
				Ammonium persulphate (% w/v)	TEMED† (% v/v)	DMAPN‡ (% w/v)	
Sample (large pore)	—	6.7	0.5	—	0.058	—	1
Small-pore gel	—	8.9	—	0.07	0.039	—	
Sample (large pore)	—	6.9	0.5	—	0.06	—	2
Small-pore gel	—	8.9	—	0.07	0.06	—	
Sample (large pore)	8	~7.0	0.5	—	—	—	3
Small-pore gel	8	~9.0	—	0.07	0.06	—	
Upper (4% acrylamide)	8	9.9	—	0.031	0.15	—	
Lower (4% acrylamide)	8	9.9	—	0.032	0.13	—	
Upper	8	4.9	0.005	—	0.019	—	
Lower	8	4.8	—	0.057	0.16	—	
Sample (large pore)	—	6.8	0.5	—	0.057	—	4
Small-pore gel	—	4.3	—	0.14	0.5	—	
5% Acrylamide	—	8.9	—	—	0.04	0.04	5

† Tetramethylethylenediamine.
‡ β-Dimethylaminopropionitrile.
* Irradiation with UV light required to set gel.

1 DAVIS, B. J. (1964) Ann. N.Y. Acad. Sci 121, 404
2 JOVIN, T., A. CHRAMBACH and M. A. NAUGHTON (1964) Anal. Biochem. 9, 351
3 DUESBERG, P. H. and R. R. RUECKERT (1965) Anal. Biochem. 11, 342
4 REISFELD, R. A., U. J. LEWIS and D. E. WILLIAMS (1962) Nature 195, 281
5 HERMANS, P. E., W. F. McGUCKIN, B. F. McKENZIE and E. D. BAYRD (1960) Staff Meetings Mayo Clinic 35, 792

(1964) states that the setting of sample gels containing protein is more reliable in presence of TEMED.

Polymerisation of acrylamide occurs rapidly at room temperatures if ammonium persulphate and TEMED are both present. In such solutions free oxygen radicles produced from the persulphate by a base catalysed reaction transform sufficient of the monomer to the free radicle state to initiate polymerisation. In the absence of excess O_2 the reaction continues until gelation is complete. Equally satisfactory results have been obtained with other bases, such as β-dimethylamino-propionitrile in place of TEMED. Gelation takes place more slowly at lower pH values because the free form of the base is required to catalyse the reaction. The concentrations of ammonium persulphate, TEMED and β-dimethylaminopropionitrile which have been found to give convenient times of setting are shown in table 2.3. Gelation can be delayed most conveniently by holding the solution of acrylamide and catalysts at a temperature near 0 °C. Because of the rather considerable concentrations of catalyst residues which remain in gels set by means of ammonium persulphate, TEMED and β-dimethylamino-propionitrile it is often desirable that these should be removed before the electrophoresis is carried out. Fortunately this can easily be done by soaking the gel in the required buffer solution or by electrophoresis before applying the sample. By this means traces of acrylamide remaining as monomer or soluble lower homologues are also removed. This is an advantage in experiments in which the UV adsorption of eluates from acrylamide gel are to be measured because of the high UV adsorption of acrylamide (cf. p. 64).

Proportion of bisacrylamide to total acrylamide

The differing properties of gels containing various proportions of bisacrylamide have already been discussed (cf. p. 11). For most purposes 5 % bisacrylamide gels are very suitable. However, it should be noted that Davis (1964) recommends 2.6 % bisacrylamide in the small-pore and 25 % in the large-pore gel.

Subject index p. 145

CHAPTER 3

Apparatus and techniques

Choice of apparatus

Choice of the most suitable apparatus for electrophoresis in acrylamide gel is often governed by the scale on which the separation needs to be conducted. Thus equipment is sometimes divided into 'analytical' and 'preparative scale' on the basis of the amount of material which can be successfully separated. In fact this division is difficult to justify because however small the apparatus, elution of segments of the gel will yield small amounts of the separated substances. A more fundamental division is between those methods in which the substances remain in the gel throughout and are revealed by staining or detection of radio-activity and methods in which the separated substances leave the gel either during the electrophoresis or when it has been completed. The methods which permit recovery of the separated substances may be subdivided into those in which each substance moves out of the intact gel by electrophoretic transport and others in which the gel must be cut into appropriate sections after the separation has been completed. In these cases recovery of the separated substances is brought about by one of several methods certain of which involve a further stage of electrophoresis in an apparatus designed especially for this purpose (see pp. 77 and 129).

Apparatus suitable for gels which are to be stained

On grounds of simplicity the apparatus used by Davis (1964) and Ornstein (1964) which consists simply of one or more vertically mounted straight glass tubes and an upper and a lower buffer vessel fitted with suitable electrodes may well be chosen (fig. 3.1). Optimum results will be obtained if the electrode vessels are constructed in such a manner that the tubes are surrounded from top to bottom by the buffer solutions. A circular apparatus constructed of Perspex, (otherwise known as Lucite and Plexiglass) of the type shown in fig. 3.1 will accommodate six tubes each of i.d. 8 mm. If used in a room at an even temperature little or no difference will be found between the pattern of bands formed when the same sample has been applied to each of the tubes. When temperature gradients are to be expected the addition of a magnetic stirrer inside the lower electrode vessels is necessary to provide even cooling of the tubes. A rectangular apparatus large enough to contain 72 5-mm i.d. tubes has also been described (Matson 1965).

With apparatus of this kind 0.1–0.2 mg of a mixture of proteins can often be resolved into as many as 20 bands (or discs). The number of components present and a qualitative estimate of their relative concentrations can be made by inspection of the stained gel. More quantitative data concerning the concentrations of the various components can be obtained by scanning the stained gel in a suitable densitometer (p. 123). Recovery of a small part of each of the separated substances can also be achieved by subdivision of the gel and diffusion into appropriate volumes of water. Rather larger amounts can be separated by the use of tubes of internal diameter up to 8 mm.

It is claimed by Clarke (1964) that two samples can be subjected to electrophoresis side by side in a single tube so that the identity or non-identity of a particular component can be demonstrated. To make this possible the two samples must be kept apart by means of a strip of waxed paper above the gel.

When amounts of more than 1 mg of protein are to be separated or when the gel containing the separated proteins is to be subjected to further treatment, i.e. immunoelectrophoresis, more complex equipment is needed. This is usually constructed so as to contain a rectangular slab of gel in which a number of samples can migrate side by side. In this way also optimum conditions can be provided for

Subject index p. 145

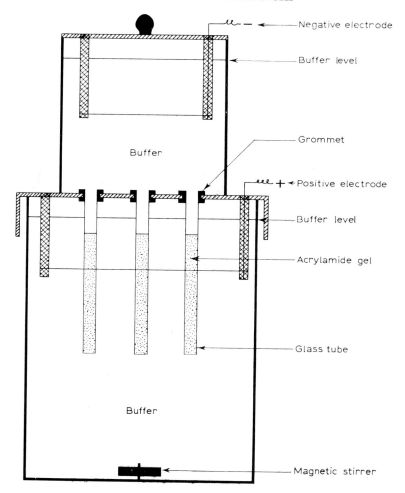

Fig. 3.1. Apparatus for 'disc electrophoresis'. The upper electrode vessel is made from Perspex tube attached to a sheet of the same material. In this there are six holes, equipped with rubber grommets in which the glass tubes must fit tightly. For six tubes of i.d. 8 mm the apparatus should be large enough to hold 2 l buffer in the lower vesse!.

demonstration of identity or non-identity of individual components.

Very many such apparatuses have been described. Among the most useful are those of Raymond (1962), Lorber (1964), and Ritchie et al. (1966) (pp. 29–32). Whereas in some the gel rests horizontally, in others it is held vertically, usually between cooling plates. When a vertical gel is used slots are generally provided along its upper edge to accommodate small volumes of the solutions to be investigated. Fortunately the rubbery nature of acrylamide gel permits the formation of rows of slots, the edges of which are less subject to breakage than in the case of starch gel. The use of a vertical gel with sample slots along its upper edge undoubtedly provides the most convenient means for neat sample application and the subsequent formation of regular bands.

In the apparatuses of Raymond (1962) and Ritchie et al. (1966) a rather deep sample slot is used. After the samples have been run into these slots the upper electrode buffer is very carefully added. In this method of working a slight loss of sample may occur as a result of the upper layer of the sample mixing with the upper buffer solution. However, especially in the apparatus of Ritchie et al. in which a spacer gel is used, the separation starts from a very narrow band of protein. The sample slots in the Lorber apparatus are shallow so that overlayering with buffer would be impracticable. To avoid this difficulty a gel bridge which touches only one lip of the sample slot is used for the initial period of the electrophoresis (fig. 1.6.A). Unfortunately in practice the positioning of this bridge requires considerable attention. Furthermore if contact with the main gel slab is imperfect part of the sample remains at the origin. This difficulty, with sufficient care, need not lead to distortion of the final pattern but it must be considered in relation to the other advantages of the apparatus and especially to the fact that catalyst residues can be removed and any chosen buffer introduced by preliminary soaking.

The tough and rubbery consistency of acrylamide gels makes neat slicing by means of a razor blade much more difficult than is the case with starch gel. Thus the insertion of filter paper previously wetted with sample solution into slots cut in a horizontal gel usually leads to unsatisfactory results. Despite the intrinsic difficulty of this method of sample application successful separations have sometimes been achieved, for example by Hermans et al. (1960) and by Work (1964).

Optimum conditions for electrophoresis in vertical glass tubes; 'disc electrophoresis'

Although the apparatus required to carry out electrophoresis by the 'disc' method of Davis (1964) and Ornstein (1964) is extremely simple, the time required to prepare each experiment according to the directions given by Davis is very considerable. This is due to the use in each tube of three separate gel layers, each containing a different buffer. The purpose of the uppermost or sample gel is prevention of loss of the sample by convection (i.e. by mixing with the upper buffer solution). The middle or spacer gel permits concentration of the sample prior to separation of the components present. Only in the lower gel does the separation actually occur. The name of 'disc electrophoresis' was given to the method because of the extreme sharpness of the starting zone or disc which is formed at the upper surface of the lower gel. The thickness of this zone has been estimated to be no more than 25 μ. A general account of the conditions of pH and ionic strength under which such a remarkable concentration effect can be obtained has been given on p. 25. In practice no difficulty is to be expected in reproducing the concentration effect and thus obtaining an extremely sharp starting zone. However, an initial zone of adequate sharpness to allow separations at least as refined or those obtainable by the 'disc' method can be obtained in a much simpler manner than that described by Davis and it is doubtful whether the complications introduced by him can be justified.

An example of a simple system has been given by Hjerten et al. (1965) who used a single gel containing 0.37 M Tris at pH 9.5. Buffer of the same molarity and pH was also employed in the electrode chambers but the sample was diluted with 2.5 vol. of water before use. As only 4 μl of serum was used, even after dilution with water, the depth of the initial zone was less than 0.4 mm. Under these conditions the proteins move into the gel from a region of lower conductivity

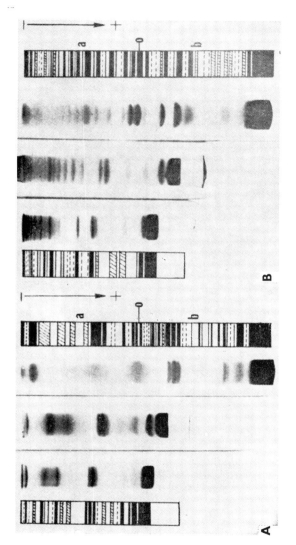

Fig. 3.2. 'Disc electrophoresis' with separations occurring successively in gels of different porosity (Wright and Mallmann 1966). (A) Comparison of separation of bovine serum in standard 7% gel (left). 4.75% gel (middle), and differential gel (right). Cross hatched areas and dotted lines indicate lightly stained and fine bands, respectively. O: origin of 10% separation gel; a: 4.75% gel; b: 10% gel. (B) Comparison of separation of human serum in standard 7% gel (left), 4.75% gel (middle), and differential gel (right). Cross hatched areas and dotted lines indicate lightly stained and fine bands, respectively. O: origin of 10% separation gel; a: 4.75% gel; b: 10% gel.

with the result that the starting zone becomes even narrower. Comparison with the final pattern thus obtained with that given by the same serum when analysed by the method of Davis (1964) and Ornstein (1964) showed the same number of bands. A similar degree of resolution is also obtainable if a buffer of much lower molarity is used in the electrode chambers. Thus it may be concluded that if a concentrated solution of proteins is available the use of a single gel containing a buffer of relatively high molarity will permit analysis into as many bands as can be obtained by the 'disc' method at least when the separation proper takes place in only one layer of the gel.

A system of potential value has recently been described (Wright and Mallmann 1966) based on that of Davis and Ornstein. In this the separation takes place in two gel layers. The upper of 4.75% acrylamide concentration is set between the small-pore gel (10% acrylamide) and the spacer layer. Since 44–50 components in human serum can be separated by the use of this method, fig. 3.2, it would seem to offer higher resolution than can be attained by means of either a single gel or by the Davis–Ornstein system itself. However, even if this is true further work will be required to establish whether the inclusion of the spacer gel layer is essential. Certainly the principle of separation in superimposed layers of gel of more than one porosity must be of value. Even greater resolution may well be achieved by the use of gradients of gel concentration.

In addition to a considerable saving of time during the setting up of the electrophoresis another advantage of the single gel system must be noted. Unlike in the procedure given by Davis and Ornstein the sample is not mixed with a solution of unpolymerised acrylamide so that there is no possibility of damage to labile proteins during the polymerisation reaction.

Preparation of gel (an example)

A stock solution of acrylamide and bisacrylamide in suitable proportions (cf. p. 11) to give the required final gel concentration may be stored at 2 °C. Thus for preparation of gels containing 12.5% acrylamide the following solution may conveniently be used. 14.3% acryla-

mide (with in addition any desired concentration of bisacrylamide) in
0.37 M Tris buffer at *p*H 8.8. Immediately before use dissolved air
must be removed from this solution *in vacuo*. To each 10 ml of this
solution is next added 0.72 ml of 0.5% TEMED, and 0.72 ml of 0.06%
ammonium persulphate. Without delay the solution thus obtained is
run into the glass tubes to a depth of 7 cm. A hypodermic syringe
equipped with a long needle has been found to be most convenient for
this purpose. In this regard *it cannot be over-emphasised that pipetting
by mouth of acrylamide solutions is dangerous* (cf. p. 93). The bottom
ends of the tubes are closed by means of a short length of rubber
tubing and a rubber bung or by parafilm secured with a rubber band.
The acrylamide solution is covered by a layer, at least 3 mm in depth,
of degassed water. This water which should contain a trace of a
detergent to prevent drop formation on the tube wall, must be added
carefully to avoid disturbance of the acrylamide surface. For this
addition a small hypodermic syringe equipped with a length of no. 1
polythene tubing is very useful. The tip of this polythene tubing, bent
to form a right angle, touches the tube wall approximately 2 mm above
the surface of the acrylamide. After the addition of water has been
started the tip is gradually raised. An alternative method by which a
water layer may be applied without disturbance of the still liquid
acrylamide solution involves the use of a Pasteur pipette with a thread
projecting for 2 or 3 mm from its tip. After setting, which should
occur within 20 min, the water layer is removed, and the space above
the gel is filled with electrode buffer. The gel will then be ready for use
after standing for a period of 2 to 3 hr.

Electrode buffer
0.05 M Na borate at a *p*H of 9.2.

Sample solution
This should contain 7.5 mg/ml of sucrose and protein at a total
concentration of 1–2 mg/ml. A volume of 50–80 μls in each tube gives
satisfactory results.

Subject index p. 145

Addition of sample solution

Immediately before use the buffer solution which is on top of the gel should be changed twice thus removing the more concentrated buffer which will have diffused out of the gel during standing. A layer 2–3 mm deep of sample solution is carefully introduced at the gel water interface by means of a fine Pasteur pipette with a tip bent at right angles. As a result of the added sucrose the density of this solution is sufficient to prevent mixing with the buffer solution in the top part of the tube.

The tubes are placed in the apparatus (fig. 3.1) before addition of the sample solutions to avoid possible mixing with the overlying buffer during transfer. Finally the upper buffer vessel is carefully filled avoiding disturbance of the liquid in the tubes. In this apparatus the tubes are completely surrounded with buffer solution. Not only does this provide an ample supply of buffer so that the products of electrolysis are well diluted but also the tubes are more effectively cooled, than if surrounded by air. As mentioned above it is advantageous to stir the lower buffer by a magnetic stirrer so as to ensure uniform temperature.

Time and current required for electrophoresis

Excellent results are obtainable by the use of a current of 1 mA per tube (i.d. 7 mm). The time required for optimum development of the pattern must depend on the proteins and buffers in use. With 0.37 M Tris buffer as described above, Hjerten et al. (1964) used a current of 3 mA for 1.5 hr. By this procedure 15 well separated bands were obtained from a sample of human serum.

Removal of gel cylinders from glass tubes

Because of the marked tendency of acrylamide gel to adhere to glass some difficulty may be found in removing the gel cylinders intact from the tubes after the electrophoresis is finished. This is greatly facilitated by the use of precision bore glass. In such tubes little difficulty is to be expected if water is injected between the gel and glass of the tube from a long 26 gauge needle attached to a hypodermic syringe. For the more adherent gels the water injection must be repeated several times so that almost the whole surface of the gel is freed. The gel cylinder will then slide out of the tube when only slight pressure is applied. Gels containing buffers at low pH values have been found to be specially difficult to remove, but with patience even these can be secured unbroken by the above technique.

An alternative but much slower method is to immerse the tubes containing the gels in a solution containing methanol. Under these circumstances and at a rate which will be partly determined by the concentration of methanol actually employed, the gels will shrink. Such gels which may be stained simultaneously by inclusion of amido black in the methanolic solution have very smooth surfaces especially suitable for densitometry.

Use of longer gels suitable for disintegration by extrusion

When it is intended to employ the mechanical extrusion device of Maizel (1966) gels 0.6×20 cm are convenient. Summers et al. (1965) have described the use of such gels containing 0.5 M urea and 0.1% SDS for separation of various proteins from HeLa cells (cf. p. 69). The samples (vol. less than 0.35 ml) contained 60% of sucrose (an undesirably high concentration see p. 53) to prevent mixing with the electrode buffer. It should be noted that no spacer gel was employed. Numerous sharp bands were obtained the radioactivity of which was estimated after extrusion into scintillation fluid (cf. p. 69).

Staining and destaining

To stain for proteins the gel cylinders should be immersed in a 0.05% solution of amido black* dissolved in 7% aqueous acetic acid for a period of at least 2 hr. If the gels are then transferred to 7% acetic acid the excess dye will diffuse out in 24 hr. By electrophoretic destaining (cf. p. 61) dye removal can be greatly accelerated.

* Also called naphthalene black 10B.

Vertical slab between cooling plates

Electrophoresis in acrylamide gel when required purely as an analytical method may be conducted very conveniently in the apparatus described by Raymond (1962, 1964). Among the advantages of this type are that, because the gel is no more than 3 mm thick, sufficient cooling to prevent band distortion can be obtained by the circulation of tap water through the cooling plates. Also as many as ten samples can be separated side by side which allows accurate matching of the position of individual components. Finally by removal of a strip of gel containing the separated components and re-insertion across the top of a new gel a two dimensional pattern may be obtained. The apparatus is simple in design and may be constructed without difficulty from perspex. The main features of this apparatus are shown in fig. 1.5. A rather similar apparatus used by Ritchie et al. (1966) is shown in fig. 1.7. In this the sample solutions are run into a series of deep pockets in a spacer gel which is set above the main gel in which the separation takes place. An alternative apparatus in which the gel is set in a separate container and then transferred to the one containing the cooling plates is shown in figs. 1.6. A–E. Certain advantages of this type of apparatus (Lorber 1964) are mentioned on page 26.

Preparation of gel and leakage check

The apparatus of Raymond is filled with the solution of acrylamide in the horizontal position, particular care being taken to avoid trapping of bubbles between the plates. By prior insertion of a strip of plastic sponge between the appropriate edges of the plates, placed so that it projects into the lower buffer chamber, the acrylamide solution is prevented from running into this chamber. After filling, the apparatus is laid horizontally with the slot former in place. When the gel has set the slot former is carefully removed and also any small pieces of gel which may have remained in the sample spaces. Next the apparatus is brought into the vertical position and filled with sufficient buffer to cover the electrode in the lower chamber and to fill the upper chamber to a level 1 cm above the upper edge of the gel slab. Before proceeding further the constancy of the buffer levels must be carefully checked. Only if these remain unchanged is it certain that leakage from upper to lower chamber is not taking place. The occurrence of any such leakage is likely to be the result of a partial inhibition of gelling due to the presence of bubbles of air between the plates.

The gel for the Lorber (1964) apparatus is set in a special container of appropriate shape. After removal from this container and, if desired, soaking in any chosen buffer solution for a period of 5 days to ensure complete equilibrium with the selected buffer, the gel is inserted between the cooling plates. Care is necessary to make sure that the lip of the gel enters the slot of the rear cooling plate without any distortion. Sufficient squeeze should next be applied to the gel by means of the wing nuts shown in fig. 1.6.B to cause it to extend to about 1.3 times its normal length. The extension must be downwards so that the sample slots in the gel remain precisely at the top of the front cooling plate. If necessary, excess length of gel can be cut off from the bottom so that the gel will rest easily on the plastic sponge on top of bar B shown in fig. 1.6.A. Next the electrode vessels and upper sections of gel are arranged for the low voltage phase as shown in fig. 1.6.A.

Entry of proteins into gels by preliminary passage of current

In both the types of apparatus mentioned in the last paragraph this is carried out for at least 20 min. In the apparatus of Raymond (1962) the same voltage and current as are to be used later for the electrophoresis proper are employed. In the apparatus of Lorber (1964) a voltage gradient of 15 V per cm of gel should be applied for 30 min.

Sample insertion

Solutions which are to be analysed in the apparatus of Raymond (1962) must be of a considerably higher density than is the buffer solution. If this is not already the case, sufficient sucrose should be added to bring the density of the sample solution up to that of a 2% solution of sucrose. The optimum volume of sample added to each slot is determined by the degree of resolution needed and the nature of the mixture. With serum 20–50 µl added to each of six slots each 1.5 cm wide will give satisfactory results.

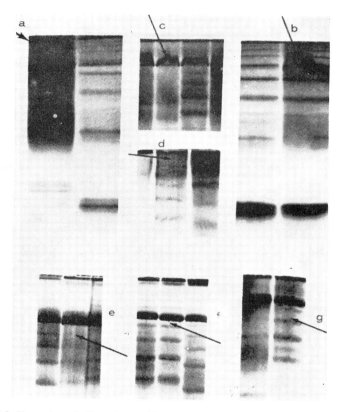

Fig. 3.3. Examples of distortion artifacts, described by Ritchie et al. (1966), in acrylamide gels. a: slanting line at origin (arrow) due to layering of water from a single point; b: distortion due to bubble rising during polymerization, large molecular species most affected; c: distortion due to irregular pore size at the interface origin; d: streaming of proteins from precipitates at the origin; e: distortion due to agitation of the liquid sample layer; f: distortion due to variation in pore size deep in gel slab (too rapid polymerization); g: major distortions due to 'bombing' of the gel interface during layering.

Mixing with electrode buffer is insignificant if the addition of the sample solution is carried out carefully by means of a Pasteur pipette the tip of which is inserted into the slot.

For the apparatus of Lorber (1964) the density of the sample solutions is unimportant. However, the volumes of these solutions should be sufficient (0.04 ml per cm of gel width) to fill the slots almost to capacity. While the adequacy of the separations which are achieved must depend on the proteins actually present, if more than 1 mg of serum protein per cm width of gel is used the results obtained are likely to be unsatisfactory.

Possible reasons for distortion of bands

In fig. 3.3 are shown the patterns found to occur as a result of certain errors in technique. The distortions shown are those reported by Ritchie et al. (1966) using a spacer gel to concentrate the sample before separation. Distortions of these kinds are not usually seen when a single pre-set gel is used as in the apparatus of Lorber (1964).

Voltage, current and time of electrophoresis

The current and voltage required depend on the concentration of buffer ions in the gel itself and in the buffer vessels. Up to 150 W can be dissipated by the cooling system which is incorporated in the apparatus of Raymond (1962) before band distortion begins to be noticeable. To provide adequate cooling tap water should be allowed to flow at a rate of 2–5 l/min. If 0.1 M Tris buffer is used in the gel as much as 500 V may be applied. Separation of up to 15 components of serum will then occur in 3 hr. Changes of pH in the electrode compartments can be prevented by recirculation of buffer by means of a pump. As shown in fig. 1.5 the buffer solution drains back continuously from the upper to the lower electrode compartment.

With the apparatus of Lorber (1964) after insertion of the samples (carried out with the gel arranged for the low voltage stage (fig. 1.6.A) a voltage gradient of 15 V/cm is applied for 30 min. This causes the proteins to enter the gel. When this has occurred the position of the upper electrode buffer vessel and the upper gel are altered to that

Subject index p. 145

shown in fig. 1.6.A for the high voltage phase. Using a tris borate buffer of 0.1 M and pH 8.7 and coolant at 0 °C circulating through the plates at 2 l/min, a voltage gradient of 25 V/cm may be used. Under these conditions the current should not exceed 250 mA.

Two-dimensional techniques

(a) Electrophoresis on paper followed by electrophoresis in acrylamide. Any convenient apparatus for electrophoresis on paper may be used to perform the separation in the first dimension. As an example, an experiment in which 30 μl serum were separated by Hermans et al. (1963) on a 3 cm wide strip of Whatman 3 mm paper using a Spinco–Durrum type of apparatus may be quoted. These authors then cut the strip of paper which they had thus obtained into three 1 cm wide strips and inserted these together (side by side) into a slot across the origin of a horizontal acrylamide gel which had been placed in a water cooled pressure plate apparatus.

(b) Electrophoresis first in acrylamide gel of one concentration and then in acrylamide gel of another concentration.   As already mentioned this method has been investigated by Raymond (1964) who used the same apparatus as that previously employed for the parallel separation of multiple samples. In an investigation of the lactic dehydrogenases of serum, 0.01 ml of an undiluted serum which had not been dialysed, and which contained a high concentration of these enzymes was placed in a slot 2 cm wide in the top of the gel. After the usual period of electrophoresis in a 5% gel, a strip 0.5 cm wide containing the partially separated components was cut out and reset in a position along the starting line of another acrylamide gel, which this time was of a concentration of 8%. In this way in the second dimension the movement of the larger proteins was relatively retarded owing to the increased sieving effect of the more concentrated gel.

(c) Electrophoresis in two acrylamide gels of the same concentration but of different pH.   Preliminary reports of work with this system are also given by Raymond (1964) using haptoglobin.

Staining methods

A considerable advantage of acrylamide gel as a matrix for electrophoretic separations is its transparency and the ease with which areas
containing proteins as well as numerous other classes of substance can
be revealed by staining. For proteins it is sufficient that the gel be
placed in a solution of amido black 10 B * and then destained by
soaking in 7 % acetic acid. The optimum concentration of the dye and
the time required for completion of this process depends mainly on
the thickness of the gel. If insufficient time is allowed so that only the
surface layers of the gel contain the dye-stuff there is considerable
danger of misleading patterns being obtained. As already mentioned
(cf. p. 33 and fig. 1.8) it is even possible for an apparent separation to
be indicated by the existence of two coloured bands when only one
band of protein is present. At higher temperatures entry of dye-stuff
is expedited as is also the clearing of the blank areas when the gel is
transferred to the wash bath. Even more rapid destaining can be
achieved by a simple electrophoretic procedure. To achieve this it is
sufficient for the gel to rest between two horizontal stainless steel
electrodes 2 or 3 cm apart immersed in 7 % acetic acid. Passage of
current (2 or 3 A) at a low voltage will lead to rapid destaining.

For optimum results an arrangement such as that of Ferris et al.
(1963) should be employed so that the bubbles of gas which are
produced do not cut off the current from certain parts of the gel. A
very simple apparatus suitable for electrolytic destaining of small gels
and in particular the cylinders used for disc electrophoresis has been
described by Richards and Gratzer (1967). In this the gels lie horizontally on top of one another in a rectangular space between two
sheets of Vyon** porous plastic. These sheets are held in place in a
vertical Perspex frame which stands between carbon electrodes in a

* Also called naphthalene black 10 B.
** $1/_{32}$″ thick porous polyethylene sheet. Obtainable from Porous Plastics Ltd.
Dagenham Docks, Essex, England.

Subject index p. 145

TABLE 3.1

Detection methods for enzymes after separation in starch or acrylamide gel

Enzyme	Detection method used in		Procedures	Ref.
	Starch gel	Acrylamide gel*		
Red cell acid phosphatase	+		Phenolphthalein diphosphate followed by alkali	1, 5
Phosphoglucomutase	+		Reduction of the tetrazolium salt of MTT	2
Placental alkaline phosphatase	+		β-Naphthyl phosphate and diazo salt of fast blue RR	3, 4, 5, 11
β-Glucuronidase	+		8-HO-quinoline glucuronide + blue RR salt	5
Cholinesterase	+		6-Bromo-2-naphthylcarbonaphthoxycholine iodide + blue B salt	5
Glucose-6-phosphate dehydrogenase	+		Application of an agar overlay containing a tetrazolium salt	6
6-Phosphogluconate dehydrogenase	+		Application of an agar overlay containing a tetrazolium salt	7
Cytochrome oxidase	+		α-Naphthol + dimethylparaphenylenediamine	5
Esterases	+	+	α-Naphthyl butyrate + diazo salt of fast blue RR	5, 11
Lactic and malic dehydrogenases	+	+	Reduction of a tetrazolium salt (nitro blue tetrazolium)	5, 9
Acid phosphatase	+	+	Sodium α-naphthyl acid phosphate + diazo salt of 5-chloro-o-toluidine	11
Phosphorylase		+	Silver phosphate is reduced to metallic silver by UV light	10
Succinic dehydrogenase	+		Reduction of a tetrazolium salt (nitro blue tetrazolium)	5
β-HO-butyric dehydrogenase	+		Reduction of a tetrazolium salt (nitro blue tetrazolium)	5
Glutamic dehydrogenase	+		Reduction of a tetrazolium salt (nitro blue tetrazolium)	5
Catalase	+		Inhibition of starch iodide reaction	8
Caeruloplasmin	+		O-dianisidine	8, 12
Leucine aminopeptidase	+		Alanyl-β-naphthylamide + diazotised O-aminoazotoluene	5, 13
Haemoglobin as peroxidase	+		Benzidine + H_2O_2 (cf. page 122 for details)	5, 13

* Detection methods used in starch gel may be expected to work equally well in acrylamide gel.
References, see p. 63.

bath of 7% acetic acid. Destaining should be complete after passage of 0.5 A for 30–45 min.

Because of the absence of reactive groups in acrylamide gels a very wide variety of staining methods can be applied. Thus the positions occupied in the gel by enzymes of all kinds can be ascertained by the use of appropriate substrates, either themselves coloured or capable of reacting to form a coloured substance. Some of the reactions of this kind which have proved useful are given in table 3.1. A particular advantage of acrylamide over starch gel is that because the former gel is entirely free from carbohydrates the detection of glycoproteins and carbohydrates is possible by the normal staining methods.

Bands of haemoglobin both in the free state and when combined with haptoglobin can be revealed most conveniently by soaking the gel in a solution containing benzidine and hydrogen peroxide (Baur 1963). For further information about this technique which was developed for use with starch gel, cf. p. 122. Location of bands of lipoproteins can be carried out by the staining methods similar to those used for these proteins after they have been separated in starch gel (cf. p. 122). Alternatively after addition of a suitable stain, they can be separated without loss of colour in large pore acrylamide gels.

References to table 3.1

1 HOPKINSON, D. A., N. SPENCER and H. HARRIS (1963) Nature *199*, 969

2 SPENCER, N., D. A. HOPKINSON and H. HARRIS (1964) Nature *204*, 742

3 BOYER, S. H. (1961) Science *134*, 1002

4 ROBSON, E. B. and H. HARRIS (1965) Nature *207*, 1257

5 LAWRENCE, S. H., P. J. MELNICK and H. E. WEIMER (1960) Proc. Soc. Exptl. Biol. Med. *105*, 572

6 FILDES, R. A. and C. W. PARR (1963) Biochem. J. *87*, 45P

7 FILDES, R. A. and C. W. PARR (1963) Nature *200*, 890

8 BAUR, E. W. (1963) J. Lab. Clin. Med. *61*, 166

9 GOLDBERG, E. (1963) Science *139*, 602

10 FREDRICK, J. F. (1963) Phytochem. *2*, 413

11 ALLEN, J. M. and R. L. HUNTER (1960) J. Histochem. Cytochem. *8*, 50

12 OWEN, J. A. and H. SMITH (1961) Clin. Chim. Acta *6*, 441

13 DUBBS, C. A., C. VIVONIA and J. M. HILBURN (1961) Nature *191*, 1203

Thus Raymond et al. (1966) were able to obtain a very sharp band in the β-lipoprotein region from serum plus a 1% solution of lipid crimson in diethylene glycol (2:1, vol/vol) after electrophoresis in a 3% gel.

Protein containing bands can be located by means of staining with great ease. If, however, a quantitative estimate is to be made of the amount of protein present in any area of the gel great care must be taken to ensure completeness of staining and subsequently appropriate corrections are required to compensate for unequal uptake of dye by individual proteins. Information concerning methods for densitometry of stained starch gels is given on p. 126. These techniques are also applicable to acrylamide gels. However, because of their inherent transparency these latter gels do not need any pretreatment such as is usually applied to starch gel. The cylinders of acrylamide gel which have been used for disc electrophoresis present certain special problems in regard to densitometry. Thus because many of the separated regions of protein (the discs) are very close to one another a densitometer with a very narrow beam and a rapid response must be used. If densitometry of the complete gel cylinder is attempted difficulties may arise due to non-parallelism of the discs. Despite this possibility the densitometry of the whole cylinder can be expected to give better results than densitometry of slices prepared as described on p. 67. This is because of the uneven slice thickness almost always obtained from gels of rubbery consistency.

Spectrophotometry of acrylamide gels

Unfortunately the absorption of light by acrylamide gels increases rapidly in the ultraviolet. This is shown in fig. 3.4 which is the absorption curve obtained from a gel after extensive washing to remove catalyst residues. As a result of the high absorption by the gel itself detection of ultraviolet-absorbing substances present in the gel is usually impracticable. At longer wavelengths because of background absorption from the gel, scanning of cylinders or strips of acrylamide is best carried out in an instrument which provides compensation from a blank gel. Such a method using a modified Beckman DU spectrophotometer for scanning gel cylinders containing cytochrome C has been described by Taber and Sherman (1964).

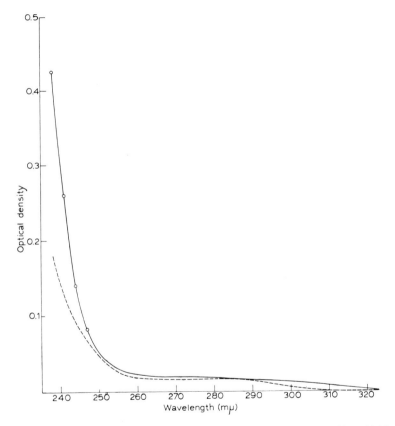

Fig. 3.4. Solid line: Adsorption in the ultraviolet by an 8% acrylamide, 3% bis-acrylamide gel, approximately 0.5 mm thick, which had been washed exhaustively in water to remove catalyst residues and traces of unpolymerized monomer. Broken line: Adsorption of solution used for washing the same gel. The values have been adjusted to give the same optical density at 285 mμ as that shown by the gel.

Subject index p. 145

Drying and storage of stained acrylamide gels

After staining with amido black gels can be kept for long periods without any apparent change if immersed in 7% acetic acid. Since, however, the wet gels are bulky and difficult to store and also because of the possibility of fading, photographic recording is usually preferred. Despite the convenience of such photographs, densitometry of the stained gel, because it provides quantitative information concerning band strength, undoubtedly yields the most valuable records. Thus if densitometry of the stained gel cannot be carried out at once, storage in a form which will permit this to be done later may be desirable. For this purpose it is sufficient for the gel to be soaked for an hour in a solution containing substances which will prevent cracking during drying. A convenient mixture of such plasticisers has been described by Hermans et al. (1960):

Arlex* 60 ml,
Pycal* 40 ml,
Acetic acid (glacial) 40 ml,
Renex 698* 20 ml,
Glycerine 20 ml,
Distilled water to a total volume of 2 l.

The whole gel after soaking in this solution may be placed on a piece of glass and covered with a wet sheet of cellophane. If thus treated the edges of the cellophane are then folded over the glass and held in place with tape. After evaporation of water, which can be speeded up by means of a stream of warm air, the dried gel and cellophane can be stripped off the glass. In this form gels can be stored and densitometry can be carried out at any time. However, the above method is somewhat tedious and much faster drying of gel strips can be achieved by drying *in vacuo* on porous polythene as described on p. 67.

* Available from Atlas Powder Co., Wilmington, Delaware, USA.

Autoradiographs

The positions of bands containing ^{131}I, ^{59}Fe, ^{32}P and other emitters of penetrating radiation in slabs of acrylamide gel may be located with ease by means of autoradiography. After electrophoresis the gel is covered with a sheet of thin polythene and placed in contact with a sensitive X-ray film (e.g. Ilfex X-ray film). When this is developed blackened areas will be found corresponding with the areas in the gel which contain the radioactive substances. If the exposure time is to be more than a few hours the gel should be placed in a polythene bag rather than under a sheet of polythene to prevent evaporation of water from the gel and thus the possibility of distortion. For maximum image sharpness the exposure should be carried out at 0–2 °C. With ^{59}Fe and ^{64}Cu in combination with plasma proteins it is important that the gel should be stained after autoradiography because under the acid conditions used for the staining, some loss of the radioactive isotope will occur. Suitable exposure times with ^{131}I are such that a total of 6×10^5 counts/cm^2 will have accumulated.

Autoradiography of bands containing ^{14}C may also be carried out but only after the gel has been dried. However, before drying the gel if thicker than 2 mm should be sliced. With cylinders of gel as used for disc electrophoresis this may be successfully achieved by means of cutting wires which are held taught in a frame (fig. 3.5). The slices of gel thus produced after soaking in the solution of plasticisers, mentioned on p. 66, are then dried by suction on a vacuum filter plate (Fairbanks et al. 1965). It is important that the surface on which the gel rests during this process and through which suction is applied should be smooth. Porous polythene has been found to be specially suitable for this purpose. The gel if dried down on a sheet of this material will remain smooth and good contact with the photographic film will be possible. To retain the gel on the suction plate during drying the whole surface of the filter plate must be covered with a sheet of wet cellophane the edges of which are secured by means of a rubber band. If thus treated the gel when dry will adhere to the cellophane and may be

Subject index p. 145

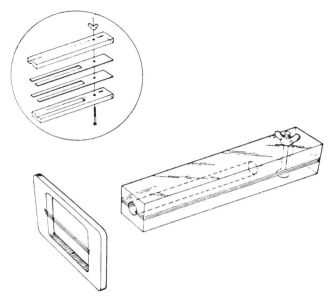

Fig. 3.5. Apparatus of Fairbanks et al. (1965) for longitudinal slicing of cylindrical polyacrylamide gels. Over-all dimensions of Plexiglass gel holder: $1 \times 1 \times 6$ inch; cavity diameter: $^9/_{32}$ inch. Wire separation and spacer thickness: $^1/_{16}$ inch.

stripped off from the suction plate. In a warm atmosphere slices of gel can be dried completely in a few hours. For autoradiography the dried gels are placed in direct contact with the photographic film. If both the autoradiograph and the stained gel from which it was made are scanned with a microdensitometer an estimate of the relative amounts of radioactivity in the bands may be obtained. Because of the close proximity of the bands after separation by the disc method the instrument used should be capable of a high degree of resolution. Fairbanks et al. (1965) used a Joyce–Loebl microdensitometer Model E 12 Mk III for this purpose.

As an indication of the amount required for the production of autoradiographs it can be stated that slices of gel made as above from 8 mm i.d. gel cylinders will lead to a suitable degree of film darkening if the bands before slicing each contained 8,000–10,000 d.p.m. of ^{14}C. Tritium if present will not be detected by the above technique.

Estimation of radioactivity in acrylamide gel

The most suitable method for estimation of the radioactivity of substances present in discrete areas of gel, as for instance in the bands obtained by electrophoresis, depends primarily on the nature of the isotope concerned. If penetrating radiation such as that from ^{131}I or ^{32}P is to be measured the continued presence of the gel is unimportant. Transfer of gel sections into glass tubes can be followed by estimation in any suitable counter. When weak β-emitters such as ^{14}C and tritium are to be estimated the radioactive materials must either be eluted from the gel as described on p. 127 or the gel must be homogenised and then mixed with a suitable scintillation fluid before estimation in a Tricarb or similar counter. Because of its rubbery character the homogenisation of pieces of acrylamide gel is difficult especially if the gel concentration is over 10%. The most convenient method for homogenisation of these gels is passage under pressure through a small orifice. With dilute gels, after cutting up into appropriate sections, sufficient dispersion may be achieved by means of a hypodermic syringe.

Gels of cylindrical cross section can be homogenised very conveniently without previous subdivision, in an apparatus described by Maizel (1966) which consists essentially of a cylinder inside which the gel fits exactly (fig. 3.6). By means of a motor driven piston the gel is forced through a needle valve situated at the other end of the cylinder. After passage through this orifice the disintegrated gel is swept out of the apparatus by a rapid stream of buffer solution. In this way a series of consecutive samples may be obtained from a cylinder of gel. In fig. 3.7 the results obtained with this device are compared with those obtained by sectioning a similar gel by hand. For this purpose 5% gels 10×0.6 cm were used. Estimates of the radioactivity of the disintegrated sections of gel may be obtained either after mixing each with an appropriate volume of scintillation fluid or more simply by

Subject index p. 145

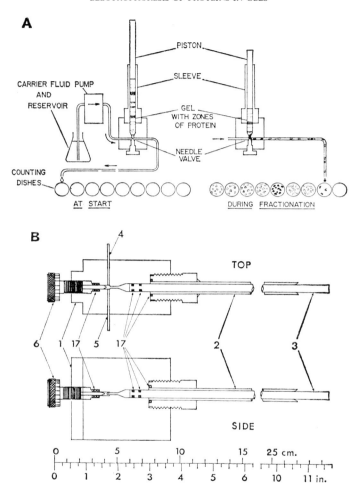

Fig. 3.6. Apparatus for homogenization of cylindrical acrylamide gels (Maizel 1966). (A) Schematic diagram of the mechanical fractionator system. (B) Details of the gel fractionator chamber. (C) Over-all details of the gel fractionator and drive mechanism: 1: gel-extrusion block; 2: stainless-steel sleeve; 3: stainless-steel plunger; 4: inlet for carrier fluid; 5: outlet for gel and fluid; 6: needle valve; 7: fractionator supports; 8: drive screw; 9: threaded half-block; 10: block to hold and drive plunger; 11: thumbscrew to clamp the threaded half-block; 12: guides

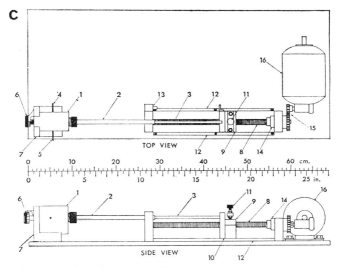

for the plunger-driving block; 13: microswitch to stop the motor; 14: thrust bearing and collar; 15: reduction gears; 16: motor; 17: O-ring seals. The extrusion block, with adjustable orifice, was machined from transparent Plexiglass to enable constant observation of the gel column. The sleeve, 2, to retain and guide the gel during fractionation was of commercial stainless-steel tubing (nominal bore, 0.25 inch (6.4 mm)); the plunger, 3, was made from 0.25-inch stainless-steel rod. For easy assembly and disassembly of the sleeve and extrusion block, a collar with a knurled grip and a $\frac{7}{8}$ inch-14 thread was soldered to the end of the sleeve that engaged the block. The gel orifice was made adjustable by fitting the block with a stainless-steel micrometer needle valve of $\frac{1}{8}$ inch (3.18 mm) tip diameter and $\frac{1}{8}$-inch taper; the valve stem had 40 threads per inch and a knurled knob with 25 graduations, giving 0.001-inch (0.025-mm) displacement of the valve tip for one division of rotation. Inlet and outlet, 4 and 5, for diluting carrier fluid were provided by drilling $^1/_{16}$-inch holes and press-fitting short lengths of No. 16 hypodermic tubing so that about $\frac{1}{2}$ inch (12.7 mm) protruded for the connection of plastic tubing. O-ring seals, 17, at the seat of the sleeve, at the end of the plunger, and around the needle valve prevented leaks. The motor was a 10-rpm constant speed motor (Bodine type NSY-12R), 16, with 2 to 1 reduction, 15, coupled to a $\frac{1}{2}$ inch-20 thread brass drive screw, 8. A threaded steel half-block, 9, engaged the drive screw and moved a block, 10, to drive the plunger. By means of a thumb screw, 11, and springs, the threaded half-block could be easily released to adjust or reset the position of the block. A switch, 13, stopped the motor when the plunger was near bottom, in order to prevent damage.

Subject index p. 145

extrusion on to planchets, drying and counting in a gas flow counter. An example of results obtained by the latter method with 5% acrylamide gels containing ^{14}C is given by Schapiro et al. (1966).

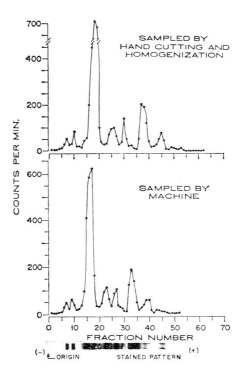

Fig. 3.7. Comparison of electrophoretic pattern of adenovirus type-2 proteins obtained by manual-sectioning, by automatic fractionating using the apparatus of Maizel (1966), and by staining with Coomassie blue (top, center, and bottom, respectively). The stained pattern was photographically reduced to obtain agreement with the plot of the machine-fractionated gel; because of different fraction size, the plot of the manually sectioned gel is somewhat longer but has the same proportionate distribution.

CHAPTER 4

Methods allowing recovery of separated materials (preparative methods)

Advantages and disadvantages of acrylamide gels

Recovery of material can be carried out either continuously during an electrophoresis or from sections of gel obtained when the separation has been completed. For either of these procedures to be conducted successfully it is important that the following properties of the gel should be taken into account.

Insolubility

To avoid contamination of the separated materials the gel itself, at least after sufficient preliminary treatment, should be completely insoluble. This is much more nearly the case for acrylamide than for any of the other gels which have been used in electrophoresis except for silica gel, the pore size of which is too small to permit the passage of large molecules.

The amount of soluble materials which can be eluted from acrylamide gels has been found to depend greatly on the freshness of the solution of acrylamide monomer used for preparation of the gel (Gordon and Louis 1967). If this solution has been stored for any considerable period the amount of soluble material originating from the acrylamide gel is sufficient for estimation either by dry weight or by taking advantage of absorption at 280 mμ. The existence of soluble UV-absorbing material can most easily be demonstrated by allowing pieces of gel to stand in water for a few hours. Alternatively if the gel forms part of an apparatus such as that of Jovin et al. (1964) the

 Subject index p. 145

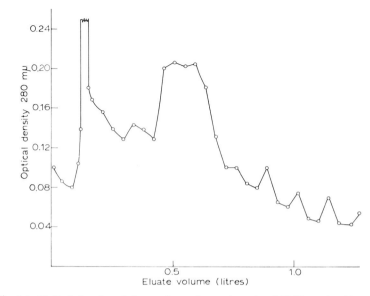

Fig. 4.1. Optical density of eluates from electrophoresis of 12 % acrylamide 3.8 % bisacrylamide gel made from a solution of acrylamide and bisacrylamide kept at 2 °C for several days. The experiment was carried out in the apparatus of Gordon and Louis (1967) cf. page 81. Gel height 5.0 cm. Flow rate of elution buffer 35 ml/hr. 75 mA for 35 hr.

pattern of UV absorption in the stream of elution buffer will be found to consist of a preliminary sharp peak followed by a region with lower but still easily measurable UV absorption (fig. 4.1). If, however, a freshly made up solution of acrylamide and bisacrylamide is employed then once the initial sharp peak has been eluted the UV absorption of the buffer solution which follows will be very low.

Flexibility and resistance to cutting

The flexibility and resistance to fracture of acrylamide gels has several advantages. Thus because slabs of acrylamide gel can be transferred with ease from one apparatus to another preliminary soaking of gel slabs before insertion into an apparatus such as that of Lorber (1964) can be done without any difficulty. In this way the soaking required for removal of a great part of the UV-absorbing material and catalyst residues originally present in acrylamide gels may easily be carried out.

Not only can slabs of acrylamide gel be handled without danger of fracture but after insertion between cooling plates they can be expanded by application of a suitable pressure by as much as 20–30%. When squeezed in this way all danger of buffer flow between the supporting plate and the gel is obviated. In short the mechanical properties of the gel are such that there is little danger of gel fracture. Yet the cutting out of individual bands can be done without serious difficulty although not with as much ease as is the case with starch gel.

A disadvantage of the rubbery texture of acrylamide gels is that the slicing of a slab to obtain two or more layers is difficult. However, the ease with which gels can be cut is improved by cooling. Thus at 2 °C an extruded cylinder may be neatly sectioned transversely if pressed down on to a set of razor blades in a suitable holder. Unfortunately even at a low temperature the slicing of slabs of gel is more difficult to carry out than is the case with starch gel.

Resistance to disintegration

The freezing of acrylamide gel does not lead to break up of the gel and thus to improved elution of contained solutes as is the case with starch gel. If so required, acrylamide gels can be dispersed by passage through a needle valve. Details of this procedure followed by suspension in a scintillation fluid and estimation of radioactivity are described on p. 69.

Stickiness and adherence to glass

In many apparatuses the gel is allowed to set in the space in which it is to remain during the electrophoresis. When used in this way the stickiness of acrylamide gel is a great advantage. However, as mentioned on pp. 9–16 the adherence of acrylamide gels to glass depends on several factors and cannot be expected to prevent detachment of the gel from the supporting wall under all conditions. The adherence of acrylamide to solids depends greatly on the nature of the solid in question. If the surface is unwettable adherence is low. Thus a gel with a flat surface can be obtained, for instance at the end of a glass tube, by standing the tube on a waxy surface and then filling the inside with a solution of acrylamide. A suitable surface of this kind is easily obtained by stretching a sheet of parafilm over a flat plate. After setting of the gel the flat plate and parafilm may be slid away leaving behind a gel surface of excellent smoothness.

Swelling

Gels containing urea present a particularly difficult problem because as the urea concentration changes a marked degree of swelling usually occurs. Such a change, if it occurs in an apparatus designed for continuous elution may lead to blocking of the channel through which the buffer flow must take place. In the apparatus of Duesberg and Rueckert (1965) this difficulty has been ingeniously overcome by arranging for the lower surface of the gel, at which swelling would otherwise occur, to be contained within the pores of a sintered glass disc.

Formation of gels with a flat upper surface

A disadvantage of acrylamide is that gel formation is inhibited by the presence of more than traces of O_2. Because of this property which is described in more detail on p. 43 special precautions are necessary if gels with a flat upper surface are to be formed. Exclusion of O_2 by overlayering with water is by far the most convenient procedure by which this difficulty may be overcome. Thus gels with surfaces of excellent flatness may be set in tubes of less than 1 cm diam. by this method with little difficulty. The overlayering with water may be carried out by hand with a hypodermic syringe to which is attached a flexible tube with a suitable tip (cf. p. 53). When the gel surface which is required has a larger area the apparatus should be placed on a very firm base because even slight vibration, if continued during the period of setting, may lead to a rough gel surface or one showing a pattern of standing waves. An alternative means by which cylinders of gel with flat upper and lower surfaces may be obtained is by casting in a closed cylinder made from a convenient plastic material. Because acrylamide gels show little adherence to surfaces such as that of Perspex, gels may

be cast in containers made from this material and then transferred to a
suitable tube for electrophoresis (Brownstone 1968).

Methods of employment and types of apparatus

Elution from sections of gel before or after disintegration

As indicated above experiments involving recovery of separated
materials can be carried out in any apparatus in which electrophoresis
in acrylamide is possible. This is because, however small the gel may
be, it can always be subdivided after electrophoresis and at least some
of the separated material can then be recovered. Often recoveries will
be found to be disappointingly low but by repeated experiments or
the use of larger gels enough of a given material may be obtained. The
recovery of proteins from sections of a gel may be undertaken either by
simple diffusion or by means of a second stage of electrophoresis, a
process which is often referred to as an electrophoretic elution. If
diffusion alone is to be utilised some advantage can be obtained by a
preliminary disintegration of the gel. If the volume of the gel sections
is sufficient a homogeniser may be used. Alternatively as already
mentioned gels of lower concentrations may be disintegrated by means
of a hypodermic syringe. After such treatment if the sludge is mixed
with water a proportion of the proteins originally present in the gel
will be found to diffuse into the water. As much as 60% of bovine
growth hormone has been recovered by this method by Lewis and
Clark (1963). With serum proteins lower recoveries must be antici-
pated. Higher recoveries of proteins from disintegrated gel may be
achieved by electrophoretic elution. A device for this purpose which can
be attached to the same tube in which the primary electrophoresis has
been carried out has been described by Sulizeanu and Goldman (1965).
If, however, electrophoretic elution is to be used little extra advantage
can be expected to result from preliminary disintegration of the gel.
In a suitable apparatus elution can be carried out directly on pieces of
gel cut out from the original slab in which the separation was conducted. An apparatus which has proved suitable for this purpose is

Subject index p. 145

that used by Gordon (1962) with sections of starch gel (cf. p. 129). With an apparatus of this kind recovery of materials from separated bands contained in pieces of gel $0.8 \times 1.2 \times 10$ cm may be carried out. Somewhat larger or smaller sections of gel can also be accommodated so that recovery from gels used in apparatuses such as those of Raymond (1962) or Lorber (1964) are also possible. The information required for the location of particular bands in a slab of acrylamide gel can most easily be obtained by cutting off both the longitudinal edges and then revealing the pattern of bands which are present, by means of the usual staining method. By this means rather accurate localisation of unstained bands may be achieved.

Vertical columns with end elution

Recovery of individual bands after separation either by chromato-graphy, by electrophoresis or by any other means can be achieved if these bands are made to flow one after the other into a zone from which they are then removed by a steady stream of buffer solution. A suitable experimental arrangement for this purpose was first devised by Porath et al. (1958) who were able to recover proteins by means of a transverse stream of buffer after separation by electrophoresis in a column packed with powdered cellulose. In this apparatus the stream of buffer solution flowed transversely through a short region at the lower end of the column. Subsequently numerous modifications of this basic design have been suggested to allow sequential elution from electrophoresis columns containing both powders and gels. When the substances have been separated in a gel such as acrylamide the zone from which elution takes place may be filled with the eluting liquid only or may, in addition, be packed with an inert powder. The ad-vantage of packing this part of the apparatus with a powder is that this prevents any tendency of the gel to swell during the course of the electrophoresis and thus to block the flow of elution liquid. Fortu-nately the physical properties of acrylamide gels are such that packing of the elution zone is not always required. In the case of the more dilute gels support of some kind is required to ensure retention of the gel in the tube in which it has been set. This can best be provided as described below, by means of Pevikon or another inert granular material. When recovery by this system of elution is carried out from gels containing urea, special measures are needed to control the tendency to swell which is characteristic of such gels in the presence of high concentration of this or similar substances.

Several apparatuses designed to allow collection of separated bands of protein in a stream of buffer are described below. In order to facilitate the assessment of the elution diagrams which are obtained with this type of apparatus some of the factors determining band shape and resolution will be mentioned.

Shape and degree of separation of peaks obtained by continuous elution
Assuming optimum experimental arrangements for elution and monitoring of bands as they arrive at the end of an electrophoresis column, the shape of the elution curves thus obtained will reflect closely the shape of the bands themselves just before exit from the column. For this to occur a sufficient rate of flow of elution buffer must be assumed. An unduly slow flow of elution buffer will lead to an elution curve of the kind shown in fig. 4.2 in which peaks A and B (dotted line) are incompletely separated. The size of the fractions into which the eluting solution is divided will have a similar effect on the shape of the peaks. Thus if too large fractions are taken the resulting adsorption curve will fail to reach the base line even though the peaks before leaving the column may have been completely separated. An elution cell of too large a volume will have the same effect. A pattern of this kind will also be obtained if the bands in the column are tipped or curved. During the course of an electrophoresis if the flow rate of the elution buffer is constant two bands of the same breadth at the time of exit from the column will give elution peaks of width inversely proportional to the mobility of the bands (e.g. peaks A and B in fig. 4.2). The height of the peak due to the substance of lower mobility will of course be less as shown in fig. 4.2 so that the areas of the two peaks will remain constant. If, however, the rate of flow of the eluting buffer is increased the concentration of the eluted substances will be reduced. As shown

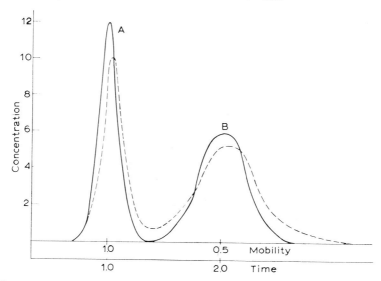

Fig. 4.2. Elution diagram of two bands A and B with mobilities 1 and 0.5. The ordinate is concentration and the abscissa mobility and time. The solid line shows the concentrations expected if elution conditions are satisfactory. The dotted line shows the effect produced if the elution cell has too large a volume or if the bands are tipped or curved. A similar effect is produced if the flow rate of the elution buffer is insufficient or if the fractions are too few.

in fig. 4.3 this will appear as a decrease in peak height and a maintenance of peak width if in the diagram the abscissa is time.

Probably the most important point to be noted is that reduction of elution buffer flow rate will only cause loss of resolution if carried to the point at which elution from the column becomes inefficient. Since bands always broaden as a result of diffusion so long as they remain in the column those with the lowest mobilities must be the broadest when they finally reach the zone from which elution takes place. This effect has to be added on to that already mentioned concerning the inverse proportionality of band width and mobility. These two effects which together result in excessively broad peaks from proteins of low mobility can be restricted or even reversed by increasing the mobility

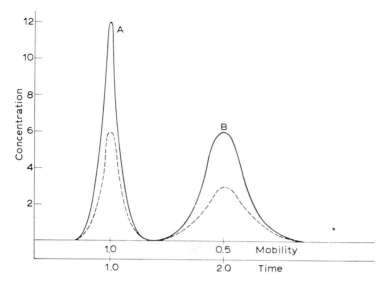

Fig. 4.3. Elution diagram of bands A and B. Band B with mobility half that of band A is collected during a period twice as long as that required for band A. Increase in rate of flow of the elution buffer leads to decreased concentrations for both bands but no change in the widths of the bands. Solid line shows concentration for elution rate 1, dotted line concentrations for double this rate of elution.

of these bands at the time of collection. Unfortunately the increased voltage gradient required for this purpose is necessarily associated with increased production of heat in the column. Thus an upper limit for the permissible voltage gradient is determined by the effectiveness of the cooling arrangements and avoidance of bands with curved fronts.

*Apparatus of Gordon and Louis (1967)**

In principle this apparatus is similar to that of Jovin et al. (1964). Electrophoresis takes place downwards through a vertical cylinder of gel. The separated substances emerge one after another from the lower face of the gel and, if of molecular size too large to pass through a cellophane membrane, are removed in a stream of buffer. All other

* Available from Quickfitt and Quartz Ltd., Stone, Staffordshire, England.

molecules travel through the cellophane membrane into the lower electrode chamber.

An important feature of the present apparatus (fig. 4.4) is that the cellophane membrane is stretched tightly over a rigid Perspex grid

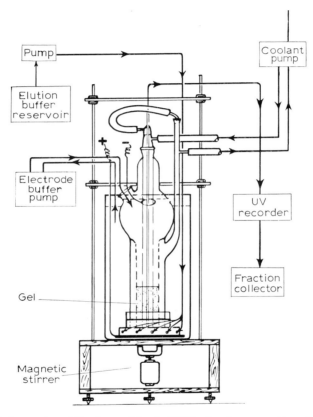

Fig. 4.4. Apparatus of Gordon and Louis (1967), showing connections for elution buffer, electrode buffer mixing pump and coolant. The glassware and electrode buffer jar are held in place by clamps attached to the vertical bars of the framework (not shown). The elution buffer which is degassed just before use is pumped from the reservoir through eight polythene tubes. The exit tube to the fraction collector should be at the same level as that of the buffer solution in the electrode vessels in order to maintain hydrostatic equilibrium.

(fig. 4.5). Bubble trapping in the grid is prevented by the action of a magnetic stirrer. Because the cellophane membrane is rigidly supported it can be fixed in its holder before attachment of the elution cell, of which it forms a part, to the glass cooling jackets. When this is done the membrane is held exactly 3 mm below the lower surface of the gel. Elution buffer is pumped into the circumference of the disc shaped space between the cellophane membrane and the bottom of the gel via eight entry tubes. The convergent streams of buffer after passage across the lower face of the gel join and flow upwards through the central capillary tube and finally exit into a fraction collector.

Before attachment of the elution cell the gel must be set in the space between the inner and outer cooling jackets. To achieve this a sheet of Parafilm is stretched across the lower end of the apparatus. Then with the cooling jackets standing in an exactly vertical position the solution of acrylamide is poured in and overlayered with water.

A single gel 5–10 cm in height containing a rather concentrated buffer (0.37 M Tris at pH 8.8) is used together with buffer of a much lower molarity (0.05 M) in the electrode chambers and for elution. Under these conditions a considerable degree of band sharpening occurs if the sample, which should previously have been dialysed against a dilute buffer (0.01 M), is added as a layer 3 or 4 mm in depth. As shown in fig. 4.6 substances with mobilities down to approximately half that of albumin at pH 8.8 can be successfully recovered. The permissible loading is from 60–100 mg of protein. Unfortunately larger amounts cannot be used because of the likelihood of contraction of the upper layers of the gel (cf. p. 17).

Control experiments in this apparatus in which acrylamide gel only was subjected to electrophoresis revealed very much smaller amounts of substances absorbing at 280 mμ when freshly made up acrylamide was used as compared with the absorption found if the acrylamide solutions had been allowed to stand for some time before the setting of the gel. It is of interest that electrophoresis using a gel of this kind yielded eluates containing both material of rapid mobility and also smaller amounts of slower moving substances. Thus as shown in fig. 4.1 with gels made from solutions of acrylamide unless these have been

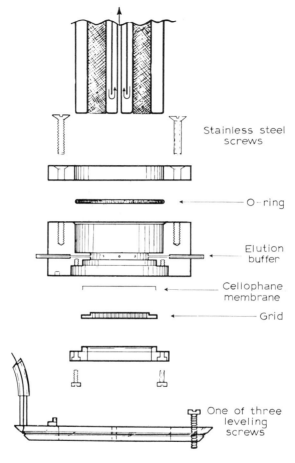

Stainless steel
screws

O - ring

Elution
buffer

Cellophane
membrane

Grid

One of three
leveling
screws

Fig. 4.5. Parts of elution cell used in apparatus of Gordon and Louis (1967). The cell is held on to the outer cooling jacket by an O-ring which is compressed by the upper Perspex ring. The screws which hold this O-ring in place are of stainless steel. The other screws are nylon. The grid is just small enough to fit in place together with the edge of the cellophane membrane. Silicone grease is used here to ensure a water-tight fit. Grease is not required at any other point. The electrode holder is secured to the base of the elution cell by nylon screws (not shown).

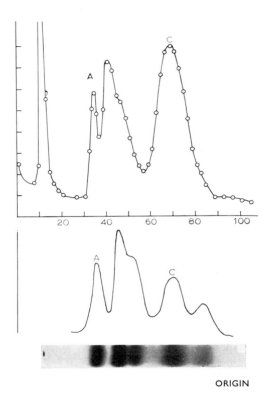

ORIGIN

Fig. 4.6. Apparatus of Gordon and Louis (1967). Upper curve: elution diagram obtained with 60 mg of a concentrate of rat α-globulins containing a little albumin (peak A) separated on an $8 \times 3\%$ acrylamide gel 4.5 cm in height. The elution buffer flow rate was 18 ml/hr. Each fraction consisted of 4.0 ml. A current of 50 mA was passed. The abscissa is the number of fractions collected, each of 4 ml. Lower curve: densitometer curve obtained by scanning an 8-mm cylinder of the same gel in which the same mixture has been separated and then stained with Amido Black 10B. The abscissa with zero at right-hand side represents distance moved. The scale has been adjusted to make the positions of peaks A and C in the two curves correspond. At the bottom is shown a photograph of the stained gel cylinder.

Subject index p. 145

prepared immediately before use, a preliminary electrophoresis cannot be expected to remove as a single peak all soluble ultraviolet absorbing substances. With fresh acrylamide solution absorption (O.D.) at 280 mμ was less than 0.04 for an elution rate of 20 ml/hr and especially after dialysis of the eluates only traces of background material could be detected by weighing (0.015 mg per hour for an 8 % acrylamide gel 8 cm in height of total volume 100 ml).

Evidently it is advantageous to use as dilute as possible buffer solution both in the gel and for elution because in this way a considerable voltage gradient can be employed without the passage of a high current and thus the evolution of a large amount of heat. However, there are several factors which limit the use of very dilute buffer solutions. Thus if a dilute buffer is used in the gel a rough gel surface is liable to occur even though careful overlayering with water has been carried out. In addition the band sharpening effect just mentioned will be more difficult to achieve. The use of very dilute elution buffer is also disadvantageous because as mentioned by Altschul et al. (1964) under these conditions considerable adsorption of albumin on the cellophane membrane must be expected.

Apparatus of Hjerten et al. (1965)

In this apparatus the lower end of the column in which electrophoresis takes place ends in a bed of Pevikon grains through which elution buffer is pumped. Since the diameter of the column is only 1 cm, a sufficiently low temperature in the gel is obtained by external cooling only. As shown in fig. 4.7 the elution chamber forms a unit with the cooling jacket and electrophoresis tube. The whole apparatus is constructed from Perspex (Lucite) except for the two porous polyethylene discs D1 and D2 in fig. 4.7. When in use the column is immersed in buffer solution in a large vessel which also contains the anode. By means of the pump, buffer is slowly drawn in through the disc D1 and across the bottom of the column of acrylamide gel and then out through disc D2. In this way collection is achieved of everything emerging from the lower end of the column irrespective of its molecular size. A special tube T is provided which when attached to

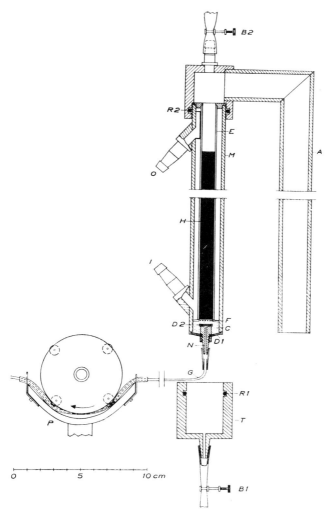

Fig. 4.7. Apparatus of Hjerten et al. (1965) for electrophoresis in acrylamide with provision for continuous elution from the lower end of the column (if not otherwise stated, the material is Perspex). E: electrophoresis tube (i.d. 1.0 cm); H: gel column; M: cooling mantle; I: inlet for cooling liquid; O: outlet for cooling liquid; C: elution chamber, packed with Pevikon powder (Müller-Eberhardt and Nilsson 1960); A: side arm; B1, B2: screw clips; D1, D2: porous polyethylene discs; P: peristaltic pump; R1, R2: O-rings; F: filter paper; N: nipple; G: polyethylene tubing (i.d. 0.5 mm); T: tube used for closing elution chamber C during preparation of gel column H.

the bottom of the elution chamber allows filling with Pevikon and setting of the gel. With this attachment in place and filled with a 6% solution of sucrose the Pevikon is added via the electrophoresis tube. After the bed of Pevikon has been consolidated by means of a vibrator and a disc of filter paper has been laid on its surface, the electrophoresis tube is carefully filled with a solution of acrylamide. The main advantage of this apparatus is that as a result of the support

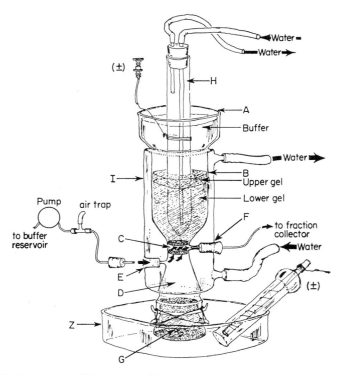

Fig. 4.8. Apparatus of Duesberg and Rueckert (1965) for preparative electrophoresis in acrylamide gels containing urea. The sample migrates in an electric field from the top through the body (B) of a prepolymerized acrylamide gel into the collection chamber (C). As the bands leave the gel and enter the collection chamber, they are flushed out to a fraction collector by a continuous upward flow of buffer entering (C) through a porous bottom disc.

provided by the Pevikon the column of gel cannot slip downwards. It is thus possible to use very soft gels, such as those which have been shown to be suitable for fractionation of ribosomes. Cf. Loening (1967) for gels of acrylamide concentration as low as 2.2%.

Apparatus of Duesberg and Rueckert (1965)

The special advantage of this apparatus is that it makes possible the use of acrylamide gel containing 8 M urea. The gel is set between the inner and outer glass cooling jackets which are shaped as shown in fig. 4.8. Since the thickness of the gel is only 0.75 cm, sufficient cooling is obtained with tap water at 12–15 °C. As in the apparatus of Hjerten et al. (1965) the elution buffer is supplied through the pores of a sintered disc. However, in this apparatus sintered glass rather than porous polyethylene is used in order to facilitate cleaning. An additional reason for the use of sintered glass for the lower porous disc mentioned by Duesberg and Rueckert is the prevention of adsorption of proteins on this part of the apparatus as has sometimes been found to occur when a cellophane membrane is employed (Altschul et al. 1964). The sintered discs used are each 4 mm thick. Before addition of the acrylamide solution a solution of 8 M urea and 20% sucrose also containing a dye-stuff is forced upwards from compartment C (fig. 4.8). The acrylamide solution is then gently added without disturbance of this dense layer. Before the acrylamide has set the level of the urea sucrose solution is lowered until the interface with the acrylamide is approximately half way through the disc. A solution containing 9.3 M urea is used for the elution buffer. The authors emphasise the importance of removal of ions from the 10 M urea solution by stirring for 1–2 hr with 'mixed bed resin' (Bio-Rad Laboratories)*. With this apparatus several successful separations were achieved. These included 4-mg amounts of trypsin and chymotrypsin and tobacco mosaic virus protein from the acetylated form of the same virus protein.

* Bio-Rad Laboratories, 32nd and Griffin Avenue, Richmond, California, USA.

Apparatus of Brownstone

This apparatus consists of a thick disc of gel placed at the bottom of a glass tube 17 cm in height. The gel is retained in the tube by a cellophane membrane which is stretched tightly across the lower end of the glass tube.

Electrophoresis takes place downwards in the cylinder of gel. Because the diameter of this cylinder is as much as 9 cm, 500–600 mg of protein can be handled at a time. The height of the gel is not more

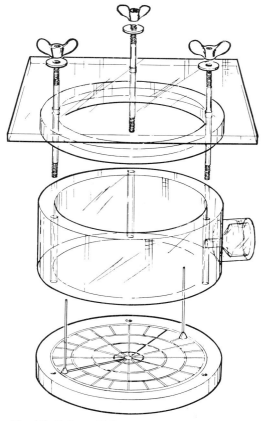

Fig. 4.9. Gel mould for apparatus of Brownstone.

than 6 cm so that a sufficient rate of heat loss occurs mainly from the upper and lower surfaces of the gel. The two requirements that the upper surface of the gel must be flat and that there must be good contact between the gel and the glass cylinder in which it is housed are both met by casting the gel in a separate mould of slightly larger diameter than that of the glass cylinder. As shown in fig. 4.9, this

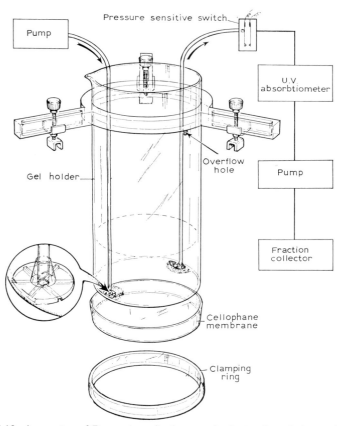

Fig. 4.10. Apparatus of Brownstone for large scale electrophoresis in acrylamide gel. When in use the gel holder hangs vertically inside a buffer containing electrode vessel (not shown). Buffer is pumped continuously from this vessel into the space above the gel from whence it returns through the overflow hole.

Subject index p. 145

mould has a pattern of radial ridges at one end. The grooves which are thus formed in the gel allow passage of the elution buffer across the lower face of the gel. In order to collect the eluted proteins in a minimum volume, inflow and outflow pumps controlled by cam operated switches repeatedly inject, and then after a pause suck out, suitable volumes of buffer. Because the length of the pause between injection and pumping out can be varied (e.g. from 5 to 60 min) substances with different rates of exit from the gel can be collected in more nearly equal volumes of elution buffer. In order to prevent damage to the gel or membrane the functioning of the outflow pump is limited by a pressure sensitive switch. In this way the membrane is sucked tight against the bottom of the gel and remains thus until the injection of a fresh volume of elution buffer. For gels of less than 6% acrylamide a disc of nylon bolting cloth is placed between the lower end of the gel and the membrane. This latter is held in place by the clamping ring shown in fig. 4.10. A magnetic stirrer placed centrally in the buffer vessel prevents accumulation of gas bubbles on the lower face of the membrane. Polyvinylchloride tubing O.D. 3 mm, I.D. 1 mm, is used for the elution buffer supply and outflow tubes. Each of these terminates in the conical end piece shown in the diagram. These are a push fit and are placed in position after the buffer tubes have been pressed through the two vertical holes present in the gel.

As in most apparatuses of this kind the solution to be separated is layered on to the surface of the gel after addition of sufficient sucrose to prevent convection. Care is necessary to avoid the presence in the initial solution of too high a concentration of proteins of very low mobility as these may form a gelatinous layer on the surface of the gel through which a large part of the material to be fractionated cannot pass.

For separation of human serum a 4% acrylamide gel containing 0.05 M glycine and 0.03 M Tris adjusted to pH 7.8 with acetic acid proved satisfactory. With the same buffer in the electrode vessels 6 ml of serum diluted to 25 ml with the buffer plus sucrose was applied. After 15 hr at 250 mA the γ-globulin started to emerge and was collected in a state of almost complete homogeneity.

CHAPTER 5

Starch gel

Introduction

Numerous mixtures of proteins may be separated equally well by electrophoresis either in starch or in acrylamide gels. Since 1955 when starch gel electrophoresis was first described (Smithies 1955) almost every available mixture of proteins has been thus investigated. A list of the reports of this work down to 1964 has been published (Connaught Medical Research Laboratories 1964). In view of the large body of information already available concerning the separation of particular mixtures in starch gel the use of this medium may often be preferred to the use of acrylamide. A further reason for choosing starch gel is the simplicity of the system. Thus in addition to the starch itself the only reagents required are those needed for the buffer solutions. Finally the completely non-toxic character of potato starch must be contrasted with the toxicity of acrylamide monomer (Fullerton and Barnes 1966).

Pretreatment of granular starch in acid acetone

Conversion of granular potato starch to the gel form used for electrophoresis is a process consisting of two stages. Firstly a partly hydrolysed material is produced by warming potato starch in acetone containing 1 % by volume of concentrated HCl (cf. p. 99). After drying, the partially hydrolysed starch may be stored indefinitely. The second stage in which this material is converted to a gel requires a somewhat

Subject index p. 145

higher temperature. In practice a suspension of the partially hydrolysed starch in an appropriate buffer is heated and at the same time
stirred or swirled vigously (Poulik and Smithies 1958). As the temper-

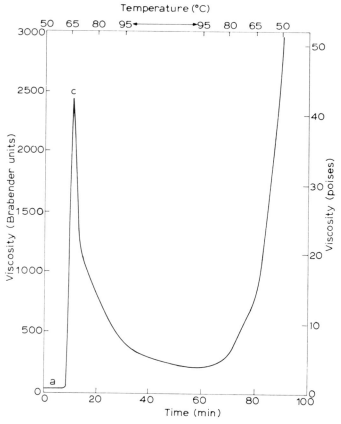

Fig. 5.1. The changes in viscosity, determined with a Brabender Amylograph,
during the preparation of a typical borate buffer starch gel (13.0 g lot A 28 A
'starch-hydrolysed'/100 ml 0.023 M boric acid, 0.0092 M sodium hydroxide).
Automatic heating and cooling cycles are provided by the apparatus. The viscosity
is shown on the vertical axes; the corresponding temperatures and times are shown
on the horizontal axes (Smithies 1959b).

ature rises the viscosity increases and then falls sharply (fig. 5.1). Once this has occurred a gel will be formed on cooling with properties suitable for the electrophoretic separation of proteins. Close control of both these processes is necessary to produce a starch gel with suitable properties for electrophoresis of proteins. The hydrolysed starch available from Connaught Medical Research Laboratories is made for this purpose and will provide gels of excellent properties. However, as mentioned by Morris and Morris (1964) a different degree of hydrolysis may be necessary to provide starch of optimum resolving power for certain mixtures of proteins.

Choice of appropriate starch gel

The mobilities of proteins or other charged molecules in starch gel differ from those existing in free solution as a result of the sieving action of the gel. Thus the choice of an appropriate gel for any given separation must take into account both the retardations resulting from the pore size of the starch gel and the free solution mobilities of the substances being separated. Since the mobilities of the substances in question are also determined by the voltage gradient in the gel and the net charges of the molecules undergoing electrophoresis, the pH and concentration of the buffer solution contained in the gel are two other important factors. Of these the pH of the buffer is most important because of its role in determining the charges carried by and thus the mobilities of the substances being separated. The final pH reached after addition of the buffer to the starch should be checked as residual acid in the starch may bring about some alteration in the original pH value of the buffer.

Pore size

In the absence of any reliable direct estimate of the range of pore sizes existing in starch gels of different concentration certain indirect evidence must be considered. This consists of the relative mobilities of pairs of proteins in the starch gel and in acrylamide gel. As a result of the work of Fawcett and Morris (1966) the mobilities of a number

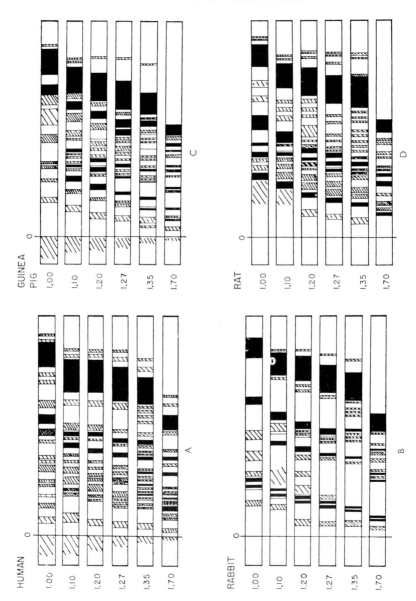

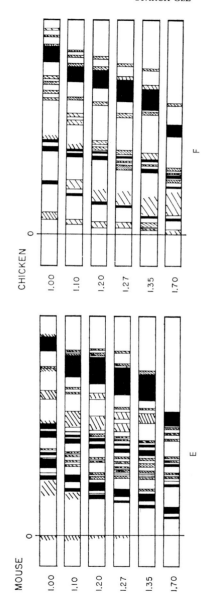

Fig. 5.2. A–F. Diagrammatic representation of the variations in one-dimensional vertical gel-electrophoresis patterns of human, rabbit, guinea pig, rat, mouse and chicken sera as a function of starch concentrations between 11.8 and 20.2%. The concentration of starch used, expressed proportionately to that recommended by the manufacturer (1.00) appears at the left of each pattern. (From Krotoski et al. 1966.)

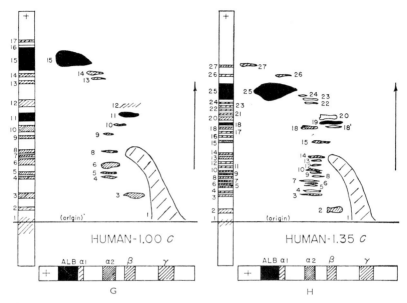

Fig. 5.2. G, H. Two-dimensional electrophoresis patterns of human serum at starch concentrations. Left, recommended for the continuous borate buffer system (1.0c); right, optimum for the discontinuous Tris–citrate and borate system (1.35c). In both cases the paper electrophoresis was conducted in 0.075 M veronal buffer and the Tris–citrate–borate system of Poulik (1957) was used in the starch gel. (From Krotoski et al. 1966.)

of proteins in acrylamide gels of widely different total acrylamide concentrations are now known. Thus it is not difficult to ascertain the concentration of acrylamide gel which gives the same relative mobilities for a pair of proteins as those found when the same two proteins undergo electrophoresis in a particular starch gel. Identity of buffer pH and concentration and a correction for electroendosmosis in the starch gel are of course assumed. In the case of an acrylamide and a starch gel which give the same relative mobilities for a pair of proteins in such circumstances it would seem reasonable to assume, at least as a first approximation, an identity of pore sizes. Albumin in the monomer and dimer forms is an example of such a pair of proteins the relative mobilities of which are known in both kinds of gel. Thus for instance Pert and Pinteric (1964) report that the relative mobility of the two forms of albumin is 0.56 in starch gel (presumably of 13% starch concentration).

According to the data of Morris (1966) the same two forms of albumin have relative mobilities of 0.56 in an acrylamide gel with a concentration of approximately 7.5%.

If mixtures of proteins of very various sizes are to be separated the most suitable gel will retard the larger molecules to a considerable degree and those of average size to a lesser extent. Inevitably the smaller protein molecules will have almost the same mobilities as if they were in free solution. In the case of the serum proteins a careful study of optimum starch concentration has been made by Krotoski et al. (1966). Optimum pore size as indicated by maximum resolution was obtained using gels containing between 13% and 16% of starch. The effects of the different concentrations of starch on the patterns obtained are shown in fig. 5.2. By electrophoresis in one dimension the presence of as many as 27 components were thus demonstrated in human serum. If is of interest that these authors obtained optimum separations of plasma proteins at a starch concentration considerably higher than that recommended by the manufacturers.

The pore size in a starch gel can be varied most conveniently simply by alteration of the concentration of the starch. For most purposes gels of a sufficient degree of resolving power can be obtained in this way by using the hydrolysed starch commercially available from Connaught Medical Research Laboratories. However, as mentioned above a different degree of hydrolysis may sometimes provide starch gel of more suitable properties. To make this possible the recommendations of Poulik and Smithies (1958) concerning hydrolysis conditions are relevant. These are that test quantities of Danish potato starch should be suspended in acetone containing 1% by volume of concentrated HCl and maintained at 37 °C for periods from $\frac{1}{2}$ to $2\frac{1}{2}$ hr. Subsequently the hydrolysis should be terminated by addition of Na acetate and then the starch washed with water and acetone and dried.

Subject index p. 145

TABLE 5.1
Starch gels

Buffer solutions — In gel			Buffer solutions — In electrode vessels			Materials investigated (examples only)	Results
Buffer ions	M	pH	Buffer ions	M	pH		
Borate†*	0.025	8.5	Borate	0.3	8.5	Serum[1]	Citrate borate boundary is seen as a brown band
Tris Citrate†	0.076 0.005	8.6	Borate	0.3	8.5	Serum[2,3], diphtheria toxin[2], horse radish peroxidase[2], haptoglobins[5] and transferrins[6]	
						Haemoglobins[4], human and animal sera[7], staphylococcal enterotoxin B[16]	The electrophoresis is over in less time compared to borate only
Tris Borate† EDTA	0.045 0.025 0.002	8.4	Tris Borate EDTA	0.013 0.075 0.006	8.4	Haemoglobins[12,13,14] Serum[17]	Hb A and F are separated
Tris Maleate† EDTA MgCl₂	0.01 0.01 0.001 0.001	7.4	Tris Maleate EDTA MgCl₂	0.1 0.1 0.01 0.01	7.4	Haemolysates investigated for phosphoglucomutase[20]	
Glycine	0.05	8.9	Borate	0.3	8.9	Myeloma γ-globulin[8]	Five bands
Citrate† Borate† Tris Lithium	0.0027 0.0076 0.0144 0.0020	8.0	— Borate — Lithium	— 0.38 — 0.10		Anterior pituitary hormones[15]	
Tris HCl	0.03 —	8.4	Tris HCl	0.05 —		Tissue dehydrogenases[21]	
Acetate	0.1	5.0	—	—		Pepsin and gastricsin[23]	The enzymes were recovered from the gel

For footnotes see table 5.2.
References, see p. 102.

TABLE 5.2

Starch gels containing urea

	Buffer solutions							Materials investigated (examples only)	Results
	In gel				In electrode vessels				
Buffer ions	M	pH	Urea M		Buffer ions	M	pH		
Formate	0.05	3.0	8		Formate	0.2	2–3	γ-Myeloma, heavy chains[10], antibodies[18]	Slightly sharper bands were obtained if alkylation was done as well as reduction
Aluminium lactate	0.05	3.1	3		Aluminium lactate			Gliadin[11]	
Glycine	0.035	7–8	8		Borate	0.3	8.2	γ-Globulin heavy and light chains[9]	Light chains well separated
Borate†	0.025	8.5	8		Borate	0.3	8.5	Haptoglobins[19]	Without prior reduction urea has no effect
Tris Citrate†	0.076 / 0.005	8.6	7		Borate	0.3	8.6	α- and β-casein[22,25]	Urea treatment of α crystallin, without reduction, leads to formation of many bands
Acetate	0.0365	5.6	6		—	—	—	E.coli ribosomal proteins[24]	At least 14 bands

† Molarities based on weight of orthoboric (H₃BO₃) or other acid taken. When no cation is given the acids have been adjusted to the pH shown by addition of NaOH.

* For optimum results use borate concentration recommended for each invidual batch of starch.

References, see p. 102.

Buffer solution in the gel

Much of the information given on p. 38 and in table 2.1 concerning buffers suitable for use in acrylamide gels is also relevant to electrophoresis in starch gel. The buffers which have been used most successfully in the latter gel are listed in tables 5.1 and 5.2 together with

---

References to tables 5.1 and 5.2

[1] SMITHIES, O. (1955) Biochem. J. *61*, 629

[2] POULIK, M. D. (1957) Nature *180*, 1477

[3] POULIK, M. D. (1959) J. Immunol. *82*, 502

[4] DE GROUCHY, J. (1958) Rev. Franc. Etudes Clin. Biol. *3*, 877

[5] GIBLETT, E. R., A. G. MOTULSKY and G. R. FRAZER (1966) Am. J. Human Genet. *18*, 553

[6] HARRIS, H., E. B. ROBSON and M. SINISCALCO (1958) Nature *182*, 452

[7] KROTSKI, W. A., D. C. BENJAMIN and H. E. WEIMER (1966) Can. J. Biochem. *44*, 545

[8] ASKONAS, I. (1961) Biochem. J. *79*, 33

[9] COHEN, S. and R. R. PORTER (1964) Biochem. J. *90*, 278

[10] EDELMAN, G. M. and M. D. POULIK (1961) J. Exptl. Med. *113*, 861

[11] WOYCHICK, J. H., J. A. BOUNDY and R. J. DIMLER (1961) Arch. Biochem. Biophys. *94*, 477

[12] WINTERHALTER, K. H. and E. R. HUEHNS (1964) J. Biol. Chem. *239*, 3699

[13] HUEHNS, E. R., N. DANCE, G. H. BEAVEN, J. V. KEIL, F. HECHT and A. G. MOTULSKY (1964) Nature *201*, 1095

[14] CHERNOFF, A. I. and N. M. PETTIT (1965) Blood *25*, 646

[15] FERGUSON, K. A. and A. L. C. WALLACE (1961) Nature *190*, 629

[16] BAIRD-PARKER, A. C. and R. L. JOSEPH (1964) Nature *202*, 570

[17] POULIK, M. D. (1966) In: D. Glick, ed.; Methods of Biochemical Analysis (Interscience Publishers) vol. 14, p. 455

[18] EDELMAN, G. M., B. BENACERRAF and Z. OVARY (1963) J. Exptl. Med. *118*, 229

[19] SMITHIES, O. and G. E. CONNELL (1959) In: Biochemistry of Human Genetics (Churchill, London) p. 178

[20] SPENCER, N., D. A. HOPKINSON and H. HARRIS (1964) Nature *204*, 742

[21] TSAO, M. U. (1960) Arch. Biochem. Biophys. *90*, 234

[22] WAKE, R. G. and R. L. BALDWIN (1961) Biochim. Biophys. Acta *47*, 227

[23] TANG, J., S. WOLF, R. CAPUTTO and R. E. TRUCCO (1959) J. Biol. Chem. *234*, 1174

[24] WALLER, J. P. and J. I. HARRIS (1961) Proc. Natl. Acad. Sci. *47*, 18

[25] BLOEMENDAL, H., W. S. BOUT, J. F. JONKIND and J. H. WISSE (1962) Nature *193*, 437

some of the mixtures of proteins for the separation of which they have been employed. It will be noted that buffers of rather low ionic strength are often used and that successful separations are possible in starch gel over the whole range of *p*H from 2 to 11. The importance of the precise ionic strength at least for optimum separation of the plasma proteins is indicated by the recommendation of Smithies (1959) that 0.026 M borate buffer should be used in his vertical apparatus whereas previously (Smithies 1955) in the horizontal apparatus, 0.023 M borate was considered to be best.

The importance of the ionic strength and constitution of the buffer in starch gels containing urea at an acid *p*H has been investigated by Azen et al. (1966). Using stromal proteins as a test system these authors found that altered concentration of buffers from 0.01 to

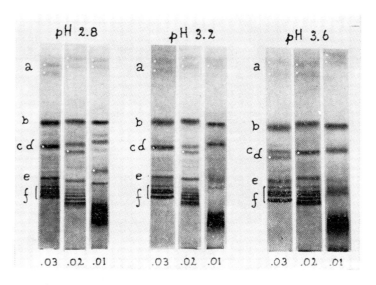

Fig. 5.3. Buffer concentration and *p*H in starch gel (Azen et al. 1966). Effects on stromal protein separations of varying ionic concentration and *p*H in a single buffer system (barium lactate). The buffer *p*H of each group of three patterns is indicated at the top of the patterns, and the buffer cation molarity is shown at the bottom of the patterns.

0.03 M led to important differences in the patterns which they obtained (fig. 5.3). As might be expected change of pH (2.8 to 3.6) also made some difference. On the other hand the substitution of a wide range of different anions and/or cations led to little or no change in the patterns.

During the process of electrophoresis in starch gel as first shown by Smithies (1955) very considerable variation in voltage gradients occur in the regions occupied by bands of protein especially if these are present at a considerable concentration. See fig. 5.4 for the voltage gradient observed by Smithies (1955) in a gel containing human serum. The effects of a voltage profile of this kind are complex but at least in certain regions greatly increased resolution of components occurs. A rather similar situation can be created in another way by the use of a different buffer solution in the gel and in the electrode

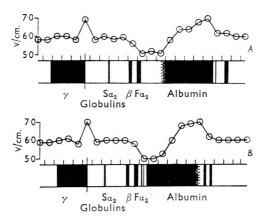

Fig. 5.4. Potential gradients observed at 5-mm intervals along the gels and corresponding protein distributions obtained after 6-hr electrophoresis of a group I serum in (A) a 12.5% starch gel, and (B) a 15% gel. The marks along the upper edges of the diagrams of the gels represent the electrode positions. The circles on the graphs show the mean potential gradient between the corresponding adjacent electrode pairs. The cross hatching indicates regions where the protein concentration changes slowly. The positions of the filter papers used for sample insertion are shown by a line extending above and below the diagrams. (Smithies 1955.)

chambers. Since the work of Poulik (1957) numerous very refined separations have been brought about by systems of this kind which are often referred to as 'discontinuous buffers'. The effects obtained in this way are due largely to the passage of a front of increased voltage gradient through the gel.

Effect of urea when present in starch gel

When urea is present in starch gel in which proteins are undergoing electrophoresis there are important effects both on the proteins themselves and on the starch gel. Some of the effects on the proteins have been mentioned above (p. 26). According to the structures of the protein molecules which are present treatment with urea may lead either to a larger or to a smaller number of bands. Thus in presence of urea, and without any other addition, at least one extra component is formed from caeruloplasmin (Poulik 1962) and α-crystallin has been shown by Bloemendal et al. (1962) to form numerous sharp bands when thus treated. Haptoglobin and γ-globulin on the other hand are relatively little effected by treatment with urea only. However, when treated with urea and a reducing agent haptoglobin divides into fewer bands whereas certain γ-globulins as a result of s–s cleavage may split up into as many as 10 bands. For separation of light chains cf. Cohen and Porter 1964.

The remarkable sharpness of these bands in gels containing concentrated urea may be due to restricted diffusion of the unfolded protein subunits. That slower rates of diffusion are likely to occur in these circumstances is to be expected from the observations already mentioned on p. 19 of Craig et al. (1965) who have measured diffusion through cellophane of protein in presence and absence of urea.

Urea when present in starch gel has two effects both of which are of some importance in relation to the use of the gel for electrophoresis. These relate to the time required for setting of the gel and its transparency. Thus gels which contain a high concentration of urea set relatively slowly. According to Porter (1966) starch gel containing more than 8 M urea cannot be used satisfactorily for electrophoresis.

Subject index p. 145

This limitation does not apply to acrylamide gels. When the setting of starch gels is complete they are almost as transparent as is acrylamide gel and of a more rubbery character than in absence of urea.

Buffer systems for particular proteins (starch gel)

The following information is additional to that contained in table 5.1:

Liver proteins.   Both continuous and discontinuous buffer systems have been used with some success for the separation of liver proteins. Thus Kalant et al. (1964) using 0.021 M borate at pH 8.2 in a vertical starch gel obtained 15 bands (cf. Smithies 1959a). De Grouchy and Rosselin (1962) used the discontinuous system of Poulik (1957) to separate transferrin from the other proteins of a liver homogenate.

Proteins of milk.   The complexity of both α- and β-caseins has been well demonstrated by Wake and Baldwin (1961) who used the discontinuous buffer system of Poulik (1957) in 11.4% starch gel containing 7 M urea. α-Lactalbumin and β-lactoglobulin have been found to separate well in starch gel at pH 3.0 containing 0.05 M formate buffer and 5 M urea (Robbins and Kronman 1964).

Muscle proteins.   Muscle extracts have been shown to give as many as 35 bands after electrophoresis in a vertical starch gel containing borate buffer (Skopes and Lawrie 1963). Hartshorne and Perry (1962) who investigated rabbit sarcoplasm also used borate buffers. For investigations on myosin Mueller and Perry (1962) used 0.022 M borate in 8 M urea at pH 9.1. 8 M urea with 0.012 M glycine at pH 8.5 was used by Carsten and Mommaerts (1963) for investigation of actin.

Wheat proteins.   Gehrke et al. (1964) used the aluminium lactate buffer system of Woychik et al. (1961) (cf. table 5.2) with 7 M instead of with 3 M urea for characterisation of wheat proteins. They found that the best separations were obtained using 9.24% starch and 0.1 M aluminium lactate buffer at pH 3.1. More than 20 components were thus obtained.

Heat-denatured collagen. Nanto et al. (1965) investigated the optimum conditions for separation in starch gel of the subunits of neutral salt soluble collagen. Because the isoelectric points of the sub-units are differently affected by the ionic strength of the medium the buffer concentration in the gel was found to be critical. Optimum separations were obtained in 0.017 M acetate buffer at pH 4.7 in the gel and electrode compartments. The concentration of starch in the gel was 14.7%.

Haemocyanin. Crayfish serum has been subjected to electrophoresis in 12.5% starch gel by Whittaker (1959) who reported two bands containing haemocyanin. The conditions were similar to those of Smithies (1955) except that 0.02 M borate at pH 8.03 was used in the gel.

Preparation of starch gel

The preparation of a starch gel involves the following stages:
(1) Mixing the dry starch with the appropriate buffer solution to form a lump free suspension;
(2) heating the suspension in a round bottomed flask until it has thickened and then become less viscous;
(3) degassing by partial evacuation;
(4) pouring on to a glass plate or into any other suitable container;
(5) covering the surface before setting has taken place.

After the gel has set the glass or plastic cover is carefully removed in order to permit insertion of the samples which are to be investigated. Since the methods for the insertion of the samples differ considerably according to the type of apparatus in question the procedures involved are described below following the description of each apparatus.

Further details concerning the above five procedures necessary for the formation of a starch gel will now be given:
(1) In general the amount of starch used should be that recommended by the manufacturer for the particular batch of starch. When stirred with buffer solution at room temperature hydrolysed starch will

readily form a smooth suspension. The total volume of this suspension should be at least one and a half times the volume of the tray or other container in which the gel is to be set. The starch and buffer solution should be mixed in a round bottomed flask of which the volume is at least 5 times that of the resulting suspension.

(2) The heating may be conducted either in a water bath or with care over an open flame. As shown in fig. 5.1 after a sharp initial rise in viscosity with further increase in temperature a fall in the viscosity of the solution of starch will take place. Especially during the period of high viscosity, sticking of starch on to the flask bottom must be avoided by a rapid swirling motion.

(3) Once the viscosity of the starch has begun to fall decisively the contents of the flask should be rapidly degassed by a brief application of vacuum. No further heating or swirling is needed during this degassing process which should be carried through in the course of approximately 1 min.

(4) Without delay the now transparent and still rather viscous solution should be poured onto the centre of the glass plate or into any other container which is to form the base of the gel. If glass is used for this purpose the best results will be obtained if it has been cleaned by means of chromic acid. A rectangular Perspex frame previously placed on the glass is a simple and effective means for retaining the viscous solution.

(5) Without waiting for the corners of the frame to be filled up the cover plate is lowered smoothly on to the starch in such a way as to avoid entrapment of bubbles. Excess starch is allowed to escape over one end of the frame and finally the cover is slid completely into position and is pressed firmly down and retained by means of a weight.

After setting has taken place which occurs in the course of half an hour the cover is carefully removed. If glass has been used for this purpose a knife blade should first be inserted at a number of points. The gel will be ready for use as soon as it has reached room temperature.

Certain special precautions are necessary when starch gels containing concentrated urea are to be prepared. Thus care must be exercised to avoid an unwanted increase in pH and conductivity as a result of the decomposition of cyanate ions, traces of which are always present in solutions of urea.

Because under acid conditions cyanate ions decompose to CO_2 and ammonia, gels containing urea and a buffer solution at any pH below 7.0 should be used as soon as possible after setting. The equilibrium between urea and ammonium cyanate is not itself effected by the pH of the solution. Furthermore because decomposition of cyanate only occurs to a significant extent below pH 7 and because after loss of CO_2 the ammonia remaining behind tends to increase the pH the change is self limiting. However, in acid gels containing urea some increase in pH and conductivity must be expected. In order to minimise these changes the period during which decomposition of cyanate can occur should be kept as short as possible. In order to achieve this, starch and 'Analar' urea should be thoroughly mixed in the dry state. Next the powder thus formed should be added to the buffer solution and heated in a water bath held at 70 °C. After 5 min at this temperature the flask should be removed from the bath and shaken vigorously. After a further 2 min heating the flask should again be removed and shaken. Several repetitions of this process will render the solution ready to degass which can be done as described above. According to Smithies (1962) with gels containing urea the degassing process may be omitted. 10–12 hr after pouring into the tray the setting will be complete. Because of the changes in pH and conductivity mentioned above gels containing concentrated urea at pH values below 7 should be used within 24 hr of preparation.

An alternative means by which NH_4^+ can be removed from solutions of starch and urea has been described by Melamed (1967). During dissolution of the urea and starch but before addition of the buffer a suitable quantity of Zeocarb 225 in the H^+ form is added and then removed by filtration. As shown in fig. 5.5 in presence of the resin (2 g Zeocarb 225 H^+, 16–50 mesh for 500 ml of 8 M urea) little change of either pH or conductivity occurred on heating to 80 °C. Thus this procedure allows the preparation of urea containing starch gels of suitably low conductivity.

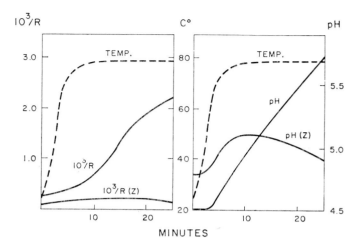

Fig. 5.5. Effect of heating 9.5 M urea solution at 80 °C. The pH and resistance (R-measured in a standard conductivity cell) of a 9.5 M solution of urea was measured as the solution was heated in an 80° bath. The curves marked with (Z) were obtained in solutions containing 2 % (w/v) Zeocarb 225 H$^+$ resin (16–50 mesh). (Melamed 1967.)

Choice of apparatus

As originally described (Smithies 1955) electrophoresis in starch gel was conducted in a horizontal gel. The container for the gel was a Perspex tray 2 cm wide, 25 cm long and 0.65 cm in depth. The bottom of the tray was only 1.5 mm thick to allow a sufficient rate of heat loss. Although excellent separations can be obtained with this simple apparatus precautions must be taken to prevent irregularities in the shapes of the bands due to electrodecantation of the protein solution in the sample slot. To avoid the occurrence of this phenomenon a vertical apparatus was later introduced (Smithies 1959a). Especially when used in a refrigerator or cold room very refined separations have been obtained by this means. In choosing which of these two types of apparatus will be most appropriate for a particular purpose the following points may be considered:

(1) The horizontal apparatus is the simpler both in construction and in use. Thus a sheet of glass and a rectangular Perspex frame are sufficient support for the gel. Furthermore a special slot former is not needed. Methods for sample insertion in these gels will be described in detail below. Because the sample solution is usually introduced already soaked into rectangles of filter paper accurate levelling of the horizontal apparatus as is essential with the vertical type is not required. (2) Because the vertical apparatus allows for an equal rate of heat loss from both sides of the gel, especially with thin gels (e.g. up to a thickness of 3 mm) rather high voltage gradients can be employed and excellent separations can be achieved. However to make this possible, after the samples have been run into the slots the whole surface of the gel must be covered with an even layer of petroleum jelly. Cooling may also be provided by means of water jackets. If these are used and the gel thickness is 3 mm potential gradients of as much as 20 V/cm can be employed (Smithies 1959b).

Horizontal apparatus (normal size)

As mentioned above the gel can be set most conveniently between two sheets of glass separated by a rectangular frame. After detachment of the upper sheet of glass the gel is ready for the insertion of the samples. This can be carried out most easily by the use of pieces of thick filter paper (Ford A4)* previously wetted with the solutions. These are inserted into individual vertical cuts in the gel made with a suitable razor blade. Each piece of paper is pressed into the cut before the razor blade is removed. The vertical height of these pieces of filter paper should be slightly less than the thickness of the gel. Any possibility that the filter paper will be drawn out with the blade can be obviated by laying a rectangular glass bar across the gel in contact with the razor blade and over the slot containing the filter paper.

According to Smithies (1959b) the regularity and straightness of the

* Obtainable from Carlson Ford Sales Ltd, 16 Heneage Street, London E.I., England.

Subject index p. 145

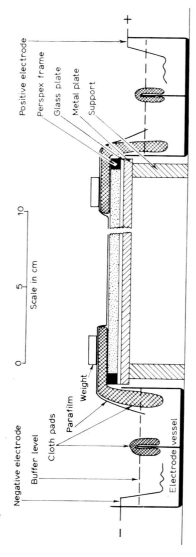

Fig. 5.6. Cross section of apparatus for electrophoresis in a horizontal slab of starch gel. The gel is set on a thin sheet of glass and is retained by a Perspex frame. The electrode vessels are each divided into two compartments to prevent changes of *pH* originating at the electrodes from spreading into the gel. The current passes from the electrode vessels into the gel via pads of folded cloth which are damped with the buffer solution before the electrophoresis is started. The purpose of the Parafilm is to prevent evaporation from these pads and from the surface of the gel. A convenient length for the gel is 25 cm. Gels of any thickness up to 0.9 cm may be used with success.

bands with mobilities less than that of the slow α_2 is improved by the use of granular starch rather than filter paper for stabilisation of the sample solutions. For this method of application slots 1 to 2 mm in width should be cut out of the gel.

Sample slots of up to 5 mm in width have sometimes been used to accommodate larger volumes of solution. If this is done an inert powder such as granular starch should also be added to prevent band distortion due to electrodecantation effects. A more convenient technique is the use of more than usually concentrated protein solutions soaked into the rectangles of filter paper. By this method with Ford A4 filter paper and a 9 mm thick gel up to 5 mg protein per cm width of gel may be used (Gordon 1962). After addition of the samples, the surface of the gel except for the final 4 cm at each end is covered with a sheet of Parafilm. Next the covered gel is placed between the electrode vessels as shown in fig. 5.6. Connection with the buffer solution in the electrode vessels is established by means of thick cloth pads which have been well damped with the same solution. Good contact with the surface of the gel is maintained by weights which are placed on the ends of the pads. In order to allow a rapid rate of heat loss from the gel the sheet of glass on which the gel is set should rest on a metal plate during the electrophoresis.

Horizontal apparatus (micro scale)

As already mentioned electrophoresis in starch gel can be carried out successfully in slabs no more than 0.9 mm in thickness. The advantages of working with such thin gels are not only that very minute amounts of proteins can be separated but also that the whole procedure including staining and destaining can be carried out in 20 min. This is possible in an apparatus described by Daams (1963) because very efficient cooling is provided. The gels adhering to the underside of glass coverslides make contact with two blocks of agar. As shown in fig. 5.7 the central compartment of the apparatus is filled with pentane which provides cooling by evaporating in an air stream induced by a water pump. In these circumstances a voltage gradient of 85 V/cm

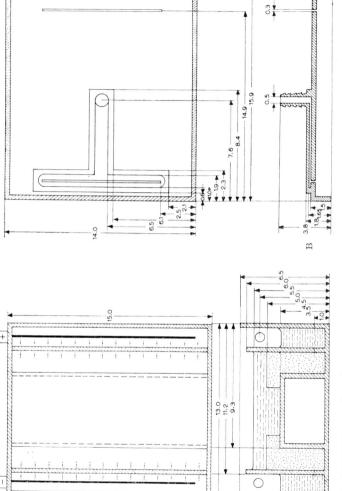

Fig. 5.7. (A) Electrophoresis apparatus of Daams (1963) without cover shown from above and in transverse section. Measurements in centimeters. Material is Perspex, 3 mm thick. Mid- and side-compartments are shown filled with agar overlaid with pentane, and electrode buffer respectively. Holes between compartments have a diameter of 1 mm. (B) Cover of the electrophoresis apparatus; cf. (A). Views shown are from above, in longitudinal and in transverse section. Cooling is provided by evaporation of the pentane which is speeded up by means of the stream of air withdrawn continuously through the centre of the lid.

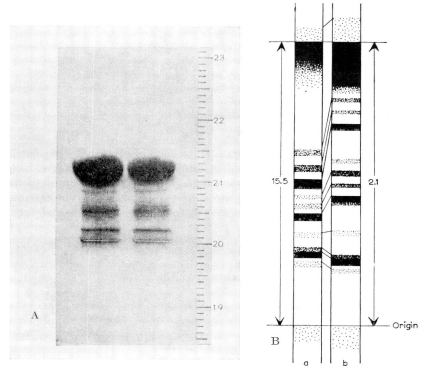

Fig. 5.8. (A) Electropherogram of mouse serum after micro starch-gel electrophoresis. Both slits contained ± 0.2 μl of C₅₇BL male serum. Duration of electrophoresis is 15 min. Staining: Amido Black 10B. Ruling in cm. (B) Comparison of electropherograms obtained with, a, macro and, b, micro starch-gel electrophoresis. For
both electropherograms identical mouse serum was used. (Daams 1963.)

can be applied without raising the operating temperature above
10 °C. It should be noted that for optimum separations such as shown
in fig. 5.8 the concentration of the gel must be 1.25 times higher than
that recommended by the manufacturers of the starch. Separations in
starch gel containing 8 M urea have also been successful in this
apparatus.

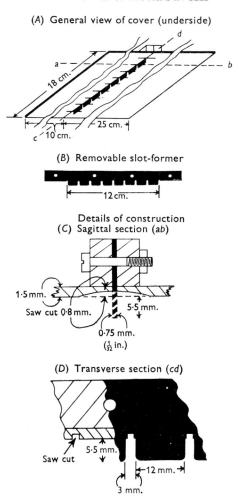

(A) General view of cover (underside)

(B) Removable slot-former

Details of construction
(C) Sagittal section (ab)

(D) Transverse section (cd)

Fig. 5.9. General view (A), and constructional details (C and D), of the plastic cover used to form the eight sample slots during the casting of the gel. The removable slot-former (B), shown throughout the figure in black, is made from linen-based phenol-formaldehyde resin ($^1/_{32}$-inch sheet); other plastic parts are made from Plexiglass.

Vertical apparatus

The gel should be set in a plastic tray with detachable ends of the kind described by Smithies (1959a). After filling with the heated and de-gassed starch solution the cover and slot former should be quickly placed in position. Care must of course be taken to exclude bubbles. This may be achieved the more easily if the cover is preheated to approximately 70 °C before use. The design of cover and slot former (fig. 5.9) recommended by Smithies (1959a) may be simplified with advantage by omission of the saw cuts between each sample slot. In

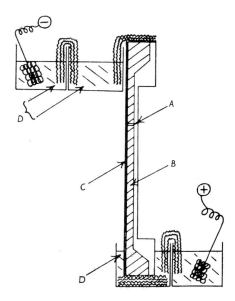

Fig. 5.10. Experimental arrangement for vertical starch-gel electrophoresis. A: position of sample slots; B: gel; C: petroleum jelly seal; D: trays containing bridge solution (0.3 M boric acid, 0.06 M NaOH). Approximately 10 thicknesses of filter paper are placed as shown at the lower end of the gel and as bridges. Although reversible Ag/AgCl electrodes were originally used by Smithies (1959a) platinum wires in bridge solution are satisfactory.

Subject index p. 145

practice, if the samples are carefully placed in the slots no mutual contamination will occur. Furthermore depressions such as saw cuts in the underside of the cover are difficult to free from bubbles and if present may lead to breakage of the gel at the stage when the cover is removed. After addition of the samples the surface of the gel is covered with an even layer of melted petroleum jelly. When this has cooled the ends of the trough are removed and it is stood on end in the electrode chamber containing the anode (fig. 5.10). Great care must be taken to ensure that the slots containing the sample solutions are level (in both dimensions). When the ends of the gel have been connected to the electrode chamber by means of cloth pads or many layers of filter paper the passage of current may be commenced.

Separations in two dimensions

In general two dimensional separations are resorted to only when a mixture is so complex that separation is incomplete after only a single stage. Thus a separation by electrophoresis in starch gel may be used subsequently to any other method of separation if this has been of insufficient resolving power and has been conducted in a suitable medium. In practice, cf. p. 120, electrophoresis on paper is the only method which has been made use of as a first stage preceding electrophoresis in starch gel. A typical pattern obtained from human plasma by this two-dimensional technique is shown in fig. 5.11. Alongside is the pattern given by the same plasma when subjected to electrophoresis in the starch gel only. By the more complex method 22 instead of 16 components have been revealed. In more recent work in which starch gel and the discontinuous buffer system of Poulik (1957) was used a further 11 components were identified by electrophoresis in one dimension only. Surprisingly only 24 of these 27 components could be identified when the same serum was investigated two-dimensionally (Krotoski et al. 1966) (fig. 5.2.H). Thus because of the very much greater resolving power of the starch gel no advantage in respect to the number of substances identified was obtained by application of the two-dimensional technique. As may be seen in fig. 5.2.G, and H this was

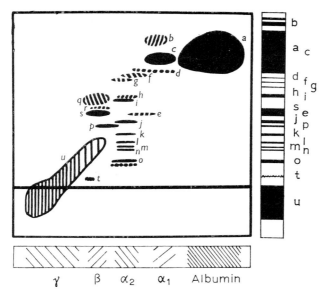

Fig. 5.11. A diagrammatic representation of the results of a two-dimensional electrophoresis experiment with serum of haptoglobin type 2–1 and transferrin type C. The corresponding filter-paper electrophoresis separation is shown below the two-dimensional diagram; the corresponding one-dimensional starch-gel separation is shown to the right. The zones which have been specifically identified are: (a) albumin; (b) acidic α_1-glycoprotein 'orosomucoid'; (h, j, k, l, m, n) haptoglobins; (o) heat-labile glycoprotein '$S\alpha_2$-globulin'; (s) transferrin C; (t) high molecular weight β-lipoprotein; (u) γ-globulins.

equally true for separations using either the continuous borate buffer system of Smithies (1955) or the discontinuous Tris citrate–borate system of Poulik (1957) in the starch gel. Probably the main value of the two-dimensional method is that it provides an easy approach to the identification of the individual proteins present in the classical α-, β- and γ-globulin bands obtained by either of several other procedures.

Subject index p. 145

Two-dimensional apparatus

Separation in the first dimension may be carried out in any apparatus suitable for paper electrophoresis. Strips of filter paper, for instance Schleicher and Schull 598 YD or Whatman 3 MM, with width slightly less than the thickness of the gel, are employed. For the next stage the damp strip is placed in a slot cut in a starch gel of width somewhat greater than the length of the paper strip carrying the partially separated protein mixture. To facilitate insertion the starch gel may be cut into two sections and the smaller one withdrawn a few mm to form a wide slot into which the filter paper strip can be slipped. When this has been done the gel is pressed back so that the strip is held firmly in place. Optimum results are likely to be obtained if between 0.010 and 0.020 ml serum is employed for the paper electrophoresis and the strip thus obtained then transferred to a starch gel 6 mm in thickness. Either the horizontal or the vertical starch gel apparatus may be used.

Treatment of starch gel after electrophoresis

Slicing

A great advantage of starch gel as a medium for electrophoresis is the ease with which it can be divided into thin slices very suitable for staining. Especially if the bands of protein after separation are not rectangular in cross section it is important to stain a layer of minimum thickness. If the central layer only is stained, possible irregularities existing at the top and bottom of the gel will be avoided. In addition the time required for staining and destaining will be minimised.

Fortunately starch gels can be sliced very conveniently by either one of two methods. Thus either a tightly stretched wire of 0.009 inch diam. or a razor blade slightly longer than the width of the gel may be used. If the former method is employed the wire should be stretched at an appropriate height above a smooth surfaced platform. By means of such a wire gel slices no more than 1.5 mm thick may be obtained. After cutting, the slice can be handled most easily if it is allowed to adhere to a thin sheet of polythene. Traces of starch should not be allowed to dry on the wire or its cutting efficiency will be reduced.

Slicing with a razor blade can be carried out in a similar manner. Alternatively if a gel holder with walls lower than the total thickness of the gel is available the blade may be drawn smoothly from end to end of the gel. The use of a double frame with a removable top section which allows slicing in this way was introduced by Moretti et al. (1957). The apparatus of Hori (1966) is very similar as the gels are cast in rectangular Perspex frames resting on a glass plate. Several frames are used and after the electrophoresis, by removal of one or more frames, the gel is left surrounded by a suitable lower wall along the top of which the razor blade can be slid.

Staining

The presence of protein in any part of a starch gel can be revealed very conveniently by briefly soaking a thin slice of the gel in a concentrated solution of naphthalene black 10B (1%) dissolved in methanol: water:acetic acid, 5:5:1, by vol. After 1 to 2 min in this stain the gel is transferred to the same solvent mixture without the dye-stuff. After several hours soaking in a large volume of the solvent the gel is transformed into an opaque solid strong enough for convenient handling. The areas which contain protein remain a dark blue colour and contrast well with the white background. The destaining process may be considerably speeded up by the passage of an electric current. For a suitable apparatus cf. p. 61. Unfortunately however such gels unless treated further as described below are not sufficiently transparent for densitometry. A few proteins such as insulin which form soluble complexes with Naphthalene Black require the use of other dyes (Smithies 1959b).

Loss of the protein dye complex from the gel during washing may sometimes be prevented by the use of an alternative solvent mixture. Both methanol:water:acetic acid 75:25:2 and ethanol:water 6:4 are mentioned by Morris and Morris (1964) p. 703 for this purpose. The same authors also report (p. 704) that by the use of 0.1% nigrosine in 3% aqueous trichloroacetic acid as little as 5 μg protein per cm

Subject index p. 145

width of gel can be detected. Unfortunately, however, they find that with this stain decolorisation of the rest of the gel is difficult.

Many other staining methods can be adapted to reveal the presence of proteins and other substances in starch gel. For instance, lipo-proteins will take up fat soluble stains such as oil red O (cf. Pert and Kutt 1958). The ability of haemoglobin to catalyse the oxidation of substances such as benzidine by H_2O_2 has been made use of to allow detection of haemoglobin both free and combined with haptoglobin in starch gel.

For this purpose the gel should be briefly immersed in a solution containing 0.2 g benzidine, 0.5 ml glacial acetic acid and 0.2 ml of 30% H_2O_2 in 100 ml of water. The H_2O_2 should be added immediately before use. In gels treated in this way areas containing haemoglobin become blue. The colour remains stable if the gel is finally washed thoroughly with water. Baur (1963) employed a similar solution which in addition contained 0.2% of sodium nitroprusside. He noted the formation of shades of colour characteristic of free haemoglobin and of the haemoglobin haptoglobin complex. In order to preserve these colours, the gel was immersed for 3 to 4 min in 3% aqueous sodium pyrophosphate and then for 4 min in absolute methanol followed by washing in water. Subsequently, if a plasticising solution was used containing 1% sodium nitrate, the contrasting colours were retained in the dry gel.

Location of enzymes even in trace amounts in starch gel can be achieved if appropriate coloured substrates or reaction products of substrates are available. Details of a number of such methods are given in table 3.1.

Because starch gels treated with methanol:water:acetic acid, 5:5:1, during staining shrink to approximately 85% of their original size they cannot be used directly to indicate the position of bands in the corresponding slices of untreated gels. However, shrinkage can easily be corrected for by reference to a series of cuts made at intervals of 1 cm along the edge of the gel before staining.

Densitometry

By means of densitometry quantitative estimates of the amounts of colour present in different parts of a stained starch gel can readily be obtained. However, only if each protein is known to bind the dye-stuff to the same degree can such estimates be used for calculation of the

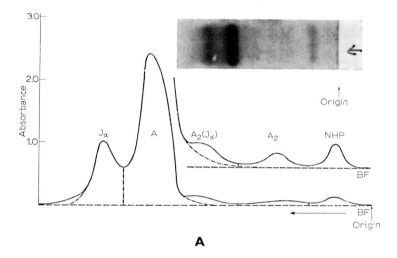

A

Fig. 5.12. Densitometry of haemoglobin bands after separation on starch gel. Buffer system, Tris/EDTA/borate, pH 8.6. Gels stained with Naphthalene Black 10B and differentiated in glycerol/water/acetic acid solvent system (Gratzer and Beaven 1960) and finally transferred to glycerol before transmission densitometry. (A) Hae-molysate containing normal human adult haemoglobin (Hb-A), normal minor component (Hb-A$_2$) and normal non-haemoprotein (NHP) carbonic anhydrase), and also abnormal haemoglobins Hb-J(α) and Hb-A$_2$(Jα) containing variant α^J-chains. Densitometered on Joyce–Loebl recording microdensitometer using Ilford 304 blue filter (B.F.), or Ilford 304 red filter (R.F.) to increase sensitivity for measure-ments of minor components; areas of zones obtained by manual planimetry of densitometer record, and total planimeter count (501, excluding NHP) taken as 100%. Planimeter reading for NHP zone (10) calculated as % relative to total haemo-globin. Balancing wedge range 0–3 optical density units; scan expansion on original record relative to gel X5; scanning slit size at gel 4×0.3 mm width, using special cylindrical condenser lens; objective lens 50 mm ($\times$ 5 mag.); detector slit size 8×14 mm width. Filter conversion factor (red to blue) $\times \frac{1}{3}$ rd. Inset: Stained gel. *(See next page.)*

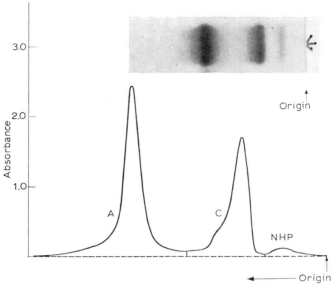

(Fig. 5.12 cont.)   **B**

(B) Haemolysate containing Hb-A, Hb-A₂ and NHP, and also abnormal haemoglobin Hb-C containing variant βc-chains. The Hb-A₂ minor component has the
same electrophoretic mobility as Hb-C and is therefore not resolved from it.
Densitometered on Joyce-Loebl 'chromoscan' recording densitometer with automatic electronic integration of densitometric record. Integrator counts corrected as
shown for base-line counts recorded when recorder pen is kept at the level (indicated by – – –) of the base-line of the starch-gel pattern. Balancing wedge range
0–3 optical density units; nominal wavelength of filter at maximum transmission
465 mμ; scanning slit ca. 5 × 0.5 mm; scan expansion on original record relative
to gel, X3.

A		**B**	
Area		Areas under peaks	
J_α = 127 = 25.4 %		A = 181 − 31 = 150 = 61 %	
A = 358 = 71.4 %		C = 114 − 18 = 96 = 39 %	
$A_2(J_\alpha)$ = 7 = 1.4 %			
A_2 = 9 = 1.8 %		246	
501 100 %		NHP = 11 − 8 = 3 = 1.2 %	
NHP = 10 = 2.0 %			

relative concentrations of the separated proteins. Unfortunately, it is only with mixtures of very similar proteins, such as the haemoglobins which may exist in a number of different forms (fig. 5.12.A, B), and isoenzymes (fig. 5.13) that equal uptake of dye can be assumed. In the case of heterogeneous mixtures of proteins of which the serum proteins are an important example where unequal uptake of dyestuff must certainly occur, the only estimates that can be made concern changes in concentration of a particular protein in the same serum.

The densitometry of separated haemoglobins can be done either

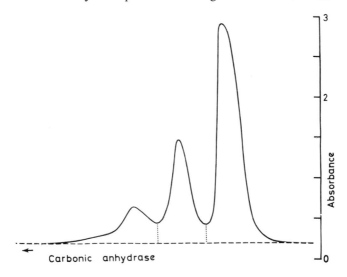

Fig. 5.13. Densitometry of carbonic anhydrase (Light–Koch) after separation on starch gel. Conditions for electrophoresis, staining and densitometry same as given in fig. 5.12A. The blue filter was used in the Joyce–Loebl recording microdensitometer. For amounts of protein in bands to be proportional to zone areas equal dye uptake is assumed.

Areas under peaks
Slow zone $= 304 = 64.5\%$
Medium zone $= 138 = 29.2\%$
Fast zone $= 30 = 6.3\%$
$\overline{472}$

direct or after the gel has been stained. In practice staining with naphthalene black is usually carried out prior to densitometry in order to take advantage of the far greater stability of the colour which is thus obtained.

Before densitometry such stained gels should be rendered transparent by soaking first in water:glycerol:acetic acid (5:5:1 v/v) and then overnight in pure glycerol (Gratzer and Beaven 1961). Because minor haemoglobin components may often be present at very low concentrations it is important that the densitometer used should respond proportionately over a range of transmission of at least 1 to 1,000 (i.e. 0–3 optical density units). As shown in fig. 5.12.A the sensitivity of instrument may be changed for the scan of the main peaks as compared with that used for the minor components. This may be done very conveniently by means of a change of filters.

After the densitometer curve has been obtained the next step is to estimate the areas contained under each of the peaks. This may be done by planimetry. By means of the appropriate filter factor (cf. fig. 5.12.A) the areas under the minor peaks if these have been recorded on a more sensitive range are converted to the range used for the main peaks. Finally the areas under each peak may be expressed as a percentage of the total area.

Patterns obtained by densitometry can be divided into those where there is little overlap of bands and those in which band resolution has been incomplete. For patterns of the former type fig. 5.12.B a densitometer such as the Joyce–Loebl 'Chromoscan' is particularly convenient. With this and other instruments which incorporate automatic integration of the densitometer record, hand measurements of the areas under the peaks with a planimeter are unnecessary. When a considerable degree of band overlapping is present as in fig. 5.12.A the curves must be extrapolated by hand to permit estimation of the total areas. In fig. 5.12.A,B details are given of slit widths and other settings used with the 'Chromoscan' and the Joyce–Loebl recording microdensitometer.

Autoradiographs

Autoradiographs may be obtained from starch gels by means of the same methods as are described on p. 67 for acrylamide gels. The possible loss of radioactivity which may occur with ^{59}Fe and ^{64}Cu when acrylamide gels are subjected to acid conditions required for staining has already been mentioned (p. 67). However, as with acrylamide gels staining should precede autoradiography unless there is a reason against this order of events. This is because once the gel has been stained there is no further possibility of bands of protein broadening as a result of diffusion. For an indication of the length of exposure required for detection of areas containing ^{131}I and ^{14}C, cf. pp. 67 and 68.

With ^{14}C and other emitters of weak radiation owing to the importance of self adsorption the amounts required for autoradiographs depend primarily on the gel thickness. This should be minimised by drying the gels.

Diffusion and thus band broadening can be prevented by freezing the gels and retaining them in this state during exposure of the autoradiograph. For optimum results a thin slice of gel should be rapidly frozen by being placed on a precooled metal plate. If frozen in this way the ice in the gel will have a microcrystalline structure which does not adversely effect the autoradiograph. This method is only useful with isotopes emitting penetrating radiation.

Special adaptations for the recovery of materials after separation in starch gel

Certain of the methods which are used for the recovery of substances after they have been separated by electrophoresis in acrylamide gel are equally applicable when starch gel is used. However, because starch gel is more soluble in aqueous solutions than is acrylamide special measures are sometimes required to remove the appreciable amounts of soluble starch which are always present (cf. p. 132). As already described for acrylamide gel two general methods for recovery of proteins are available thus the electrophoresis may be completed and

Subject index p. 145

then the recovery of proteins carried out from appropriate sections of the gel, alternatively means may be provided for continuous elution from the gel during the course of the electrophoresis. Unfortunately,

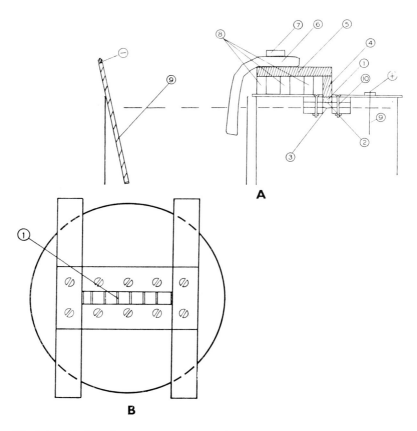

Fig. 5.14. (A) Complete apparatus with elution cell resting on top of a 3-l filtrate jar. Only the upper part of this is shown. 1: section of gel being eluted; 2: polythene bridges; 3: cellophane membrane; 4: vertical rectangular slab of starch gel (starch pillar); 5: horizontal slab of starch gel; 6: wet folded muslin; 7: glass weight; 8: Perspex supports for gel bridge; 9: platinum electrodes; 10: brass screws. (B) Plan of elution cell showing polythene bridges (1) which support the piece of gel during elution. (Gordon 1960.)

however, the physical properties of starch gel render this very difficult to carry out successfully.

Consideration will be given first to recovery of proteins from sections of the gel which have been cut out after completion of the electrophoresis. Recovery from such sections of gel may be achieved most easily if the gel structure is disintegrated by freezing and thawing. As a result of this treatment the gel becomes sponge-like in structure. When in this state the proteins can be recovered by mixing the disintegrated starch with buffer and then centrifuging.

Higher recoveries of most proteins can be obtained by electrophoretic elution. By means of a special cell (Gordon 1960, 1962) current may be passed through one (fig. 5.14) or more sections of the gel and the proteins present caused to migrate into a small volume of buffer solution. Because of the presence of a cellophane membrane passage of protein into the large volume of buffer surrounding the positive electrode (fig. 5.14.A) is prevented. For successful elution 0.02 M phosphate buffer at pH 8.3 should be used in the electrode vessels. In this way almost complete recovery of albumin from starch gel can be achieved. Unfortunately recoveries of proteins of lesser mobility are lower. Thus Gordon (1960) succeeded in 2 hr in recovering only 70 % of the β-globulin from rat plasma which had been labelled with [131]I.

Several authors have described methods which make possible recovery of separated substances from channels which have been cut in the starch gel either before the beginning of the electrophoresis or at a later stage before the separations are complete. In principle most of these methods resemble that of Gordon et al. (1950) who investigated recovery of proteins from an agar gel. In order to recover the separated proteins a transverse channel is cut across the gel. During electrophoresis the proteins migrate into this channel but are prevented from leaving it because of the presence of a strip of cellophane or other semipermeable membrane which forms a barrier at the far side of the channel (fig. 5.15.B). The membrane must of course be arranged in such a way that little or no leakage of buffer solution can occur. Proteins will accumulate in a channel of this kind whether it is

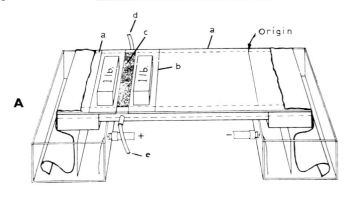

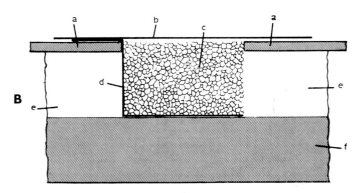

Fig. 5.15. (A) General view of starch-gel electrophoresis apparatus of Crispin Smith et al. (1966), modified for continuous elution during electrophoresis. a: glass plates; b: cellulose acetate sheet; c: polyurethane sponge filling elution trough; d: elution buffer inlet; e: elution buffer exit; d and e are connected to a proportioning pump delivering and withdrawing buffer from the elution trough at the same rate. (B) Cross section of the region of the transverse elution trough of the apparatus shown in (A). a: glass plate; b: cellulose acetate sheet; c: polyurethane sponge; d: dialysis membrane; e: starch gel; f: floor of Lucite gel mold. The anode is to the left.

filled with buffer solution only or with buffer and cellulose powder or some other anti-convection medium. The chief disadvantage of this rather simple arrangement for the recovery of bands of protein is uncertainty concerning the time required for the entry of a given band into the channel. Thus whereas excellent results can easily be obtained with coloured substances, in the absence of colour, incomplete recovery or admixture with the next band may well occur. By means of continuous elution from a channel this difficulty may be avoided. Thus if a stream of buffer solution is caused to flow at a sufficient rate from end to end of the channel and from thence into a fraction collector complete separation of bands can, in principle, be achieved. In practice, however, quantitative recovery of materials by this method is difficult and satisfactory results are unlikely unless very great care is taken. A detailed description of a technique suitable for this purpose has been given by Crispin Smith et al. (1966). As recommended by these authors the first part of the electrophoresis is carried out in a vertical starch gel apparatus. Then after a period of 2 hr at 8–10 mA the gel trough is brought into the horizontal and a transverse channel $12.5 \times 1.5 \times 0.5$ cm is carefully removed at a position in the gel which has not yet been reached by the band or bands which are to be collected. Next the floor of this channel is dried and covered with a layer of silicone grease. On top of this layer is placed a rectangular piece of dialysis membrane lying so that it is against the wall of the channel distant from the origin. As shown in fig. 5.15.B this membrane is wide enough to reach on to the top of the gel on the far side of the channel. Next the channel is filled with an exactly fitting piece of porous polyurethane foam wetted with the gel buffer solution. Finally this area of the gel is covered with a piece of cellulose acetate sheet held down by weights as shown in fig. 5.15.A. Elution is carried out by means of a transverse flow of buffer delivered into one end of the channel and sucked out from the other end by a proportioning pump. For this purpose special holes in the trough wall are needed. With this apparatus, using a flow of 1.2 ml/min of buffer, Crispin Smith et al. (1966) achieved a good separation and recovery of thyroxine binding prealbumin.

Subject index p. 145

Removal of soluble starch

Because of the appreciable solubility of starch gel, solutions of proteins or other substances which have been recovered from this medium are always contaminated with considerable amounts of soluble starch. If such solutions are incubated with a trace of amylase and then subjected to dialysis the concentration of starch and starch degradation products will be considerably reduced. However, for complete removal of soluble starch adsorption of the protein or other substance on an appropriate ion exchanger is necessary. Since the choice of ion exchanger must necessarily be determined by the nature of the substances which have been recovered from the starch gel no general indication can be given. With plasma proteins other than γ-globulin DEAE Sephadex can be employed. With this exchanger such proteins are adsorbed whereas the starch and starch degradation products are not retarded. After the passage of one column volume of buffer (0.0175 M phosphate buffer at pH 6.4) the protein can be eluted with a buffer of higher molarity.

Acknowledgements

While writing the present manual I have sought and received advice from many of my colleagues. I am indeed most grateful for their numerous useful suggestions and for much information which I could not otherwise have obtained. I wish to thank particularly Professor C. J. O. R. Morris for allowing me to quote certain unpublished results and Dr. G. H. Beaven for information concerning densitometry and the use of two figures. I am also very grateful to Dr. P. A. Charlwood and to Mr. L. N. Louis who have both helped me in a number of different ways.

Many of the illustrations and diagrams in this book have been obtained from other publications. In all cases reference is made to the original publications in the figure caption. A full bibliography of these sources can be found in the reference list.

The permission for the reproduction of this material is gratefully acknowledged.

Appendix

TABLE A1

Buffer solutions. Values of pH obtainable with substances most often employed in buffers used for electrophoresis of proteins. Each is listed only at values of pH at which the buffer in question is appropriate. Information concerning amounts of constituents needed for each solution are given in table A2. The pK value of each buffer appears in brackets.

pH					
2.2	Glycine (2.3) ————	a			
2.4	a	b			
2.6	b	c			
2.8	c	d	a		
3.0	Citric acid (3.08)— d		b		
3.2	e		c		
3.4	f		d		
3.6	g		e		
3.8			Formic acid (3.75)— f		
4.0	h				
4.2	i		a		
4.4	j		b		
4.6	Citric acid (4.74)— k		c		
4.8	l		Acetic acid (4.75)— d		
5.0	m		e		
5.2	n		f		
5.4	Citric acid (5.4) — o			a	
5.6	p			b	
5.8	q			c	
6.0	r			Maleic acid (6.07)— d	
6.2			a	e	
6.4			b	f	
6.6			c	g	
6.8			d		
7.0			e		
7.2	a		Phosphoric f		
7.4	b		acid* (7.21)— g		a
7.6	c		h		b
7.8	Veronal (7.96)— d		i		c
8.0	e		j		Tris (8.1)— d
8.2	f				e
8.4	g				f
8.6		a			
8.8		b			
9.0		c			
9.2		Borate (9.14)— d			e
9.4		e			f
9.6		f			g
9.8		g		Glycine (9.87)— h	
10.0					i
10.2					j
10.4					k

* pK_2.

TABLE A2

Constituents required to make up buffer solutions at values of pH as given in table A1. E.g. the volumes of 0.1 M glycine and M HCl given below under glycine (a) will give a glycine buffer of pH 2.2 as indicated in table A1, pH 2.2, glycine (a).

Glycine.	0.05 M with respect to glycine. All quantities in a final volume of 100 ml.	
	ml 0.1 M glycine $+$	ml M HCl
a	50	4.4
b		3.24
c		2.42
d		1.68
	ml 0.1 M glycine $+$	ml M NaOH
e	50	1.20
f		1.68
g		2.24
h		2.72
i		3.20
j		3.86
k		4.55

Subject index p. 145

Citrate.	0.1 M in respect to citrate. All quantities in a final volume of 100 ml.	

	ml M citric acid	+	ml M NaOH
a	10		1.51
b			2.62
c			3.96
d			5.4
e			6.75
f			8.1
g			9.45
h	10		12.3
i			13.8
j			15.15
k			16.65
l			18.0
m			19.5
n			20.85
o			22.35
p			23.7
q			25.2
r			26.55

Acetate.	0.05 M with respect to acetate. All quantities in a final volume of 100 ml.	

	ml M acetic acid	+	ml M NaOH
a	5.0		1.33
b			1.85
c			2.45
d			2.95
e			3.50
f			3.95

Formate.	0.05 M with respect to formate. All quantities in a final volume of 100 ml.	

	ml M formic acid	+	ml M NaOH
a	5.0		0.565
b			0.851
c			1.25
d			1.71
e			2.17
f			2.80

Maleate.	0.05 M with respect to maleate. All quantities in a final volume of 100 ml.	

	ml 0.2 M NaH maleate	+	ml M NaOH
a	25		1.05
b			1.53
c			2.08
d			2.69
e			3.30
f			3.80
g			4.16

Phosphate.   0.05 M with respect to orthophosphate. All
quantities in a final volume of 100 ml.

	ml 0.1 M KH_2PO_4 +	ml M NaOH
a	50	0.81
b		1.16
c		1.64
d		2.24
e		2.91
f		3.47
g		3.91
h		4.24
i		4.45
j		4.61

Sodium 5,5′-diethylbarbiturate (veronal sodium; barbitone sodium).
0.05 M with respect to diethylbarbiturate. All quantities in
a final volume of 100 ml.

	ml 0.1 M sodium diethylbarbiturate +	ml N HCl
a	50	4.17
b		3.82
c		3.35
d		2.87
e		2.35
f		1.80
g		1.30

Tris.	0.05 M with respect to tris. All quantities in a final volume of 100 ml.		

	ml 0.1 M tris +	ml 1 M HCl	$pH_{\frac{1}{2}}$*
a	50	4.2	− 0.02
b		3.85	
c		3.45	
d		2.92	− 0.02
e		2.29	
f		1.72	− 0.01
g		1.24	

Borate.	0.0125 M with respect to orthoborate. All quantities in a final volume of 100 ml.		

	ml 0.025 M $Na_2B_4O_710H_2O$ +	ml M HCl or NaOH	$pH_{\frac{1}{2}}$*
a	50	1.35	
b		0.94 } HCl	+ 0.04
c		0.46	+ 0.02
d		—	
e		0.62	+ 0.01
f		1.11 } NaOH	+ 0.01
g		1.50	+ 0.01

* $pH_{\frac{1}{2}}$ = increase (+) or decrease (−) in pH of buffer when diluted withn a equal volume of water

References

ACKERS, G. C. (1964) Biochemistry *3*, 723

ALLEN, J. M. and R. L. HUNTER (1960) J. Histochem. Cytochem. *8*, 50

ALTSCHUL, A. M., W. J. EVANS, W. B. CARNEY, E. J. MCCOURTNEY and H. D. BROWN (1964) Life Sci. *3*, 611

ARONSSON, T. and A. GRÖNWALL (1957) Scand. J. Clin. Lab. Invest. *9*, 338

ASKONAS, I. (1961) Biochem. J. *79*, 33

AZEN, E. A., R. A. NAZHAT and O. SMITHIES (1966) J. Lab. Clin. Med. *67*, 650

BAIRD-PARKER, A. C. and R. L. JOSEPH (1964) Nature *202*, 570

BAUR, E. W. (1963) J. Lab. Clin. Med. *61*, 166

BLOEMENDAL, H. (1963) Zone Electrophoresis in Blocks and Columns, Elsevier

BLOEMENDAL, H., W. S. BOUT, J. F. JONKIND and J. H. WISSE (1962) Nature *193*, 437

BOYER, S. H. (1961) Science *134*, 1002

BROWNSTONE, A. (1968) Anal. Biochem. (in press)

CANN, J. R. (1966) Biochemistry *5*, 1108

CARSTEN, M. E. and W. F. H. MOMMAERTS (1963) Biochemistry *2*, 28

CHERNOFF, A. I. and N. M. PETTIT (1965) Blood *25*, 646

CHOULES, G. L. and B. H. ZIMM (1965) Anal. Biochem. *13*, 336

CLARKE, J. T. (1964) Ann. N.Y. Acad. Sci. *121*, 428

CLELAND, W. W. (1964) Biochemistry *3*, 480

COHEN, S. and R. R. PORTER (1964) Biochem. J. *90*, 278

CONNAUGHT MEDICAL RESEARCH LABORATORIES (1964) Starch Gel Electrophoresis, University of Toronto, Toronto, Canada

CRAIG, L. C., J. D. FISHER and T. P. KING (1965) Biochemistry *4*, 311

CRISPIN SMITH, J., G. BERNSTEIN, M. I. SURKS and J. H. OPPENHEIMER (1966) Biochim. Biophys. Acta *115*, 81

DAAMS, J. H. (1963) J. Chromatog. *10*, 450

DAVIS, B. J. (1964) Ann. N.Y. Ac. Sci. *121*, 404

DE GROUCHY, J. (1958) Rev. Franc. Etudes Clin. Biol. *3*, 877

DE GROUCHY, J. and G. ROSSELIN (1962) Rev. Franc. Etudes Clin. Biol. *7*, 844

DUBBS, C. A., C. VIVONIA and J. M. HILBURN (1961) Nature *191*, 1203

DUESBERG, P. H. and R. R. RUECKERT (1965) Anal. Biochem. *11*, 342

EDELMAN, G. M. and M. D. POULIK (1961) J. Exptl. Med. *113*, 861

EDELMAN, G. M., B. BENACERRAF and Z. OVARY (1963) J. Exptl. Med. *118*, 229

FAIRBANKS, G., C. LEVINTHAL and R. H. REEDER (1965) Biochem. Biophys. Res. Commun. *20*, 393

FAWCETT, J. S. and C. J. O. R. MORRIS (1966) Separation Studies *1*, 9

FEINSTEIN, A. (1966) Nature *210*, 135

FERGUSON, K. A. and A. L. C. WALLACE (1961) Nature *190*, 629

FERRIS, T. G., R. E. EASTERLING and R. E. BUDD (1963) Am. J. Clin. Pathol. *39*, 193

FERRIS, T. G., R. E. EASTERLING and R. E. BUDD (1964) Anal. Biochem. *8*, 477

FILDES, R. A. and C. W. PARR (1963) Nature *200*, 890

FILDES, R. A. and C. W. PARR (1963) Biochem. J. *87*, 45P

FREDRICK, J. F. (1963) Phytochemistry *2*, 413

FULLERTON, P. M. and J. M. BARNES (1966) Brit. J. Ind. Med. *23*, 210

GEHRKE, C. W., Y. J. OH and C. W. FREEARK (1964) Anal. Biochem. *7*, 439

GIBLETT, E. R., A. G. MOTULSKY and G. R. FRAZER (1966) Am. J. Human Genet. *18*, 553

GOLDBERG, E. (1963) Science *139*, 602

GORDON, A. H. (1960) Biochim. Biophys. Acta *42*, 23

GORDON, A. H. (1962) Biochem. J. *82*, 531

GORDON, A. H., B. KEIL, K. SEBESTA, O. KNESSL and F. SORM (1950) Collection Czech. Chem. Commun. *15*, 1

GORDON, A. H. and L. N. LOUIS (1967) Anal. Biochemistry *21*, 190

GRATZER, W. B. and G. H. BEAVEN (1960) Clin. Chim. Acta *5*, 577

GRATZER, W. B. and G. H. BEAVEN (1961) J. Chromatog. *5*, 315

HARRIS, H., E. B. ROBSON and M. SINISCALCO (1958) Nature *182*, 452

HARTSHORNE, D. J. and S. V. PERRY (1962) Biochem. J. *85*, 171

HERMANS, P. E., W. F. MCGUCKIN, B. F. MCKENZIE and E. D. BAYRD (1960) Proc. Mayo Clin. *35*, 792

HJERTEN, S., S. JERSTEDT and A. TISELIUS (1965) Anal. Biochem. *11*, 211

HJERTEN, S., S. JERSTEDT and A. TISELIUS (1965) Anal. Biochem. *11*, 219

HOPKINSON, D. A., N. SPENCER and H. HARRIS (1963) Nature *199*, 969

HORI, J. (1966) Anal. Biochem. *16*, 234

HUEHNS, E. R., N. DANCE, G. H. BEAVEN, J. V. KEIL, F. HECHT and A. G. MOTULSKY (1964) Nature *201*, 1095

JENSEN, K. (1965) Scand. J. Clin. Lab. Invest. *17*, 192

JOVIN, T., A. CHRAMBACH and M. A. NAUGHTON (1964) Anal. Biochem. *9*, 351

KALANT, H., R. K. MURRAY and W. MONS (1964) Cancer Res. *24*, 570

KOHLRAUSCH, F. (1897) Ann. Physik *62*, 209

KROTOSKI, W. A., D. C. BENJAMIN and H. E. WEIMER (1966) Can. J. Biochem. *44*, 545

LAURENT, T. C. and J. KILLANDER (1964) J. Chromatog. *14*, 317

LAURENT, T. C. and H. PERSSON (1963) Biochim. Biophys. Acta *78*, 360

LAWRENCE, S. H., P. J. MELNICK and H. E. WEIMER (1960) Proc. Soc. Exptl. Biol. N.Y. *105*, 572

LEWIS, U. J. and M. O. CLARK (1963) Anal. Biochem. *6*, 303

LOENING, U. E. (1967) Biochem. J. *102*, 251

LONGSWORTH, L. G. (1941) Ann. N.Y. Acad. Sci. *41*, 267

LORBER, A. (1964) J. Lab. Clin. Med. *64*, 133

McDOUGAL, E. I. and R. L. M. S. SYNGE (1966) Brit. Med. Bull. *22*, 115

MAIZEL, J. V. (1966) Science *151*, 988

MATSON, C. F. (1965) Anal. Biochem. *13*, 294

MELAMED, M. D. (1967) Anal. Biochem. *19*, 187

MORETTI, J., G. BOUSSIER and M. F. JAYLE (1957) Bull. Soc. Chim. Biol., Paris *39*, 593

MORETTI, J., G. BOUSSIER and M. F. JAYLE (1958) Bull. Soc. Chim. Biol., Paris *40*, 59

MORRIS, C. J. O. R. (1966) In: H. Peeters (ed.) Protides of the Biological Fluids (Elsevier, Amsterdam) p. 543

MORRIS, C. J. O. R. and P. MORRIS (1964) Separation Methods in Biochemistry (Pitman Ltd., London)

MUELLER, H. and S. V. PERRY (1962) Biochem. J. *85*, 431

MÜLLER-EBERHARDT, H. J. and U. NILSSON (1960) J. Exptl. Med. *111*, 4

NANTO, V., J. PIKKARAINEN and E. KULONEN (1965) J. Am. Leather Chemists' Assoc. *60*, 63

OGSTON, A. G. (1958) Trans. Faraday Soc. *54*, 1754

ORNSTEIN, L. (1964) Ann. N.Y. Acad. Sci. *121*, 321

OSTER, G. K., G. OSTER and G. PRATI (1957) J. Am. Chem. Soc. *79*, 595

OVERBEECK, J. Th. G. (1950) Advan. Colloid Sci. *3*, 97

OWEN, J. A. and H. SMITH (1961) Clin. Chim. Acta *6*, 441

PASTEWKA, J. V., A. T. NESS and A. C. PEACOCK (1966) Clin. Chim. Acta *14*. 219

PERT, J. H. and H. KUTT (1958) Proc. Soc. Exptl. Biol. N.Y. *99*, 181

PERT, J. H. and L. PINTERIC (1964) Ann. N.Y. Acad. Sci. *121*, 310

PHELPS, R. A. and F. W. PUTNAM (1960) Chemical Composition and Molecular Parameters of Purified Plasma Proteins. In: F. W. Putnam (ed.) The Plasma Proteins, Vol. 1 (Academic Press) p. 163

PORATH, J. (1956) Biochim. Biophys. Acta *22*, 151

PORATH, J., E. B. LINDNER and S. JERSTEDT (1958) Nature *182*, 744

PORTER, R. R. (1966) Brit. Med. Bull. *22*, 164

POULIK, M. D. (1957) Nature *180*, 1477

POULIK, M. D. (1959) J. Immunol. *82*, 502

POULIK, M. D. (1962) Nature *194*, 842

POULIK, M. D. (1966) In: Glick (ed.) Methods of Biochem. Anal. (Interscience) Vol. 14, p. 455

POULIK, M. D. and A. G. BEARN (1962) Clin. Chim. Acta 7, 374

POULIK, M. D. and O. SMITHIES (1958) Biochem. J. 68, 636

PUN, J. Y. and L. LOMBROZO (1964) Anal. Biochem. 9, 9

RAYMOND, S. (1964) Ann. N.Y. Acad. Sci. 121, 350

RAYMOND, S. (1962) Clin. Chem. 8, 455

RAYMOND, S., J. L. MILES and J. C. J. LEE (1966) Science 151, 346

RAYMOND, S. and M. NAKAMICHI (1962) Anal. Biochem. 3, 23

REISFELD, R. A., S. DRAY and A. NISONOFF (1965) Immunochem. 2, 155

REISFELD, R. A., U. J. LEWIS and D. E. WILLIAM (1962) Nature 195, 281

RICHARDS, E. G. and W. B. GRATZER (1967) In: J. Smith (ed.) Chromatographic and Electrophoretic Techniques (Heinemann) Vol. 2

RITCHIE, R. F., J. G. HARTER and T. B. BAYLES (1966) J. Lab. Clin. Med. 68, 842

ROBBINS, M. F. and M. J. KRONMAN (1964) Biochim. Biophys. Acta 82, 186

ROBSON, E. B. and H. HARRIS (1965) Nature 207, 1257

SCHAPIRO, A. L., M. D. SCHARFF, J. V. MAIZEL and J. W. UHR (1966) Nature 211, 243

SHEPHERD, G. R. and L. R. GURLEY (1966) Anal. Biochem. 14, 356

SKOPES, R. K. and R. A. LAWRIE (1963) Nature 197, 1202

SMALL, P. A., W. F. HARRINGTON and W. W. KEILLEY (1961) Biochim. Biophys. Acta 49, 462

SMALL, P. A., R. A. REISFELD and S. DRAY (1965) J. Mol. Biol. 11, 713

SMITHIES, O. (1955) Biochem. J. 61, 629

SMITHIES, O. (1959a) Biochem. J. 71, 585

SMITHIES, O. (1959b) Advan. Protein Chem. 14, 65

SMITHIES, O. (1962) Arch. Biochem. Biophys., Suppl. 1, 125

SMITHIES, O. and G. E. CONNELL (1959) In: Biochemistry of Human Genetics (Churchill, London) p. 178

SPENCER, N., D. A. HOPKINSON and H. HARRIS (1964) Nature 204, 742

SULIZEANU, D. and W. F. GOLDMAN (1965) Nature 208, 1120

SUMMERS, D. F., J. V. MAIZEL and J. E. DARNELL (1965) Proc. Natl. Acad. Sci. 54, 505

SYNGE, R. L. M. S. and A. TISELIUS (1950) Biochem. J. 46, xli

TABER, H. W. and F. SHERMAN (1964) Ann. N.Y. Acad. Sci. 121, 600

TANG, J., S. WOLF, R. CAPUTTO and R. E. TRUCCO (1959) J. Biol. Chem. 234, 1174

TSAO, M. U. (1960) Arch. Biochem. Biophys. 90, 234

VOS, J. and H. J. VAN DER HELM (1964) J. Neurochem. 11, 209

WAKE, R. G. and R. L. BALDWIN (1961) Biochim. Biophys. Acta 47, 227

WALLER, J. P. and J. I. HARRIS (1961) Proc. Natl. Acad. Sci. 47, 18

WHIPPLE, H. E. (ed.) (1964) Ann. N.Y. Acad. Sci. 121, 305

WHITTAKER, J. R. (1959) Nature 184, 193

WINTERHALTER, K. H. and E. R. HUEHNS (1964) J. Biol. Chem. *239*, 3699

WORK, T. S. (1964) J. Mol. Biol. *10*, 544

WOYCHICK, J. H., J. A. BOUNDY, R. J. DIMLER (1961) Arch. Biochem. Biophys. *94*, 477

WRIGHT, G. L. and W. L. MALLMANN (1966) Proc. Soc. Exptl. Biol. Med. *123*, 22

YOUNG, R. W. and H. W. FULHORST (1965) Anal. Biochem. *11*, 389

Subject index

AN INTRODUCTION TO
GEL CHROMATOGRAPHY

L. Fischer

Pharmacia Fine Chemicals AB
Uppsala

Contents

CHAPTER 1

What is gel chromatography?

1.1. Gel chromatography – a biochemical separation method

The history of chemistry is to a remarkable extent the history of the separation and purification of substances from one another. In many discoveries the decisive step has been the right solution of a separation problem. Examples may be cited from every branch of chemistry, but the branch of chemistry that has relied most heavily on various separation methods is no doubt biochemistry. Although much interesting information can be obtained by observation of intact cells and organisms, it is also essential that these complex structures be taken apart and the various parts studied separately. However carefully the parts have been separated from the cells, a complex mixture of substances will always result. The success of further investigations will then depend on refined methods for separation.

The various separation methods available will sort the substances with respect to different parameters. In some cases the variable involved is easy to pinpoint. Isoelectric separation (electrophoresis in stable pH gradients, see for instance Vesterberg and Svensson 1966; Haglund 1967) sorts the substances according to their electric charge, while preparative ultracentrifugation fractionates them with respect to their diffusion coefficients, their masses and their buoyancy factors. In other cases it is more difficult to define the variables governing the separation. For precipitations it is very difficult to relate the order in which the molecules precipitate to the basic molecular parameters.

Subject index p. 391

When separating a complex mixture it is essential that the different methods used should be based on different principles with as little overlap as possible. Thus, methods which ultimately depend on the same property of the substances, such as electrophoresis, ion exchange chromatography and isoelectric separation, all take advantage of the charge of the molecules and it is unprofitable to apply all three in succession.

When gel chromatography was introduced, it was found that the separation was based on a property that was new among biochemical fractionation methods: it is a separation method based on differences in molecular dimensions. It is true that the separation obtained with the preparative ultracentrifuge also depends on molecular weight, together with the diffusion coefficient and a buoyancy factor. This method is, however, rather complicated and does not give very sharp separations. It is limited to substances of fairly high molecular weight. Ultracentrifugation also is very time-consuming and has a very limited capacity. Dialysis can also be said to give a separation according to molecular weight, although this separation is rather coarse.

1.2. The mechanism of gel chromatography

As indicated by the name, gel chromatography is a chromatographic technique. Before going into the more specialized subject of gel chromatography, it seems appropriate to give a brief description of the mechanism by which separation is obtained in chromatography.

The tool for obtaining a separation is the chromatographic bed. The bed consists of minute particles usually packed into a tube. In the more specialized technique of thin-layer chromatography, the particles are spread in a layer over a solid support. The space between the particles is occupied by a liquid which is made to flow through the bed. The substances to be separated are carried through the bed by the flow of the liquid. The stationary phase retards the progress of substances through the bed. Different substances are retarded to a varying extent and so migrate through the bed at different velocities. If two substances are applied at one end of the bed mixed with each other, they will leave the bed separated from one another, the faster moving leaving the bed first, followed by the slower moving substance.

The retardation is effected by partitioning of the substances between the liquid and the stationary phase. When a molecule is in the gel phase, it does not move in the direction of the liquid flow, as all the flow of the liquid takes place between the gel grains and there is no bulk flow of liquid through the gel particles.

The rate at which a solute passes through the bed is proportional to the mean time, calculated on a statistical basis, that the molecules spend in the liquid between the gel grains. This average time is determined by the partition coefficient for the substances between the gel phase and the liquid phase, as the average for a given molecule over a period of time is equal to the average for a large number of molecules at a given time.

The characteristic property distinguishing gel chromatography from other types of partition chromatography is that the grains that form the stationary phase in the chromatographic bed consist of an uncharged gel. This gel is swollen in the same solvent as that percolating through the bed. Typically, the gels consist of macromolecules with great affinity for the solvent used. These have been cross-linked to form a three-dimensional network, thereby making them insoluble. Instead of dissolving in the liquid, they swell, taking up large amounts of liquid.

Gel chromatography separates substances according to their molecular size; large molecules will emerge first from the bed, while smaller molecules are retarded Few substances will, however, be retarded so strongly that their elution volume will be higher than the total column volume. For many groups of substances a very close correlation is found between molecular weight (or molecular size) and elution behaviour, and for practical purposes the elution volume is usually determined entirely by the molecular weight. This can be explained by the simple model for gel chromatography, introduced by Flodin (1962a). According to him, the partition coefficient of the solute between the gel phase and the liquid phase is governed exclusively by steric effects. He points out that the gel matrix occupies a great deal of space in the immediate environment of the cross-links.

Subject index p. 391

Large molecules cannot penetrate into these regions, while small molecules can approach the cross-links more closely. Small molecules have access to all the space between the chains of the gel matrix and will consequently be distributed fairly evenly between the free liquid and the liquid in the gel. Large molecules have access to less space within the gel, and the partition coefficient is shifted in favour of the liquid outside the gel grains. This induces large molecules to emerge from the chromatographic bed earlier than smaller ones.

Although the model of Flodin explains the elution behaviour of most substances, certain exceptions have been observed. The model does not account for elution volumes larger than the total volume of the liquid in the chromatographic bed (the sum of the amount of liquid in the gel and between the gel grains). Although few substances are so strongly retarded that they are difficult to elute, elution volumes larger than this theoretical maximum have often been observed. Aromatic substances (including heterocyclic aromatic substances) are known to give elution volumes larger than those expected (Gelotte 1960). A number of other substances with higher elution volumes than those expected from the steric model have been reported by Marsden (1965). This author also gives an example of a case, where the higher members of a homologous series have higher elution volumes than the lower ones: among the normal alcohols, the higher the molecular weight, the stronger is the retardation on a dense dextran gel.

If the separation were a steric effect only, it would be described thermodynamically as an entropy effect. This would mean that temperature effects would be absent. Marsden (1965) examined the temperature dependence of the elution volume and found considerable temperature effects for certain substances.

Although deviations from the general pattern can thus be observed, the following picture of gel chromatography will be sufficient for practical purposes: The molecules are carried down the chromatographic bed by the flow of the liquid between the gel grains. Large molecules are for steric reasons unable to penetrate into the gel grains and travel at the same rate as the liquid. The smaller molecules can penetrate into the gel grains. Molecules inside the gel grains are stationary. The average velocity in the direction of the flow is proportional to the time spent in the space between the gel grains. Small molecules will consequently travel at a lower rate. The principle is illustrated in fig. 1.1.

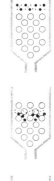

Fig. 1.1. Principle of gel chromatography. A sample containing a mixture of small and large molecules is applied to a gel column. The small molecules (small dots) can pass into the gel beads (open circles) and lag behind the large molecules (large dots) that cannot penetrate into the beads. From 'Sephadex – gel filtration in theory and practice', by Pharmacia Fine Chemicals.

1.3. Characteristic properties of gel chromatography

There are several reasons why gel chromatography was very rapidly adopted as a standard procedure after its introduction around 1960. The following features are probably those which have contributed most strongly to its rapid progress:

Gel chromatography is technically simple to perform. It is remarkably insensitive to composition of the eluant and to temperature. Even very labile compounds may be treated with little risk of destruction. The gel matrices in gel chromatography generally do not cause denaturation, and the procedure can be performed under very mild conditions.

Gel chromatography fractionates substances of very high molecular weight. By varying the contents of gel matrix in the gel, the fraction-

Subject index p. 391

ation range can be varied within wide limits. The most dense micro-reticular gels fractionate substances in the region below mol. wt. 1,000; with other gels, fractionation ranges extending up to molecular weights of several millions can be attained.

With gel chromatography certain standard problems in biochemistry can be solved in a very rational way. Well-known examples are de-salting of solutions of protein and other high molecular weight sub-stances, and determination of molecular weights of macromolecules, particularly proteins.

The chromatographic beds in gel chromatography usually need no regeneration and can be used over and over again. The materials are remarkably stable, and the same gel can be used for years without change of chromatographic properties, provided bacterial growth is avoided.

Gel chromatography has been introduced only recently but it is now a standard method in almost every biochemical laboratory. The very rapid development of the method illustrates the need for a separation method of this kind.

CHAPTER 2

Basic concepts

2.1. Some definitions

Before going more deeply into the technical details of gel chromato-graphy, a short discussion of the terminology used may contribute to the understanding of the subject, especially for those who are not fa-miliar with chromatography. Like many other branches of science, gel chromatography has a nomenclature with a number of synonyms and ambiguities. A number of scientists have introduced nomenclatures of their own. In this work, the commonest terms will be used as far as possible. In certain cases common terms have been used rather re-strictively to avoid ambiguity.

The technique itself has been given different names by scientists wanting to stress different aspects of the technique. Porath and Flodin (1959) called the technique *gel filtration*, while Fasold et al. (1961) pre-ferred to call it *molecular sieve filtration*. Steere and Ackers (1962) used the term *restricted diffusion chromatography*, Pedersen (1962) *exclusion chromatography*, Hjertén and Mosbach (1962) *molecular sieve chromato-graphy*, and Moore (1964) *gel permeation chromatography*. The desig-nation used in this book, *gel chromatography*, was proposed by Deter-mann (1964). It seems preferable to use the word chromatography instead of the word filtration. The technique undoubtedly is a chro-matographic technique, and the designation filtration is misleading. Even if the designation gel filtration is most commonly used, that of gel chromatography has been preferred for the sake of clarity.

Two different principles have been used to designate chromatographic methods. The name can refer either to the material in the bed or to the mechanism by which separation is achieved. In gel chromatography the mechanism is probably more complex than is implied by names relating the method entirely to steric mechanisms. Many cases are known where steric mechanisms alone cannot give the result obtained, and no entirely satisfactory account of gel chromatographic mechanism has yet been reported which takes into account all the factors that should contribute to the separation. It is therefore rather arbitrary to make a methodological distinction between the cases where 'adsorption' and other possible mechanisms contribute to the separation, and those cases where only steric effects are involved. The two cases cannot be distinguished from the point of view of experimental technique and methodology. For this reason, the term gel chromatography seems to be preferable to the others.

In the literature on gel chromatography, the term *adsorption* has been used to describe a stronger retardation of a substance than that which would be expected from the steric model. The term may lead to some ambiguity. Adsorption chromatography is the term used where retardation of a substance on the chromatographic bed is caused by its adsorption on the surface of the particles, in contrast to partition chromatography, where the substances are distributed through the bulk of the stationary phase (Giddings 1965, p. 2 and 9). From this point of view, gel chromatography is a special case of partition chromatography (except possibly in some very few exceptional cases). Here, the term adsorption will be used very restrictively and only when its meaning is completely clear.

A certain confusion exists with regard to the use of the words *chromatographic bed*, *chromatographic tube* and *chromatographic column*. Here, the word chromatographic bed refers exclusively to the column packing material and the interstitial liquid. The word column will be used for the hardware encasing the chromatographic bed and also for the totality of hardware and bed where no confusion will arise. The word tube will be used exclusively as a designation for the hardware. The granulated or beaded gel material in the bed is designated *packing material* or *bed material*. In theoretical discussions the word *stationary phase* is used, as the solutes are distributed through the whole gel phase, at least on a macroscopic scale. The liquid, percolating through the bed between the gel particles, is called *eluant* or, in theoretical discussions, *mobile phase*.

The solution of the substances to be separated is called *sample*. For the sake of variation, the substances to be separated will also be called *solutes*, although the term solute would, strictly speaking, refer to any substance dissolved in the liquid.

2.2. Parameters used to characterize the bed

When an experiment is described and the results are evaluated, it is necessary to select the relevant parameters, as it would be impossible to describe a complete experimental set-up in every detail. In chromatographic experiments, the geometry of the bed and the flow rate are the most important variables determining the results.

The meaning of the terms *bed height* and *bed diameter* is quite clear and does not require much explanation. It should be pointed out, though, that the bed height (or the *bed length*) extends from the bed support to the upper gel surface (not to the top of the tube). In calculations of the experimental results, the volume of the chromatographic bed, V_t (the *total bed volume*), is one of the main parameters. To calculate this from the length and diameter of the bed by the formula for the volume of a cylinder requires a very accurate determination of the diameter of the bed, as this parameter is squared and the relative error involved is doubled. It should also be remembered that the tube may be uneven, with a cross section that is not perfectly round, and that the cross-sectional area may vary over the length of the tube. For this reason it is recommended that in accurate work the volume of the tube should be determined separately (described in § 5.7.4).

Another important parameter, used in the evaluation of the experimental results, is the *void volume* (*hold-up volume* or *dead volume*), V_0, of the chromatographic bed. This is the volume of the liquid in the interstitial space between the grains in the bed. It can be determined by chromatography of a substance that is not retarded by the bed material

Subject index p. 391

(that is completely excluded) and measurement of its elution volume. This gives a relatively accurate determination of the void volume, as substances that are completely excluded are eluted in very sharp peaks. In gel chromatography, substances of high molecular weight, for example high molecular weight proteins, can be used for the purpose. A material, especially intended for the purpose, Blue Dextran 2000, with a weight average molecular weight of two millions, is prepared by Pharmacia Fine Chemicals AB (Manufacturers, see appendix 1). In accurate work it may be necessary to take into account that the void volume measured in this way includes the dead space below the bed support and the volume of the tubes between the column and the detector or the fraction collector.

It can be shown that if the bed consists of hard beads of the same size, the void volume would be approximately 35 per cent of the bed volume (Susskind and Becker 1966). However, the particles of the packing material are always more or less soft, and the size of the grains varies quite considerably, even if the material has been well sieved. For this reason, the void volume is lower than this maximum. It varies with the packing method and with the operating pressure (§ 2.3).

The volume of the gel in the bed, V_x, is obtained as the difference between the total bed volume and the void volume. V_0, V_t and V_x are

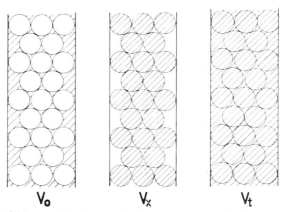

Fig. 2.1. Variables used to characterize the chromatographic bed: V_0, V_x and V_t.

shown schematically in fig. 2.1. The partial volume of the liquid in the gel phase is termed the inner volume, V_i. It can be estimated by subtracting the partial volume of the gel matrix from the volume of the gel:

$$V_i = V_x - m_g v_g, \tag{2.1}$$

where m_g represents the weight of gel matrix in the bed and v_g is the partial specific volume of the gel matrix. The inner volume can also be obtained without a separate determination of V_x, if the water regain, W_r, (§ 2.6), of the gel is known:

$$V_i = m_g W_r. \tag{2.2}$$

This expression for V_i includes the error from the determination of W_r. As accurate determinations of W_r are very difficult to perform, this equation should be avoided in accurate work.

Some other equations for the determination of V_i can be derived (Flodin 1962a). However, they offer no specific advantages.

2.3. Parameters used to characterize the flow

The flow rate through the chromatographic bed is usually measured in ml/min or ml/hr. When comparing experiments performed on columns of different diameter, the flow rate per unit cross-sectional area of the chromatographic bed is calculated. It has the unit ml.hr^{-1}. cm^{-2}, or the equivalent measure cm.hr^{-1}.

To obtain the linear rate of migration on the chromatographic bed of a substance that is completely excluded, the flow rate per unit cross-sectional area is divided by the fraction of the bed volume that is occupied by the void volume.

To maintain the flow rate, it is possible either to use a pump or a difference in level between the inlet and the outlet of the bed. In each of these cases the flow is causing a pressure drop over the bed. This pressure drop is called the operating pressure or the driving pressure. It should be noticed that this is not the hydrostatic pressure in the column. It is essential to control the operating pressure to avoid

Subject index p. 391

compacting of the bed with soft gels. The operating pressure is discussed more thoroughly in ch. 5.

2.4. Parameters used to characterize solute behaviour

In the course of a chromatographic experiment the concentration of
the substances in the sample is determined in the effluent from the bed.
The primary data obtained from the experiment are used to plot the
concentration of the substances in the effluent (or some suitable variable related to the concentration) versus the volume of eluant collected
after the sample application. From this elution curve it is possible to
characterize the behaviour of the various substances on the chromatographic bed. The most important variable to be determined is the
elution volume of a substance, V_e. This is theoretically the volume of
eluant that is, on the average, required to carry the molecules of the
substance through the column. The elution volume should, ideally, be
independent of the flow rate. In practice, different criteria have been
used to determine the elution volume. Although some of them are
doubtful from a theoretical standpoint, they can often be used with
success for practical purposes. As there are several ways of measuring
elution volume, an indication of the method used to determine the
elution volume from the elution curve is valuable in accurate work.

For small sample volumes that can be neglected in comparison with
the elution volume, the volume of liquid that has passed the column
between the application of the sample and the elution of the maximum
concentration of substance is the elution volume, if the elution curve
is symmetrical. As pointed out above, the dead volume from the supporting net to the point of collection should always be subtracted in
accurate work. If the sample volume is so large that the elution curve
reaches a plateau region, the elution volume is the volume eluted from
the onset of sample application to the inflection point or half the height
of the front of the elution curve. For samples of intermediate size, not
forming plateau regions in their elution curves, the elution volume
should be measured from the point where half the sample volume has
been applied until the maximum of the elution curve is reached.

All these criteria theoretically require that the elution curves are symmetrical. For practical purposes they are in most cases sufficient, even if the elution curves are not symmetrical. Substances moving with the void volume have a tendency to give more spreading on the rear side than at the front. This, however, does not generally give rise to difficulties.

For certain applications and for theoretical purposes, other parameters, related to the zone broadening and to the form of the elution curve, are of importance. An account of these would, however, be far beyond the scope of this treatise. The reader, interested in these questions, is referred to the excellent work by Giddings (1965).

The elution volume can be used to characterize a substance, as described above. However, the elution volume alone has limited significance as it depends on the geometry of the chromatographic bed. To characterize the behaviour of the solute in a way independent of the geometric dimensions of the column, the following parameters are most commonly used:

V_e/V_0, the relative elution volume, is easy to determine with a minimum of measurements. It may vary slightly from column to column, even if the same packing material and the same eluant are used, as it is influenced by the packing of the bed. If high operating pressures are used or if the bed is compressed in some other way, the void volume is diminished. In this case the value of this parameter is increased. This variation is, however, in practice of relatively little importance.

R, the retention constant, is the inverse of V_e/V_0. It is of interest because of its close relationship to the relative migration rates used to characterize the chromatographic behaviour of substances in thin-layer chromatography.

V_e/V_t is also easily calculated. As with V_e/V_0 it is susceptible to variations in the packing of the gel bed, although the variation in V_e/V_t should theoretically be smaller than that in V_e/V_0.

As indicated earlier, gel chromatography should be regarded as a special type of partition chromatography. The theory of partition chromatography provides a correlation between the elution behaviour of a substance and its partition coefficient between the stationary phase and the moving phase (see ch. 9):

$$V_e = V_0 + K \cdot V_s, \tag{2.3}$$

where K is the partition coefficient between the phases and V_s is the volume of the stationary phase. The partition coefficient, K, derived from this equation, can be used as a parameter to characterize the behaviour of a given solute.

In gel chromatography, two different partition coefficients are used. The difference between them lies in the definition of the stationary phase. If the entire gel phase is assumed to be the stationary phase, the partition coefficient

$$K_{av} = \frac{V_e - V_0}{V_x} \tag{2.4}$$

is obtained. If, on the other hand, only the liquid imbibed in the gel

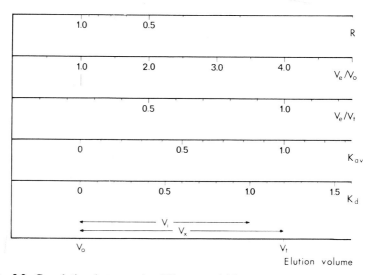

Fig. 2.2. Correlation between the different variables used to characterize solute behaviour.

is assumed to be the stationary phase and the volume of the gel matrix is subtracted from the total gel volume, the partition coefficient

$$K_d = \frac{V_e - V_0}{V_i} \tag{2.5}$$

results. From a theoretical point of view these parameters are equally useful for characterization of substances. They are proportional to each other and the proportionality constant depends only on the properties of the gel. From a practical standpoint, K_{av} is often preferable, as the determination of V_i involves measurements with considerable uncertainties. However, for historical reasons, K_d has been much used and is found in the majority of the early papers on gel chromatography. The relationship between R, V_e/V_0, V_e/V_t, K_{av} and K_d is illustrated in fig. 2.2.

2.5. Graphic representation of the relationship between molecular parameters of solutes and elution properties

In gel chromatography, chromatographic behaviour can to a fair degree of accuracy be related to the molecular size of the solute or other molecular parameters closely connected to the molecular size, such as the Stoke's radius or the molecular weight. Different graphical representations for this relationship have been proposed by different authors. In most cases the graphical representation is chosen to illustrate the author's theoretical assumptions about the mechanism of gel chromatography.

For practical purposes the representation proposed by Andrews (1964, 1965) is most suitable. Here, one of the parameters linearly related to the elution volume (V_e/V_0, V_e/V_t, K_d, K_{av}) is plotted as a function of the molecular weight on a logarithmic scale. The advantages of this representation from a practical standpoint are that the errors are relatively constant along both axes and that the representation gives a very clear picture of the working ranges of the various gels. The use of a logarithmic scale for the molecular weight also

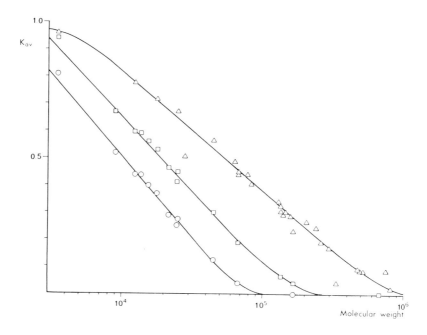

Fig. 2.3. Relationship between elution behaviour and molecular properties: K_{av} versus molecular weight for globular proteins on different types of Sephadex. △ Sephadex G-200, □ Sephadex G-100, ○ Sephadex G-75. The following proteins were used in the measurements: Glucagon, M 3,500; *Pseudomonas* cytochrome c-551 M 9,000; horse heart cytochrome c M 12,400; ox pancreas ribonuclease M 13,700; α-lactalbumin M 15,500; sperm whale myoglobin M 17,800; soya bean trypsin inhibitor M 21,500; horse heart cytochrome c dimer M 24,800; chymotrypsinogen M 25,000; ovomucoid M 28,000 (below the curve for Sephadex G-200; not included in the measurements on Sephadex G-75 and Sephadex G-100); ovalbumin M 45,000; foetal calf serum feotin M 47,000 (below the curve for Sephadex G-200; not included in the measurements on Sephadex G-75 and Sephadex G-100); pig heart malate dehydrogenase M 63,000; bovine serum albumin M 76,000; bovine transferrin M 67,000; *Escherichia coli* phosphatase M 78,000; cow's milk lactoperoxidase M 83,000; rabbit muscle triosephosphate dehydrogenase M 130,000; serum albumin dimer M 135,000; rabbit muscle dehydrogenase M 135,000; yeast alcohol dehydrogenase M 140,000; rabbit muscle aldolase M 145,000; human ceruloplasmin M 157,000; bovine gamma-globulin M 165,000; human gamma-globulins M 165,000 (the gamma-globulins fall below the curve for Sephadex G-200; not in-

Continue on page 173

makes it possible to include the whole range of molecular weights without loss of detail at the low molecular weight end.

Fig. 2.3 is a typical diagram showing the relationship between molecular weight and K_{av} for globular proteins. Below a certain molecular weight the curve is almost horizontal. In this region all substances are eluted together at a volume close to the total column volume. The central part of the curve has an inclination downwards. A variation in molecular weight here corresponds to a variation in elution volume, resulting in separation of substances with different molecular weights. This part of the curve represents the working range of the gel. At molecular weights above the fractionation range, the curve is again horizontal. In this region all substances move with the void volume, corresponding to $K_{av} = 0$. The molecules are so large that they cannot penetrate into the gel. The point where the curve reaches $K_{av} = 0$ (or $V_e = V_0$) is called the *exclusion limit* of the gel.

For many gels, especially of the microreticular types, the curve is fairly linear over a large part of the working range. This is, however, not always the case, and among the gels of the macroreticular types the curve may be markedly non-linear over part of the fractionation range (microreticular and macroreticular, see § 3.1).

The slope of the curve is a very important characteristic for a given gel type. A gel that has a very steep curve within the working range will be very efficient for fractionation of substances within that range. However, the fractionation range will be much narrower for this type of gel. A reasonable compromise between steepness and fractionation range is desirable.

---

cluded in the measurements on Sephadex G-75 and Sephadex G-100); pig heart fumarase M 205,000; ox liver catalase M 240,000; R-phycoerythrin M 260,000; α-conarachin M 295,000; bovine fibrinogen M 335,000 (below the curve for Sephadex G-200; not included in the measurements on Sephadex G-75 or Sephadex G-100); apoferritin M 475,000; urease M 490,000; *Escherichia coli* galactosidase M 520,000; bovine thyroglobulin M 670,000; horse spleen ferritin M 750,000; bovine α-crystallin M 810,000. The molecular weights given are in some instances relatively uncertain. The data used to compile this diagram are taken from Andrews (1964, 1965).

Subject index p. 391

2.6. Parameters used for the characterization of gels

The most important parameters used for characterization of gels are those connected with the chromatographic properties of the gels. The parameters most commonly used for this purpose are the fractionation ranges of the gels (sometimes only the upper limit of the fractionation range, the exclusion limit). For Styragels ®, the manufacturer (Waters Associates) gives the exclusion limits as the Stoke's radius of the molecules rather than their molecular weight. When the exclusion limits or the fractionation ranges are given, it should be stated for what types of substances these data have been determined, as the numbers will vary from one type of substance to another. Within a given group (globular proteins, polysaccharides etc.) they are fairly constant.

For xerogels (§ 3.1) the water regain, W_r, is the most common measure of the swelling capacity of the gel. The water regain represents the amount of water (in ml), imbibed by one gram of dry xerogel, on swelling. It does not include the interstitial liquid between the grains. For dextran gels and polyacrylamide gels, it has been found that there exists a close relationship between the water regain and the fractionation properties. A low water regain corresponds to a fractionation range at low molecular weight. For agarose gels, the percentage of gel matrix in the gel grains is given instead of the water regain. For gels working in non-aqueous solvents, the solvent regain, S_r, is defined by analogy with the water regain.

Finally, the particle size of the gel grains is an important variable. It influences the degree of zone broadening, the resolution, the dilution and the flow rates that can be attained.

CHAPTER 3

Gels for chromatography

3.1. Definition of the term gel

In everyday language the term gel is quite clear. It refers to a fairly soft, elastic material containing water. In technical contexts the term acquires a wider meaning. A gel consists of a three-dimensional structure or three-dimensional network. A structural material, often consisting of cross-linked polymers, gives the gel mechanical stability (or at least a preference for a certain form). The space within the gel not occupied by structural material is filled with liquid. The liquid mostly occupies the main part of the space in the gel. The mechanical properties of gels vary widely. Some gels are soft and deform easily under external forces, thus corresponding to the popular picture. Others are rigid or even brittle.

There are many natural substances capable of forming gels. These include polysaccharides from fruits and roots, proteins from animal tissues, inorganic silicates and phosphates. By cross-linking with a suitable cross-linker almost any macromolecule, synthetic or natural, can be induced to form a gel in some suitable solvent. Different gels react differently to removal of the liquid in them. The group called xerogels shrink on drying to a compact material, containing only the gel matrix. The aerogels, on the other hand, do not shrink; instead, the surrounding air penetrates into the gel. When a dry xerogel is brought into contact with a liquid which is compatible with the gel matrix, it takes up liquid, swells, and returns to the gel state. In aerogels the air in the gel can be substituted by liquid, when the dry gel is exposed

175 Subject index p. 391

to liquid. All gels do not return to the original state in this process, and many gels change their properties when dried and re-wetted.

From the point of view of their chromatographic properties – and also from their general properties – two different gel types can be distinguished: macroreticular and microreticular gels (Kun and Kunin 1964). Macroreticular gels have properties indicating that the microstructure is strongly heterogeneous, with regions where the matrix material is aggregated and regions where there is very little gel matrix present. This structure, with large spaces within the gel virtually free from gel matrix, allows large molecules to enter. The regions of high density form a skeleton that stabilizes the gel and makes it rigid. The microreticular gels, on the other hand, have properties that indicate that the gel matrix is relatively evenly distributed throughout the gel. They fractionate in lower molecular weight ranges than the macroreticular gels, and the gels are usually softer. The macroreticular gels are usually aerogels, while the microreticular gels usually seem to be xerogels.

3.2. Important properties of gels for chromatography

Out of the many gels that exist or could be synthetized, only relatively few are suitable for gel chromatography. In addition to the chromatographic requirements, there are also some practical demands that should be met.

The matrix of the gel must be inert. Chemical interaction between the bed material and the solutes may lead either to irreversible binding of solutes to the bed material or to chemical alterations of labile substances. In biochemistry the risk of denaturation of proteins and nucleic acids is considerable; fortunately, there are several gel types which interact very little with these substances. Gel chromatography is one of the rather few separation methods in biochemistry, capable of giving virtually quantitative yields.

Weak reversible interactions between the solute and the matrix give larger retention volumes than those expected from the molecular size of the molecule (adsorption). This effect does not in general cause any departure from linearity of the partition isotherms (the partition coefficients remain independent of the solute concentration), and the molecules will usually be eluted in sharp narrow bands in the presence of this type of interaction. In some circumstances these weak interactions may improve the separation of substances normally difficult to separate. Such weak interactions are for instance those between aromatic substances and dextran or polyacrylamide gels in aqueous solutions.

The gels must be stable chemically. The gels used in practice are stable for long periods of time so that they can be used over and over again for months or years. In some cases, the same bed has been used for accurate measurements for years without even being repacked. The gels should be stable over a fair range of pH and temperature to allow free choice of experimental conditions. Leaching of material from the bed should be very low, otherwise the substances subjected to chromatography may be contaminated with leached material.

Low content of ionic groups is required to avoid ion exchange effects. Charged groups will give rise to bad yields of charged solutes chromatographed in low concentrations and to asymmetric elution curves for charged solutes, particularly so when the work is conducted at low ionic strength. It is impossible to avoid charged groups completely. The amount of charged groups is, however, very low in the commercially available chromatographic gels. In accurate work, it is nevertheless necessary to work at ionic strengths that are not too low (0.02 or higher) to avoid ion exchange and ion exclusion effects. Regarding Donnan effects in this connection, see ch. 9.

A wide choice of gel types with the same general chemical constitution but with different fractionation ranges is desirable to facilitate the adaptation of the method to different problems. For microreticular gels the fractionation range is mainly determined by the swelling properties. Gels with low contents of dry substance in the gel give access to larger molecules than those with high contents of dry substance. The content of dry substance in these gels can be varied from approximately 50% w/v to 5% w/v ($W_r = 1$ to $W_r = 20$). This corresponds to a variation of the exclusion limit from molecular weight around 1,000 to molecular weight around 500,000 (determined for peptides and proteins). With macroreticular gels, the content of dry substance is no longer the only variable which determines the fractionation range of the gel; here, the structure of the gel is important. Gels can be produced with the same content of dry substance but with widely varying properties.

The particle size and the particle size distribution must be very carefully controlled. A bed consisting of small particles will generally give good resolution. The reason is that the mechanisms that give rise to zone broadening are amplified, as the particle size is increased. With large particles, diffusion in and out of the particles takes longer. The flow pattern in a bed of large particles is inferior, giving rise to more remixing. On the other hand, the resistance to flow in a bed packed with large particles is lower and the maximum flow rate that can be attained is higher. For this reason a compromise with respect to particle size should be reached, giving maximum zone resolution under the flow conditions required.

No known chromatographic material has an absolutely homogeneous particle size. As the resolution will be determined mainly by the large particles, while the flow characteristics are dominated by the small particles, it is essential for satisfactory function of the material that the particle size distribution be as narrow as possible. For special purposes it may be necessary to use narrower particle size distributions than those of the material commercially available. This may be achieved by wet or dry sieving or by elutriation. The easiest method is dry sieving, if possible. Elutriation gives the sharpest fraction. Wet sieving should only be attempted when no other means are possible. (For practical aspects of sieving and elutriation see § 5.2.)

The gel materials commercially available are usually delivered in beaded form as the flow properties are superior in a bed packed with beaded material. The bead form of the particles has been obtained by synthetizing the gels in suspension in an excess of organic solvent. Some materials are, however, still delivered as crushed powders. Such materials are synthetized in blocks and powdered afterwards in mills or other special devices (see for instance Hjertén 1962a).

The mechanical rigidity of the gel grains should be as high as possible, as they will otherwise tend to be deformed by the forces caused by the flow of liquid through the bed. This will cause the beds to compact reversibly or irreversibly, thus increasing the resistance to flow through the bed. This will, in many cases, limit the flow rate. As gels with small contents of dry substance and a correspondingly high exclusion limit tend to be mechanically weak, this sets an upward limit to the fractionation range that can be reached with many types of gel.

The manufacturers of chromatographic gel have usually tried to make gels with fractionation ranges extending to as high molecular weights as possible. The gel types fractionating at very high molecular weights usually require some technical skill in handling.

3.3. Synthesis of gels for gel chromatography

Scientists, who are particularly interested in the methodology of gel chromatography, may wish to manufacture their own bed material; others are advised to use commercial products. The gels on the market have reproducible properties corresponding to standards of quality that would be difficult to obtain in small scale synthesis. As this book is mainly intended as a guide for those who use gel chromatography as a tool rather than as a research subject, the synthesis of gels will not be discussed. Those who have special interests in the synthesis are referred to other sources for a description of synthetic procedures. A general survey has been given by Determann (1967). The synthesis of dextran gels (Sephadex ®) has been described by Flodin and Ingelman (1959), and Flodin (1962a). The synthesis of dextran gels in beaded form has been described by Flodin (1962b), polyacrylamide gels by Lea and Sehon (1962), Hjertén and Mosbach (1962), Sun and Sehon (1965), and Fawcett and Morris (1966), agarose gels by Polson (1961), Killander et al. (1964), Hjertén (1962b, 1964), Bengtsson and Philipson (1964), and Russel et al. (1964), macroreticular polystyrene gels by Moore (1964), cross-linked polymethylmetacrylate gels by Determann et al. (1964), substituted Sephadex ® gels by Determann (1964) and by Nyström and Sjövall (1965a, b, 1966a).

Subject index p. 391

3.4. Dextran gels, Sephadex®

The first gels to have their chromatographic behaviour systematically investigated were the dextran gels (Flodin 1962a). Dextran gels have exceptionally good chromatographic properties, and they have kept a dominating position in this field since their introduction.

Dextran is a polysaccharide, built up from glucose residues. It is produced by fermentation of sucrose. The microorganism used for this fermentation is *Leuconostoc mesenteroides* strain NRRL B512. The native dextran has high molecular weight and a very wide molecular weight distribution (mol. wt. $(10-300)\cdot 10^6$) (Arond and Frank 1954). The raw dextran is extensively purified, partly hydrolyzed and finally fractionated by ethanol precipitation to yield a product of suitable average molecular weight and a narrow molecular weight distribution. The glucose residues are joined by α-1,6-glucosidic linkages. The chains are to a certain extent branched. The branches are joined to the main chain by 1–2, 1–3 or 1–4-glucosidic linkages. In the dextran produced by *Leuconostoc mesenteroides*, strain B512, the branches are joined by 1–3-glucosidic linkages. The chemistry of dextran has been reviewed by Neely (1960), Ricketts (1961) and Jeanes (1966). Dextrans dissolve readily in water. When the dextran is cross-linked to form a gel, the polysaccharide chains of the gel form a three-dimensional network. The product is insoluble unless it is broken down chemically. In solvents, capable of dissolving dextrans, the cross-linked dextrans swell, taking up liquid into the grains. The degree of swelling is determined by the degree of cross-linkage and also, to some extent, by the conditions of the cross-linking reaction.

Dextran gels for chromatography are available from Pharmacia Fine Chemicals AB (for manufacturers, see appendix 1) under the trade name Sephadex®. Sephadex is manufactured by a bead polymerization process. In this process an alkaline solution of dextran of suitable molecular weight distribution is suspended in an organic solvent immiscible with water. Stabilizers have been added to stabilize the suspension. When the suspension has been stirred so that a suitable emulsion has been formed, epichlorohydrin is added. The epichloro-

ydrin reacts with the dextran matrix forming glyceryl links between
ie chains (Flodin 1962a). After the reaction has gone to completion, the
:action product is washed extensively and allowed to shrink in alcohol
water mixtures with successively increasing alcohol concentration,
nd dried. It is delivered dry as a free-flowing powder, consisting
f regular beads. When suspended in water the beads swell. Drying
nd swelling of Sephadex is reversible, and the material retains its
hromatographic properties after repeated drying and reswelling. The
iethod of drying Sephadex will be described in § 5.5.

Sephadex is very stable chemically. Its weakest points are the
lucosidic linkages, which may be hydrolyzed at low pH. However,
ie material is still intact after 6 months in 0.02-M HCl (Cruft 1961).
ephadex is also stable in alkaline solutions. Sephadex G-25 was found
ɔ be intact and working well after 2 months in 0.25-M NaOH at 60 °C.
'his makes it possible to remove contaminants, such as denatured
iroteins or lipids that may have precipitated on the gel, by treatment
vith strong alkali. Prolonged exposure to oxidizing agents may cause
n increase in the content of carboxyl groups. As carboxyl groups
mpair the chromatographic properties of Sephadex, oxidizing agents
hould be avoided. Sephadex can be heated to 110 °C in the wet state
vithout change in properties. In the dry state it can be heated to 120 °C.

Sephadex is available in eight different types. These types differ in
heir degree of cross-linkage and thus in their swelling properties. The
various types are characterized by the letter G followed by a number
Sephadex G-10 to Sephadex G-200). The numbers correspond to the
vater regain value of the gel multiplied by a factor 10 (water regain,
iee § 2.6). The special kind of Sephadex called Sephadex LH-20,
ntended for polar organic solvents, will be dealt with separately. For
:ach type of Sephadex different particle size grades are available. The
nanufacturer's technical data for Sephadex are given in table 3.1.

Subject index p. 391

TABLE 3.1
Technical data for Sephadex gels*

Designation		Particle diameter** (μ)	Fractionation ranges (mol. wt.)		Water regain (ml/g dry gel)	Bed volume (ml/g dry gel)	Minimum swelling time (hr)	
			Peptides and globular proteins	Dextrans			At room temperature	On boiling water bath
Sephadex G-10		40–120	<700	<700	1.0±0.1	2–3	3	1
Sephadex G-15		40–120	<1,500	<1,500	1.5±0.2	2.5–3.5	3	1
Sephadex G-25	coarse	100–300	1,000–5,000	100–5,000	2.5±0.2	4–6	3	1
Sephadex G-25	medium	50–150						
Sephadex G-25	fine	20–80						
Sephadex G-25	superfine	10–40						
Sephadex G-50	coarse	100–300	1,500–30,000	500–10,000	5.0±0.3	9–11	3	1
Sephadex G-50	medium	50–150						
Sephadex G-50	fine	20–80						
Sephadex G-50	superfine	10–40						
Sephadex G-75		40–120	3,000–70,000	1,000–50,000	7.5±0.5	12–15	24	3
Sephadex G-75	superfine	10–40						
Sephadex G-100		40–120	4,000–150,000	1,000–100,000	10.0±1.0	15–20	72	5
Sephadex G-100	superfine	10–40						

TABLE 3.1 *continued*

Designation	Particle diameter** (μ)	Fractionation ranges (mol. wt.) Peptides and globular proteins	Dextrans	Water regain (ml/g dry gel)	Bed volume (ml/g dry gel)	Minimum swelling time (hr) At room temperature	On boiling water bath
Sephadex G-150 Sephadex G-150 superfine	40–120 10–40	5,000–400,000	1,000–150,000	15.0 ± 1.5	20–30	72	5
Sephadex G-200 Sephadex G-200 superfine	40–120 10–40	5,000–800,000	1,000–200,000	20.0 ± 2.0	30–40	72	5

* Data taken from 'Sephadex – gel filtration in theory and practice', from Pharmacia Fine Chemicals.

** The diameter given is the dry particle diameter. The wet particle diameter can be calculated by multiplication with the factor $(1 + W_r \cdot d)^{\frac{1}{3}}$, where W_r is the water regain of the gel and d is the density of the dry gel, about 1.64 g/ml for the dextran gels.

3.5. Chromatographic properties of Sephadex

Dextran gels (Sephadex) were the first for which a close relationship between molecular size and elution behaviour was established (Granath and Flodin 1961). The relationship is illustrated for proteins in fig. 2.3. The corresponding diagrams for soluble dextrans are given in fig. 3.1. The behaviour of polyethylene glycols on the most tightly cross-linked members of the Sephadex series is given in fig. 3.2. From these diagrams it can be seen that the Sephadex series includes gels with fractionation ranges distributed over a very wide interval of molecular

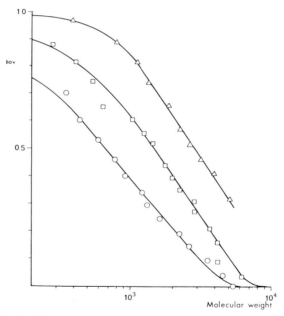

Fig. 3.1. Relationship between elution behaviour and molecular properties: K_{av} versus molecular weight for dextrans on cross-linked dextran gels with different water regain. $\triangle$ $W_r = 8.7$; $\square$ $W_r = 4.3$; $\bigcirc$ $W_r = 2.3$; the molecular weights are $\overline{M}_n$ for the fractions obtained on fractionation of a dextran with a broad molecular weight distribution. The data used to compile this diagram are taken from Granath and Flodin (1961)

weights, from Sephadex G-10 (mol. wt. 0–700) up to Sephadex G-200 (5,000–800,000).

Some differences exist between the fractionation properties of Sephadex for different groups of substances, as can be seen from table 3.1, and figs. 2.3, 3.1 and 3.2. In most cases these differences are relatively limited, and the general shape of the fractionation curves are similar. If the molecular weight of a substance is known, its chromatographic behaviour can usually be predicted with a fair degree of accuracy. This greatly facilitates the choice of gel type for a given problem.

Some general conclusions as to the range of applications of the gel

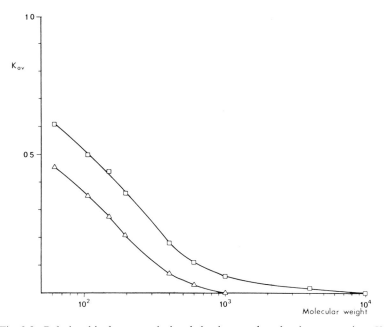

Fig. 3.2. Relationship between elution behaviour and molecular properties: K_{av} versus molecular weight for oligomers of ethylene glycol on Sephadex G-10 and Sephadex G-15. △ Sephadex G-10; □ Sephadex G-15. The elution volumes determined by chromatography of polyethylene glycol preparations with very narrow molecular weight distributions. The data used to compile the diagram are taken from 'Sephadex G-10 and G-15' by Pharmacia Fine Chemicals.

Subject index p. 391

types can be drawn from the list of fractionation ranges in table 3.1 and the figures. For the fractionation of proteins (with molecular weights higher than 10,000) Sephadex gels with water regain between 7.5 and 20 (Sephadex G-75 to Sephadex G-200) should be used. Sephadex gels with lower water regain (Sephadex G-10 to Sephadex G-50) are intended for fractionation of peptides and for group separation (desalting etc.). The gel type most commonly used for desalting proteins is Sephadex G-25. This gel type is easy to handle and gives fast and efficient desalting with little loss and low dilution. The choice of the right gel type for a given separation problem will be dealt with in more detail in § 5.1. Special techniques for specific purposes will be described in ch. 8.

Certain molecular species deviate strongly from the general elution behaviour described above. Notably, aromatic substances (homocyclic or heterocyclic) show greater affinity to the gel matrix than to the solvent (Gelotte 1960). They are retarded to varying extents compared with non-aromatic substances of similar size. This effect is particularly notable on the tightly cross-linked Sephadex gels such as Sephadex G-25, while it is scarcely noticeable with the higher numbered members of the series.

In some types of solvent this effect is strongly attenuated or completely absent. Carnegie (1965) was able to determine the molecular weights of peptides on Sephadex G-25 without disturbance by aromatic groups in the peptides, using phenol–acetic acid–water (1:1:1 w/v/v) as eluant. Aqueous NaOH and acetic acid–pyridine buffers (Eaker and Porath 1967) as well as urea and potassium thiocyanate solutions (Gelotte and Porath 1967) have also been found to attenuate the aromatic effect.

Some other substances have also been found to be more retarded on Sephadex than would be expected from their molecular size, although these effects are less pronounced than the aromatic effect. Marsden (1965) found an 'aliphatic adsorption' effect on a very tightly cross-linked dextran gel, closely similar to Sephadex G-10. For normal primary alcohols he found that the members of the series following ethanol are more retarded with increasing molecular weight – the verse to what would be expected for steric reasons. He also found that thiourea, urea and formamide are retarded considerably more than would be expected from steric models of the mechanism of gel chromatography. This could be confirmed by measurement of the temperature effects in chromatography of these compounds. If the chromatographic behaviour were governed by the steric hindrance in the gel only, no temperature effects should be noticed. Kirret et al. (1966) found that the temperature effects are very small for proteins on Sephadex G-100 columns and that the effect decreases with increase in the molecular weight of the proteins. Marsden found that substances that exhibit a non-ideal behaviour (normal alcohols, urea, certain benzoic acid derivatives) have K_d-values that vary strongly with temperature.

The dry Sephadex powder contains varying quantities of free dextran. The amount present in the tightly cross-linked gels is very low, while Sephadex G-200 may contain up to 10% free dextran. The dextran is released very rapidly, and after the passage of 2–3 column volumes of eluant virtually all the free dextran has been washed away. After this initial period, 0.002–0.003% of the Sephadex matrix is released per day as dextran from the Sephadex gels G-25 to G-75, while 0.005% per day is released from Sephadex G-200 (Granath 1964). This quantity is so small that the effluent from Sephadex columns gives little or no background when the anthrone reaction for carbohydrates is used, and even very small quantities of carbohydrates can be investigated on Sephadex columns without interference from the material released from the bed material (Granath and Kvist 1967).

3.6. Polyacrylamide gels, Bio-Gel

Cross-linked polyacrylamides form gels with water which have been used in various biochemical separations. The use of acrylamide gels in electrophoresis is treated in detail in the companion volume by A. H. Gordon 'Gel electrophoresis'.

The use of granulated polyacrylamide gels for gel chromatography was proposed by Lea and Sehon (1962) and by Hjertén and Mosbach (1962). In contrast to the dextran gels, the polyacrylamide gels are

Subject index p. 391

TABLE 3.2
Technical data for Bio-Gel*

Designation	Mesh	Particle diameter** (μ)	Operating range† (mol. wt.)	Water regain†† (ml/g dry gel)	Bed volume (ml/g dry gel)	Minimum swelling time (hr) at room temperature
Bio-Gel P-2	50–100	150–300				
Bio-Gel P-2	100–200	75–150				
Bio-Gel P-2	200–400	40–75	200–2,600	1.5	4	2–4
Bio-Gel P-2	<400	<40				
Bio-Gel P-4	50–100	150–300				
Bio-Gel P-4	100–200	75–150				
Bio-Gel P-4	200–400	40–75	500–4,000	2.4	6	2–4
Bio-Gel P-4	<400	<40				
Eic-Gel P-6	50–100	150–300				
Bio-Gel P-6	100–200	75–150				
Bio-Gel P-6	200–400	40–75	1,000–5,000	3.7	9	2–4
Bio-Gel P-6	<400	<40				
Bio-Gel P-10	50–100	150–300				
Bio-Gel P-10	100–200	75–150				
Bio-Gel P-10	200–400	40–75	5,000–17,000	4.5	12	2–4
Bio-Gel P-10	<400	<40				
Bio-Gel P-30	50–100	150–300				
Bio-Gel P-30	100–200	75–150	20,000–50,000	5.7	15	10–12
Bio-Gel P-30	<400	<40				

Table 3.2 continued

Designation	Mesh		Particle diameter** (μ)	Operating range† (mol. wt.)	Water regain†† (ml/g dry gel)	Bed volume (ml/g dry gel)	Minimum swelling time (hr) at room temperature
Bio-Gel P-60	50–100		150–300				
Bio-Gel P-60	100–200		75–150	30,000–70,000	7.2	20	10–12
Bio-Gel P-60	<400		<40				
Bio-Gel P-100	50–100		150–300				
Bio-Gel P-100	100–200		75–150	40,000–100,000	7.5	20	24
Bio-Gel P-100	<400		<40				
Bio-Gel P-150	50–100		150–300				
Bio-Gel P-150	100–200		75–150	50,000–150,000	9.2	25	24
Bio-Gel P-150	<400		<40				
Bio-Gel P-200	50–100		150–300				
Bio-Gel P-200	100–200		75–150	80,000–300,000	14.7	35	48
Bio-Gel P-200	<400		<40				
Bio-Gel P-300	50–100		150–300				
Bio-Gel P-300	100–200		75–150	100,000–400,000	18.0	40	48
Bio-Gel P-300	<400		<40				

* Data taken from price list S, February 1, 1967, from Bio-Rad Laboratories.

** Not indicated whether this refers to wet or dry particle diameter; see note in table 3.1.

† The operating range indicated here does not correspond to the fractionation range; the fractionation range can be seen to be considerably wider from a diagram in the brochure.

†† The water regain values are given with ±10% accuracy.

entirely synthetic. Acrylamide, $H_2C = CH - CO - NH_2$, a solid, is soluble in water and insoluble in non-polar organic solvents. It can polymerize in two modifications. By polymerization of the acrylamide with heat, a solid is obtained that is insoluble in all the common solvents. By vinyl polymerization of acrylamide, a linear water-soluble polymer is obtained (Jones et al. 1944). By copolymerization with methylene-bis-acrylamide, $H_2C = CH - CO - NH - CH_2 - NH - CO - CH = CH_2$, a material can be obtained where polyacrylamide chains are cross-linked. The reaction mixture can be induced to form a gel, if suitable reaction conditions are chosen. The concentration of monomers in the reaction mixture and the proportion of cross-linker in the monomer can be varied, giving different swelling characteristics and chromatographic properties to the gels. *The monomers used in polyacrylamide synthesis are toxic, and should be handled carefully.*

Polyacrylamide gels for gel chromatography are available from Bio-Rad Laboratories, under the trade name Bio-Gel. Bio-Gel has been produced by bead polymerization. It is delivered as a dry powder, which has a rather marked tendency to form clumps and stick together. Like Sephadex, Bio-Gel is a xerogel. On addition of water to the dry powder, it swells spontaneously to form the gel particles that are used for chromatography. The matrix chains of Bio-Gel are very inert, as they are held together mainly by carbon–carbon bonds. The weakest points of the material are the amide groups that may be hydrolyzed at extremes of pH; on hydrolysis carboxyl groups are produced that give the gel more or less pronounced ion exchange properties. The manufacturer states that the material is stable in the pH range 2–11.

Bio-Gel is delivered in 11 types with different swelling characteristics and different fractionation ranges. The types are characterized by the letter P and a number (Bio-Gel P-2 to Bio-Gel P-300). The number is intended to indicate the exclusion limit for the gel, calculated for globular proteins or peptides and given in 1,000 atomic units. For each type different particle size grades are available. Technical data for Bio-Gel, taken from the manufacturer's technical bulletins, are given in table 3.2.

3.7. *Chromatographic properties of Bio-Gel*

As the literature about Bio-Gel is not as extensive as that for Sephadex, information on its chromatographic behaviour is much more limited. The fractionation properties seem to be very similar to those of Sephadex. Fractionation ranges are very close to those of the Sephadex types with the corresponding water regain. Aromatic compounds have been found to be retarded on Bio-Gel. No extensive study of the retardation of aromatic compounds on Bio-Gel has been published, but the sparse information available indicates that the effects are approximately as large as on Sephadex gels with similar water regain (see for instance Determann 1967, pp. 87–89). This is rather astonishing, as the chemical constitutions of the two types of gel matrix are so different.

As with Sephadex beads, Bio-Gel beads with low water regain are rather hard, while the types with high water regain are very soft. Beads of Bio-Gel P-300 are so soft that they cause great technical difficulties. Recently Bio-Rad Laboratories have announced the introduction of a new quality of Bio-Gel. Little information is yet available about this material. No investigation on the breakdown of the gel has been reported in the literature.

3.8. *Agar and agarose gels*

Shortly after the introduction of gel chromatography as a standard separation method in biochemistry, Polson (1961) published a study on the chromatographic properties of agar gels. These were found to be very interesting, combining fractionation ranges at very high molecular weights with good mechanical stability. These properties should make them suitable as a supplement to the dextran gels and the polyacrylamide gels. The agar gels with the lowest fractionation ranges that can be used practically correspond approximately in their fractionation properties to the dextran or polyacrylamide gels with the highest fractionation ranges. Agar gels fractionate far into the region intermediate between molecules and particles.

Agar, or agar-agar, as it was called earlier, is obtained from various species of sea-weed. It is a mixture of linear polysaccharides composed mainly from D-galactose and 3.6-anhydro-L-galactose residues. Agar dissolves readily in boiling water; on cooling, the solutions form gels even at very low agar concentrations (below 0.5%). This property has led to a number of applications, notably in the food industry. Agar is also used in scientific work to solidify solutions without changing their physico-chemical properties noticeably. In some of these appli cations, advantage is taken of the fact that the gel can be penetrated by molecules of considerable size. This property is a prerequisite for the use of agar gels in gel electrophoresis, in immunodiffusion and in immunoelectrophoresis. The use of agar gels in immunodiffusion and immunoelectrophoresis is described in the companion volume by J Clausen 'Immunological techniques for the identification and esti mation of macromolecules'.

In contrast to the gel types described earlier, the macromolecules in the gel matrix of agar are not bound together by covalent bonds The molecules are thought to be held together by hydrogen bonds (see for instance Wieme 1965, pp. 102–110). As the gels are remarkably re sistant to hydrogen bond breaking agents, some other mechanism may be holding the molecules together. The great mesh width of the gels and their stability indicate that the mechanism may be the formation of microcrystallites.

Agar has some disadvantages as a chromatographic material, and it has taken some time to develop agar gel chromatography into a standard method that can be used in chromatographic practice. The main drawback is the presence of a considerable amount of charged groups in the material. These charged groups are to a large extent sulphate groups, but carboxyl groups have been found also to be present. Because of the contents of charged groups, it is usually neces- sary to work at very high ionic strength to suppress ion exchange ef- fects.

Araki (1937, 1956) showed that agar consists of two groups of poly- saccharides that he termed agaropectin and agarose. Agaropectin is the fraction of the agar that carries the charged groups, while the agarose is virtually uncharged. Araki's original method for separation of agarose and agaropectin, acetylation followed by shaking out of the agarose into a chloroform phase and regeneration of the polysaccharides, is too complicated to be practically useful. The polysaccharides can be separated from one another more easily by fractional precipitation with polyethylene glycol (Russel et al. 1964) or by precipitation of the agaropectin with cetylpyridium chloride (Hjertén 1961; see also volume by J. Clausen). Both procedures give agarose preparations well suited for gel chromatography. Agarose has the capacity of giving stable gels at very low concentrations (lower than the original agar). Agarose gels were found to fractionate at high molecular weight in a similar way to agar, although without interference from the charged groups.

One disadvantage of agar and agarose for gel chromatography stems from the fact that the agar chains are not linked by covalent bonds. This makes the agar gels chemically less stable than, for instance, the dextran gels. Agar and agarose dissolve in water at raised temperatures; if the temperature of the agarose gels is increased above 50°C, they gradually loose their stability and melt. Therefore, in work with these gels the temperatures must be kept low, and heat sterilization of the material is impossible. Agar gels are also less stable to extremes of pH than the gels described earlier. Values of pH outside the range 4.5–9 should be avoided. This does not in general limit the usefulness of the agarose. Most proteins and other biochemical substances have their range of stability within this region and can be chromatographed on the material.

Agents known to disrupt hydrogen bonds, such as urea, decrease the mechanical stability of the gel. The effect is, however, much less pronounced than one would expect, and the gels will not be destroyed by moderate concentrations of urea. Nor will the gels be influenced by organic solvents such as acetone or ethanol. It is possible to treat agarose gels with pure acetone without change of their properties. Dextran gels or polyacrylamide gels shrink completely, when treated with this solvent.

The structure of agarose gels makes it impractical to dry and reswell them. Once the gel has been prepared, it should be stored in the

TABLE 3.3

Technical data for commercial agarose gels*

Designation	Mesh	Particle diameter** (μ)	Fractionation range millions a.u.	Agarose concentration (%)	Manufacturer†
Sagavac SAG 2		66–142 (F)	0.5–150	2	
Sagavac SAG 4		142–250 (C)	0.2–15	4	
Sagavac SAG 6			0.05–2	6	Seravac
Sagavac SAG 8			0.025–0.7	8	
Sagavac SAG 10			0.010–0.25	10	
Sepharose 4B††		40–190	0.3–3	4	Pharmacia Fine Chemicals
Sepharose 2B		60–250	2–25	2	
Bio-Gel A-0.5m	50–100	150–300			
Bio-Gel A-0.5m	100–200	75–150	<0.010–0.5	10	Bio-Rad Laboratories
Bio-Gel A-0.5m	200–400	40–75			
Bio-Gel A-1.5m	50–100	150–300			
Bio-Gel A-1.5m	100–200	75–150	<0.010–1.5	8	Bio-Rad Laboratories
Bio-Gel A-1.5m	200–400	40–75			
Bio-Gel A-5m	50–100	150–300			
Bio-Gel A-5m	100–200	75–150	0.010–5	6	Bio-Rad Laboratories
Bio-Gel A-5m	200–400	40–75			

TABLE 3.3 continued

Designation	Mesh	Particle diameter** (μ)	Fractionation range millions a.u.	Agarose concentration (%)	Manufacturer†
Bio-Gel A-15m	50–100	150–300			
Bio-Gel A-15m	100–200	75–150	0.04–15	4	Bio-Rad Laboratories
Bio-Gel A-15m	200–400	40–75			
Bio-Gel A-50m	50–100	150–300	0.10–50	2	Bio-Rad Laboratories
Bio-Gel A-50m	100–200	75–150			
Bio-Gel A-150m	50–100	150–300	1–>150	1	Bio-Rad Laboratories
Bio-Gel A-150m	100–200	75–150			
2% Gelarose suspension				2	
4% Gelarose suspension				4	
6% Gelarose suspension				6	Litex
8% Gelarose suspension				8	
10% Gelarose suspension				10	

* Data all taken from the manufacturers' technical information material. Sagavac is delivered as crushed material, while the other types are beaded.

** Wet particle diameters.

† Appendix 1.

†† A third type, Sepharose 6B, available within short (Oct. 1968).

wet state. The gel seems to be very stable mechanically, and if microbial growth is prevented, the gel suspensions can be stored for long
periods of time without changing their properties to any noticeable
extent.

Four brands of agarose gels for chromatographic purposes are
available commercially: Sagavac (earlier called Sagarose), Sepharose ®, Bio-Gel A and Gelarose.

Sagavac, from Seravac Laboratories, is available in different types,
designated SAGA 2 F ... 10 F and 2 C ... 10 C. The numbers used in
the designations of the Sagavac types refer to the percentage of dry
material in the gels. The letter F stands for fine and C for coarse. Sagavac is prepared in blocks and is delivered as a crushed material. According to the information given by the manufacturer the agarose is
prepared by polyethylene glycol fractionation of natural agar by a
modification of the method of Russel et al. (1964). The material has
a particle size of 66–142 μ (F) and 142–250 μ (C).

Sepharose ®, from Pharmacia Fine Chemicals, is available in two
types, designated Sepharose 2B and Sepharose 4B. The numbers de-
note the percentage of dry material in the gels in the same way as for
Sagavac. Sepharose is produced in beaded form by a modification of
the method of Hjertén (1964). The agarose is prepared by cetylpyridium chloride precipitation of the agaropectin from the natural agar
by the method of Hjertén (1962c). The particle size is 40–190 μ for
Sepharose 4B and 60–250 μ for Sepharose 2B.

Gelarose, from Litex, is available in five types, containing 2%, 4%,
6%, 8% and 10% of dry substance. Gelarose is prepared in beaded
form. No information is available regarding the methods of preparation of the material or the technical characteristics of it.

Bio-Gel A, from Bio-Rad Laboratories, is supplied in six types, each
in three sieve fractions. The various types, designated A-150m to A-
0.5m, contain 1, 2, 4, 6, 8 and 10% of agarose in the gel.

Technical data for the agarose gels that are commercially available
are given in table 3.3. The data are taken from the manufacturers'
technical information.

3.9. Chromatographic properties of agarose gels

As mentioned earlier, agarose gels have fractionation ranges at considerably higher molecular weights than expected by comparison with dextran or polyacrylamide gels. This can probably be explained from the structure of the agarose in the gel. The agarose chains can be expected to align themselves to form fibres of a considerably greater

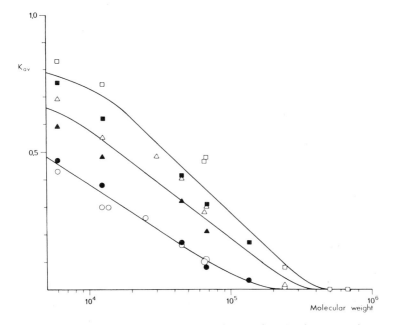

Fig. 3.3. Relationship between elution behaviour and molecular properties: K_{av} versus molecular weight for proteins on different types of Bio-Gel P. □ Bio-Gel P-300, △ Bio-Gel P-200, ○ Bio-Gel P-100. The following proteins were used in the measurement: Insulin, M 6,000; horse heart cytocrome c, M 12,400; ribonuclease, M 13,700; chymotrypsinogen, M 25,000; pepsin, M 35,000; ovalbumin, M 45,000; hemoglobin, M 65,000; bovine serum albumin, M 67,000; bovine serum albumin dimer, M 134,000; ox liver catalase, M 240,000; edestin, M 310,000; urease, M 490,000; thyroglobulin, M 670,000. The molecular weights are in some instances relatively uncertain. The data used to compile the diagram are taken from Batlle (1967).

Subject index p. 391

thickness than that of the single agarose chain (Laurent 1967). In these fibres the separate chains can be expected to be kept in position by crystallite formation. This picture of the agarose structure is supported by the properties of the gel, its stability to hydrogen bond breaking agents and its mechanical rigidity. This will also explain the variations of the fractionation properties of the gels with the method of preparation: the process of crystallite formation will be influenced by the conditions under which the gel is prepared. This will make it possible to prepare gels with the same contents of dry substance but differing properties (Laurent 1967; Öberg and Philipson 1967).

In fig. 3.4 the relationship between chromatographic behaviour and molecular weight is given for Sepharose. It can be seen that the curve is less steep than it is for the gels from dextran and polyacrylamide (figs. 2.3, 3.3). This seems to be a general characteristic for gels of macroreticular character.

On agarose gels there seems to be still less interaction between solute and matrix than with the other types of gels. Hjertén (1961) reports that even crystal violet, which is notorious for its tendency to stick to chromatographic materials, is not attached to agarose. As mentioned earlier, the agarose gels have very good mechanical properties. The particles are much more rigid than the dextran gels or the polyacrylamide gels with the same contents of dry substance. The agarose gels are, however, not completely rigid, and the gel types with low contents of dry substance (2% or less) may easily compact in the bed and clog the column. The compacting has a different character from the irreversible clogging of dextran or polyacrylamide gel beds which necessitates repacking of the column. The agarose gel beds compact under the influence of the flow, but return partly to an expanded state when the flow is stopped. Although gel beds packed with gels containing more than 4% agarose do not easily get clogged, the movement of the bed makes it difficult to obtain reproducible results without very careful control of the chromatographic conditions. Some suggestions on the specific experimental technique with agarose gels will be found in § 5.8.

Although the agarose chains are not cross-linked by covalent bonds,

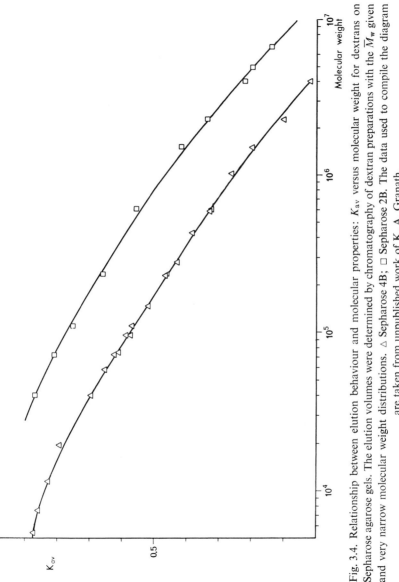

Fig. 3.4. Relationship between elution behaviour and molecular properties: K_{av} versus molecular weight for dextrans on Sepharose agarose gels. The elution volumes were determined by chromatography of dextran preparations with the $\overline{M}_w$ given and very narrow molecular weight distributions. △ Sepharose 4B; □ Sepharose 2B. The data used to compile the diagram are taken from unpublished work of K. A. Granath.

agarose beds release very little bed material to the eluant. For
Sepharose the bleeding from the bed material is less than 1 μg/ml in
the effluent from a 1-m bed at a flow rate of 4 cm/hr.

3.10.   Other types of gels for use in aqueous solutions

Porous glass as gel medium for gel chromatography was proposed by
Haller (1965). The glass is very rigid and fractionates at large molecular size (Haller reports fractionation of virus). The glass beads, however, seem to carry somewhat too large quantities of charged groups
and possibly also to interact in other ways with the solutes. This effect
is said to be reduced to some extent by treatment of the material with
hexamethyldisilazane. So far, too little information is available regarding this material to judge about its possible range of applications.
Porous glass is commercially available from Bio-Rad Laboratories
under the trade name Bio-Glas.

Polystyrenes are used for gel chromatography in organic solutions
(see § 3.11). Recently, attempts have been made to convert these materials for use in aqueous solutions as well. Thus, Dow Chemical
Company has recently introduced a gel type called Aqua-Pak and Bio-
Rad has introduced a gel type called Bio-Beads SM. Both types are
so new that no information is available in the literature on their
characteristics or possible applications.

3.11.   Gels for use in organic solvents

Very soon after the first successful results of Porath and Flodin (1959)
had been reported, attempts were made to adapt the method to use in
organic solvents, as a chromatographic method for separation according to molecular weight would be a benefit for scientists working
in polymer chemistry and also for many organic chemists.

It was very soon found that cross-linked dextrans (Sephadex) could
be used for this purpose in a few organic solvents, notably in glycol,
formamide and dimethylsulfoxide (Flodin 1962a, p. 30). Dimethylsulfoxide has been used to some extent for determination of molecular

weight distributions of lignins from wood (Enkvist et al. 1966; Ekman and Lindberg 1966; Lindberg et al. 1965). Sephadex does not swell in pure alcohols. It swells to a certain extent in mixtures of the lower alcohols and water. For ethanol–water mixtures, the solvent regain is approximately proportional to the percentage of water in the mixture.

Vaughan (1960) reported the use of cross-linked polystyrenes as chromatographic media with aromatic hydrocarbons as solvents. A macroreticular polystyrene gel with fractionation ranges extending up to very high molecular weights was developed by Moore (1964). A material of this type is manufactured by Dow Chemical Co. and sold by Waters Associates, under the trade name of Styragel®. This material has mainly been used for the determination of molecular weight distributions of organic polymers, but may be interesting for biochemists for the fractionation of lipid-soluble natural substances. Styragel is available in 11 different types with exclusion limits ranging from molecular weights around 1,600 up to around 40,000,000. Styragel is delivered suspended in diethylbenzene. The beads are rigid and the solvent can easily be exchanged even after the bed has been packed, as the beads are said not to change their volume with change of solvent. These polystyrene gels are intended for use in non-polar organic solvents mainly, though the manufacturers of Styragel claim that the material can be used even in dimethylsulfoxide.

Recently a similar material was made available by Bio-Rad Laboratories under the name Bio-Beads S. It is delivered in three types, with fractionation ranges up to 2,700 in molecular weight. Bio-Beads S are delivered dry.

For the purpose of developing a material suitable for gel chromatography in polar organic solvents, Nyström and Sjövall (1965a, b) have produced a methylated Sephadex derivative. With this material Sjövall and his co-workers have separated a considerable number of lipids, steroids, protected oligopeptides and vitamins of the K group (Nyström and Sjövall 1966a, b; Sjövall and Vihko 1966a, b; Vihko 1966). At the same time, Pharmacia Fine Chemicals independently developed a hydroxypropyl derivative of Sephadex with properties very similar to those of the methylated Sephadex derivative (Joustra et al. 1967). This material is commercially available under the trade name of Sephadex LH-20. The letters LH refer to the fact that the gel matrix is compatible with lipophilic as well as with hydrophilic solvents. Sephadex LH-20 has a solvent regain value of approximately 2 ml/g in water, chloroform and the lower alcohols. The technical data for the material can be found in table 3.4. Sephadex LH-20 is delivered as a dry powder.

TABLE 3.4
Technical data for Sephadex LH-20*

Solvent	Approx. solvent regain (ml/g dry gel)	Approx. bed volume (ml/g dry gel)
Dimethylformamide	2.2	4.0–4.5
Water	2.1	4.0–4.5
Methanol	1.9	4.0–4.5
Ethanol	1.8	3.5–4.5
Chloroform, stabilized by 1 % ethanol	1.8	3.5–4.5
Chloroform	1.6	3.0–3.5
n-Butanol	1.6	3.0–3.5
Dioxane	1.4	3.0–3.5
Tetrahydrofurane	1.4	3.0–3.5
Acetone	0.8	
Ethyl acetate	0.4	
Toluene	0.2	

* Data taken from 'Sephadex – gel filtration in theory and practice'.

Sephadex LH-20 has slightly different fractionation properties in different solvents. The lower limit of the fractionation range lies around a molecular weight of 100 and the exclusion limit somewhere between 2,000 and 10,000. The relationship between molecular weight and the elution behaviour is illustrated in fig. 3.5 for polyethylene glycols in ethanol. Some effects related to specific functional groups of the solutes have been noticed. In chloroform, substances containing hydroxyl or carboxyl groups are retarded relative to substances not containing these groups. This is probably the reason for the anomalous behaviour of polyethylene glycols on Sephadex LH-20 in chloroform (fig. 3.5). On the other hand, the retardation of substances containing aromatic groups found with ordinary Sephadex in aqueous solutions is much diminished on Sephadex LH-20 in alcohol and is completely absent when chloroform is used as eluant (Wilk et al. 1966).

With Sephadex LH-20, a rather special technique has to be used for

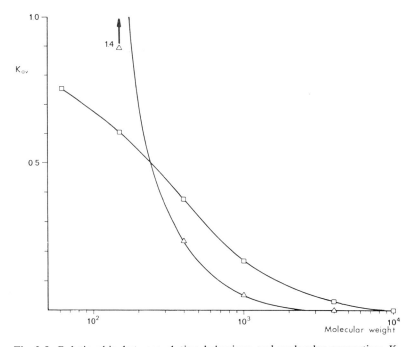

Fig. 3.5. Relationship between elution behaviour and molecular properties: K_{av} versus molecular weight for polyethylene glycols in ethanol and chloroform on Sephadex LH-20. △ chloroform; □ ethanol; the elution volumes determined by chromatography of polyethylene glycol preparations with very narrow molecular weight distributions (ethylene glycol, triethylene glycol, polyethylene glycols with $M = 400$, 1,000, 4,000, 10,000). The data used to compile the diagram are taken from 'Sephadex LH-20' by Pharmacia Fine Chemicals.

Subject index p. 391

chromatography in chloroform. The chloroform is denser than the swollen gel, and the gel floats in the liquid. For this reason it is necessary to work with the gel bed enclosed between plungers. The bed can either be packed upwards or by a strong downward flow forcing the gel downwards in spite of its tendency to float. A description of the packing technique will be given in § 5.8.

CHAPTER 4

Equipment for gel chromatography in columns

4.1. General

The principle of chromatography is simple, and certain experiments of a qualitative nature can be performed with very simple equipment. For accurate experiments, where the experimental conditions must be carefully controlled and where optimal resolution is desired, a considerable amount of equipment is required. It may seem unnecessary to buy equipment costing several hundred dollars to start chromatography, where the principal phenomenon is that substances are separated when they are washed down a tube by a liquid. This is, however, in most cases necessary, and it is wise to choose the equipment with care from the very beginning so that it covers the requirements for some time to come.

The equipment required for different kinds of chromatography varies, and no set-up covers all types of experiments. It is therefore appropriate to devote a chapter to the equipment required for gel chromatography. As the situation in the market for chromatographic equipment is rapidly changing, it is not intended to give a complete list of the instruments that can be obtained, but rather to give a picture of what equipment is required and to discuss the advantages and disadvantages of different types of equipment for gel chromatographic applications. The discussion is mainly limited to equipment for gel chromatography of substances of biological origin in aqueous solvents.

 Subject index p. 391

4.2. The chromatographic column

A chromatographic column consists of a straight tube with a bed support at the bottom. The bed support is permeable to allow the liquid to pass while the bed material is retained. Below the support there should be some arrangement to permit collection of the effluent. The top of the column is designed to allow the eluant reservoir to be connected.

The simplest columns consist of a straight glass tube with a constriction at the bottom end. The bed support is arranged by inserting a plug of glass wool into the bottom end of the tube and by covering the glass wool with quartz sand or glass beads (fig. 4.1). If this simple type of column is handled carefully, very good results can be obtained.

In a slightly modified version of this simple column arrangement, a porous glass plate is fused into the tube to serve as bed support (fig. 4.2). This construction is inferior to the one just described. The glass plate is easily clogged, and the dead space below will cause remixing of the zones. On the other hand, there is no risk of conta-

Fig. 4.1. Simple column construction: glass tube with constriction and glass wool plug at the lower end.

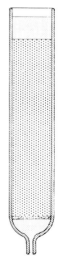

Fig. 4.2. Simple column construction: glass tube with constriction and sintered glass plate at the lower end. When a column of this type is used, there is a risk of clogging of the glass plate, and a filter paper or other protective device should be positioned over the glass plate before use. To reduce the void space below the sintered plate, glass beads can be used.

mination of the gel suspension with glass beads or sand when the column is repacked.

Chromatographic columns of more advanced design, specially constructed for gel chromatography, can be obtained from various manufacturers. Most of the columns that are commercially available have plunger(s) (adapters) at the top or, better, at both ends or can be equipped with such plungers. These plungers are necessary if the column is used in upward flow or recycling experiments. They are also valuable in routine work, where simple and reliable sample application is required. An example of a column of this type is

Fig. 4.3. Advanced column construction. The column is equipped with a jacket for thermostating and with two plungers. The bed support material of the plungers is nylon net. The void space below the bed support has been reduced to a minimum. The plungers can be tightened to the walls of the tube by an expansion mechanism operated by the nut at the outer part of the plunger (column K 50/100, Pharmacia Fine Chemicals).

shown in fig. 4.3. In all chromatographic work, the column must be chosen with great care to obtain optimal results. Although a column is in principle a very simple piece of equipment, there are several requirements to be taken into account. The cost of the column is a small part of the total cost of chromatographic equipment, and it is well worth buying a good column.

The following properties are essential in a column for gel chromatography: small dead volume below the bed support, facilities for connection of the outlet from the column to a capillary tubing, bed support that does not get clogged by the gel, protection for the bed surface, freedom from materials that may cause denaturation of labile substances.

Small dead volume below the bed support: In gel chromatography, it is usually possible to obtain sharp, narrow zones. The reasons are that the partition isotherm for most substances between the gel phase and the liquid phase is linear (see § 5.11), that the equilibrium distribution of a substance between gel and liquid is established very rapidly, and that the mechanical properties of the gels allow very even packing of the bed. This is important in fractionation experiments where the differences in elution volume between the substances to be separated are relatively limited (in gel chromatography almost all substances are eluted within one bed volume, see Giddings 1967). Owing to the sharpness of the bands, a limited broadening will be very noticeable. Large dead volume in the effluent leads and below the bed support will, thus, impair the resolution in gel chromatography more than in most types of chromatography. Large dead spaces are common in columns of simple design. If such columns must be used, it is recommended that the space below the bed support be filled with small glass beads.

Facilities for connection to capillary tubing: In most experiments the column is connected to a capillary tube which either carries the effluent to a pump, or fraction collector, or monitor, or which simply regulates the flow rate in gravity feed experiments. Various nipples may be used for connecting the capillary tubing. Further comments on the design and handling of such nipples will be given in § 4.7.

Bed support that does not get clogged by the gel: Porous plates of various kinds have found extensive use as bed supports in chromatographic columns. In many cases, gel particles pass into the holes of the plate. After a short time the plate may become completely clogged so that no liquid can pass through. This has been observed most frequently with coarse sintered glass plates and soft gel types. For this reason, coarse sintered glass plates should be avoided as bed supports; if a column with this type of bed support has to be used, the bed support should be covered with filter paper (for instance rayon paper, see below).

Protection for bed surface: In gel chromatography, as in all kinds of chromatography, it is important to apply the sample evenly to the surface of the bed. When the sample is applied directly to the unprotected bed surface, even application may be relatively difficult, as the bed material has a tendency to whirl up when the sample is pipetted onto it. Gels are more difficult than most other materials in this respect, as the gels have densities that are close to the density of the liquid. For this reason it is particularly important to have the surface protected. A sheet of rayon filter paper or some other filter paper with good mechanical stability in the wet state will usually serve. (For suppliers of rayon paper, see appendix 1.) If the sample contains substances that get attached to paper, other rigid porous materials may be used. One manufacturer of columns, Pharmacia Fine Chemicals AB, equips some of the columns with a special device called sample applicator that serves to protect the bed surface. In this device, a thin nylon fabric is mounted at the end of a short piece of Perspex tube fitting inside the chromatographic tube.

Freedom from denaturing construction materials: Many proteins are denatured by contact with metal surfaces. For this reason, metals should be avoided in the construction of those parts of the columns that come in direct contact with the bed or the effluent.

Some suppliers of chromatographic columns suitable for gel chromatography are given in appendix 1.

Subject index p. 391

4.3. Equipment for regulation of the flow

4.3.1. Mariotte flask

For most chromatographic work, gravity feed of the eluant will be quite satisfactory. In this case a Mariotte flask will be needed to keep a constant operating pressure over the column. For a discussion about the operating pressure, see § 5.9. The principle of the Mariotte flask is illustrated in fig. 4.4. A simple Mariotte flask can be constructed as shown in fig. 4.5.

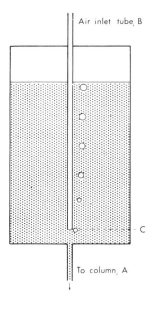

Fig. 4.4. The principle of the Mariotte flask. The container is closed. When liquid is drained from the container through tube A, the pressure above the liquid decreases and the level of the liquid in tube B, which is open to the air, sinks. When the air has reached the lower end of tube B further drainage will cause air to pass into the container as bubbles. The pressure of the liquid at level C is then equal to the external pressure.

4.3.2. Pumps

In precision experiments, where the constancy of flow obtained with gravity feed is unsatisfactory, the flow is best regulated with a precision metering pump. For laboratory scale chromatography, peristaltic pumps (Crisp and De Broske 1952) are usually to be preferred to plunger pumps. Centrifugal pumps are unsuitable, as they do not give a reproducible flow. In peristaltic pumps, the liquid comes in contact only with the tubing. For this reason there is very little risk of leakage or denaturing of proteins when this type of pump is used; nor can the eluant be contaminated by lubricants. The zone broadening and remixing caused by peristaltic pumps can for practical purposes be neglected, and for this reason peristaltic pumps can be connected to the outlet from the column. This has the advantage that the flow can be regulated by the pump also during sample application.

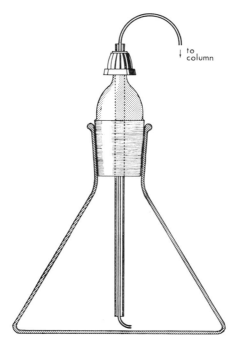

to column

Fig. 4.5. Simple and reliable design of Mariotte flask. The Erlenmeyer flask is equipped with a standard ground glass joint NS 29. The glass tube with about 6 mm outer diameter is kept in position by a Quickfit screw cap adapter St 54/13. The liquid is drained from the flask through a capillary tube with less than 2 mm outer diameter.

By the use of different diameters of tubing in the pump, a wide range of pumping rates can be obtained with one pump. This type of pump seems to be almost ideally suited to chromatography. Examples of the construction of peristaltic pumps are given in figs. 4.6, 4.7 and 4.8.

To give a constancy of the flow, superior to that obtained with gravity feed, the pump should be equipped with a motor of sufficient stability. In practice it has been found that a strong synchronous motor is required. It is advantageous to use a continuously variable gear between motor and pump to permit easy regulation of flow rate.

Some suppliers of pumps for chromatographic purposes are given in appendix 1.

Fig. 4.6. Peristaltic pump. Three rollers are mounted between the peripheries of two thin wheels. The tubing is tensioned around the rollers. When the wheels rotate, the liquid in the tube is pumped. The pump gives relatively little pulsations if the tube tension and the distance between the tube ends are correctly adjusted.

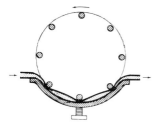

Fig. 4.7. Peristaltic pump. Design similar to that in fig. 4.6. The rollers press the tube against a round support. The pump is somewhat more difficult to adjust than that in fig. 4.6 and may cause somewhat more wear of the tubing.

Fig. 4.8. Peristaltic pump (finger pump). The fingers compress the tube successively from one end to the other.

4.4. Recording of elution curves

4.4.1. General

Until some 5–6 years ago, the amount of substance in the effluent from a chromatographic experiment was usually measured manually in the fractions collected; this was a tedious process. The accuracy of the measurements was limited by the size of the fractions which, for practical reasons, could not be made too small. During the last few years, a great number of monitors for chromatography have been developed. These record continuously some physical or chemical parameter of the effluent, such as light absorption, conductivity, refractive index, flame ionization or fluorescence. For properties that cannot be determined with a monitor, the samples can be analyzed by automatic analysers.

4.4.2. Automatic analysis

Enzymatic activities and some types of substances, notably sugars, have to be determined in separate fractions. This work has been greatly facilitated by instruments for automatic analysis. (Automated enzyme assay will be covered in a companion volume by D. B. Roodyn now in preparation.) With these instruments many samples can be analyzed rapidly without excessive work and the effluent can be separated into many small fractions so allowing better resolution of the elution curves. The number of analytical methods developed for these instruments is tremendous and they cover almost all types of substances. Some suppliers of equipment for automatic analysis are given in appendix 1.

4.4.3. Monitors

4.4.3.1. General considerations

In a monitor, some easily measurable property of the eluant is recorded continuously. Owing to the special requirements of flow monitors, their design differs radically from that of the corresponding instruments for measurements on separate samples. In some ways, there are

Subject index p. 391

greater demands on an instrument intended as a chromatographic monitor than on the corresponding instruments for general purposes. Thus, the concentration of solute in the effluent from a column is often relatively low, and the instruments must therefore be sensitive. In addition, the long-term stability must be very good, as many chromatographic experiments require considerable periods of time. Moreover the region, where the measurement is made, should be small and have a simple form without pockets to avoid zone broadening and remixing. Finally, the instrument (or the measuring cell compartment, if this is a separate unit) should take little space so as to fit easily into the chromatographic set-up without long connecting tubes.

4.4.3.2. Photometric monitors

Most of the monitors used in biochemical applications exploit the spectral properties of the solutes. Proteins and nucleic acids have considerable absorption in the ultraviolet and can be readily detected by photometry.

In proteins, ultraviolet absorption is caused by tryptophan and tyrosine and, to a smaller extent, by phenylalanine. The absorption produced by these amino acids has a maximum near 280 nm. Prostethic groups of proteins, like heme groups or flavin groups, may also show strong absorption extending into the visible region.

Nucleic acids, nucleosides and nucleotides have an absorption maximum near 260 nm. It is sometimes useful to monitor a column at both 260 and 280 nm so as to detect both protein and nucleic acid in the same effluent, although it should be pointed out that proteins have a certain absorption at 260 nm as also have nucleic acids at 280 nm.

For a discussion of Beer's law, relating light transmission through a cell and concentration of coloured substance in the cell, the reader is referred to standard textbooks on physical chemistry, such as Daniels and Alberty (1961). It should be stressed that the light intensity in the beam that has passed the cell is not a linear function of the concentration and that the transmission curve therefore does not give a fair representation of the concentration variation in the effluent (especially the high peaks reaching below 50% transmission tend to be too square and the peak height tends to be suppressed). To get the correct elution curve, the recorded curve should therefore be recalculated, although the recorded curve gives a fairly good idea of the result.

Spectrophotometers, intended for measurement of light absorption of separate samples can often be converted for flow analysis, but they are usually rather bulky and expensive pieces of equipment. In addition, the flow cells supplied for ordinary spectrophotometers have relatively large volumes. This increases the zone broadening from the column. Also, the recorders supplied with the recording types of spectrophotometers are not intended for the slow recording rates in chromatographic experiments, and an extra recorder will usually be necessary. Ordinary spectrophotometers are not manufactured for long-term experiments, and in some instances the base line stability is not completely satisfactory. In Zeiss spectrophotometers this is corrected by an automatic device that at regular intervals inserts a reference cell and adjusts its base line. In addition, this device automatically changes between two preset wavelengths.

Special spectrophotometric devices for chromatographic purposes are available commercially. These instruments are usually smaller and less expensive than the standard spectrophotometers. They are equipped with flow cells with limited volumes and with recorders adapted to the requirements of the chromatographic experiments. They are also designed to be used in cold rooms.

In standard spectrophotometers, the light is rendered monochromatic by a prism or a grating monochromator. This gives light of good spectral purity, and a free choice of wavelength within the wavelength range of the instrument. A monochromator is, however, an expensive part of the instrument. The monochromator can be dispensed with provided that high spectral purity is not required and that a limited number of wavelengths is sufficient.

Some instruments use a mercury resonance lamp radiating at 253.7 nm; a filter is inserted to remove undesired wavelengths. This is the system used in the cheaper UV monitors such as the Uvicord from LKB-Produkter AB. In a later version, this has been supplemented by a fluorescent plastic rod, converting the light of the mercury resonance lamp to 280 nm, where the proteins have an absorption maximum. This, however, gives a broader wavelength band than the original one. In other instruments, lamps are used that give a spectral continuum or a considerable number of lines (high pressure mercury lamps, hydrogen lamps) and interference filters are used to select the wavelength band. As the quality of the UV interference filters has been improved considerably in the last few years, this is a satisfactory method in measurements on substances that do not exhibit very sharp absorption peaks. Deviations from Beer's law are to be expected at low transmission values (high extinction values), as light at wavelengths removed from the absorption maximum will be responsible for a larger part of the signal in this case. The number of UV monitors on the market is large and will probably increase. Some suppliers of instruments now available are listed in appendix 1.

4.4.3.3. *Other types of monitors*

The conductometric monitors make use of the conductance of the solutes. Their range of application in gel chromatography is somewhat limited, as the conductivity of high molecular weight solutes is low and the solvents used in gel chromatography (buffers, salt solutions) conduct well. The contribution of the solute in these cases is small in comparison with the conductivity of the eluant and is difficult to detect. For certain special purposes conductometers are, however, valuable: one such is the supervision of desalting experiments, where they are invaluable detectors for the salt fraction.

Refractometric monitors are based on the differences in refractive index produced by the solutes. Although these differences are small, the refractometric monitors can be made very sensitive, as the refractive index can be measured to a high degree of accuracy. This, however, makes the method very sensitive to fluctuations in temperature and composition of the liquid, and these variables must be kept strictly under control. It is difficult, therefore, to obtain satisfactory long-term stability with a limited effort and apparatus. Refractometric monitors are usually intended for application to organic solvents, although this is not an absolute requirement.

Several other properties of the solutes can be used for determination of concentration in the eluate. Optical activity measurement, potentiometry (including pH-measurement with glass electrodes), fluorimetry, measurement of dielectric constants have been used in different connections. Also a flame ionization detector for use in liquid chromatography has been constructed (Haahti and Nikkari 1963). A similar device is commercially available from Japan Electron Optical Laboratories. W. G. Pye & Co., Ltd. has developed a monitor based on the ionization of organic substances in a stream of argon exposed to radioactive irradiation. By a special device, the products from the column are transferred to the gas stream. The apparatus cannot be used for entirely aqueous solutions, as the device for transporting the substances from the liquid stream to the gas stream cannot handle water solutions. A further limitation to flame ionization detectors as well as the argon ionization detector is that even low concentrations of non-volatile organic substances in the eluant (for instance organic buffering substances) interfere with the determination.

An exellent review of the principles for the various types of monitors can be found in Morris and Morris (1962, pp. 449–484). Some suppliers of monitors are listed in appendix 1.

4.5. Fraction collectors

The substances, separated on the chromatographic bed, should be collected separately to take advantage of the separation obtained. In principle, this could be attained by connecting the outlet from the chromatographic apparatus by valves to different containers for the different peaks eluted. This principle is used in preparative scale and large scale gel chromatography (Flodin 1962a). The equipment necessary to obtain an automatic collection of samples of this kind is, however, not of a very general kind, and in most set-ups on a laboratory scale, it is preferable to collect the effluent in small equal fractions. This is also the method of choice if the concentration of substance is not continuously recorded before collection of the effluent, and the exact positions of the peaks are not known. The construction and function of the turntable-type fraction collectors have been discussed by Morris and Morris (1964, pp. 156–161), who also include a discussion of the different principles for activating the step mechanism (by timing devices, volume measurement or drop counting). Recently another type of fraction collector has been introduced. In this type, the tubes are placed in straight tube racks; either these pass under the column outlet or the outlet is moving above the tubes. This means a considerable saving of space and makes it easier to handle the fractions after the experiment has been finished. On the other hand the construction is more complicated. The construction of a fraction collector for sterile work has been described by von Zeipel and am Ende (1966).

In addition to easy handling and small dimensions, it is essential that fraction collectors for gel chromatography be well enclosed to permit their use in humid environments. Cold rooms tend to be very destructive to electronic equipment that has not been very carefully protected. The number of fraction collectors available commercially is very large, and it is hardly worth-while mentioning any type separately.

4.6. Thermostats

If the temperature of the room, where the chromatographic experiments are carried out, is reasonably constant with fluctuations not exceeding some $\pm 2°$, no control of column temperature is usually necessary, as gel chromatography is remarkably insensitive to temperature fluctuations. In this connection it should be pointed out that whether the column is thermostated or not, draughts and direct sunlight should be avoided. In very accurate work such as molecular weight determinations, a thermostat may be required. For this purpose, almost any laboratory thermostat equipped with a circulation pump can be used. The requirements on heater capacity, cooler capacity and pumping capacity are very low, as long as the temperature of the column is not too far removed from room temperature, and any ordinary laboratory thermostat will be sufficient for work within the temperature range of interest in gel chromatography.

4.7.   Connecting tubing

To avoid remixing, the connecting tubing should be of narrow bore. For aqueous solutions, PVC tubing with about 1 mm internal diameter will usually serve well. For work with organic solvents and for special purposes, PTFE tubing of similar diameter should be used. In addition to being more expensive, the PTFE tubing has the disadvantage of being more difficult to handle. In most types of connecting nipples, the tubing needs to be flared out at the end. This requires higher temperatures with PTFE tubing. The PTFE in addition is so hard that it is difficult to make a tight seal with the connecting nipple. On the other hand, PTFE tubes do not release any UV-absorbing material, as do other types of plastic and rubber tubes.

Both PVC and PTFE tubing will be permanently deformed if they are compressed. For this reason they cannot be used in pumps, and clamps should be avoided. For applications where compression of the tubing is required other types of tubing such as Tygon or silicon tubing should be used. Most manufacturers of peristaltic pumps also supply tubing for use with their pumps.

Most of the equipment for gel chromatography has suitable nipples as standard equipment on delivery, and in these cases there is little difficulty in connecting the tubing. Fig. 4.9 shows one type of connecting nipple. In most types of connecting nipples, the tube should

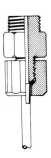

Fig. 4.9. Connecting nipple. The outer hood presses the flare of the tube against the inner cone to give a tight fit.

Subject index p. 391

be flared out before inserting it into the nipple. The manufacturers of the equipment also deliver suitable tools for flaring the tubes.

The quality of joints depends on the quality of the flare of the capillary tubing. Therefore, one should be very careful to produce an absolutely symmetrical and even flare. For production of conical flares, a simple tool, consisting of a metal rod turned in a lathe to conical shape at one end and equipped with a handle at the other is often used. This tool should be gently heated so that the plastic will be softened without melting on contact. The point is inserted into the tube with gentle pressure. Without removing the tool from it, the end of the tube is immersed in cold water. After cooling, the tool can be loosened from the tubing. The procedure is repeated until a flare of the required size has been obtained.

In some cases, the apparatus is equipped with nipples with luer cones or other special nipples. Direct connection to the tubing can then be made by insertion of the tubing into the hole at the point of the nipple. If the outer diameter of the tubing is slightly larger than the inner diameter of the hole, this joint will be satisfactory for most purposes. The insertion of the tube is facilitated if the end is cut skew before it is inserted. With PVC tubing that is too thick to be inserted as it is, the end of the tube can be drawn thin before insertion. This is possible without heating the tube. A pair of pliers is used to hold the end of the tube which is drawn gently some centimetres from the pliers. Before insertion, the end that has been crushed by the pliers is cut. PTFE tubing can be drawn after gentle heating. If the nipple can be removed, the end of the tubing is drawn out over some distance so that it reaches inside the nipple. It is then pulled into the nipple until a very tight fit has been obtained between nipple and tube. The part of the tube emerging inside the nipple is then cut off.

If the pressure of the liquid is not very high, it will usually be sufficient to insert the ends of the capillary tube to be joined into a short piece of elastic tube (Tygon or silicon) with an internal diameter slightly smaller than the outer diameter of the capillary tube.

CHAPTER 5

Experimental technique in column gel chromatography

5.1. Choice of gel type

From the point of view of methodology, two separate types of separation can be distinguished. In one type, substances with high molecular weight are separated from substances with low molecular weight. The substances with high molecular weight are completely excluded from the gel and are eluted after the void volume of the column while the low molecular weight constituents are eluted considerably later, often at a volume close to the bed volume V_t. This type of separation, which will be called group separation in the following discussion, is also often referred to as desalting, even if no salts are involved. In the other type of separation, called fractionation, the substances are more similar to one another. The gel material has to be chosen so that they do not elute either with the void volume or with the total column volume. The substances are eluted closer to one another than in group separation and may overlap. As can be deduced from the terminology, group separation separates the substances in (two) groups, those which move with the void volume and those which penetrate completely into the gel phase, while in fractionation the various substances have their partition coefficients and elution volumes within the fractionation range of the gel. A practical difference between group separation and fractionation is that in group separation the groups are eluted so well apart that large quantities of solution can be applied, while in fractionation the sample size is much more limited (see § 5.7.2). The distinction between the two types is not absolute, but

 Subject index p. 391

for practical purposes it is quite useful to differentiate between them.

The difference between group separation and fractionation can also be illustrated with reference to the diagrams relating molecular weight and chromatographic behaviour (see § 2.5). In group separation, the substances of high molecular weight fall on the horizontal part of the curve at $K_{av} = 0$. The substances with low molecular weight fall on the horizontal part of the curve close to $K_{av} = 1$. Ideally, no substances fall on the inclined part of the curve. In fractionation, on the other hand, the substances of interest should fall on the inclined part of the curve.

In group separations, only a relatively coarse fractionation of the substances in the sample is achieved. The typical case is the removal of salts or other low molecular weight solutes from solutions of proteins or other high molecular weight solutes. No separation of the high molecular weight solutes is obtained. This type of gel chromatography thus has a range of application corresponding most closely to that of dialysis.

In special cases the technique can be modified by the use of chemical complexes and other effects, to give very good purifications of specific materials (Lindner et al. 1959; Frankland et al. 1966, see § 6.3.1). The method has the advantage of being fast (considerably faster than dialysis), giving good yields and little dilution. The amount of equipment required is small, and very little work is involved.

For group separations intended to remove low molecular weight solutes from protein solutions, Sephadex G-25, Sephadex G-50, Bio-Gel P–6 or Bio-Gel P–10 should be used. Sephadex G-25 has a dominating position for this application. It is easy to handle and produces very few difficulties. For proteins of molecular weight exceeding 30,000–50,000, gels which swell somewhat more such as Sephadex G-50 could be used with advantage. They give as efficient group separations and are more economical as they swell more strongly and consequently give larger bed volumes from the same amount of dry substance. On the other hand, they are slightly more difficult to pack and give lower flow rates. For desalting of peptides and other substances of low molecular weight (molecular weight 1,000–5,000), Sephadex G-10, Sephadex G-15, Bio-Gel P–2 and Bio-Gel P–4 can be used.

In group separation, the substances to be separated are very different. If the substances have properties closer to one another and their chromatographic parameters differ less, they must be separated by fractionation. In this case, the chromatographic conditions should be chosen with more care. As a rule of thumb, the gel material should be used that gives the largest separation volume between the substances to be separated. In most cases, the substance to be fractionated and purified is contaminated with a variety of substances of both higher and lower molecular weights. A gel that has its fractionation range centered around the molecular weight of the substance under study should give the best fractionation result. In some cases, it has been found to be advantageous to use a somewhat denser gel as the denser gels tend to give less technical difficulties. Some examples of the choice of gel material will illustrate the discussion.

Group separation experiments, for example buffer exchange preceeding electrophoretic and ion exchange chromatographic experiments, desalting of protein solutions and removal of phenol from nucleic acid preparations are in most laboratories regarded as routine operations not worth reporting and are hardly ever mentioned in the literature. One group separation experiment that is interesting because it can be scaled up to industrial scale is the separation of proteins and low molecular weight components in milk. This has been reported by De Koning (1962). For this application he used Sephadex G-50 in a column with about 250 ml bed volume (4×20 cm). 50 ml skim milk (about 20% of the bed volume) could be applied and the whole experiment could be performed in little more than 1 hour.

Fractionation will be illustrated with some experiments from different fields of biochemistry and with substances of different molecular weight ranges. When Flodin and Aspberg (1961) wanted to separate the cellodextrin oligosaccharide mixture with one to six glucose units (produced by hydrolysis of cellulose) they used Sephadex G-25, the densest gel available at that time. The molecular weights of the cellodextrin oligosaccharides range from 180 to 990 and lie well within the fractionation range of Sephadex G-25 (100–5,000). The result is illustrated in fig. 5.1, where the experimental data are also given.

Subject index p. 391

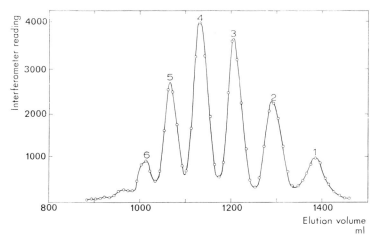

Fig. 5.1. Separation of cellodextrins produced by partial hydrolysis of cellulose on Sephadex G-25. Column dimensions 4.5 × 126 cm. Bed volume 2,000 ml. The numbers in the figure indicate the number of glucose units present in the glucose oligomer. From Flodin and Aspberg (1961).

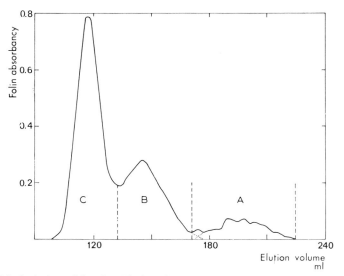

Fig. 5.2. Isolation of insulin. Elution diagram of a crude pancreas extract on a column of Sephadex G-50 in 1 M acetic acid. The insulin was recovered from peak A. Bed dimensions 2 × 120 cm. From Davoren (1962).

Davoren (1962) and Epstein and Anfinsen (1963) elaborated methods for purification of insulin from small amounts of starting material. In their methods they included gel chromatography on Sephadex. As the molecular weight of insulin is around 6,000, they used Sephadex G-50 with fractionation range 1,500–30,000 approximately. Their results are given in fig. 5.2 and 5.3, together with pertinent experimental data. The difference in their elution curves can be explained from the difference in starting material and the differences in experimental conditions. It can be noted however that in spite of the differences, the V_e/V_0 for insulin is approximately 2 in both cases (it is assumed that the first peak corresponds to the void volume).

Serum albumin has a certain tendency to form dimers and other oligomers, which diminishes its value in certain experiments, for instance as standard substance in ultracentrifugation. To study the formation of oligomers, Pedersen (1962) used gel chromatography to separate the different forms of serum albumin. Human serum albumin

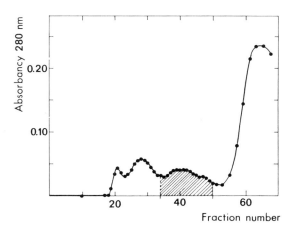

Fig. 5.3. Isolation of insulin. Elution diagram of a crude calf pancreas extract on a column of Sephadex G-50 in 0.2 M NH_4HCO_3. The insulin was recovered from the cross-hatched area. Bed dimensions 2.2×85 cm. After addition of zinc acetate, the material from the gel chromatographic run could immediately be crystallized. From Epstein and Anfinsen (1963).

has molecular weight 69,000, and the oligomers have even multiples of this (138,000, 207,000 etc.). For this separation, Pedersen found Sephadex G-150 (fractionation range 5,000–400,000) most suitable. Fig. 5.4 illustrates the separation obtained in one of the experiments.

Granath and Kvist (1967) have applied gel chromatography to the determination of molecular weight distributions of dextrans, particularly in body fluids. Such determinations give important information regarding the fate of the dextrans in the body. For this purpose, they wanted the gel material to fractionate in the molecular weight range 10,000 to 150,000. Although this range is covered for instance by the gel Sephadex G-150, this gel does not give sufficient separation in the highest

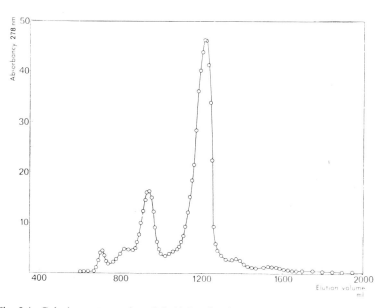

Fig. 5.4. Gel chromatography of lipid-free bovine serum albumin, showing the separation of monomer, dimer and higher oligomers, mainly trimer, on Sephadex G-150. The last peak containing the main part of the material corresponds to the monomer. Column dimensions 5×110 cm. Eluant 0.2 M NaCl–0.1 M tris buffer H 8.1. Flow rate 40 ml/hr. The concentration given in the ordinate was determined spectrophotometrically at 278 mm. From Pedersen (1962).

and the lowest molecular weight range to permit accurate determinations. For this reason the authors packed their columns with a mixture of Sephadex G-200 which fractionates well in the high molecular weight range, and Sephadex G-100 which ensures a satisfactory fractionation in the low molecular weight range. In this way a satisfactory fractionation was obtained in the whole molecular weight range which could not have been properly covered by a single gel type.

An example of a case intermediate between group separation and fractionation is the preparation of pyrogen-free albumin by gel chromatography on Sephadex G-100 (Philip et al. 1966). The pyrogens to be removed from the albumin are all completely excluded from the Sephadex gel and emerge from the column with the void volume, while the bovine serum albumin monomer is eluted later, well separated from the pyrogenic material. In this case the albumin falls within the fractionation range of the gel, while the contaminants are eluted as a group with the void volume. The reason for the choice of Sephadex G-100 instead of Sephadex G-200 is probably partly that the flow properties of Sephadex G-100 are better and partly that the low molecular weight part of the pyrogens might tail on Sephadex G-200, diminishing the advantage that has been gained by the use of the gel with the higher fractionation range.

5.2. Particle size and particle size distribution

For all the gel chromatography materials commercially available the particle size distribution is rather wide, with a factor two or three between the upper and the lower limit. For most work this is quite acceptable. For some types of gels, different sieve fractions are available. For ordinary laboratory column chromatography, the dry powders with particle size distributions centered around approx. 70 μ particle diameter are usually satisfactory. The gel materials delivered in liquid (the agaroses and the cross-linked polystyrenes) should have particle size distributions centered at approx. 150 μ particle diameter. This will give a fairly good compromise between resolution and flow

Subject index p. 391

rate for most types of gels. For crushed materials, the resistance to the flow for these particle sizes may be somewhat too high. On the other hand these materials may require a lower flow rate to give the corresponding resolution (crushed and beaded materials, see § 3.2).

The numbers given above for the particle size should not be taken as strict recommendations but rather as a general guide, and for many purposes other particle sizes will give better results. For critical fractionation purposes, the use of a finer grade material will in many cases give a considerable improvement in resolution and may even make special arrangements like recycling unnecessary. If the flow rate with the standard grade material can be increased above that required, finer grade material is recommended for columns. The finest grade material (superfine), with particle diameter lower than 40 μ, can be used with advantage in many cases. For group separations where high flow rates can be used, the coarser grades intended for industrial use may be preferable. For a discussion of the mechanisms of zone spreading, see Giddings (1965) chapter 2.

Some of the commercially available materials contain an appreciable amount of fine particles or particle fragments that will impair the flow properties of the material. These can usually be removed to a sufficient extent by repeated decantations (see § 5.3).

For special fractionation purposes, where a limited improvement of the chromatographic properties would be worth a considerable effort, the commercially available materials may be improved by further sharpening of the particle size distributions. For this purpose, elutriation or sieving may be used. Elutriation in air is the method giving the sharpest fractions. It allows separation of powders in almost infinitely sharp particle size fractions. The method takes advantage of the different Stoke's velocities in air of particles of different size. In practice, the fractionation is performed in the following way (see fig. 5.5). The dry powder to be fractionated is placed on a fine mesh support at the bottom of a relatively long tube. A carefully regulated current of dry air is blown through the support. At a relatively low air velocity, the powder forms a fluidized bed. Small particles, with falling velocities lower than the upward velocity of the air, are carried upwards through the tube and collected in a filter arrangement at the other end of the tube. When no more particles are carried away by the current of air, the filter can be changed and the air velocity increased. The particles with falling velocities between that of the air current used in the first case and that used in the second case are collected in the filter. Collection of closely graded fractions will inevitably imply collection of small fractions. The method can also be used to remove fine and coarse particles, while the bulk of the material is collected. This improves the column performance considerably even if the fraction collected is not made extremely sharp. Only dry, free-flowing powders can be treated by air elutriation. Of the gel materials intended for gel chromatography in aqueous systems, only Sephadex can be treated in this way. The Bio-Gel powders tend to stick together and form clumps, and the agarose preparations are delivered wet.

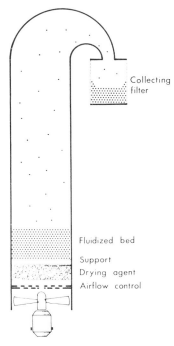

Collecting filter

Fluidized bed

Support

Drying agent

Airflow control

Fig. 5.5. Principle of apparatus for particle sizing by dry elutriation. The powder to be sized is placed on the support at the bottom of the tube. A current of dry air is allowed to pass upwards through the tube after having passed through a filter of drying agent. The powder at the bottom of the tube forms a fluidized bed and the fine particles are carried over to the collecting filter.

Dry sieving is a simple method of sharpening the particle size distribution. Although it does not give the very sharp fractionation obtained by elutriation, it has the advantage that the necessary equipment is available in most laboratories. The powders must be dry and free-flowing.

A method for wet elutriation of chromatographic materials has been described by Hamilton (1958). In this method the powder (in the liquid) is placed in a separation funnel, through which a carefully regulated flow of liquid is allowed to pass. The fractions of the powder may be collected on a Büchner funnel in a manner corresponding to dry elutriation. As the funnel is conical, the flow rate is lower at the top and consequently the material is graded in the funnel, and after the liquid flow has stopped the different layers in the funnel contain material of different particle size.

Wet sieving is the least satisfactory of the methods for separation of grains of different size. Unfortunately, this is the only method except wet elutriation that is available for agarose gels and for polyacrylamide gels. Wet sieving takes more time, and requires more complicated equipment than dry sieving. If it is carried out properly, it will, however, give fairly satisfactory results.

Equipment for dry sieving and for wet sieving can be had through most laboratory suppliers. U.S. standard mesh sieves are available in most laboratories.

5.3. *Preparation of the gels*

Sephadex and Bio-Gel are delivered as dry powders. Before they are used, they must be allowed to swell in the liquid to be used as eluant. In the early days of gel chromatography, it was recommended that the gels should be allowed to swell in distilled water and washed afterwards with the eluant liquid. This is an unnecessary complication, as the gels can very well be left to swell directly in the eluant. The required amount of dry powder calculated from the volume of the chromatographic column is weighed out before swelling. (The volume of chromatographic bed produced from each gram of dry powder can be found in tables 3.1 and 3.2.) As the powders swell considerably it is difficult to estimate the amount of powder needed without weighing. The dry powder is then mixed with an excess of liquid. As the powder mixes readily with the liquid, it is fairly unimportant whether the liquid is added to the powder or vice versa (although in principle the powder should be added to the liquid).

The classical method of swelling the powder is to leave it standing until the gel has swollen to equilibrium. This takes a considerable time for some of the gel types, as can be seen from tables 3.1 and 3.2. Even though the time given in the table has usually been calculated with a fair safety margin, methods for accelerating the swelling process are available.

The most convenient method is the 'heating method'. By warming the gel slurry in a boiling water bath to a temperature close to 100 °C, the swelling is greatly speeded up and can be completed in a couple of hours instead of days (for the loosely cross-linked gels). The method has the further advantages that bacteria and fungi present in the suspension will probably be killed and that the air dissolved in the liquid is removed, making separate de-aeration of the slurry unnecessary. After the gel has swollen to equilibrium, the slurry is left to cool (or cooled by immersing the flask in cold water) before packing. The columns should be packed at the temperature at which they are to be used. Swelling time on boiling water bath is included in table 3.1. The only case when the above method cannot be used is when the eluant solution is unstable to heating. In that case, the gel should be swollen in hot distilled water and after cooling washed repeatedly with the de-aerated eluant.

If necessary, the gel slurry should be decanted to remove the fine particles at this point of the procedure. To do this, an excess of eluant is added to the gel. After gentle stirring, the gel is allowed to stand until all the gel particles except the very fine ones have settled. The supernatant liquid and the fine particles can then be decanted and the procedure repeated if necessary. During stirring, creation of air bubbles in the gel suspension should be avoided.

Subject index p. 391

5.4.   Prevention of microbial growth: bacteriostatic agents

Some of the gel types, notably dextran gels (Sephadex) and agarose gels, may be attacked by microbes (bacteria or fungi). The microbes may cause degradation of the gels. Polyacrylamide gels (Bio-Gel) will not themselves be attacked by microbes. Nevertheless microbial growth may occur in gel suspensions and on gel beds. Such microbial growth will impair the chromatographic properties of the material and cause decreased yields and infection of the solutions eluted from the column. For this reason, microbial growth should always be prevented.

Microbial growth does not often appear on beds while they are running. Gel slurries or packed columns, however, should not be left standing without a satisfactory protection against bacteria and fungi. If the bacteriostatic agent is to be eluted before the column is used, any efficient germicide may be used that does not react with the gel material. If the column is used for protein chromatography, the germicide should preferably not denature or precipitate protein solutions, as the sample solution may accidentally come in contact with it. Driedger et al. (1967) have proposed the use of 2.5 % I_2 in half saturated KI for sterilization of gel chromatography columns. Various substances, like toluene, phenol, cresol, formalin and chloroform (Flodin 1962a, p. 47) have been proposed as germicides. Phenol, cresol and formalin have a marked tendency to precipitate irreversibly almost any protein. Chloroform may in some instances change the degree of swelling of gel materials and thus interfere with the function of the bed. It also dissolves in most types of plastics. This removes the chloroform from the solution. The mechanical strength of the plastics is diminished and the plastic parts may swell or be deformed.

Very often the need may arise to use the bacteriostatic agent in the solutions during the experiments. For such applications the germicide should fulfil other requirements in addition to those mentioned above. The germicide should be compatible with the substances to be chromatographed without denaturation, precipitation or reduction of biological activity. If the substances are to be detected by ultraviolet spectroscopy, the germicide should not absorb appreciably in the ultraviolet. The following substances are satisfactory for many applications.

Sodium azide, NaN_3, is a commonly used preservative for serological material. A concentration of 0.05–0.1 % has been recommended for this purpose (Batson et al. 1950). However, a considerably lower concentration, around 0.02 %, seems to give satisfactory protection to gel chromatographic columns, although streptococci have been reported to grow at this concentration in some instances. Sodium azide is easily soluble in water (about 40 % at 20 °C). The azide is precipitated by heavy metals, forming explosive insoluble salts. It does not interact notably with proteins or carbohydrates. Thus, antibody activity is not impaired by the use of sodium azide (Batson et al. 1950). Nor does sodium azide change the chromatographic behaviour of proteins or carbohydrates. Its interference with fluorescent marking of proteins (Lachmann 1964) seems to be due to a reaction between the azide and the fluorochrome. Sodium azide also interferes with the anthrone reaction. Being anionic, it cannot be used in connection with anion exchangers. A 0.02 % solution has about 90 % transmission in a 3-mm cell and about 60 % transmission in a 1-cm cell at 254 nm, while the light absorption at 280 nm is low at this concentration (see fig. 5.6).

Chloretone, trichlorobutanol, $Cl_3C\text{-}C(OH)(CH_3)_2$, is used as preservative for injectables. For this application concentrations of 0.3–0.5 % are recommended. Considerably lower concentrations, 0.01–0.02 % seem to provide satisfactory protection against growth on gel chromatographic columns. Chloretone is most efficient as a germicide in weakly acidic solutions. It decomposes in strongly alkaline solutions or on heating to temperatures above 60 °C. If the heating method for swelling of the gels is used, the chloretone should be added after the swelling. The solubility in water (20 °C) is about 0.8 %. Chloretone is uncharged and consequently does not interact with polyions or ion exchangers. It does not interfere with the chromatographic behaviour of carbohydrates or with the anthrone reaction. The light absorption is very low in the entire range of the ultraviolet region that is used for spectrophotometric analysis of water solutions.

Merthiolate ®, *Thimerosal, ethylmercuric thiosalicylate*, is used as

Subject index p. 391

preservative for injectables. For this application, 0.005–0.01 % solutions are recommended. Its effect against spore-forming bacteria is, however, limited. It is most effective in weakly acidic solution. Merthiolate is precipitated by heavy metal ions. Trace amounts of cupric ions may cause decomposition in the absence of EDTA (Davisson et al. 1956). Merthiolate is bound to and inactivated by substances containing thiol

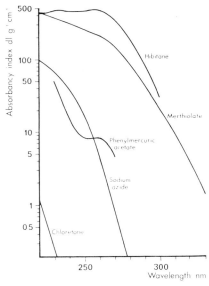

Fig. 5.6. Ultraviolet spectra of some bacteriostatic agents. The absorbancy index (extinction coefficient) on weight basis, $a = A_{1 cm}/c$, is plotted in a semilogarithmic diagram against the wavelength. c is the concentration in per cent w/v. The measurements were performed on a Bausch & Lomp 600E spectrophotometer with 1 cm quartz cell. The substances were those commercially available and measured without further purification. The solvent in all cases was distilled water, and the measurements were performed at room temperature. The transmission through a solution can be calculated from the absorbancy index by Beer's law: $T = 100 \log^{-1}(-a \cdot l \cdot c)$, where T is the transmission in per cent and l the light path. The details of the experiments were: Sodium azide, Merck, batch 6184772, 0.01 %, 0.02 % and 0.5 %; phenyl mercuric acetate, commercial purum quality 0.001 %; Merthiolate, commercial quality, 0.001 %, 0.005 % and 0.05 %; Chloretone, Merck, batch 913731, 0.3 %; Hibitane acetate, ICI, 0.0004 %, 0.001 %, 0.004 % and 0.2 %.

groups. This includes proteins which attenuate the bacteriostatic effect of merthiolate to varying extents. Merthiolate is also taken up by rubber, and if solutions of merthiolate are left standing in contact with rubber, the bacteriostatic effect is gradually attenuated. Merthiolate is easily soluble in water (up to about 50%). It has been used as preservative for sera and vaccines and does not alter the chromatographic properties of the proteins. Neither does it interfere with the chromatographic properties of carbohydrates or with the anthrone reaction. Merthiolate is anionic and should not be used in connection with anion exchangers. It is delivered as the sodium salt. A 0.005% solution transmits about 9% of the light through a 1-cm cell and 40% through a 3-mm cell at 254 nm. A solution of this concentration transmits about 40% through a 1-cm cell and 75% through a 3-mm cell at 280 nm.

Phenylmercuric salts (acetate, nitrate, borate), are used as preservatives for injectables. For this application, 0.001–0.01% solutions are used. Phenylmercuric salts are most bacteriostatic in weakly alkaline solution. Halogen and nitrate ions may cause precipitation, particularly from fairly concentrated solutions, on prolonged storage. Reducing agents may cause decomposition. Ammonia and ammonium salts inhibit the bacteriostatic effect. As with Merthiolate, substances containing thiol groups (including proteins) attenuate or inhibit the bacteriostatic effect. Solubility in water (20°C): nitrate about 0.07%, borate about 0.8%, acetate about 0.17%. As phenylmercuric salts are cationic they interact with polyanions like carboxymethyl cellulose or dextran sulphate and with soaps and anionic detergents. They should not be used in connection with cation exchangers. A 0.002% solution transmits about 70% through a 1-cm cell and about 90% through a 3-mm cell at 254 nm, while the light absorption at 280 nm can be neglected at this concentration.

Hibitane ®, *Chlorhexidine* (ICI). A very efficient bacteriostatic that was found to inhibit the growth of all test bacteria tried at 0.0013% concentration. Growth of *Pseudomonas* in 0.05% Hibitane has, however, been reported (Burdon and Whitby 1967). The effect against fungi is less pronounced, but the growth of many types was inhibited by concentrations between 0.1% and 0.01%. For gel chromatographic purposes, 0.002% concentration should be sufficient in most cases. Hibitane is incompatible with only very few substances. From the biochemical point of view, the carboxymethylcelluloses (and probably other polyanions as well) are probably the most important ones. Hibitane is cationic and should not be used in work with cation exchangers. The chloride and the sulphate have low solubilities, and precipitation may occur on prolonged storage of Hibitane in solutions with appreciable concentrations of chloride or sulphate ions (although not from very dilute Hibitane solutions). For the same reason, it may be difficult to dissolve Hibitane in these solutions, and it is recommended that it is dissolved separately in pure water and subsequently added to the solution. Increased temperatures cause decomposition of Hibitane, particularly in relatively concentrated solutions. Solutions containing 0.1% or less can, however, be boiled and even sterilized by autoclaving. Hibitane is delivered as 20% gluconate solution, crystalline diacetate or crystalline hydrochloride. The diacetate is soluble in water to 1.9% and the hydrochloride to 0.06%.

The ultraviolet spectra of commercial samples of the bacteriostatic substances mentioned are given in fig. 5.6. As a general rule, the solution should transmit more than 30–40% in order not to decrease the signal-to-noise ratio excessively in UV monitors and to make it necessary to work with excessive slit width and bad stray light conditions. In work with UV monitor under conditions where the bacteriostatic absorbs noticeably, it is important to keep the concentration of the bacteriostatic very constant.

Bacteriostatics generally seem to start causing hemolysis in concentrations close to the concentrations effective for bacteriostatic purposes. This indicates an interaction with the structural elements in the red cell walls. Some bacteriostatics mentioned above were found to cause hemolysis at the following concentrations: Chloretone 0.26–0.32%, Merthiolate 0.05–0.50%, phenylmercuric nitrate 0.001–0.003%, Hibitane 0.02–0.1%. The lower limits are those causing trace hemolysis and the upper limits are those causing complete hemolysis of rabbit erythrocytes. For hemolysis of human erythrocytes, somewhat higher concentrations are required. The data are taken from Ansel and Cadwallader (1964) and from Ansel (1967).

The concentrations given in the discussions of the bacteriostatic agents are in many cases not bactericidal and definitely not fungicidal. However, inhibition of growth is satisfactory in most cases, and germicidal conditions may necessitate inconveniently high concentrations of the germicide.

It is worth mentioning that even if a certain germicide does not interfere with the chromatographic or physico-chemical properties of a protein, it may nevertheless inhibit its biological activity. Although the bacteriostatics mentioned are generally very mild in their effects and are known in some cases not to affect antibody activity etc., some cases are known where enzymatic activity is inhibited. The mercury compounds inhibit enzymes with free thiol groups in their active centers. Azide also is known to inhibit certain enzymes (Curzon 1966; Duffey et al. 1966).

Most of the general information regarding Chloretone, Merthiolate and phenylmercuric salts has been taken from Münzel (1959). Information regarding Hibitane mainly stems from the manufacturer. Other written sources of information have been Merck's index, Wallhäusser and Schmidt (1967) and Jaspersen (1963).

5.5. Drying of gels

As the gels can be stored in the wet state, it is not necessary to dry them except for special purposes (concentration of protein solutions and similar non-chromatographic processes). Agarose gels should not be dried, as it may be difficult to bring them back to their original state. Dextran gels (Sephadex) and acrylamide gels (Bio-Gel) can be dried without damage and returned to the wet state without difficulty. For Sephadex the manufacturer gives the following instructions for drying.

'The swollen gel is washed on a Büchner funnel with excess water to remove salt and contaminants. To shrink the gel, alcohol is then added at intervals under gentle suction. When the shrunken Sephadex has been sucked dry, it can be dried at 60–80 °C. Clumps appearing during this process do not matter, as they will disperse during reswelling of the gel material. A very slow shrinking procedure will prevent clump formation.' It is worthwhile to stress in this connection the importance of careful washing of the gel with distilled water before shrinkage to avoid inclusion of impurities in the dry gel. The slow shrinking procedure mentioned can be brought about by washing the gel suspension carefully with 50% ethanol before the addition of 96% ethanol which makes the gel shrink completely. A final wash with ether will make the powder dry rapidly without clump formation.

5.6.   Avoiding contamination, rinsing contaminated gels

As chromatographic gels have little tendency to bind irreversibly to substances likely to be present in samples of biological origin, there is usually no need for special procedures for rinsing or regeneration of the gels. Under certain conditions, very small amounts of Blue Dextran (see § 5.10) attach themselves to the gel. This is particularly the case with the dense gel types at very low ionic strength. The Blue Dextran (and possibly some other substances that may get attached in small quantities) can be removed by running a zone of serum albumin through the column.

If the samples to be fractionated contain suspended macroscopic particles, these will in most cases remain in the top layer of the chromatographic bed. They will impair the flow properties. To avoid such contamination it is advisable to filter or centrifuge samples containing macroscopic contaminants before the sample is applied. To remove such impurities from a gel bed it is usually sufficient to remove the top layer of gel. The contaminants and the gel particles can in most cases be separated from one another by sedimentation and decantation.

In work with proteins, some proteins (especially lipoproteins) have a tendency to precipitate on the gel particles. By suitable choice of experimental conditions, this can largely be avoided and it is possible to study lipoproteins by gel chromatography (Franzini 1966). Margolis and Langdon (1966) used 0.5 M NaCl + 1.0 mM EDTA + 1.0 mM potassium phosphate buffer in their study of the behaviour of human β-lipoproteins on a Sephadex G-200 column. Where lipoproteins are not directly under study, they can be removed before the chromatographic experiment by ultracentrifugation (De Lalla and Gofman 1954) or by precipitation with some suitable agent, for instance dextran sulphate (Oncley et al. 1957; Burstein and Samaille 1958; Walton and Scott 1964). For this purpose, the following working procedure has been found suitable: for each ml of serum, 0.02 ml of a 10% solution of a high molecular weight dextran sulphate is added. After addition of 1 M $CaCl_2$, the precipitate of β-lipoproteins and dextran sulphate formed can be removed by centrifugation. 0.1 ml of $CaCl_2$ solution for each ml of serum is sufficient to give more than satisfactory precipitation. Dextran sulphate with $\overline{M}_w = 0.5 \cdot 10^6$ has been found suitable for the procedure. With these working conditions, the β-lipoproteins and the chylomicrons are quantitatively removed from the serum, possibly together with a small proportion of the α-lipoproteins.

Should it be necessary to wash gel materials, the limits of stability of the different gel types must be considered. Sephadex and dextran gels are the only gels for use in aqueous solutions that can be treated with alkali, while agarose gels and polyacrylamide gels (Bio-Gel) will be destroyed by such treatment. 1% NaOH at elevated temperature has been found to be very efficient in removing denatured proteins, while it has little or no effect on the Sephadex gel (see § 3.4).

5.7. The column dimensions, the sample size and the flow rate

5.7.1. The influence of column length

The design of the column has been discussed in § 4.2. For all experiments, it is essential to choose a column of suitable dimensions. The length of the column determines the resolution that can be obtained; the longer the column, the better the resolution. The scope of this treatise does not permit any lengthy discussion of these matters, and the interested reader is referred to Giddings (1965, 1967). Svensson (1966) has discussed the meaning of the term resolution in chromatography. It should be mentioned though that the resolution of small samples will be improved approximately in relation to the square root of the length of the bed. Long beds, on the other hand, also imply

Subject index p. 391

longer time for the experiment and larger sample dilution. In practice, the proper column length is usually best found by systematic trial and error. The following may serve as starting points:

For group separation experiments the separation of the substances is already adequate when short beds are used. Beds 20–30 cm in height will be sufficient for many laboratory applications. Fractionation experiments require longer columns to give the required separation. For most normal experiments, columns of 100 cm length are sufficient, but considerably longer columns have been reported. Long columns are very difficult to handle. If very long columns are required, some special techniques may be used; these are described in § 5.14.

5.7.2. The volume of sample

When the experiment is planned, the volume of the sample must be taken into consideration. For analytical purposes, where the main objective is to obtain as good a separation as possible, the starting zone should be made narrow. This can be accomplished by applying a small sample. The gain in resolution will, however, be very limited, if the sample size is made smaller than 1–2% of the bed volume. On a preparative scale, the sample volume should be the maximum which will give the required separation. This will cause least dilution and permit the use of the smallest bed volume. The sample size is determined by the difference in elution volume of the substances eluted most closely together. This difference in elution volume is called the separation volume:

$$V_{sep} = V_{e1} - V_{e2},$$

where V_{e1} and V_{e2} are the elution volumes for the various substances.

Fig. 5.7 illustrates the elution curves obtained at different sample sizes. The figure shows that the sample size depends on the separation volume, but that the whole separation volume cannot be 'filled' with sample. The zone broadening would give a considerable remixing of two substances, if a sample was applied with a volume that fills the whole separation volume (see the centre elution curve in fig. 5.7). In fractionation experiments, where the separation volumes are small, the samples applied will necessarily be small also. In analytical applications, there is usually little to be gained by applying samples smaller than 1–2% of the total bed volume. In group separation experiments, samples as large as 25–30% of the total column volume can often be applied.

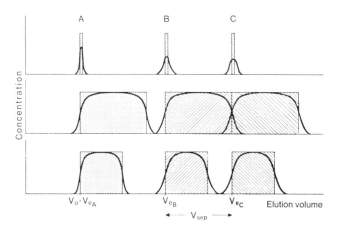

Fig. 5.7. Elution curves for different sample size. The top diagram corresponds to the application of a small sample. The centre diagram corresponds to the maximum sample size that would give complete separation if no zone spreading were to take place. The bottom diagram corresponds to the maximum sample volume to be applied to obtain complete separation under the conditions of the experiment. The cross-hatched areas correspond to the elution profiles that would be obtained if no zone spreading were to take place. From 'Sephadex – gel filtration in theory and practice' by Pharmacia Fine Chemicals.

5.7.3. The column diameter

In analytical applications a usual column diameter is 10 mm. Still thinner columns have been used. Thus, Nyström and Sjövall (1966b) used teflon tubes 1.5–2.3 mm in diameter in some experiments. Such thin columns are useful, when only small amounts of material are available. If the amount of sample is not too limited, it is easier to work with columns of larger diameter, 20–30 mm being suitable for most types of work. These columns are easier to use and usually give somewhat better resolution than those of the same length and smaller diameter. This is probably due to the greater influence of wall effects in thin columns.

For preparative purposes the diameter should be chosen to give the column sufficient capacity. Increase of diameter does not significantly impair the separation properties of the column even at very large diameters. Columns with diameters of 5 cm or more should preferably be equipped with plungers designed to give an even application of the sample over the whole bed surface. Columns with diameters up to 100 cm have been tried with success (Samuelsson et al. 1967a, b). Therefore one has an almost complete freedom to choose the column diameter to give the capacity that is required for a given experiment. Columns for gel chromatography are commercially available with diameters ranging from about 1 cm to 20 cm.

5.7.4. The bed volume

Although the volume of the chromatographic bed can be calculated from its length and diameter, it is advisable to determine the volume by separate calibration, since there are considerable errors in calculations from linear measurement of the column. To determine the volume, the column is filled with water. The water is drawn from the column in portions and weighed. The weight of water is then plotted against the level of the water in the column.

5.8.   Packing of the column

Column packing is of primary importance in chromatographic experiments. Many different methods have been tried. Some of them cannot be used in gel chromatography, because of the specific properties of the gels. Any attempt to pack the dry powder into the column followed by the liquid will result in cracked or exploded columns due to the swelling of the gel.

The most common method for packing columns is to attach a large container to the top of the column; the column is filled with eluant and a very thin slurry of chromatographic material is poured into the funnel, where it is stirred. The material gradually sediments into the column and packs to a bed. This method does not give even packing in gel chromatography (and possibly not in other types of chromatography either) except in thin columns. The reason is that the material sedimenting down the column will drag liquid along; this will give rise to con-

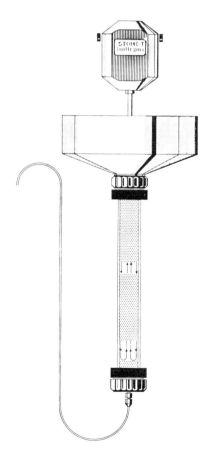

Fig. 5.8. Packing of chromatographic bed from a thin suspension. The arrows indicate schematically the convection currents in the tube during sedimentation.

vection currents in the tube as illustrated diagrammatically in fig. 5.8. At the bottom of the tube, the current is directed radially. The stirrer in the container is not sufficient to break up these convection currents. The coarse particles sediment first and will be enriched at the wall of the tube. The fine material will be carried in toward the centre. As the flow rate will be higher at the wall where the coarse material is enriched, this type of column packing will give rise to zones that are bent. If the funnel arrangement happens to favour an upward current at the wall the result will be the opposite. The magnitude of the effect will depend on the geometry of the arrangement and the thickness of the slurry.

The method for packing the columns should differ for the various gel types. With the soft gel types more careful packing will be required, while the hard gel types will pack well with fewer precautions. The following packing procedure has been found to work well for the soft gel types (Sephadex G-75 to Sephadex G-200, Bio-Gel P–30 to Bio-Gel P–300, agarose gels) on columns with more than 2 cm diameter (on thinner columns the method described earlier can usually be used). The column is mounted vertically. Small deviations from the vertical position will usually not interfere seriously. However, the vertical alignment is easily adjusted and can be checked with a plumb line or with a level. An extension tube is mounted on top of the column. This tube should have a length of approximately $\frac{1}{3}$ to $\frac{1}{2}$ of the length of the column. The diameter should be approximately the same as that of the column. A funnel with the same outlet diameter as that of the column and a very small angle could be used instead of the extension tube (see fig. 5.9). The volume of the funnel should in this case correspond to the volume of the extension tube. The outlet from the column is fitted with a piece of capillary tubing sufficiently long to reach to a point some 5 cm below the top of the extension tube. If the column is to be run by a metering pump attached to the outlet of the column and the optimum flow through the column is known, the pump can be attached at once. In this case it is not necessary to use long capillary tubing, as this is intended for regulation of the flow. The space below the bed support is filled with liquid. This can usually be done by injecting liquid from the outlet end with a syringe. This should be done carefully to avoid formation of bubbles under the bed support. If bubbles are formed, they can usually be removed by forcing the liquid back and forth through an inverted pipette or a glass tube. When sufficient liquid has been added to fill the space below the bed support and a few cm above it, the outlet is closed.

A gel slurry of suitable thickness for packing the column is produced by the following procedure: The gel is allowed to swell (§ 5.3). If the swelling is carried out at elevated temperature, the slurry is allowed to cool. If the slurry has not been heated, it is de-aerated under vacuum. The gel is then allowed to settle. The supernatant liquid is sucked off until the volume of the remaining supernatant liquid is approximately half the volume of the sedimented gel. The gel and supernatant are remixed gently and form a suspension that has the right consistency

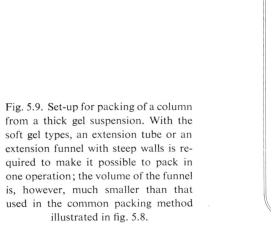

Fig. 5.9. Set-up for packing of a column from a thick gel suspension. With the soft gel types, an extension tube or an extension funnel with steep walls is required to make it possible to pack in one operation; the volume of the funnel is, however, much smaller than that used in the common packing method illustrated in fig. 5.8.

for packing the bed. Stirring should be gentle, so that air is not mixed into the slurry.

The column is filled with the slurry by pouring down a rod, avoiding splashing. Gentle stirring of the upper part of the slurry in the tube during the filling will allow air bubbles to rise to the surface. If the amount of gel weighed out is correct and the slurry has been prepared in the right way, all the gel necessary to produce the bed can be added at one time. Packing of the bed in sections should be avoided, as this procedure may give rise to uneven beds. After the slurry has been added, the bed is left to settle for a short time and then flow through the column is started. The length of the period for settling is not critical and the flow can be started after 5 min (Sephadex G-25 and corresponding) to 15 or 20 min (Sephadex G-200 and corresponding). The flow rate should initially not be too high and in all circumstances it should be lower than the flow rate to be used during the experiments. (For regulation of the flow rate, see § 5.9.) During packing, liquid should be added very carefully to avoid disturbance of the gel surface. As the bed packs, the flow rate is gradually increased to its final value. When the gel surface has passed well below the extension tube, this can be emptied and removed from the column.

When liquid is added during column packing (before any protection device has been inserted), one should be careful not to disturb the top layer of the bed. The use of a pipette (even with a bent tip) will easily cause disturbance, as the speed of the liquid in the constriction at the end is considerable even at low rate of addition of liquid. Liquid can be added for instance through a wide tube and the flow regulated with a glass bead in the tube as described in § 5.12, or from a syringe with a piece of tubing attached. To permit continuous, even addition of liquid over a long period of time, it is recommended that a Mariotte flask is connected to the column (fig. 5.10).

When the gel has packed and the gel surface has become stationary or is only moving very slowly, the protection device is positioned on top of the bed. If a plunger is used, it should be inserted at this stage. Air bubbles in the plunger and in the leads to the plunger must be avoided.

The hard gels (Sephadex G-10 to Sephadex G-50, Bio-Gel P–2 to Bio-Gel P–20) are easier to pack. The procedure is in principle the same. These gels do not, however, require so much liquid to form slurries of the right consistency. For this reason, it may even be possible to dispense with the extension tube. The beds pack more quickly with these gels, and the regulation of the flow rate is not as critical as with the soft gel types.

Agarose gels are delivered as wet suspensions. These are usually too thick to be directly packed into the column. They are therefore best mixed with some buffer. As this type of gel melts on heating, the slurry

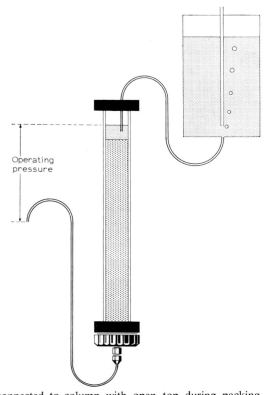

Fig. 5.10. Mariotte flask connected to column with open top during packing.

Subject index p. 391

should be de-aerated under vacuum. After this, the packing procedure corresponds to that for the soft gels.To prevent the agarose gel beds from moving and to obtain reproducible results, columns with plunger should be used. When the bed has stabilized at the highest flow rate that will be used on the bed, the plunger is moved into contact with the bed surface and the bed is compressed *very slightly* (some few mm).

The gels for use in organic solvents are packed in the corresponding way as those in aqueous solutions. If the solvent is denser than the gel, as with Sephadex LH-20 in chloroform, the bed is best packed upwards. In this case, a column equipped with plungers from both ends should be used. The gel slurry is poured into the column, with the lower plunger positioned close to the bottom of the tube filled with eluant. After the slurry has been added, the upper plunger is immediately inserted, moved down to the surface of the slurry, and secured in position. A flow of liquid upwards through the column is started. When the bed has stabilized, the lower plunger is moved upwards until in contact with the gel surface. During this adjustment, the lower outlet from the column should be open. If the plunger has a tightening mechanism, this should not be opened too far, as air leaking into the bed this way is impossible to remove without repacking the bed.

5.9.   Regulation of the flow rate

Two methods are commonly used for regulation of the flow rate. The simplest one is a gravity feed in which the inlet to the column is at a higher level than the outlet. For more precise measurements a metering pump may be connected to the outlet of the column to keep the flow at a predetermined rate.

The gravity feed method is commonly used and in most cases it gives a satisfactory stability of flow rate. The short-term stability of the flow is very good, without pulsations or other irregularities. The flow rate may, however, decrease slowly even after the column has been packed for a long time. In gravity feed experiments the flow rate is regulated by adjusting the operating pressure. The operating pressure is the pressure that is needed to overcome the resistance to the flow in the chromatographic bed. If the resistance to the flow of the connecting tubings is neglected, the operating pressure corresponds to the difference in liquid level between the inlet and the outlet side. If the column is connected to an ordinary open container with eluant, the operating pressure will vary in the course of the experiment due to the variation of the level of liquid in the container. To keep the operating pressure constant, a Mariotte flask may be used (§ 4.3.1).

Fig. 5.10 illustrates the operating pressure in a simple set-up during column packing. Fig. 5.11 gives the operating pressure in an upward

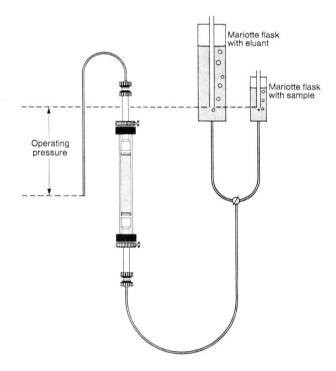

Fig. 5.11. Schematic diagram illustrating the set-up of a gel chromatographic experiment. The column is operated in upward flow. The sample application is performed by turning the valve. From 'Sephadex – gel filtration in theory and practice' by Pharmacia Fine Chemicals.

Subject index p. 391

flow experiment with a Mariotte flask. In experiments, where the column has not been filled with liquid to the top, the height of the gas column at the top of the tube should be subtracted from the vertical distance between inlet (or Mariotte flask tube) and outlet.

When hard gel types are used, the bed packing will usually be fairly insensitive to variations in operating pressure. Resistance to flow will remain relatively constant irrespective of the operating pressure, and the flow will be approximately proportional to the operating pressure. This is not the case for soft gels. Beds packed with these gels will be compressed under the influence of flow, giving increased resistance to flow at higher operating pressure. In these cases the flow rate will level off when the operating pressure is increased and eventually an increase in operating pressure will result in a decrease in flow rate. This is illustrated in fig. 5.12 for two agarose gels of different agarose concentration. The maximum flow rates are obtained at approximately the following operating pressures: Sephadex G-200: 10% of bed height; Sephadex G-150: 15% of bed height; Sephadex G-100: 30% of bed

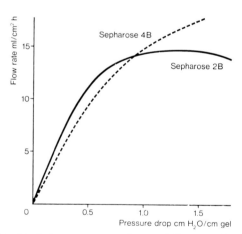

Fig. 5.12. Relationship between pressure drop and flow rate for Sepharose. The data were obtained with columns of 2.5 cm diameter. The pressure was increased at intervals of two hours. At a pressure of 20 cm water, the bed heights were 40.5 cm and 39.5 cm. From 'Sepharose' by Pharmacia Fine Chemicals.

height; Sephadex G-75: 100 % of bed height. These values are valid for ordinary laboratory columns (maximum diameter 5 cm, maximum bed height 1 m). The flow rates that can be obtained with Sephadex gels on beds of varying dimensions can be found in appendix 4.

When a column is operated by gravity feed, the set-up can easily be arranged to make the flow stop automatically when the eluant has been used up without any risk of the column running dry. This is done by allowing the tubing from the eluant container to pass below the level

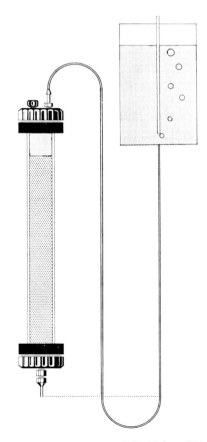

Fig. 5.13. If the flow in a chromatographic column is maintained by gravity feed, the flow can be made to stop when the eluant has been used up for instance by arranging the tube to the inlet so that it passes below the level of the outlet.

of the outlet from the column before it is connected to the inlet to the column. This is illustrated in fig. 5.13.

If the flow is regulated by a metering pump, slight pulsations in the flow will usually be noticed. These pulsations can be kept low by the use of suitable pumps. On large columns bubble traps will also serve to damp pulsations from the pump (see fig. 5.14). As mentioned above, there is also a limit to the flow rate that can be achieved, when soft gels are used. If one tries to exceed this maximum flow rate, the chromatographic bed will compact, obstructing the flow completely. The gels may pass through the bed support and if the pump is connected to the inlet side the pressure building up inside the column may cause rupture of some part of the set-up. The column should therefore first be allowed to stabilize using gravity feed and the flow rate of the pump should then be adjusted to well below the maximum flow rate that can be obtained by gravity feed.

If the samples are applied manually, the pump is usually best connected to the outlet end of the column (see § 4.3.2). For this mounting

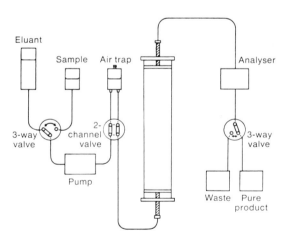

Fig. 5.14. Scheme for the connection of a preparative scale column. During sample application, the two channel valve should be turned so that the liquid does not pass through the air trap. From 'Sephadex column K100/100' by Pharmacia Fine Chemicals.

it is necessary to use a peristaltic pump, as plunger pumps would cause remixing of the zones that have already been separated. Usually it is most convenient to connect the pump to the outlet side of the column also when the bed is enclosed between plungers and the sample is applied through the plunger. In large scale work, however, when high operating pressures are used, it is often advantageous to connect the pump to the inlet side to avoid the formation of a vacuum in the column,

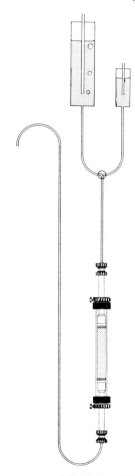

Fig. 5.15. When operating a column with a volatile eluant, it is sometimes difficult to avoid formation of bubbles in the bed. To some extent the situation is improved if the hydrostatic pressure in the column is increased for instance by raising the inlet and the outlet to a high level compared to the column. This can be done without changing the operating pressure.

Subject index p. 391

as this may lead to the formation of gas bubbles in the bed. Fig. 5.14 gives a scheme for the connection of a large scale column.

To avoid formation of gas bubbles in the column, it is sometimes desirable to keep the eluant container at a temperature somewhat above that of the column (15–30 °C). In this way the liquid is not saturated with air, when it is introduced into the column. Mariotte flasks otherwise cause saturation of the liquids with air, as air is constantly bubbling through the liquid. At the flow rates used in laboratory experiments, the liquid has sufficient time to come to column temperature during the passage through the tubings. The temperature of the liquid can be increased easily by placing an incandescent lamp below the eluant reservoir.

Solvents with high vapour pressure, notably chloroform, have a great tendency to form bubbles in the bed. To a certain extent the situation can be improved by keeping the column at increased hydrostatic pressure. This can be done by keeping both the inlet and the outlet above the column, see fig. 5.15.

5.10. Checking the column packing

The separation result is entirely dependent on the quality of the column packing. Before the column is used, the packing of the bed should therefore be checked.

A visual inspection may reveal heterogeneities in the bed or air bubbles trapped during the packing. With agarose gels and with strongly swollen dextran or polyacrylamide gels, the bed is more or less transparent. In these cases it is often very useful to observe the bed in transmitted light (by putting a lamp on the opposite side of the column).

As a final check a coloured test sample should be run on the column and the progress of the coloured zone observed. The zone should move through the bed as a straight band without excessive tailing. Usually, it is sufficient to apply a sample of completely excluded substance, for instance Blue Dextran available from Pharmacia Fine Chemicals. For use on agarose gels that give access to Blue Dextran, coloured *Esche-*

richia coli cells available from Seravac Laboratories may be used. As these coloured substances have relatively high molecular weight, the concentration used should not be too high to avoid viscosity zone broadening (see § 5.11). For Blue Dextran, 0.3 % solutions give sufficient colour intensity. The volume of the test sample should be at least 0.5–1 ml solution per cm² column cross sectional area.

Flodin (1961) gives the quantitative criterion that on a reasonably well-packed column, a sample of completely excluded substance with a volume corresponding to 10% of the bed volume should be eluted with a volume corresponding to twice the volume of the sample. Considerably better results can, however, be expected.

The procedure described for checking the column packing with a solution of Blue Dextran or coloured *Escherichia coli* cells can also be used for void volume determinations. In practice, both are usually performed simultaneously. When determining the void volume, it is necessary to make sure that the bed has been stabilized and does not settle any further. For this purpose, one should put a mark on the column at the surface of the bed. This mark can also be used for the determination of the total bed volume (see § 5.7.4). It should be noted that to behave properly on the bed, Blue Dextran requires an ionic strength of at least 0.02 (for instance 0.02 M NaCl). If the salt is not desired in subsequent experiments, it can be eluted with distilled water after the void volume determination. Regarding small amounts of Blue Dextran that may get attached to the gel, see § 5.6.

5.11. *Influence of sample composition*

In gel chromatography the partition isotherms are linear (the partition coefficients between gel and liquid are independent of the sample concentration) up to very high concentrations of solute (Porath 1967). In the case of certain proteins the partition isotherm has even been found to be bent slightly upwards (Winzor and Nichol 1965). This effect could, however, only be observed at very high sample concentrations. The linearity of the partition isotherm may be ascribed to the absence of specific sites on the material that can be saturated by the solute. The linearity of the partition isotherm also implies that very high concentrations of sample may be used. In practice the limiting factor is the viscosity of the sample relative to the eluant: if this is high, the flow pattern in the bed becomes irregular. This can be seen if coloured substances are chromatographed. The zone very soon becomes irregular and uneven. The spreading of the zones is illustrated in fig. 5.16, showing the elution curves for hemoglobin and NaCl in samples, where the viscosity has been increased by addition of dextran. That the zone spreading depends on the relative viscosity of the sample rather than the absolute viscosity is illustrated in fig. 5.17. The experiments where the sample and the eluant have the same viscosity give sharp, narrow zones independent of their absolute viscosity, while the experiment with increased viscosity of the sample relative to the eluant shows considerable zone broadening. As a general rule viscosities of the sample relative to the eluant exceeding 1.5–2 should be avoided in laboratory experiments. The relative viscosity is the ratio of the viscosity of the solution to that of the eluant. It is easily obtained in a capillary viscometer as the ratio of the time required by the solution for emptying the bulb to that required by the pure solvent. For a

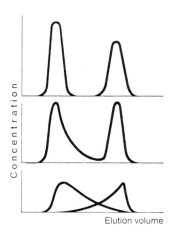

Concentration

Elution volume

Fig. 5.16. Elution diagrams obtained when hemoglobin and NaCl were separated. Experimental conditions were identical except that the viscosities were altered by the addition of increasing amounts of dextran. An increasing zone spreading becomes apparent. For the upper experiment no dextran was added, and the viscosity of the sample relative to the eluant is 1. In the lower two experiments, the sample contained 2.5% and 5% resp. of dextran with $\overline{M}_w$ 250,000. The relative viscosities were 4.2 and 11.8 respectively. From 'Sephadex – gel filtration in theory and practice' by Pharmacia Fine Chemicals.

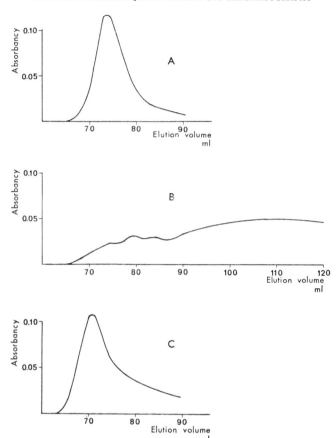

Fig. 5.17. Elution curves for albumin on a column of Sephadex G-25 fine at different combinations of viscosity of sample and eluant. The bed dimensions were 2.5 × 35 cm. As eluant water with 0.1-M NaCl was used. The sample with 5 ml volume contained 0.2% human serum albumin. In experiment B, 3.5% dextran with $\overline{M}_w$ 500,000 was added to the sample, increasing its viscosity relative to the eluant to 4.09. In experiment C, 3.5% dextran was added to both the sample and the eluant. From the figure it can be seen that when the relative viscosity of the sample is equal to that of the eluant, no viscosity zone spreading occurs. The flow rate in all experiments was about 0.6 ml/min. The protein concentration was monitored with a Uvicord (LKB-Produkter AB).

Subject index p. 391

dextran with $\overline{M}_w = 0.5 \times 10^6$, a 1 % solution has relative viscosity around 1.5, while a 1 % solution of dextran with $\overline{M}_w = 40,000$ has relative viscosity around 1.2 and serum albumin, $M = 69,000$, has relative viscosity 1.065 in a 1 % solution. The relative viscosity, however, rises fairly fast with increasing concentrations of macromolecule.

5.12. Sample application

The oldest and best known method for applying the sample is the one in which the sample is directly applied to the drained surface of the bed. Most of the liquid on top of the bed is removed by a pipette and the rest drained into the surface leaving a thin layer on the surface. Then the flow should be stopped, care being taken to prevent the column running dry and the sample carefully added onto the bed. If the surface is too dry, the sample will be sucked down at the point where it is applied. This will give an uneven front to the zone. As mentioned earlier (§ 4.2) the application of the sample is facilitated, if the bed surface is equipped with a protecting sheet.

When the sample has been applied to the top of the gel bed, the flow is restarted and the sample is allowed to pass into the bed. Then a small volume of eluant is carefully pipetted onto the bed to wash the last of the sample into the bed. After the surface has been washed in this way once or twice, the top of the column is carefully filled with eluant and the eluant reservoir is connected. It may be difficult to add liquid to the drained bed top without disturbing the surface, even if it has been protected. It is essential that the liquid be added at a slow, even rate. The use of a pipette with a bent tip has been recommended for this purpose (Flodin 1962a). Even with this method considerable technical skill is required to keep the flow rate even. Alternatively the liquid can be pumped onto the surface with a peristaltic pump (Flodin 1962a, p. 45). A simple arrangement that will give equally satisfactory results is to connect a piece of silicon tubing to a suitable container for the liquid. A glass bead with a diameter slightly greater than the inner diameter of the silicon tubing is inserted into the tube. The silicon tube is connected to a tube leading the liquid to the bed surface and the whole arrangement is mounted above the top of the column. By pressing slightly on the silicon tubing at the glass bead an even and easily controlled stream of liquid from the container is obtained. A syringe and a piece of plastic tube can also be used.

A very elegant way of applying the sample that is particularly suited to gel chromatography was described by Flodin (1962a, p. 45). It is based on the observation that two liquids of different density can be easily layered on top of one another without notable mixing, even if the liquids are miscible. (The observation has for long been used by bartenders in preparation of certain drinks.) In practice, the procedure is as follows: If the density of the sample is not already higher than the density of the eluant, glucose or sucrose is added to a concentration of about 1 %. (The sugar will usually be eluted later than the substances of interest and will not disturb the experiment.) The eluant above the surface of the bed is removed until a layer about 1 cm thick remains. The sample is then carefully delivered through thin tubing below the surface of the liquid some millimeters above the surface of the bed. The sample solution, which is denser than the eluant, displaces it and forms an even layer on top of the bed and is then carried into the bed by the flow. When the sample has passed into the bed, the space above the top of the bed is filled with eluant and the column is connected to the eluant reservoir. To prevent contamination of the eluant with sample when the tubing is inserted and extracted, a small air bubble should precede the sample when the sample addition is started and some eluant should be sucked back into the tubing before it is removed from the column.

The most reproducible way of applying the sample is by the use of a plunger. This also requires least technical skill. The arrangement used is illustrated in fig. 5.11. Before sample application, make sure that plunger and bed are in close contact. If the sample application is performed by a three-way-valve as illustrated in the figure, the flow need not be interrupted during sample application. To start the sample application the inlet is connected through the valve to the sample container. The sample container should be graduated to permit an estimate of the sample size. After the sample application the inlet is

Subject index p. 391

again connected to the container for the eluant. The three-way-valve should have a bore equal to that of the tubing, to avoid remixing. Valves intended for injection syringes can be obtained from companies dealing with medical equipment. For special applications electromagnetic valves may be used. In preliminary experiments it may in some instances be easier to apply the sample through a plunger without the use of a valve. In this case the flow is stopped and the inlet tube is transferred from the eluant container to the sample container. After the sample has been fed into the column the flow is stopped anew and the inlet tube is returned to the eluant container. This method is particularly simple, if the inlet tube is not permanently connected to the eluant container. One example of a Mariotte flask suitable for this type of sample application was given in fig. 4.5. When this type of sample application is used, one must be careful to avoid air bubbles entering the tubing.

5.13. Preparation of the bed for a new experiment

A characteristic feature of gel chromatography is that in general all substances are eluted without change of eluant. Thus the bed requires no regeneration and can be used immediately for the next experiment. If contamination of the bed with dust particles or other impurities is avoided, the bed can be used without repacking for a very large number of experiments.

If the column is clogged by dust particles or other contaminants, the flow may be obstructed or the chromatographic properties impaired. The procedure in rinsing the column will depend on the character of the contaminants and on the type of gel used. In many cases it will be sufficient to remove the top layer where the dust has accumulated and, if necessary, to add fresh gel slurry instead. Gels contaminated with dust can often be rinsed by decantation. To remove bacteria and certain other contaminants such as denatured proteins, washing with alkali has been found very efficient for gels that can stand this treatment (§ 5.6).

If the packed column has been standing for some time, it should be inspected in transmitted light for irregularities in the packing, indicating bacterial growth or other defects (§ 5.10).

5.14.   Increase of the effective column length

5.14.1.   Connecting columns in series

If the separation between two substances in gel chromatography is incomplete due to insufficient separation volume, a longer chromatographic bed should be used (§ 5.7.1). This may, however, involve the use of an inconveniently long single bed. Beds of lengths exceeding 1 m or 1.5 m are difficult to pack. They also have low flow rates, particularly if they are packed with a soft gel type. Instead, batteries of columns in series may be used. To connect columns in series, they must be equipped with plungers. The columns are packed separately. After packing, the outlet from one column is connected to the inlet of the next by narrow tubing, avoiding air bubbles. With this arrangement, higher flow rates are obtained than with long single columns. The set-up is also easier to handle. To obtain less dilution of the samples it has been proposed that the liquid should be concentrated by evaporation or by ultrafiltration between the columns. This, however, seems to introduce unnecessary complications without giving much better results.

5.14.2.   Recycling chromatography

An interesting approach to the problem of increasing the effective column length without the use of excessively long columns was proposed by Porath and Bennich (1962). This method, called recycling chromatography, is particularly suited to chromatographic processes where no gradients are used and where the velocities of all the substances in the sample are relatively close to one another. It has been used in gel chromatography of proteins with good results. The principle of the method is relatively simple. The liquid emerging from the column is pumped back into the inlet and allowed to pass through the same column several times.

Subject index p. 391

One disadvantage is that if there are several components present in the sample, some of which are moving considerably faster or slower than the substances that need recycling to be separated, the faster substance may overtake a slower substance within a single cycle and

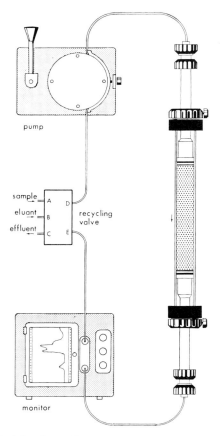

Fig. 5.18. The principle of recycling. The block designated 'recycling valve' may consist of one or two valves. During sample application, the port A is connected to D, and C to E. In the recycling position, ports D and E are connected. During elution of the substances from the system, port B is connected to port D, and port C to port E.

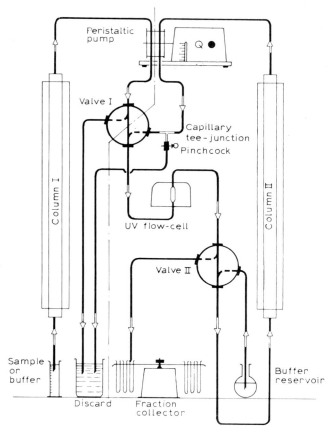

Fig. 5.19. Two-column set-up for recycling chromatography. The sample is first applied to column I, followed by buffer. In column I, a preliminary separation is obtained and the substances that are easily separated are led to the container marked 'Discard' with valve I in the position other than that indicated. During the elution from column I of the substances to be recycled, valve I is shifted to the position indicated in the figure. After they have been fed into the recycling loop, valve I is returned to the opposite position of that indicated in the figure. The substances are then recycled in column II until separated. They can then be eluted to the fraction collector by turning valve II. The lead with the pinchcock serves to feed the effluent from column II to the 'Discard' container when valve I is in the position indicated and the sample is introduced into column II. From Chersi (1964, erratum). (LKB-Produkter AB)

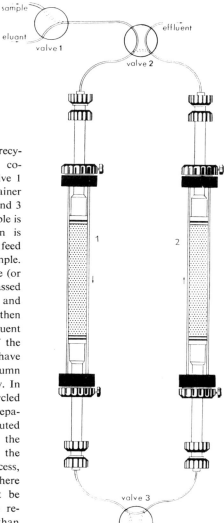

Fig. 5.20. Schematic set-up for recycling chromatography with two columns. To put on the sample, valve 1 is set to connect the sample container with the columns. With valves 2 and 3 in the positions indicated, the sample is fed into column 1. The elution is started by switching valve 1 to feed eluant into the system instead of sample. When the substances in the sample (or at least the interesting ones) have passed into column 2 by valve 3, valve 2 and valve 3 are changed. The eluant is then passing into column 2 while the effluent from column 1 is passing out of the system. When the substances have passed from column 2 back into column 1, valves 2 and 3 are shifted anew. In this way, the sample can be recycled until the substances have been separated. The substances are then eluted from the system by not changing the valves after they have passed into the other column. To supervise the process, a monitor should be inserted somewhere in the loop. As the valves must be shifted for each cycle, the set-up requires somewhat more attention than the set-up in fig. 5.18.

thus the substances may be remixed although their separation volumes are more than satisfactory. This disadvantage can to a certain extent be overcome by removing the substances that have already been completely separated at an earlier stage. The principle for the original construction of Porath and Bennich is shown in fig. 5.18. In this construc-

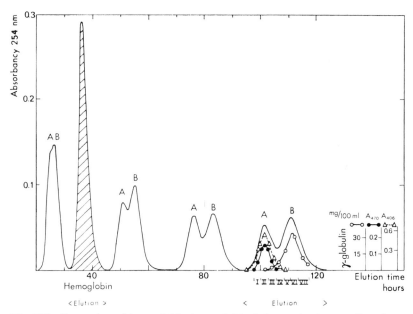

Fig. 5.21. Separation of hemoglobin–haptoglobin 1–1 complex by recycling chromatography on Sephadex G-200. Hemoglobin (80 mg) in excess of the binding capacity of the haptoglobin was added to the pooled and concentrated fractions (8 ml) containing haptoglobin (type 1–1) from previous gel chromatographic separations of human serum. Four cycles were run on a column 4.2 × 96.5 cm packed with Sephadex G-200 in 0.1 M tris–HCl buffer pH 8.0 containing 0.5 M NaCl at a flow rate of 25 ml/hr. Protein is monitored by the light absorption at 254 nm. I, II .... VII indicate the fractions subsequently collected. A represents the hemoglobin–haptoglobin complex determined by the light absorption at 406 nm and by its peroxidase activity (A_{470}). B contains the other proteins of the sample, mainly 7-S-γ-globulins, determined by an immunochemical method. 'Elution' represents fractions that were not recycled. Cross-hatched areas represent the excess hemoglobin. From Killander (1964b).

tion, the liquid is pumped directly from the outlet of the column back to the inlet. In this construction it is therefore necessary to let the liquid pass through the pump each cycle, and a pump that does not cause any remixing is required (see §4.3.2). By changing the position of the valve, sample or eluant can be pumped into the inlet of the column and the liquid emerging from the column be eluted (for instance to a fraction collector at the end of the experiment when the substances have been separated). A somewhat more advanced set-up is shown in fig. 5.19. The material that is easily separated is here removed in a separate column prior to recycling.

Other constructions have been proposed. Fig. 5.20 shows a set-up consisting of two columns. In this set-up, the liquid does not need to pass through the pump every cycle, and gravity feed may be used. On the other hand, the valves must be reset each time the substances have passed through a column and consequently the set-up must be attended to more carefully.

In all set-ups, a monitor must be included in the circuit to supervise the course of the experiment and to indicate when the substances that have been separated can be removed from the system.

Recycling chromatography has for instance been used by Killander in his work with plasma proteins (Killander et al. 1965; Killander and Philipson 1964; Killander 1964b). Fig. 5.21 shows the separation of haptoglobin and hemoglobin–haptoglobin 1–1 complex. A complete set-up for recycling chromatography according to Porath (fig. 5.18) can be obtained from LKB-Produkter AB (see appendix 1).

5.15. *Upward flow chromatography*

Beds packed with the soft gel types have a certain tendency to pack giving rise to decreased flow rates. In the traditional type of chromatography the flow is directed downwards. In this case flow and gravity co-operate to pack the bed downwards (at least as long as the bed packing material has greater density than the liquid). The tendency of the bed to pack can be decreased by the use of upward flow in the column, as gravity then works in the opposite direction to the flow.

When upward flow is used, the column must be equipped with a plunger, preferably one at each end. The column should be packed from the top in the ordinary way with the bottom plunger in position. When the column has been packed and the flow is directed upwards, the lower plunger is adjusted to compensate for any additional packing of the bed that would otherwise give rise to a void space between the lower bed support and the bed. On large columns, with soft gel material, the flow rate decreases gradually even when upward flow is used. By inverting the column after a number of chromatographic runs and reversing at the same time the flow to maintain upward flow, the flow rate can be maintained almost indefinitely without repacking. Fig. 5.22 shows a flow scheme for a set-up of this type, and fig. 5.23 shows a column with a stand facilitating inversion. Fig. 5.11 illustrates how a column is run in upward flow. As can be seen, the sample is applied and the experiment is performed essentially in the same way as with other experiments where a plunger is used.

The advantage of upward flow is that higher flow rates can be used on beds of the soft gel types than would otherwise have been possible.

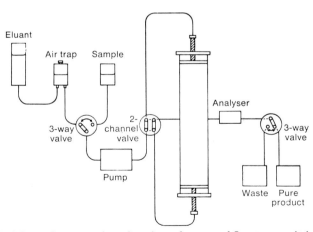

Fig. 5.22. Scheme for connection of a column for upward flow to permit inversion. When the column is inverted, the flow is reversed by the two-channel valve. From 'Sephadex column K100/100' by Pharmacia Fine Chemicals.

Subject index p. 391

The technique is therefore recommended for protein fractionation on the soft gel types. Upward flow should not be attempted, if the sample has considerably higher density than the eluant (mostly in desalting experiments), as the sample may be applied in an uneven fashion in this case. In desalting experiments on dense gels, downward flow should be used also when a plunger technique is used.

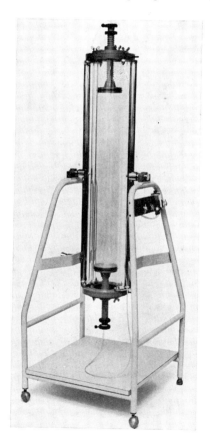

Fig. 5.23. Preparative column with stand that permits the column to be inverted (column K100/100, Pharmacia Fine Chemicals).

CHAPTER 6

Some applications of gel chromatography

6.1.   General

This chapter on applications has not been made encyclopedic in any way. The very large fields of enzyme purification, purification and characterization of antibodies, separation and purification of peptide and protein hormones are fairly uniform from a methodological point of view and are dealt with in the form of a limited number of examples from the literature. These examples, which are intended to illustrate methods and procedures that are common in everyday practice have been described in some detail. In addition some procedures that are not self-evident and that illustrate a new aspect of gel chromatography have been included.

The chapter has been divided into two major parts: analytical applications and preparative applications. The division between the groups is not very clear-cut and some applications could be included in either. Thus it is for instance questionable whether the separation of fluorescent antibodies from unreacted dye should be included in the one or the other of the sections. Nevertheless, the division contributes to the clarity of the treatment.

6.2.   Analytical applications

6.2.1.   Analytical group separation

Gel chromatographic group separation is a very common practice for removal of interfering substances before the final determination. For

   Subject index p. 391

this application very small columns and simple equipment can be used. Particularly it has proved very useful in removing low molecular weight interfering substances before determination of a macromolecular component in a mixture. A typical case where group separation has been used for removal of interfering substances is in the determination of proteins in spinal fluid, described by Patrick and Thiers (1963). The protein concentration in spinal fluid is generally low and the samples available small. As the extinction coefficient of proteins at 220 nm is very high (much higher than at 280 nm) spectrophotometric measurement at 220 nm would be a very simple and sensitive method. The determination is, however, disturbed by low molecular weight aromatic substances, mainly amino acids, in the spinal fluid. To remove these interfering substances, a small column was constructed (fig. 6.1). The bed volume is 5 ml. The column is packed with Sephadex G-25 gel up to the constriction in the tube. The function of the constriction is to stop the flow in the column when the liquid level has reached this point. The capillary forces, acting over the small surface of the con-

Fig. 6.1. Column for determination of protein in spinal fluid according to Patrick and Thiers (1963).

striction, are sufficient to balance the gravity forces on the liquid and the column can be left without attention until the liquid in the upper container has passed.

The experiment is performed in the following way: After the level of liquid in the column has reached the constriction and the flow has stopped, the column is positioned above a clean test tube. If the column is constructed in the way indicated in the figure with a larger diameter of the upper container than of the lower, it can simply be inserted in a test tube in a tube rack, without any need for separate stand for the column, as the upper container will rest on the rim of the test tube. 0.2 ml spinal fluid is applied with a micropipette. When this sample has penetrated into the bed, 2.8 ml of physiological saline is added and the column is left standing until the liquid flow has stopped. The proteins then have been quantitatively eluted into the test tube in a volume of exactly 3 ml. After mixing the contents of the test tube the extinction at 220 nm is measured in a spectrophotometer and the protein concentration calculated. The container at the top of the column is filled with physiological saline that is allowed to pass to wash out low molecular weight substances and the column can be re-used immediately.

It is often desirable to determine polysaccharides like inulin, amylose or dextran without interference from low molecular weight sugars. One important case is the inulin clearance test on renal function. In this test, the inulin in the urine is determined to see how large quantities pass through the kidneys. Particularly in diabetics, the glucose present in the urine interferes with the determination. To remove glucose, the sample may be incubated with yeast or digested with hot concentrated NaOH before the determination (Davidson et al. 1963). As these methods are not entirely satisfactory, Östling (1960) proposed the use of gel chromatography for this purpose. Jacobsson (1962) and Davidson et al. (1963) worked out procedures for determination of inulin in urine and blood. For their experiments they used Sephadex G-25 in fairly small columns. Fig. 6.2 shows the separation of high molecular weight substances from glucose in the procedure of Jacobsson. In this connection it is worth pointing out that Granath and Kvist (1967) have

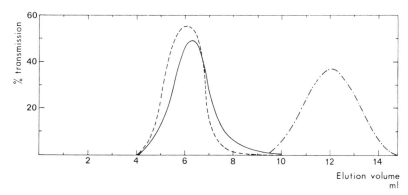

Fig. 6.2. Determination of inulin in serum. The serum was chromatographed on a 1.1 × 17 cm column of Sephadex G-25 in water. After the void volume, 4–5 ml, the high molecular weight substances (proteins, – – – ; inulin, ————) are eluted. They are followed later by the low molecular weight material (glucose, — · — · — ·). From Jacobsson (1962).

developed a method for determination of quantities and molecular weight distributions of carbohydrates in biological fluids (see § 6.2.5).

The very sensitive microbiological methods for determination of vitamin B_{12} do not function at sea-water salinity, making it difficult to determine the (very low) concentrations of this vitamin in salt water. In spite of the difference in molecular size, Daisley (1961) found it impossible to separate the vitamin and the salts by gel chromatography. After addition of a minute amount of intrinsic factor, the peptide that specifically binds vitamin B_{12} very strongly, he was able to achieve a separation on a column packed with Sephadex G-25, and subsequently to determine the content of vitamin B_{12} in the sea-water.

Gel chromatography was used by Englander (1963) in an interesting study of the exchange kinetics of exchangeable hydrogen in ribonuclease. In his experiments, he incubated the ribonuclease with tritiated water. In this way, the exchangeable hydrogen was partly exchanged by tritium. The incubation mixture was then applied to a 3 × 6 cm column of Sephadex G-25 coarse. When the ribonuclease had passed through half the column the flow was stopped. The tritiated ribonuclease was then

completely separated from the free tritium. This separation of ribonuclease from tritium was completed within about two minutes, a period so
short that the loss of bound tritium from the protein in this time is
negligible. In the column, the tritium is passing out from the protein.
After a suitable time the flow was restarted and the fractions collected.
The ribonuclease is then separated from the tritium set free. From the
radioactivity of the ribonuclease on elution, the amount of tritium exchanged for hydrogen during the interval when the flow was stopped can
be calculated. The method cannot be used for long-time experiments as
the free tritium from the incubation mixture diffuses through the bed to
remix with the ribonuclease on prolonged incubation in the column.
For longer term experiments, the chromatography was carried through
without stopping the flow, the protein emerging was collected and
aliquots of the tritiated ribonuclease thus prepared at intervals run
through another column to determine the amount of tritium set free.
The uptake reaction was studied by incubating the ribonuclease for
varying times with tritiated water before chromatographing for the
first time. By these experiments, four different types of exchangeable
hydrogen could be detected. The method of measurement was found
to compare well with other methods for this type of measurement,
both from the point of view of accuracy and freedom from artifacts.

Gel chromatography naturally can be used for removal of high molecular weight interfering substances also, although this has not been
used as much. Potter and Guy (1964) used gel chromatography for
removal of proteins before the determination of plasma salicylate.

The method of Beling for concentration and purification of conjugated urinary oestrogens, although methodologically different from
other gel chromatography (see § 8.6), is a special method for removal
of interfering substances.

The methods for study of equilibria, protein binding and related
methods can be considered as analytical group separation procedures.
They will, however, be treated separately.

6.2.2. Analytical fractionation

Fractionation experiments cover a whole range. At the one end of the scale are experiments, in which the substances in the sample are completely separated and can be determined separately. At the other end are the cases, where the various substances overlap one another to a very large extent, and the elution curve forms a profile that can be used to characterize the sample without determination of the concentrations of the various ingredients.

An example of the first type is the separation of sugars from cellulose hydrolysate by Flodin and Aspberg (1961, see § 5.1).

Another example of an analytical fractionation experiment where the substances have been completely separated from one another has been described by Nyström and Sjövall (1966b): To determine the various types of vitamin K (2-methyl-1-4-naphthoquinone with side chains of varying length in the 3 position) they used a methylated Sephadex G-25 superfine gel (see § 3.11). In one experiment the gel was packed into a capillary column made from teflon tubing with 1.5 mm inner diameter and about 2 m length. The eluant used was chloroform–methanol–heptane 1:1:2 and a specially constructed flame ionization detector was used to monitor the substances (Haahti and Nikkari 1963). The result of one of their experiments is shown in fig. 6.3.

An example of a fractionation experiment, where the substances were eluted in the 'wrong' order (the small substances eluted first) has been given by Wilk et al. (1966). In this experiment, polycyclic aromatic hydrocarbons were chromatographed on Sephadex LH-20 in chloroform and isopropanol. In chloroform, they all were eluted very close to each other, which is what one would expect, as their size lies below the fractionation range of the gel type. In isopropanol they seem to interact with the gel matrix, although the interaction is less pronounced than the interaction of aromatic substances with Sephadex in aqueous solution. Fig. 6.4 shows the elution curve obtained for these aromatic substances on Sephadex LH-20 in isopropanol.

The most important applications of analytical fractionation, however, come closer to the 'fingerprint' end of the scale with the substan-

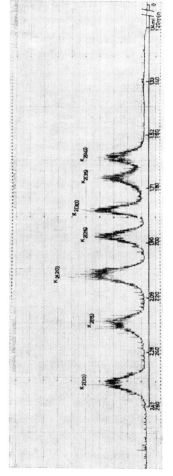

Fig. 6.3. Separation of about 20 μg each of vitamins $K_{2(40)}$–$K_{2(10)}$ on a capillary column of methylated Sephadex. For details about the experiment, see the text. From Nyström and Sjövall (1966b).

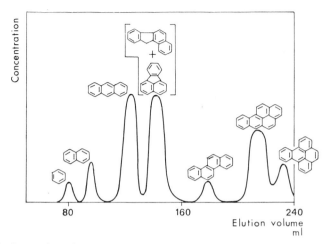

Fig. 6.4. Separation of a mixture of aromatic hydrocarbons on Sephadex LH-20 in isopropanol. Column dimensions 1.1 × 112 cm. Flow rate 2.5 ml/hr. From Wilk et al. (1966).

ces overlapping to a large extent. Many biological fluids have been characterized by gel chromatography. The most important among these is plasma. The elution behaviour of plasma proteins in gel chromatography has been extensively investigated by the group of Killander. The behaviour of some plasma proteins on Sephadex G-200 is indicated in fig. 6.5.

The normal elution pattern changes strongly under the influence of certain diseases, thus gel chromatography can be used as a diagnostic tool. This has been studied by many authors. The first investigations on the elution patterns in different pathological conditions were published by Roskes and Thompson (1963), Killander (1963), and Harboe and Drivsholm (1963). A comprehensive study was performed by Rivera et al. (1965). Other articles on the subject have been published by Wirth et al. (1965), Killander et al. (1965), Kyle and McGuckin (1966) and Prellwitz and Hammar (1966). The article by Hanson et al. (1966a) will be discussed in § 7.8.

It may still be too early to estimate the potential value of this method as a general diagnostic tool comparable to gel electrophoresis or immuno-electrophoresis. However, by gel chromatography it is possible to characterize some diseases when the electrophoretic methods are less reliable. Thus it is possible to distinguish macroglobulinemia (for instance Waldenström's disease), characterized by large amounts of 19S paraproteins in the plasma, from hyperglobulinemia (for instance plasmocytoma) where an excess of paraproteins of lower molecular weight is present in the plasma. To distinguish unequivocally between these conditions, an ultracentrifuge or an immunological test would otherwise have been required. Fig. 6.6 shows the elution pattern in

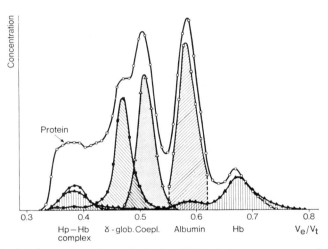

Fig. 6.5. Gel chromatography on Sephadex G-200 of a human serum to which was added both hemoglobin in excess of the binding capacity of the haptoglobin (type 2–1) and ceruloplasmin. 3.2 ml of lipoprotein-depleted human serum mixed with 1 ml of 5.3 % hemoglobin and 3 ml of a crude 5 % ceruloplasmin preparation was chromatographed on a 4.2 × 73.5 cm column of Sephadex G-200 in 0.1 M tris–HCl buffer pH 8.0 containing 1 M NaCl. The flow rate was 10–20 ml/hr and the temperature was 22 °C. Fraction volume was 10 ml. The protein concentration was determined by a modified Folin method, the heme components determined by the absorbancy at 406 nm, the peroxidase activity with guaiacol and measurement of the absorbancy at 470 nm, ceruloplasmin by the oxidase activity and albumin and gamma-globulins by immunochemical methods. From Killander (1964b).

Subject index p. 391

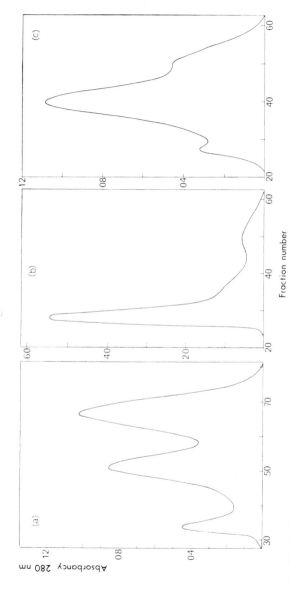

Fig. 6.6. Elution pattern obtained on chromatography of serum from one subject with hyperglobulinemia (c), compared with that from a normal subject (a), on Sephadex G-200 in 0.04 M phosphate buffer pH 7.3. The bed dimensions were 2.2 × 50 cm and the flow rate 40–45 ml/hr. The macroglobulinemic serum was obtained from a patient with multiple myeloma and the hyperglobulinemic serum from a patient with widespread metastases from a carcinoma of esophagus. The protein concentration was determined from the light absorption at 280 nm. From Rivera et al. (1965).

one case of macroglobulinemia and one case with hyperglobulinemia, compared to the pattern from normal serum.

A vast number of different mixtures, ranging from tryptic digests of
casein (Bennich 1961) to lignins (Ekman and Lindberg 1966), have been
characterized. Many of these methods also aim at the preparation of
the various substances and will be treated under § 6.3.2. The determination of molecular weights and molecular weight distributions by
gel chromatography could be included under the heading of analytical
fractionation, but these applications require a more detailed discussion
and will be dealt with separately (§ 6.2.5).

6.2.3. *Measurement of protein binding and complex formation*

Gel chromatography has found many interesting and important applications in the study of complexes between proteins and between proteins and low molecular weight solutes. If the reactants are irreversibly
bound to one another, the principle for the measurement is straight-
forward. The reaction mixture is applied to the bed and the complex is
separated chromatographically from the free reactant present in excess.

One example of this type of determination of complex formation
between proteins that is used in clinical laboratories is the determination
of the haptoglobin content of plasma. Haptoglobin is an α_2-globulin
in plasma with a molecular weight around 100,000. It forms a strong
complex with hemoglobin, and serves to bind the free hemoglobin in
plasma and to regulate the renal hemoglobin levels. The serum levels
of haptoglobin are decreased in certain hepatic disorders and in
hemolytic anemias, while some inflammatory conditions may cause
increased haptoglobin levels. Hemoglobin is eluted very late from
Sephadex columns; although its molecular weight is almost the same
as that of albumin (around 70,000), it is eluted later (see fig. 6.5). The
complex between hemoglobin and haptoglobin on the other hand is
eluted very early: although the molecular weight of the complex
(about 170,000) corresponds to that of 7S gamma-globulins, the complex is eluted close to the void volume together with the 19S gamma-
globulins. It is thus very easy to separate free hemoglobin from the
hemoglobin–haptoglobin complex by gel chromatography. Lionetti

et al. (1963) first described a method for haptoglobin determination, while Ratcliff and Hardwicke (1964) made a more detailed study and investigated possible interferences. They also made a comparison with other methods of determination of haptoglobin based on thin-layer agar electrophoresis and on the peroxidase activity of the hemoglobin–haptoglobin complex. They found that the gel chromatographic method is more reliable than the electrophoretic technique as there is no interference from hemolysis and it is simpler to perform than the enzymatic technique. Hodgson and Sewell (1965) have given a standardized procedure for the determination. Their procedure is essentially the following: a column 40×1.5 cm is packed with Sephadex G-100 in a buffer containing 9 g NaCl, 10 g NaN_3 and 200 ml Sörensen's buffer per litre. Approximately 2.5 mg hemoglobin in solution is added to 0.5 ml serum and applied to the column. The void volume, 25 ml is discarded and the 9 ml following, including the zone containing the hemoglobin–haptoglobin complex, is collected. 1 ml of cyanmethemoglobin diluent (10 times the concentration used in routine hematology) is added and the hemoglobin concentration determined with a hemoglobin colorimeter or with a spectrophotometer at 540 nm. After elution of the free hemoglobin, the column can immediately be used for the next determination.

The protein binding of insulin is also interesting clinically as it gives information about the formation of insulin antibodies in diabetics treated with insulin. The first study of the protein binding of insulin was that of Manipol and Spitzy (1962). They incubated radio-iodinated insulin with plasma and applied the incubation mixture to a column 70×1.1 cm packed with Sephadex G-75 in 0.85% NaCl. The radio-activity eluted in the void volume was used as a measure of the insulin binding capacity of the serum. This method gives information on the total protein binding but no information regarding the character of the proteins that bind the insulin. To get more detailed information on this point Rivera et al. (1965) and Toro-Goyco et al. (1966) chromatographed serum incubated with radio-iodinated insulin on columns packed with Sephadex G-200. They found that normal subjects and diabetics who have not been treated with insulin do not have any insulin-binding proteins in the blood plasma. Diabetics treated with insulin on the other hand develop insulin antibodies that can be studied by their strong insulin binding. In most cases the protein-bound insulin is eluted between the 7S and the 19S proteins in the plasma. In some cases, the protein-bound insulin is eluted entirely in the 19S peak or in two peaks, one in the same position as the 19S proteins and the other between the 19S protein peak and the 7S peak. Horino et al. (1966) have used the same technique to study experimental insulin immunity in guinea-pigs. In these animals, insulin is normally bound to some extent to proteins eluted in the albumin peak and to some extent to a protein eluted in the 19S gamma-globulin peak. In the plasma of immunized animals, the insulin is strongly bound to the antibodies and the complex is eluted in the 19S protein peak. Also the free antibodies were studied and the results were compared with electrophoretic results.

Gel chromatographic methods have been used successfully to determine protein binding of many low molecular weight compounds. For this purpose a working procedure corresponding to group separation can be adopted, while the working procedure in the study of complexes between compounds of high molecular weight corresponds more closely to fractionation.

One important application of this type of measurement is that concerned with the iodinated compounds in plasma. As the most important iodinated compound in the organism is the thyroid hormone and its complexes, this type of measurement gives information about the thyroid function and is mainly used as a diagnostic tool in metabolic disorders.

Spitzy et al. (1961) determined the concentrations of protein-bound and free iodine in plasma. In their work, they do not seem to have determined free iodothyronines, as they worked under conditions where the iodothyronines are usually retained on the column (see below). On a 1×12 cm column with Sephadex G-25 in 0.9% NaCl, they were able to separate and determine the protein-bound iodine even in enormous excess of inorganic iodine. Lissitzky et al. (1962) worked under similar conditions (Sephadex G-25 in tris–HCl buffer pH 7.4). They found that they could elute the protein-bound iodine and the inorganic iodine, while the free thyroid hormones (triiodothyronine, thyroxine) were retained on the bed. To elute them, they used an eluant consisting of tertiary amylol with 2 M NH_4OH. In this eluant the free thyroid hormones were eluted in a single sharp peak. Lissitzky et al. (1963) found that the monoiodinated and the diiodinated tyrosines could be eluted from a bed of Sephadex G-25 without the use of a separate eluant, although they were eluted after the inorganic iodine. They could not detect any of these compounds in the plasma from man or rat. Jacobsson and Widström (1962) used a similar system and compared it to other systems for determination of protein-bound iodine.

To determine triiodothyronine and thyroxine separately, Lissitzky and Bismuth (1963) digested the plasma proteins with papain before the gel chromatographic run. The thyroid hormones thus set free were retained on the column. After elution with ammonia in amylol, the substances were concentrated by evaporation of the solvent and rechromatographed on paper and the ratio between the triiodothyronine and the thyroxine determined. This somewhat complicated procedure was considerably simplified by Makowetz et al. (1966) and by Müller (1967). They found that the free thyroid hormones could be separated on a column of Sephadex G-25 in 0.015 M NaOH. The serum samples could be applied directly to the column as the protein-bound hormones were set free in the strongly alkaline environment.

In plasma under physiological conditions, the iodine concentrations are so low (in the range of 1 $\mu g/ml$) that they can only with great difficulty be determined without radioactive tracers. The direct determination of free and protein-bound iodine in plasma thus requires administration of radio-iodine to the subject of the investigation. Although this is not a problem for subjects under radio-iodine therapy, administration of radioisotopes should otherwise be avoided. Alternative routes are therefore required. Pearson Murphy and Pattee (1964) have described a method that is based on isotope dilution. In their method, the thyroid hormones in the plasma under investigation are set free by ethanol precipitation of the plasma proteins. The ethanol containing the hormones is evaporated and the evaporation residue is dissolved in water with a known quantity of radio-iodinated triiodothyronine. The mixture is incubated with a known quantity of the thyroxine-binding globulin in plasma and the incubation mixture chromatographed on Sephadex G-25. The excess thyroid hormones are retained on the Sephadex bed and the dilution of the radio-iodinated thyroxine with inactive material can be calculated from the radioactivity of the protein eluted from the column.

A technique that is in principle similar but in practice much simpler was described by Shapiro and Rabinowitz (1962). In their method it is assumed that the concentration of thyroxine binding globulin in plasma does not vary very greatly from individual to individual. In a similar way as Hamolsky et al. (1957) they incubated the plasma with radio-iodinated triiodothyronine. Although the plasma contains normally thyroxine binding globulin in quantities exceeding the quantity of hormone present, so that practically all the plasma thyroxine is protein-bound, the quantity of radio-iodinated hormone added is calculated to exceed the binding capacity of the plasma. When the plasma is subsequently chromatographed on Sephadex G-25, the excess hormone is retained on the bed and the quantity originally present can be estimated by comparing the quantity of radioactivity eluted in the protein peak with the total amount of radioactivity added to the plasma (in the method of Hamolsky et al., the excess hormone was removed with the aid of red blood cells instead). As only a relative measure of the quantity of hormone is required, the result is usually given as the percentage of the radioactive hormone that is taken up by the protein. A number of authors have discussed the method and presented clinical studies (Rabinowitz et al. 1963; Graul and Stumpf 1963; Stumpf and Graul 1963; Hocman et al. 1966; Gimlette 1967b). Hocman (1966) discussed the errors inherent in the method. Particularly he emphasized the fact that the reversible binding between hormone and the thyroxine binding globulin makes the complex dissociate partly during the passage through the column. For this reason the experimental conditions used must be very reproducible from one determination to another.

Subject index p. 391

Hvid-Hansen (1966) simplified the determination by taking up the excess hormone on Sephadex G-25 coarse added directly to the incubation mixture, washing the Sephadex repeatedly and measuring the amount of radioactivity taken up on the gel, while Gimlette (1967a) simplified the chromatographic procedure. It should be added that the hormone remaining on the bed can be eluted with fresh plasma with an excess of thyroxine binding protein. It is thus not necessary to use ammonia in tertiary amylol to remove the free hormone and to make the bed ready for the next experiment. It should also be remembered that all preparations of radio-iodinated triiodothyronine contain varying amounts of inorganic iodide and that a correction must be introduced for this iodide. The inorganic iodide can be determined separately in the chromatographic methods as it is eluted in a peak separated from the proteins and from the free hormones.

By methods similar to those described, protein-binding of dyes, drugs, metal ions and other species have been studied. As the gel chromatographic technique is very independent of the composition of the eluant, protein-binding can be studied within wide limits of concentration, pH, ionic strength and other variables.

With the methods given above, a qualitative estimate of the stability of complexes is possible. If a complex is dissociating during the passage through the bed, it is not very stable. If, on the other hand, it is eluted unchanged, it is reasonably stable under the conditions of the experiment. It is impossible, however, to calculate quantitatively the complex constant from such measurements. It is possible, however, to assess quantitatively complex constants by chromatography. For gel chromatography, this was first described by Hummel and Dreyer (1962). The method is the following: A column is packed and equilibrated with an eluant which has the pH, ionic strength etc., at which the complex constant is to be determined and which contains in addition one of the reactants, **A**. A sample is made up by dissolving the other reactant, **B**, in the eluant solution. The total concentration of reactant **A** should be exactly the same in the eluant and in the sample. As the zone of reactant **B** moves down the bed it will carry along some of reactant **A** in the form of complex **AB**. If the zone of **B** and **AB** moves with a velocity different from that of reactant **A**, it will move into fresh solution of **A**. **B** will react with reactant **A** in the eluant forming more **AB** until a steady state has been reached. In this steady state, the concentration of free **A** in the zone is the same as its concentration in the eluant. As the zone contains also some of reactant **A** in bound form as the complex **AB**, the total concentration of **A** in the zone is higher than its initial concentration. This increased concentration of **A** in the zone corresponds to a zone of decreased concentration of **A** in the part of the eluant that was passed by the zone before the establishment of a steady state. This zone of decreased concentration of **A** moves down the bed at the rate at which free **A** moves and can be collected at the outlet. The quantity of **A** that is taken up by the **B** applied to the bed thus can be assessed from the excess in the total concentration of **A** in the zone or the deficit of **A** in the zone of decreased concentration of **A**.

Some prerequisites have to be fulfilled to make it possible to use the method. One that is self-evident from the description is that the zone of **B** and **AB** should move with a different velocity from free **A**. Another prerequisite is that reactant **B** and the complex **AB** are not separated from one another. This can be achieved in different ways. Either the equilibrium between **B** and **AB** is established so fast that it prevents separation, or **B** and **AB** move with the same velocity. In either case, the establishment of the equilibrium must be so fast that a steady state can be reached before the zone has moved too far down the bed.

In gel chromatographic work, the method has mainly been used to determine protein binding of low molecular weight substances. In this case, the prerequisites are easily fulfilled. The low molecular weight substance is used as reactant **A** which is added to the eluant while the protein is used as reactant **B** which is only added to the sample. The gel type is usually chosen so that the protein is completely excluded, although this is not an absolute requirement. If both the protein and the complex move with the void volume there is no tendency for separation of them. The low molecular weight component on the other hand moves more slowly and is well separated from the zone of protein and complex. The rate of complex formation must, however, be sufficient to allow the formation of a steady state even if there is no tendency for separation of the protein and the complex.

When the steady state has been reached, the concentration of free **A** in the zone of **B** and **AB** is the same as in the original eluant. The concentration of **A** in the solution that the zone leaves behind then is also the same as in the original solution. This can be used as a criterion for the establishment of a steady state: between the zone of **B** and **AB** and the zone of decreased concentration of **A**, there should be a plateau region where the concentration of **A** is the same as in the original eluant. If there is no plateau region, a larger column should be used or less protein added to the sample. If the plateau region is very large,

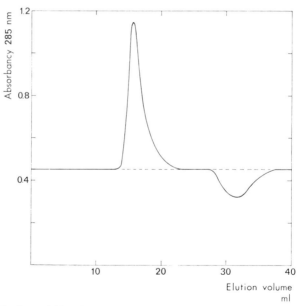

Fig. 6.7. Binding of 2′-cytidylic acid to pancreatic RNase, studied by chromatography of a sample of RNase on a 0.4×100 cm column of Sephadex G-25 in 0.1 M acetate buffer containing 9×10^{-5} M 2′-cytidylic acid. The peak contains the protein with bound cytidylic acid, the zone following, depleted of cytidylic acid, corresponds to the cytidylic acid bound to the protein. For explanations, see text. From Hummel and Dreyer (1962).

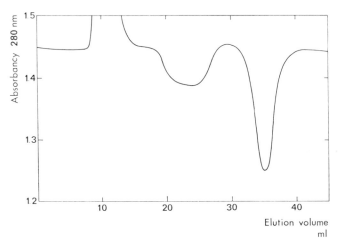

Fig. 6.8. Measurement of the competition between acetyl-L-tryptophan and acetyl-L-tryptophanamide for binding by bovine serum albumin. 20 mg of bovine serum albumin was chromatographed on a 0.5×115 cm column of Sephadex G-25 in 0.1 M NaCl containing 1.54×10^{-5} M acetyl-L-tryptophan and 2.68×10^{-4} M acetyl-L-tryptophanamide, pH 9. The temperature in the experiment was $15 °C$. The effluent was monitored at 280 nm in a Gilford UV monitor with 1 cm light path. The first trough after the protein peak corresponds to acetyl-L-tryptophan, the second to acetyl-L-tryptophanamide. From Fairclough and Fruton (1966).

the experiment could be performed in less time and with less zone broadening on a shorter chromatographic bed.

To illustrate the method, the original experiment of Hummel and Dreyer is shown in fig. 6.7. To illustrate the versatility of the method, an experiment of Fairclough and Fruton (1966) is shown in fig. 6.8. In this experiment the simultaneous binding of two low molecular weight substances to a protein was studied.

Pfleiderer and Auricchio (1964) used the method to demonstrate the binding of enzymes, in this case dehydrogenases, to coenzyme DPNH. A somewhat different method was used by Auricchio and Bruni (1964) to demonstrate the binding of a proteolytic enzyme to a protein. They used a gel type into which the proteolytic enzyme, trypsin, could penetrate. The trypsin could not be separated from ribonuclease on the column used. After some casein had been added to the eluant, the trypsin was, however, well separated from the ribonuclease as the complex of trypsin and casein moved at a higher rate than the free trypsin. Stonehill and Balis (1965) determined enzymatic activities by monitoring the degree of conversion in the effluent from a column, where a zone of enzyme had been applied to a column with an eluant containing substrate. Solute–solute interaction in gel chromatographic experiments has also been discussed by Ackers and Thompson (1965), by Winzor (1966) and by Kellett (1967).

6.2.4. *Determination of molecular weights*

One of the most important applications of gel chromatography is the determination of molecular weights, particularly of proteins. The potential use of chromatographic gels for this purpose can be deduced from the mechanism for gel chromatographic separations proposed by Flodin (see ch. 1). Later, works by a number of authors have indicated that for most proteins there is a close correlation between molecular weight and elution behaviour (Whitaker 1963; Auricchio and Bruni 1964; Leach and O'Shea 1965 and several others; see also § 7.8). Similarly, relationships between molecular weight and elution behavior can be found for carbohydrates (Granath and Flodin 1961; Roberts 1966) and for peptides (Carnegie 1965a, b, and several others). In a long series of careful measurements Andrews and his group demonstrated that very few proteins show anomalous behaviour on gel chromatography (Andrews 1962, 1964, 1965; Andrews et al. 1964; Downey and Andrews 1965). The proteins with anomalous behaviour are glycoproteins with high carbohydrate content. Fibrinogen also deviates considerably, due possibly to the long cigar shape of the protein (its molar frictional ratio is close to two, and it is among the proteins with the highest frictional ratio known). Ferritin behaves as apoferritin and the content of iron seems not to influence its behaviour. Catalase with a molecular weight of approximately 240,000 for reasons that are not known behaves as if its molecular weight were 195,000.

For molecular weight determinations, Sephadex G-100 and Sephadex G-200 have been used most frequently. Agar gels and agarose gels have also been studied (Andrews 1962; Largier and Polson 1964). Recently a study of the use of Bio-Gel P has also been made (del C. Batlle 1967).

In molecular weight estimations by gel chromatography, the technique described in ch. 5 should be used. The eluant in work with proteins is usually buffer or saline. Usually no special precautions are necessary. As long beds as possible should be used as this increases the precision of the measurement. Although calibration measurements of the various gel types are available in the literature, a separate calibration curve should be made for each gel bed. This is done with some proteins of known molecular weight as standards. A list of suitable proteins that can be used as standards is given by Andrews (1965), together with their molecular weights and their diffusion coefficients.

Siegel and Monty (1965, 1966) have found good correlation between the Stoke's radius of the proteins and their elution behaviour (see also Laurent and Killander 1964). From density gradient centrifugation and gel chromatography they are able to calculate molecular weights and frictional ratios. This, however, requires more apparatus and more complicated calculations, and even if this may improve the precision of the method for molecular weight determination to some extent it is doubtful if it is worth the extra complications involved.

It was pointed out by Ivatsubo and Curdel (1963) that the gel chromatographic method allowed molecular weight estimates to be made for impure enzymes. In most cases, absolute purity of a substance with biological activity is not required to determine it in the eluant. As other methods for molecular weight determination require that substance be prepared in pure form, this possibility is a great advantage when it is impossible or difficult to prepare samples in a pure state. Measurement of the biological activity in the eluant has been used to determine the elution volume in most estimates of the molecular weight by gel chromatography. The examples given below have been picked out at random from the vast number of experiments that have been published.

Kidney renin is a hormone that produces an increase in blood pressure by liberating anginotensin. It has been extensively purified

(Peart et al. 1966). The molecular weight of hog renin was estimated by gel chromatography by Kemp and Rubin (1964). They used columns packed with Sephadex G-100 and Sephadex G-200 in 0.5 M phosphate buffer pH 6.0. As standard substances they used radio-iodinated human gamma-globulin, radio-iodinated human albumin and pepsin. They found the same elution volume for different preparations of renin, and from their experiments they estimated the molecular weight to be 42,000 to 49,000. Warren and Dolinsky (1966) estimated the molecular weight of human renin. They used a column packed with Sephadex G-200 in citrate buffer pH 5. As standard substances they used porcine thyroglobulin, beef liver catalase, bovine gamma-globulin, human serum albumin and pepsin. They arrived at a molecular weight of 42,300, in good agreement with Kemp and Rubin.

Schane (1965) wanted to compare the properties of the phosphorylases from smooth muscle and skeletal muscle, as immunological studies indicated differences. The properties of skeletal muscle phosphorylases are fairly well known. The difficulty in obtaining sufficient quantities of material made it impossible to determine the molecular weight of smooth muscle phosphorylases by classical methods. Therefore, Schane determined the phosphorylase activity in the effluent from a column of Sephadex G-200 in 0.1 M NaF and 0.3 M NaCl. As standard substances, bovine albumin, beef heart lactic dehydrogenase, bovine thyroglobulin, glucose oxidase and pyruvate kinase were used. He arrived at molecular weights of 232,000 and 197,000 for rat uterine phosphorylase a and b, respectively. This makes the enzymes appear more similar to the liver phosphorylases than to the skeletal muscle phosphorylases.

When gel chromatography is used for estimating molecular weights of peptides, the influence of the molecular structure disturbs the measurement. The reason is that in the case of peptides, the variation in the content of aromatic groups and the steric irregularity may be greater. The gels used are the dense gels with fractionation range at the molecular weights of the peptides. Carnegie (1965a, b) has used with success an eluant proposed by Synge and Youngson (1961) and by Bagdasarian et al. (1964). This eluant, composed of equal parts of phenol, water and acetic acid, seems to reduce the interaction between solute and gel matrix and to allow peptides to be eluted in the order of molecular size. The eluant, however, is rather unpleasant to work with and the high content of phenol makes it difficult to find suitable analytical procedures for the effluent from the column. Carnegie used the ninhydrin reaction. He obtained good results with a number of peptides on a column packed with Sephadex G-25 in this eluant.

Gel chromatography for molecular weight determination has somewhat lower precision than other available methods. There is also a certain risk that the protein studied may belong to the group of proteins showing anomalous behaviour. On the other hand, the method has the advantage that the determination is rapid, easy to perform and requires only fairly inexpensive equipment. Another advantage is that molecular weights can be determined even in crude preparations if a specific reaction is available for the substance under investigation.

6.2.5. Determination of molecular weight distributions

For a polydisperse macromolecule, the molecular weight distribution curve gives the amount of material of various molecular weights, present in the material. This molecular weight distribution characterizes the material more completely than the molecular weight averages. Two types of distribution curves are used, the integral distribution curve and the differential distribution curve. The first gives the percentage of the total amount of material that has molecular weight below the molecular weight that is used as independent variable. The second is the derivative of the earlier one. Fig. 6.9 shows a typical distribution curve for a pharmaceutical dextran of molecular weight 40,000 that is used as a plasma expander and blood flow improver (Rheomacrodex, Pharmacia AB).

The earlier method for determination of molecular weight distributions is based on fractional precipitation of the molecules; the method is laborious and time-consuming. This method can be improved in various ways. This has for instance been done in the Baker–Williams column, where the precipitation is performed in a column filled with glass beads.

The relationship between molecular weight and elution behaviour on gel chromatographic columns makes it possible to determine molecular weight distributions for macromolecules in a very rapid and expedient way. In principle the molecular weight distribution is determined as follows: By gel chromatography the macromolecules are separated into several fractions. For each fraction molecular weight and amount of substance present are determined. To obtain the integral

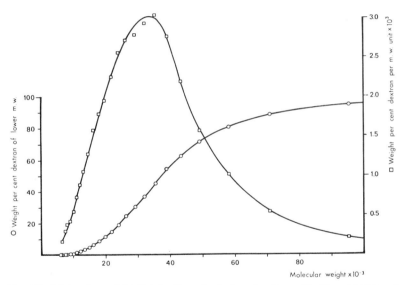

Fig. 6.9. Molecular weight distribution of a dextran fraction with $M_w = 44,100$ and $\overline{M}_n = 27,700$. The molecular weight distribution was determined by gel chromatography and the distribution curve computed from the elution curves with a computer program developed for this purpose. The average molecular weights given above were calculated from the molecular weight distribution curve; they compare well with those calculated from end group analysis and light scattering measurements $(\overline{M}_w = 43,900; \overline{M}_n = 32,700)$. This dextran fraction is used for clinical purposes as a plasma expander and blood flow improver (Rheomacrodex). The data on which the diagram is based were obtained from Dr. K. A. Granath.

distribution curve, the amount of material present in fractions containing material of lower molecular weight than a given fraction and the half of the material in the fraction itself are added and plotted as a function of the average molecular weight of the substance in the fraction. In this connection it should be noted that the low molecular weight material is eluted last from a gel chromatographic column.

The procedure given above for calculation of distribution curves from gel chromatographic elution curves would give the true distribution curve if the fractions obtained were infinitely sharp. Due to the zone broadening in the bed, this is not the case, although the gel chromatographic data seem to be more reliable than the data from other fractionation methods (see for instance Adams et al. 1966; Altgeld 1965a). Mathematical procedures to correct the distribution curves obtained for the zone broadening have been developed and tested experimentally by Tung and co-workers (Tung 1966a, b; Tung et al. 1966) and by Hess and Kratz (1966). Granath and Kvist (1967) have shown that with molecular weight distributions as broad as those normally encountered, the fractionation obtained with gel chromatography is so sharp that the error from the finite zone width is rather small and no correction is therefore necessary in most cases.

In practice, the effluent is not collected in separate fractions. The correlation between the molecular weight and the elution behaviour is determined by separate calibration, and the elution curve is continuously monitored (Moore 1964; Granath and Kvist 1967). For the calibration, a series of well characterized polymer fractions with very narrow molecular weight distribution is used. The elution behaviour from gel columns has been found to be so reproducible that the columns do not require frequent recalibration, particularly if K_{av} values are used so that variations in the column packing and the void volume are compensated. The distribution curve is calculated directly from the elution curve in a way corresponding to that suggested for the separate fractions. The calculations for converting the elution curve to the distribution curve are simple but time-consuming. Hence a computer program transforming the elution curve to integral and differential distribution curves is used in routine work (Pickett et al. 1966).

The most important applications of distribution analysis fall within the fields of synthetic polymers like plastics, rubbers (synthetic and natural) and similar materials where the mechanical properties of the materials are used. For these materials the properties are to a very large extent determined by their molecular weight distribution. As these substances are only soluble in organic solvents (if at all soluble), the polystyrene gels developed by Moore are usually used (see § 3.11). Some examples will serve to illustrate this application.

Asphalt is a very complex mixture of high molecular weight hydrocarbons and other compounds that are obtained from oil after the volatile substances have been distilled off. Altgeld (1965a, b) studied the molecular weight distribution in asphalts from different sources and found that they vary widely.

Smith et al. (1966) have studied the kinetics of polymerization of polystyrenes and methylmethacrylate by conducting the polymerization for different periods of time and determining the molecular weight distributions and the yields of polymer obtained.

By new synthetic techniques, the freedom of variation in the synthesis of rubber elastomers has increased very greatly. This has also made it necessary to introduce methods for better characterization of the products obtained. Gamble et al. (1965) and Adams et al. (1966) have used gel chromatographic techniques with great success for characterization of rubber elastomers, particularly polybutadienes.

Blundell et al. (1966) used gel chromatography to characterize the products formed when a polyethylene monolayer single crystal was degraded. From their experiments they were able to make deductions regarding the structure of the crystals.

Gel chromatography has been used to determine the molecular weight distribution of water soluble macromolecules; Sephadex gels and agarose gels have been most extensively used. The following are some examples of such measurements.

In management of surgical shock, large quantities of infusion solutions containing a suitable type of macromolecule in saline or glucose solution are given intravenously (plasma expander). The macromolecule used in this type of therapy should have compositions varying only within very narrow limits. For this reason it is essential to develop analytical procedures that allow careful characterization. Dextrans are the best known polymers for this purpose. The methods developed by Granath and co-workers for characterization of dextrans include gel chromatography on a bed of equal amounts by volume of Sephadex G-100 and Sephadex G-200 (Granath and Kvist 1967). Denatured bovine plasma proteins have also been proposed as plasma expanders. To characterize these, Přistoupil and his group (Přistoupil 1965; Přistoupil and Ulrych 1967) used Sephadex G-200. They found that although they obtained a fractionation of the modified and denatured proteins the relationship between molecular weight and elution volume for these was different from that for native proteins. For that reason they attempted to use 8 M urea as eluant to break down the tertiary structure of the native proteins. They found that under these conditions they could use native proteins for calibration of their column. Later they used the same eluant in experiments on agar beads.

6.3. Preparative applications

6.3.1. Preparative group separation

In many biochemical preparations, desalting or exchange of buffer is an important step. There is no magic about the operation. The salts and the proteins are very different in character and there is no theoretical difficulty involved. In practice, however, the operation may present considerable difficulties. The most usual way of desalting is probably dialysis. Dialysis, however, takes considerable time, which may cause losses of labile proteins. Ion exchangers cannot be used to desalt proteins, as the proteins become attached to the ion exchangers.

Gel chromatography is a simple and rapid method for desalting or change of buffer (see for instance Porath and Flodin 1959; Flodin 1961). The technique is the one described in ch. 5. The sample size can be up to 25–30% of the bed volume, and the gel bed volume should consequently be chosen 3–4 times that of the sample to be applied. Sephadex G-25 and Bio-Gel P–6 are the gel types most suited for the purpose. The gel bed should be equilibrated before the experiment with a solution with the ionic composition that is desired (distilled water in the case of desalting). The elution is performed with the same liquid. The flow rate may be high (10–20 cm/hr) making it possible to complete the whole operation within one hour and to collect the desalted material within less than one hour on beds 30–40 cm high.

When desalting is performed with distilled water as eluant, some undesired effects may become apparent. Tailing is more pronounced than at higher ionic strength and the dilution is consequently larger. For this reason it has been proposed that volatile electrolytes should be added to increase the ionic strength. These electrolytes could subsequently be removed by freeze-drying. Volatile electrolytes that have been used for this purpose are for instance pyridinium acetate and ammonium carbonate. These systems in addition act as buffers in some pH regions. The volatile electrolytes are, however, usually difficult to remove completely and may interfere in subsequent experiments. Some of them (for instance pyridinium acetate) may also cause corrosion on the freeze-dryer. The pumps should be protected with an extra cold trap and the freeze-dryer chambers themselves should preferably be made from glass. The volatile electrolytes have a strong tendency to corrode copper tubes commonly used for the coolers in the freeze-dryer.

The desalting technique is not restricted to desalting of macromolecules. Matheka and Wittman (1961) have reported desalting of virus suspensions on Sephadex G-25. Englander (1963) indicates that erythrocytes pass undamaged through the columns. The technique seems not to have gained any wide-spread application, probably because virus can be separated from salt solutions by centrifugation. To desalt solutions of high viscosity, the centrifuge desalting technique should be used (see § 8.1).

Gel chromatography is frequently used for separation of macromolecules that have been modified chemically from the free reactant. Almost immediately after the introduction of gel chromatography, several authors described procedures for separation of fluorescent antibodies from unreacted dye (Goldstein et al. 1961; Zwaan and Van Dam 1961; Killander et al. 1961; Lipp 1961; Curtain 1961; Fothergill and Nairn 1961; George and Walton 1961). The method works with the most common fluorescent markers (fluorescein isothiocyanate, Lissamine Rhodamine B 200 and diethylamino naphthalene sulphochloride; Rinderknecht 1962). It can be used with other marked macromolecules as well. Ernst and Schill (1965) have used it for purification of fluorescent dextran.

The gel types usually used are Sephadex G-25 and Sephadex G-50. Usually a buffer of neutral pH is used as eluant (very often phosphate buffers at pH very close to 7 have been reported). Very small chromatographic beds are sufficient: at 10–20 cm bed height the separation is satisfactory and the marked macromolecules can be recovered from the bed about 15 min after their application in quantitative yields and about two-fold dilution. In spite of its aromatic character, the fluorescein isothiocyanate most commonly used has been reported not to be very strongly retarded on the bed – Tokumaru (1962) determined a K_d value of 0.92 on a Sephadex G-25 bed packed with 0.15 M NaCl – 0.0175 M phosphate buffer pH 7.0. Others have reported difficulties in removing the unreacted dye from the bed, particularly on Sephadex G-25. Sephadex G-50 seems to be easier to handle from this point of view. Possibly the remaining unreacted dye can be removed by running a zone of some protein, for instance serum albumin, through the column.

Gel chromatography has been compared with other methods for removal of unreacted dye by Fothergill and Nairn (1961) and by Zwaan and Van Dam (1961). They have found that dialysis does not give a satisfactory removal of the dye even after prolonged treatment while treatment with charcoal or organic tissues results in losses of activity. For these reasons, gel chromatography is now very commonly used for this purpose.

In work with substances marked with radioisotopes, the amount of substance available is often very limited. It is therefore necessary to work with methods that give good yields even with very small amounts of substance. Very often chemical reactions can be carried out, but the separation of the products from the unreacted reactant and from each other is difficult. Gel chromatography seems to offer some possibilities in work with proteins and peptides marked with radioisotopes, as the losses in the column can be kept very low. Hunter and Greenwood (1962) and Greenwood et al. (1963) worked with radio-iodinated human growth hormone. The amount of growth hormone in each experiment was very small, about 3–4 μg. The radio-iodine was introduced by incubating the growth hormone with radio-iodide and chloramine-T. After the reaction, the excess chloramine was destroyed by addition of sodium metabisulphite. To remove the low molecular weight reactants and products (particularly the remaining radio-iodine) the reaction mixture was subsequently transferred to a 1×10 cm column of Sephadex G-50 in 0.07 M barbiturate buffer, pH 8.6. To prevent losses on the gel bed, it had previously been 'presaturated' by running a solution of crystalline bovine plasma albumin through, followed by buffer. Within 15 min after the labelled hormone had been applied to the column it could be collected in the effluent, free from unchanged iodide and other additions, in about 65 % yield.

Another example of the separation of labelled protein preparations from contaminating labelling reactants has been provided by Wood et al. (1963) and by Numa et al. (1964). They carboxylated acetyl-CoA-carboxylase with radiocarbon from ^{14}C-methylmalonyl-CoA. The $^{14}CO_2$-acetyl-CoA-carboxylase could be separated from the reactants by chromatography on Sephadex G-50 in 0.05 M potassium phosphate buffer. Subsequently the binding of the $^{14}CO_2$ could be studied and its reactions followed.

Disulphide bonds are of great importance for the tertiary structure of proteins. When the steric properties of the proteins are studied, it is important to be able to break disulphide bridges with little other changes in the molecule. This can be done by reduction of the S–S bridges to form SH groups by suitable reactants. One method for this has been given by Anfinsen and Haber (1961). In their procedure they incubate the protein with 8 M urea, adjusted to pH 8.6 with methylamine and 1 μl of mercaptoethanol per mg of protein. After the mercaptoethanol had been allowed to react with the protein for $4\frac{1}{2}$ hr at room temperature, the pH of the solution was adjusted to 3.5 by acetic acid and the protein was separated from the reactants on a 2.5×35 cm column packed with Sephadex G-25 in 0.1 M acetic acid. By this method they were able to obtain fully reduced products from trypsinogen, chymo-trypsinogen and lysozyme.

Gel chromatography has been used with good results for removal of inhibitors and cofactors from enzymes. This removal is very important in kinetic studies of enzyme reactions. It can be extremely difficult to achieve by other methods, particularly with labile enzymes that are destroyed by precipitation or by long dialysis.

Hyaluronidase in urine is partially inhibited by substances in the urine. Not only is the enzymatic activity attenuated, but the entire kinetics are different. The inhibitors of hyaluronidase may have quite high molecular weights. Thus, sulphated polysaccharides of different kinds are known to be inhibitors. By chromatography of untreated urine on a column of Sephadex G-75 in acetate buffer, Knudsen and Kofoed (1961) were able to separate the enzyme from the inhibitors. In this system the hyaluronidase was found to be completely excluded. This is unexpected, considering the low molecular weight of the enzyme. By the chromatographic run the inhibitors were sufficiently well removed to increase the activity considerably and to restore normal enzymatic kinetics.

Extracts from *Escherichia coli* have been found to catalyze a reaction between homocysteine and serine to produce methionine. The reaction requires a folic acid derivative as cofactor. To study the enzyme system, Kisliuk (1960) separated the proteins from the folic acid cofactor. This was done on a 2×12 cm column packed with Sephadex G-50. 0.01 M phosphate buffer pH 7.8 was used as eluant. A sample of 10 ml volume was eluted from the column within 30 min, completely free from cofactor as judged from the complete absence of enzymatic activity. The enzymatic activity could be restored completely after re-addition of the coenzyme. For comparison, one sample of the preparation of the original extract was dialyzed for 20 hr. After this time 54% of the original enzymic activity was still retained without addition of any cofactor preparation, indicating that this method is unsatisfactory for removal of this type of cofactor.

The enzyme system required for microbial fixation of nitrogen is a very complex one that requires several cofactors. The system must be kept under anaerobic conditions, further complicating the study of the system. Munson et al. (1965) removed the cofactors by gel chromatography under anaerobic conditions. This required very complicated equipment that is described in the article. The chromatographic bed used measured 2×25 cm. It was packed with Sephadex G-25 in tris buffer. When the *Clostridium* extract was chromatographed at pH 6.8, the enzymes were separated from all the cofactors except ferredoxin and thiamine which were too strongly bound to the proteins to be removed in this way. The enzyme system could be reactivated by re-addition of the various cofactors and the effects of the different cofactors could be studied. If the chromatographic run was performed at pH 8.3, the ferredoxin and the thiamine could be removed as well. In this case the enzyme system could only be partially reactivated.

In some cases, group separation may give extremely high purification by the use of complexes that can be split. Lindner et al. (1959) and Frankland et al. (1966) have described methods for purification of oxytocin and vasopressin from pituitary extracts, based on the binding of these peptide hormones to Van Dyke's protein, a protein from the pituitary specifically binding these peptides. The extract was first chromatographed on Sephadex G-25 to remove the low molecular weight material. The peptide hormones were then eluted together with the proteins. The bond to the protein was subsequently split by incubation at low pH. Lindner et al. treated the complex with 1 M formic acid for 10 min at 70 °C to split the complex. When the incubation mixture was subsequently chromatographed on a 2.5×50 cm column packed with Sephadex G-25 in 1 M formic acid, the peptides were eluted well separated from the proteins in good yield. Frankland et al., working with varying concentrations of formic acid, found that after incubation in 0.1 M formic acid at room temperature and chromatography on a 2×145 cm column with Sephadex G-25 in 0.1 M formic acid, the oxytocin and the vasopressin were separated from protein and from one another.

Aqueous phenol is often used to extract nucleic acids from tissues (Gierer and Schramm 1956; Kirby 1956). The phenol makes it possible to extract efficiently nucleic acids from mammalian cells with very little contaminants from the tissues. On the other hand, the phenol itself is usually an undesired contaminant in subsequent experiments. Shepherd and Petersen (1962) have reported the use of gel chromatography for removal of the phenol from a DNA preparation, while Gross et al. (1965) used a similar procedure in the purification of RNA. Sephadex G-25 or Sephadex G-50 was used in beds of 30 cm bed height or less. With phosphate buffer or saline as eluants, the nucleic acids were efficiently separated from the phenol with quantitative yields. For this purpose, gel chromatography seems to have several advantages over the ether extraction method used earlier. All the phenol is removed rapidly in one operation. Other low molecular weight contaminants that may be present after the extraction are removed in the same operation. The disadvantage would be that it is necessary to identify in some manner the portion of the effluent containing the nucleic acids, thus making it necessary to carry out several analytical determinations. With a spectrophotometer at hand this should not cause too much difficulty, and once the elution pattern from the column has been established this work can be dispensed with. Another potential disadvantage is the dilution caused by the chromatographic step.

Gel chromatography can be scaled up considerably. Columns with bed volumes of more than 1,000 l have been found to work well. In such large columns, coarse grade material makes it possible to use very high flow rates (more than 5 cm/min) and correspondingly short cycle times (down to 20 min). Such large scale processes have been developed for industrial purposes. One process that illustrates the low production costs and high capacity that can be attained is the process for production of protein enriched milk (Samuelsson et al. 1967a, b):

Dieticians claim that ordinary consumers' milk contains too much fat and sugar and too little protein. The milk can be enriched in proteins by evaporation. This, however, gives a milk that is also enriched in low molecular weight components (the excess fat can be removed by centrifugation). By the use of gel chromatography the low molecular weight components can be removed from part of the milk so that the protein content can be increased by evaporation without simultaneous increase in the content of low molecular weight components of the milk. Fig. 6.10 shows the flow scheme for the process. After the low molecular weight constituents have been partly removed from skim milk, the fraction containing the high molecular weight constituents (mainly proteins) is mixed with untreated skim milk and ordinary full milk and the mixture is evaporated to give milk of the desired composition. Fig. 6.11 illustrates the gel chromatographic step of the procedure. The use of a three-column arrangement was chosen to give almost continuous input and output flow from the unit to suit the rest of the plant. The unit illustrated in the example is a pilot-plant scale set-up. On a full scale, the process costs are calculated at 1.5 US-cents for each litre of milk treated.

If the milk is freed from sugar more completely and the protein fraction from the gel chromatographic step is directly evaporated to

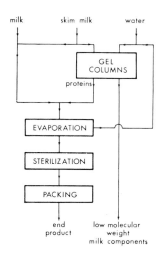

Fig. 6.10. Flow scheme for a process for production of protein-enriched milk. After Samuelsson et al. (1967a).

a suitable concentration, the product will be suitable as milk substitute for diabetics and for others on special sugar-free diet (De Koning 1962). A similar process can also be used to produce high quality proteins from sources that otherwise cannot be utilized (for instance whey) by separating them from low molecular weight contaminants that are toxic or ill-tasting and in this way make the protein capable of being used as food.

Another application of large-scale gel chromatography is the separation of pyrogenic material from drugs for injection. Philip et al.

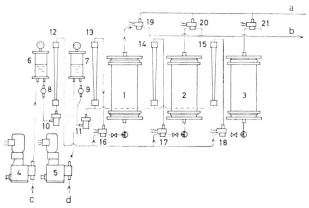

Fig. 6.11. Schematic picture illustrating the set-up of the gel chromatographic step in the process in fig. 6.10 for production of protein-enriched milk. The skim milk is pumped by pump 4, the water by pump 5. 6 and 7 are damping vessels serving to damp out the pulsations from the pumps. 8 and 9 are safety-valves preventing accidents by too high pressure at the inlet side of the columns. 12, 13, 14 and 15 are flow meters. 16, 17 and 18 are solenoid valves controlled from a central programmed switch device. 1, 2 and 3 are the columns, made from stainless steel. The solenoid valves 19, 20 and 21, operated by the central program device to collect the high M.W. fractions in one lead and the low M.W. fractions in the other. The columns are operating out of phase with one another, giving almost constant input and output flow from the gel chromatography set-up to the other parts of the equipment. (a) protein fraction; (b) low molecular weight solute fraction; (c) skim milk; (d) water. A very similar apparatus can be used for treatment of whey. From Samuelsson et al. (1967a).

(1966) have used the method for removal of pyrogenic material from serum albumin on Sephadex G-100 (see § 5.1).

Another closely related application is the removal of allergens from pharmaceutical preparations. Allergens are often compounds of high molecular weight that are completely excluded on the gel types that are most interesting in industrial connections. One example is the removal of penicillinoylated proteins from penicillin. The commonest methods for preparation of penicillins give a substance containing in addition to penicillin and penicillic acid also small quantities of proteins and peptides. These couple with the penicillins and the penicillinoylated proteins obtained are highly allergenic (Stewart 1967; Batchelor et al. 1967). These penicillinoylated proteins can be removed by dialysis or by gel chromatography (Feinberg 1967).

6.3.2. *Preparative fractionation*

For fractionation experiments, the gel type must be chosen with care to obtain satisfactory separation (§ 5.1). The sample volumes are smaller than those used in group separation work and the flow rates used usually much lower (1–5 cm/hr).

In samples containing few components of interest a rough estimate of the possible separation can be obtained from the curves relating elution behaviour and molecular weight (§ 2.5, ch. 3) if the molecular weights of the components are known. From this the sample size to be used and the column length required can be roughly estimated. One example of this is the purification of D-oxynitrilase by Becker and Pfeil (1966, see below). In complex samples, on the other hand, there is a more or less random distribution of contaminants in the elution pattern around the substance of interest. In this case it is necessary to select a sample size that is a reasonable compromise. Larger sample sizes in this case always involve a lower degree of purification – but also better yields, higher capacity and smaller dilution. If the sample is less than 1–2 % of the total column volume, the improvement in purification seems, however, to be insignificant and little is gained by applying smaller samples. One example is the purification of simian growth hormone by Peckham (1967, see below). Although all types of gels may be used in fractionation experiments, the most interesting results from the standpoint of the biochemist are undoubtedly obtained with the gels fractionating high molecular weight compounds such as proteins, polysaccharides, nucleic acids etc. The examples quoted are only intended to illustrate some features of the method and some technical details and do not cover even a small fraction of the field of applications.

Gamma-globulins have been subjects of an intense study for determination of their structure, their synthesis and the mechanism of binding antigens. In a large proportion of these investigations, gel chromatography has been used as a tool for separating the proteins, their degradation products and their complexes. One example is provided by Fleischman (1967), in a study of the synthesis of the heavy chain of rabbit lymph node cell γG-globulins. He incubated the lymph node cells with an incubation mixture containing radioactive leucine. After varying times of incubation, the cells were chilled to stop the reaction, washed to remove excess radioactive leucine and frozen to set free the gamma-globulins produced. Carrier gamma-globulin was added and the gamma-globulins were purified by ammonium sulphate precipitation, chromatography on DEAE cellulose and finally chromatography on Sephadex G-200. The heavy chains were split off from the light chains by reduction and alkylation and purified by chromatography on Sephadex G-100 in 1 M propionic acid. Subsequently, the heavy chain preparation was digested with cyanogen bromide or by papain and the fragments formed separated by chromatography on a Sephadex G-100 column in 1 M acetic acid. At a flow rate of 8 ml/hr on a column 2×103 cm, five different peptides were obtained after cyanogen bromide digestion (fig. 6.12). From the ratio between the radioactivity of the various peptides isolated after different times of incubation, conclusions could be drawn concerning the mechanism for the synthesis of the gamma-globulin heavy chain.

Isolation of antibodies to specific antigens has considerable interest, particularly in the study of the mechanism of antibody formation and binding. One way of preparing a specific antibody is to precipitate it

Subject index p. 391

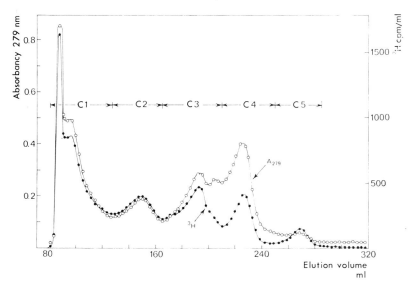

Fig. 6.12. Chromatography of cyanogen bromide fragments of the heavy chain of γG-globulins produced in vitro by rabbit lymph node cells, on a 2×103 cm Sephadex G-100 bed in 1 M acetic acid. The fragments were marked with ^{3}H-labelled lysine included in the incubation medium for the lymph node cells. By incubating the cells for varying periods and studying the radioactivity of the fragments, the order in which the fragments were produced can be determined. From Fleischman (1967).

together with its antigen, wash the precipitate free from other proteins, split the precipitate and separate the antibody from the antigen. The separation of the antibody from the antigen can often be performed by gel chromatography. Some alternatives are precipitation or digestion of the antigen. Givol et al. (1962) precipitated antibody–antigen complexes to the antigens lysozyme, egg albumin and a synthetic polypeptide. The precipitates were dissolved in 0.02 M HCl–0.15 M NaCl pH 1.8, and separation of the antigen from the antibody by chromatography of the solution on a column packed with Sephadex G-75 was tried. This was possible in the case of lysozyme, while the egg albumin and the synthetic polypeptide were not split off from their antibodies under these conditions. A slight binding could be observed also in the case of the lysozyme. Kávai et al. (1966) were able to dissociate ovalbumin and ovalbumin antibody in 1 M acetic acid so that they could be separated on a 1 × 50 cm column of Sephadex G-200 in 1 M acetic acid.

In the field of hormone chemistry, gel chromatography is frequently used for resolution of the complex mixtures of peptides obtained in the crude preparations. An example of the preparation of a peptide hormone is the isolation of simian growth hormone by Peckham (1967). The preparation illustrates the need for different fractionation methods based on different principles in purification of complex mixtures.

The starting material for the purification procedure was a crude preparation of growth hormone, produced by extraction of acetone powder of simian pituitaries. The extract was precipitated with ethanol and the precipitate resuspended in distilled water and lyophilized (fraction B, C and D of Reisfeld et al. 1962). After re-extraction

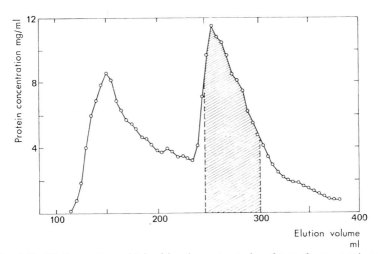

Fig. 6.13. Elution pattern obtained by chromatography of a crude preparation of simian growth hormone on a 2.5 × 100 cm column of Sephadex G-100 in 0.05 M phosphate buffer pH 6.8 containing 0.5 M NaCl. The cross-hatched area corresponds to the fractions containing growth hormone. From Peckham (1967).

Subject index p. 391

with 10 ml of the same buffer and pooling of the extracts, a small
amount of diisopropyl fluorophosphate was added to inhibit the
proteolytic enzymes in the preparation. The solution was then applied
to a 2.5 × 100 cm column of Sephadex G-100 in 0.05 M phosphate
buffer, pH 6.8, containing 0.5 M NaCl. After elution at a rate of 10 ml/
hr, the protein content and the hormonal activity in the effluent were
determined. The result can be seen from fig. 6.13. The material in the
preparation could not be resolved into individual peaks and at least
six components could be seen in disc electrophoresis. The fractions
from the gel chromatographic run that had hormonal activity were
then applied to a DEAE–Sephadex ion exchanger column equilibrated
with 0.05 M phosphate buffer, pH 6.8, and eluted without the use of a
gradient. The result of the ion exchanger experiment is given in fig. 6.14.
In the disc electrophoresis run, only trace amounts of contaminants

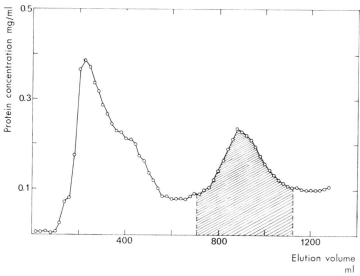

Fig. 6.14. Elution pattern obtained from the chromatography of the material obtained in fig. 6.13 on a 3.2 × 40 cm column of DEAE-Sephadex A-50 in 0.05 M phosphate buffer pH 6.8, without the use of a gradient. The cross-hatched area corresponds to the fractions containing hormone. From Peckham (1967).

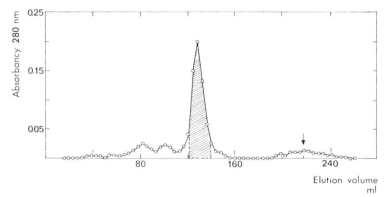

Fig. 6.15. Elution pattern obtained from density gradient electrophoresis of the material obtained in fig. 6.14. A sucrose gradient in 0.025 M tris–HCl buffer pH 8.6 was used. A current of 4–5 mA was used in a column 3×32 cm. The electrophoresis was conducted for 31 hr before elution. From Peckham (1967).

could be detected. To remove these final impurities, the material was subjected to column electrophoresis in a sucrose density gradient with tris–HCl buffer, pH 8.6. A column of Sephadex G-25 was used to change buffer. The result of the density gradient column electrophoresis experiment can be seen from fig. 6.15. The growth hormone from this experiment could be shown to be pure by polyacrylamide disc electrophoresis and gel chromatography.

One example of an enzyme isolation where the substance is obtained in pure state after gel chromatography is given by Becker and Pfeil (1966). In their study of enzymes related to emulsin from bitter almonds, they wanted to purify the D-oxynitrilases from various sources. For this purpose, seeds from various members of the genus *Prunus* were ground in a turmix and defatted with petrol ether, while the flowers of *Prunus spinosa* were treated fresh in a turmix and pressed. The enzyme is extracted from this preparation with dilute ammonia. The extract is then neutralized with acetic acid and the precipitate forming in the cold is centrifuged off and discarded. By addition of ethanol the enzyme is precipitated and centrifuged off. This crude preparation is dried in vacuum, dissolved in water and

adjusted to *p*H 7.5 with ammonia. The enzyme is taken up on DEAE
or ECTEOLA cellulose and placed on top of a column. It is then eluted
from the column with 0.1 M pyridium acetate buffer. After precipitation of the enzyme with ammonium sulphate a solution in 0.1 M acetate buffer is prepared. This solution is applied to a column 4 × 120 cm
packed with Sephadex G-100 in 0.1 M acetate buffer. A typical elution
curve is given in fig. 6.16. The first peak contains proteins of high

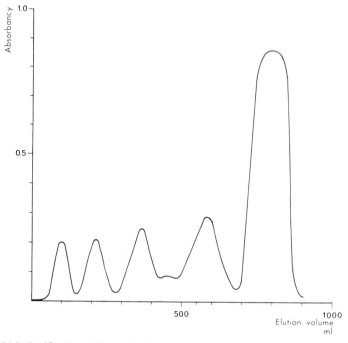

Fig. 6.16. Purification of D-oxynitrilase from sweet almond. The crude preparation
was subjected to gel chromatography on a 4 × 120 cm column of Sephadex G-100
in 0.1 M acetate buffer *p*H 5.0 containing 0.4 M NaCl. The first peak was found to
contain high molecular weight proteins with phosphatase and β-galactosidase activity. The second peak contained β-glucosidase, the third peak the D-oxynitrilase
under study, the fourth peak low molecular weight protein components and the
fifth peak pyridium acetate and other salts that had been added in earlier steps in
the procedure. After Becker and Pfeil (1966).

molecular weight, the second the β-glucosidase, the third the D-oxy-nitrilase and the two last peaks low molecular weight contaminants. After rechromatography on the same column, about 1 g of pure D-oxynitrilase is obtained per kg of starting material. This enzyme could then be characterized by immunological and by physico-chemical methods. One unusual feature of this enzyme is that it is a flavoenzyme that is not involved in any redox reaction.

Gel chromatography is very often used in the resolution of plasma proteins. Some analytical applications of this have been indicated in § 6.2.2. Fig. 6.5 gives the elution behaviour of some important plasma proteins. One elegant example of the purification of an important plasma protein, the transferrin, has been given by Killander (1964a). From fig. 6.5 it can be seen that transferrin is eluted in the first part of the albumin peak when chromatographed on Sephadex G-200. By pooling the fractions containing the transferrin and applying them to an anion exchanger column eluted with a tris – HCl gradient, it was possible to elute the transferrin separated from the albumin. The transferrin prepared in this way was shown by immunoelectrophoresis and starch-gel electrophoresis to be homogeneous. This material was less denatured than material prepared by precipitation methods. The elution patterns obtained are illustrated in fig. 6.17.

Fractionation of nucleic acids on agarose gels has been studied by Öberg and Philipson (1967). In work with different nucleic acid prepa-rations from various sources they used beaded agarose manufactured in their own laboratory. Fig. 6.18 gives the separation obtained when KB cell nucleic acids and poliovirus RNA were separated on a 2.1×60 cm column of 1 % beaded agarose in 0.002 M sodium phosphate, 0.001 M $MgCl_2$, pH 6.0. The chromatographic run allows the KB cell DNA, the ribosomal RNA and the soluble RNA to be separated from each other and from the poliovirus RNA although the bed height was not in this case sufficient to bring about complete resolution. The two types of ribosomal RNA remained unresolved in this system. The influence of the concentration of the gel matrix in the gel is given in fig. 6.19. This figure shows that the DNA which is completely excluded even on agarose gel goes with the void volume irrespective of the gel matrix concentra-

Subject index p. 391

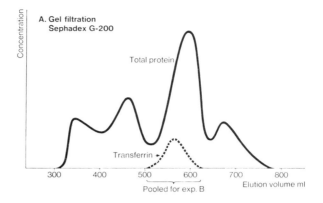

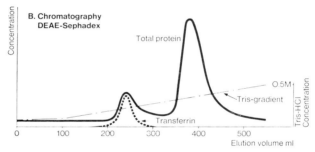

Fig. 6.17. Purification of transferrin labelled with ^{59}Fe from lipoprotein-depleted human serum by gel chromatography on Sephadex G-200 and ion-exchanger chromatography on DEAE-Sephadex A-50. The following experimental conditions were used: 6.5 ml of serum with low iron content and high transferrin concentration was incubated with ^{59}Fe-ferriammonium citrate (6.5 µg Fe) for two hours. After addition of 1 ml 5.3% hemoglobin solution, gel chromatography was performed on a 4.2×72.5 cm column of Sephadex G-200 in 0.1 M tris–HCl buffer pH 8.0, containing 1 M NaCl and 0.01% Merthiolate. The flow rate was 20 ml/hr. The protein concentration was monitored from the absorbancy at 254 nm and the transferrin was determined from the radioactivity. The fractions containing the transferrin were subsequently chromatographed on a 2.2×25 cm column of DEAE-Sephadex A-50 in 0.05 M tris–HCl buffer pH 8.0. The elution was performed with the gradient of tris–HCl buffer concentration. In this case, the protein concentration was determined by a modified Folin method and the transferrin was determined from the radioactivity. From Killander (1964a).

tion. The other nucleic acids pass into the gel increasingly when the agarose concentration is decreased in the gel. As indicated in § 3.9, the method of preparation of the gel also influences the fractionation properties. This is illustrated by the observation of Öberg and Philipson that 2 % agarose gel supplied by Pharmacia Fine Chemicals (an experimental batch of Sepharose) had the same fractionation properties as the 1 % agarose gel manufactured in their own laboratory. The influence of the composition of the buffer was also investigated. It was found that the elution characteristics of DNA and soluble RNA were unaffected by increases in salt concentration or urea concentration. Ribosomal RNA, on the other hand, was retarded by high salt concentration and eluted earlier in the presence of urea.

Fractionation of animal viruses on agar gels was reported by Bengtsson and Philipson (1964). The effect of the charged groups was counteracted by the use of fairly high ionic strength (ionic strength about 0.15, phosphate buffer containing NaCl, KCl, $CaCl_2$ and $MgCl_2$). The agar was in beaded form, produced from 2.5 % solution. On 2×30 cm beds, it was possible to separate influenza virus type A with a diameter of 100 nm and particle weight $170 \cdot 10^6$ from polio virus type 1, with a diameter of 28 nm and a particle weight of $6.8 \cdot 10^6$. ECHO virus

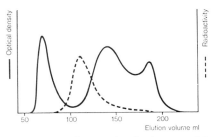

Fig. 6.18. Chromatography of a mixture of poliovirus RNA labelled with 30×10^3 cpm of ^{32}P and 1 mg of KB cell nucleic acids in 1.5 ml sample volume on a 2.1×60 cm column of 1 % agarose gel in 0.002 M phosphate buffer pH 6.0 containing 0.001 M $MgCl_2$. The KB cell nucleic acid (full line) was determined by its light absorption at 260 nm and the poliovirus RNA (dotted line), having too low concentration to be detected optically, was determined by its radioactivity. From Öberg and Philipson (1967).

Subject index p. 391

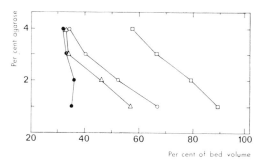

Fig. 6.19. Elution volume of different nucleic acids on agarose of varying concentration. The remaining experimental conditions correspond to those in fig. 6.18. ● KB cell DNA; ○ KB cell ribosomal RNA; △ poliovirus RNA; □ KB cell soluble RNA. From Öberg and Philipson (1967).

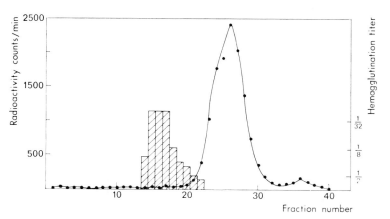

Fig. 6.20. Separation of ^{32}P-labelled poliovirus type A and influenza virus type A (Shope) on a 2×30 cm column of 2.5% agar gel in phosphate buffer containing NaCl, KCl, CaCl$_2$, MgCl$_2$ and Tween. The poliovirus (full dots) was determined from its radioactivity and the influenza virus from the hemagglutination titre (shaded squares). From Bengtsson and Philipson (1964).

type 7, with a diameter of 24 nm, and adenovirus with 80 nm diameter, could also be separated, while poliovirus (28 nm) and ECHO virus type 7 (24 nm) could not be separated by this method. Fig. 6.20 shows the separation obtained between polio virus and influenza virus. A practical application of this separation is the purification of ECHO virus from cell fragments. The cell fragments were eluted at the void volume, well separated from the virus. This method for purification of virus has been reported also for other types of virus (Čech 1962; Steere and Ackers 1962; Steere 1963) and seems to work in separation and purification of cell particles as well (Hjertén 1962b).

Fractionation processes have also been performed on a large scale, although not on the very large scale used in group separation (see § 6.3.1). The most important of these large scale applications are purification processes for plasma proteins, enzymes and hormones. When the soft gel types are used in columns with diameters larger than 5–10 cm, the flow rate often continues to decrease for a very long time. To be able to work under sufficiently good flow conditions it is therefore in these cases often necessary to use a column arrangement allowing inversion of the column at regular intervals (see § 5.15).

Subject index p. 391

CHAPTER 7

Thin-layer gel chromatography

7.1. General

In thin-layer chromatography, the chromatographic bed is formed as a layer supported by a plate. Although the principle for the fractionation is the same as in column chromatography, the technique is entirely different and the applications to a very large extent are different also.

Thin-layer chromatography has almost without exception been used for analytical purposes. For this application, it has the advantage that only very small amounts of substance are required. This is particularly important for biochemists who have often very limited amounts of substance at their disposal. For a thin-layer experiment, only a few microliters of sample solution containing some micrograms of substance are required for each experiment. The separation is rapid. This not only implies a saving of time, but makes it possible to carry through separations of sensitive substances with limited life-time. The resolution is considerably better than the resolution that would have been obtained on a column of the same length. The technique is simple and each run takes a limited time to set up. In addition, several different samples can be run on the same plate. This makes it possible to use it as a quick trial method. This is a considerable advantage when working with a large number of samples, for instance fractions from a fractionation experiment. Gel chromatography in thin-layer is also extremely useful for rapid estimation of molecular weights and the sample can be chromatographed on the same plate as the reference substances. From a practical standpoint, thin-layer chromatography is entirely different from column chromatography. Instead of having the bed enclosed in a tube, it forms a layer on the surface of a plate. The methods used for production of flow in the bed and for detection of the substances are completely different. While the flow in columns is regulated with pumps or with the level of the eluant container and the outlet, capillary forces are used to produce the flow in thin-layer chromatography on most types of chromatographic media. This method cannot, however, be used in thin-layer gel chromatography. In column chromatography, the substances are usually eluted from the column, while in thin-layer chromatography the substances are detected before elution. For this reason, the primary parameter is not elution volume but rather distance migrated.

7.2. Differences between ordinary thin-layer chromatography and thin-layer gel chromatography

Two ways of achieving the flow of liquid are used in thin-layer chromatography. The flow may be produced by capillary forces in the layer. In this case the sample is applied as small spots on a dry plate. The plate is then placed with one end in a container for the eluant. The liquid flows upwards into the layer by capillary attraction. This principle is used in chromatography on silica, alumina, cellulose etc.

The other way of producing a flow is to use the force of gravity. In this case the plate is wet during the whole operation. The liquid is transported to the plate by a strip of filter paper, and on the other end of the plate another strip of filter paper carries away the eluant that has passed through the bed. The plate is usually inclined downwards, although it may also be placed horizontally, in which case the flow is produced by the difference in levels of the liquids into which the filter paper strips are immersed.

In thin-layer gel chromatography the second of these methods is usually used to produce the flow. The reason for this is two-fold. One is entirely practical. With the gels in use at present, especially the dense ones, it has sometimes been found difficult to produce dry layers, as they tend to crack during drying. In addition many gels (notably the

agarose gels) cannot be dried and re-wetted reversibly. The second reason is of more fundamental nature. When the liquid passes through
layers of alumina into a dry region, the front advances at approximately the same rate as the liquid following later in the layer. When liquid
passes into a layer of dry xerogel, the gel at the front swells, and in
this process the particles take up water. Liquid is thus consumed at the
front. This liquid is derived from the wet part of the layer and therefore
the flow rate in the wet part of the layer is higher than the rate at
which the front is advancing. Thus, substances that are not strongly
retarded move up to the front and accumulate there (if they were not
at the front from the beginning). These substances consequently
acnnot be separated (or may give a very poor separation due to the
nfiite rate of swelling of the gel particles).

As the plates in thin-layer gel chromatography may be difficult to
dry, the chromatograms are often developed by a special technique,
where the liquid in the layers is transferred to paper and developed on
the paper in the same way as paper chromatograms.

7.3.   Equipment for thin-layer gel chromatography

For thin-layer gel chromatography, ordinary glass plates for thin-layer
chromatography can be used. Also glass microscope slides have been
sued for certain purposes.

Ordinary spreading apparatus for thin-layer chromatography may
be used. A very simple and reliable device for spreading is a straight
stainless steel rod equipped with collars at both ends. The thickness
of the collars corresponds to the thickness of the layer (0.5–1 mm
in most cases). The procedure for spreading will be described in
the section dealing with the experimental technique.

The equipment required to run thin-layer gel chromatography is not
commercially available, as downward flow thin-layer chromatography
is not a standard procedure. It can be made by the researcher himself
with various degrees of technical complication. The simplest forms of
equipment consist of some plastic strips of suitable thickness to keep
a cover some millimeters above the plate and some clamps to keep the

strips and the cover in position. In addition, two small trays are required: one for the liquid to be fed into the layer and one to collect the liquid emerging from the layer. To connect the layer to the liquid containers, strips of thick filter paper (e.g. Whatman 3 MM) are used (see fig. 7.1). One such simple sandwich-chamber has been described by Determann and Michel (1965). For the purpose of routine experiments, more advanced equipment is desirable. Fig. 7.2 shows a thin-layer gel chromatography apparatus used at Pharmacia Fine Chemicals AB. The liquid fed into the layer is placed in the upper container and that emerging from the layer is collected in the lower container. Such a device can easily be made in any laboratory workshop. The inclination can be regulated by inserting wooden blocks under the upper end. In all designs described, it is valuable to have a slit in the cover for application of the sample. In this way, the whole cover need not be removed during sample application. This will reduce the disturbance of the system due to evaporation of liquid from the layer. The slit should be covered with tape when not in use.

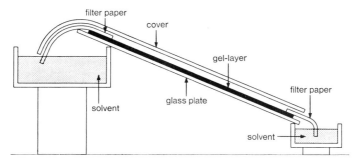

Fig. 7.1. Simple experimental set-up for thin-layer gel chromatography. The part of the cover over the plate and that over the filter paper wick are conveniently made separately. The cover should have a slit close to the upper end of the plate to facilitate sample application. The cover is kept at the right position over the glass plate by strips of some plastic material along the sides of the glass plate and clamps pressing the cover down on the plastic strips. The cover over the filter paper wick is required to keep the eluant from evaporating and changing its composition during passage. From 'Sephadex – gel filtration in theory and practice', by Pharmacia Fine Chemicals.

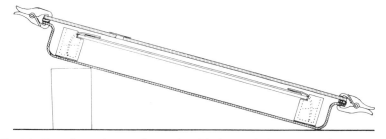

Fig. 7.2. Experimental set-up for routine thin-layer gel chromatography. A photographic tray or some other shallow tray may serve as outer container, with a perspex cover and troughs at the upper and lower end made from PVC, perspex or some other suitable material. The troughs must be equipped with grooves to keep the plate in position when the device is inclined.

For development of spots on the thin-layer chromatograms, the same equipment that is ordinarily used for development of paper chromatograms or other thin-layer chromatograms can be used.

7.4. Preparation of the plate

The gels for thin-layer gel chromatography are selected on the same principles and treated in the same manner as those for column chromatography (§ 5.1), but the finest grade material available should be used. The sieve fractions of dry powder centred around 20–30 μ are most suitable, and coarse grains are preferably sieved away.

After the gel has been allowed to swell for a sufficient time it is allowed to settle. The supernatant above the gel is decanted off almost completely except in the case of dense gels which require a small amount of liquid to be left above the gel. After gentle stirring the slurry has approximately the right consistency for spreading. The best thickness of the slurry varies somewhat with the type of gel and with the spreading device and should be found by trial and error.

The glass plate should be thoroughly cleaned by washing with hot detergent solution and rinsing in distilled water. If the plates are contaminated, the spreading of the gel will usually be unsatisfactory

Fig. 7.3. Simple spreading device consisting of a straight rod equipped with collars of electrical tape at the ends to keep it at suitable distance from the plate.

and the contamination may also interfere with the detection of the substances.

For spreading the plates, the spreading devices for thin-layer chromatography on the market can be used, as mentioned in § 7.3. The procedure of spreading is described by the manufacturers of the spreading devices. A simple spreading device that can be made from materials available from the laboratory workshop is the following: A straight rod of stainless steel of a length slightly exceeding the width of the plate is equipped with collars at both ends. The collars should have the same thickness as the layer that one plans to produce and can be made by winding PVC insulating tape around the ends of the rod. The gel slurry is placed on the plate and is spread by moving the rod back and forth over the plate with the collars sliding along the sides of the plate (see fig. 7.3). When the layer is spread, it adheres instantly to the plate without need for added fixative. The layers should be fairly thick; between 0.5 and 1 mm layer thickness is usually most suitable.

7.5.   Set-up of apparatus and chromatographic run

When the layer has been spread, the plate should be left undisturbed for a few minutes and subsequently be placed in a moist chamber to prevent evaporation. The most convenient way of doing this is usually to place the plate in position in the chamber where the run is to take place and to connect the paper wicks. It is important that the chamber be absolutely airtight, as drying will ruin the plate. If it is essential to save space and chromatographic chambers, the plates can be stored in a closed box. Before the sample is applied, the plate should be stored wet for at least 10–15 hr. The reason for this is not quite clear; it may be that during storage the liquid is evenly distributed through the layer.

After this equilibration period, the sample can be applied. Samples to be applied as spots (in contrast to lines across the plate) should have a volume of 1–5 μl. They can be applied through a micropipette or a thin glass tube which should not be allowed to touch the layer. When the sample is being applied, there is a local excess of liquid at this spot. If the plate is inclined, the liquid will tend to float on top of the layer, producing oblong spots. For this reason, the plate should be kept horizontal during sample application. Another method for sample application that seems to give satisfactory results and that is simple to perform is to cut small pieces of filter paper (1×1 mm), soak them in the sample solution, remove excess liquid by touching it to another piece of filter paper and to put the piece of filter paper on top of the gel layer. The piece of filter paper does not seem to interfere with the chromatographic run. As with column chromatography, the viscosity of the sample should not be too high, as this tends to disturb the flow pattern.

The flow rate of the liquid in the layer is adjusted by regulating the inclination of the plate. The most suitable inclination seems to be 10–20°. At this inclination substances that are completely excluded will migrate about 1–2 cm/hr. (The rate of migration of a substance that is completely excluded corresponds to the flow rate of the liquid in the interstitial space.) A 20-cm standard plate thus requires about one working day to develop.

In contrast to thin-layer chromatography on dry plates, there is no front marking the extent to which the plate has been developed. For this reason some suitable coloured marker substance should be run on the plate together with the samples under study. Various substances have been used. Blue Dextran, the standard marker substance for similar purposes, has a rather faint colour at the concentrations where it does not increase the viscosity of the sample excessively, but it can nevertheless be used. Other substances that have been used are DNP-amino acids, vitamin B_{12}, coloured proteins like hemoglobin, bromphenol blue-stained albumin or fluorescein isothiocyanate-conjugated proteins (that can be detected by their fluorescence in ultraviolet light). Fluorescein isothiocyanate-conjugated proteins seem to be best, while DNP-amino acids move too slowly to be of much use. If the marker substance penetrates into the gel grains, the progress of the 'front' can be calculated from the R-value of the substance. It may be an advantage to use a substance that falls within the fractionation range of the gel, as it can be used as a reference substance in the evaluation of the plate.

7.6. Detection of the substances

Coloured substances and fluorescent substances can be detected on the plate by visual inspection or photography of the moist plate. For other substances, staining is required. This can be carried out on the wet plate in some instances (Andrews 1964; Roberts 1966).

Like other thin-layer plates, gel plates may be dried, but the procedure is not simple: plates covered with hard gels particularly have a great tendency to crack during drying as mentioned in § 7.2. For this reason the drying should be performed under mild conditions. The plates seem to dry best and with least risk of cracking, if they are allowed to dry from the bottom, keeping the surface relatively moist. Determann (1967) indicates that the plates should be dried at about 50 °C in an atmosphere that is kept moist by placing wet filter paper in the oven. Another method that seems to work well in many instances

Subject index p.391

is to place the plate on a heated surface, for instance a slightly heated electric plate, about 50–70 °C.

After drying, the plates are stable mechanically and can be easily handled. They can be stained in solutions causing some – very limited – swelling of the gel, as this will give the stain access to the substances in the layer (see appendix 3). The most reliable method for detection and staining of the substances in the layer is to transfer the substances to filter paper and to stain them on the paper. A sheet of thick filter paper, for instance Whatman 3 MM, is laid on the plate. By starting from one side of the plate and working smoothly and relatively fast, it is possible to cover the plate without disturbing the layer excessively and without trapping any air bubbles between the paper and the plate. After about one minute, the liquid in the layer has been transferred to the paper, which can then be removed and dried. Staining is then performed by the conventional methods of paper chromatography. Enzymes may also be detected by suitable methods.

In appendix 3, some methods for staining plates and papers are given.

7.7. Two-dimensional thin-layer techniques

To obtain better resolution of complex mixtures of proteins, thin-layer gel chromatography may be coupled to electrophoresis or to immuno-diffusion to achieve two-dimensional resolution of the sample. (For techniques of immunodiffusion see manual by Clausen.)

When thin-layer gel chromatography is coupled to electrophoresis, the gel chromatographic experiment is run in the buffer used for the electrophoresis. After the chromatographic run has been completed, an electric field is applied at right angles to the direction of chromato-graphy. The apparatus for the experiment may be built to allow both the chromatography and the electrophoresis to be performed in the same chamber by just turning the plate through 90° (Hanson et al. 1966a, b). After the experiment has been completed, the plate is developed in the same way as with ordinary thin-layer gel chromato-graphy.

Gel chromatography may also be coupled to immunodiffusion to give two-dimensional patterns. Some authors have tried to apply agar to the thin-layer plate, to make it suited for the immunodiffusion, after the gel chromatographic run (Carnegie and Pacheco 1964; Hanson et al. 1966a, b; Johansson and Rymo 1966). These methods still seem to be quite complicated. Grant and Everall (1965) performed the immunoelectrophoresis without any stabilizing medium between the gel grains. Agostoni et al. (1967) transferred the proteins from the thin-layer plate to a sheet of cellulose acetate membrane, where the immunodiffusion was allowed to take place. This seems to be the easiest and best technique so far. A similar technique has been used by Williamson and Allison (1967) with agar as stabilizing medium.

7.8. *Applications of thin-layer gel chromatography*

Thin-layer gel chromatography has been used mainly for studies of proteins and peptides, although some cases have been reported where other types of substances have been fractionated: DNP-amino acids (Reith and Brown 1966), mucopolysaccharides (Roberts 1966), nucleotides (Stickland 1965).

The most important application is the estimation of molecular weights of proteins and peptides. The first report of thin-layer gel chromatography (Wieland et al. 1962) also mentions a simple molecular weight estimation of plastein (the polymers formed from amino acids and low molecular weight peptides under the influence of proteases and peptidases).

The first investigators using downward flow on a wet plate were Johansson and Rymo (1962). They studied the chromatography of amino acids, protein hydrolysates and some low molecular weight proteins on Sephadex G-25 fine, Sephadex G-50 fine and Sephadex G-75 fine. Although they discuss to some extent the relationship between molecular weight and chromatographic behaviour, they do not make any thorough study of the subject. The first methodological study of the molecular weight determination with thin-layer gel filtration was undertaken by Andrews (1964), who found a close correlation between molecular weight and chromatographic properties for proteins on

Sephadex· G-100 that could be used for molecular weight determination (fig. 7.4). Morris (1964) made a comparison between the
chromatographic behaviour of proteins on thin-layer and column. He
found a linear relationship between the R-value on the thin-layer
plates and the K-values from the columns – although there should
theoretically be a linear relationship between the inverse of the R-
value and the K-value (see § 2.4). The discrepancy may be explained
by the short range over which the R-values and the K-values are
determined.

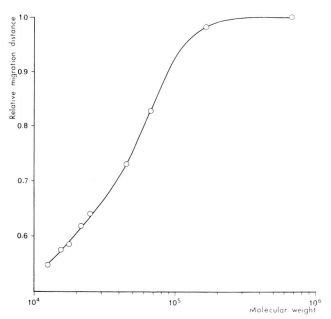

Fig. 7.4. Correlation between thin-layer chromatographic behaviour and molecular
properties: Relative migration distances for proteins as function of molecular
weight (on logarithmic scale) in thin-layer gel chromatography on Sephadex G-100
Superfine. The following proteins were used in the measurements: cytochrome c,
M 12,400; α-lactalbumin, M 15,500; myoglobin, M 17,800; soya bean trypsin inhibitor, M 21,500; chymotrypsinogen, M 25,000; ovalbumin, M 45,000; serum albumin, M 67,000; human and bovine gamma-globulins, M 165,000; thyroglobulin,
M 670,000. From Andrews (1964).

One example of the use of thin-layer gel chromatography for molecular weight estimation is provided by Ohno and Morrison (1966) in their study of the constitution of the hagfish hemoglobin. To determine its molecular weight, these authors applied a hagfish erythrocyte hemolysate to a thin-layer plate with Sephadex G-75 in 0.1 M phosphate buffer pH 7.4. As standard substances, monomer cytochrome (M 12,000), soy bean trypsin inhibitor (M 21,500), and lactoperoxidase (M 80,000) were used. For comparison, human hemoglobin and trout hemoglobin were also included in the experiment. The hagfish hemoglobin was found to have a molecular weight of 18,000, as compared to the 60,000 obtained for human and trout hemoglobin. This indicated that the hagfish hemoglobin is monomeric with only one heme group for each molecule, as compared to the tetrameric hemoglobin found in most vertebrates. As hagfish is one of the most primitive vertebrates, this gives an indication of the development of the hemoglobin molecule in the course of evolution of the vertebrates. A similar investigation by column gel chromatography (Arnheim et al. 1967) of the hagfish muscle lactate dehydrogenase indicates a tetrameric form of this enzyme in this primitive vertebrate. This is similar to the tetrameric from of the enzyme in higher vertebrates.

Another important application of thin-layer gel chromatography is the characterization of body fluids and detection of pathological proteins. As the protein composition of body fluids is extremely complex, two-dimensional techniques have been much used for this purpose. Particularly gel chromatography-electrophoresis gives very clear fingerprints and allows clear characterization of the paraproteins. Hanson et al. (1966a) have studied two-dimensional thin-layer gel chromatography-electrophoresis of normal and pathological samples of serum and spinal fluid on Sephadex G-200 plates in barbital buffers at pH 8.4. Under these conditions they were able to resolve and characterize the paraproteins on plates 20×20 cm.

Harrison and Northam (1966) used a slightly different technique in their studies of urinary proteins. After the gel chromatographic run on the thin-layer plate, they transferred the proteins on to filter paper

Subject index p. 391

and conducted the electrophoresis on the paper. From such studies, conclusions could be drawn concerning the renal function.

Another example of the use of thin-layer gel chromatography was reported by Brighton (1966). When checking the quality of commercial preparations of fluorescent antisera, he used, among other methods thin-layer technique with Sephadex G-200. In this way he could distinguish between free fluorescein isothiocyanate, fluorescent albumin and fluorescent antibodies.

CHAPTER 8

Special techniques

8.1. Basket centrifuge separation

In ordinary chromatography only solutions of limited viscosity can be treated (see § 5.11). This makes it impossible to treat concentrated solutions of macromolecules. Recently a method has been developed at Pharmacia Fine Chemicals AB, Uppsala, by which solutions with viscosities up to 2,000 centipoise may be investigated (Gelotte and Emnéus 1966; Emnéus 1968). The process is limited to group separation processes. The great advantage of the process is that it allows preparative desalting and removal of low weight constituents from concentrated solutions of high molecular weight substances. The yields are good, the dilution of the solutions is small and the process is very rapid.

For the process a basket centrifuge is required (fig. 8.1). This consists of a cylindrical perforated drum rotating around the vertical axis. A lining can be fitted inside the drum. This lining, which consists of porous plastic, allows liquid to pass, while solid particles are retained. For suppliers of material, see appendix 1. The liquid that is spun out by the rotation of the drum is collected by an outer container with an outlet. Basket centrifuges are available in varying sizes, from small table models for laboratory use to large units.

The process described here was developed for the gel type Sephadex G-25. Other types can certainly be used, but it may be necessary to change the procedure to adapt it to the gel. The process is the following: The centrifuge is filled at rest with a relatively thin suspension of Sepha-

 Subject index p. 391

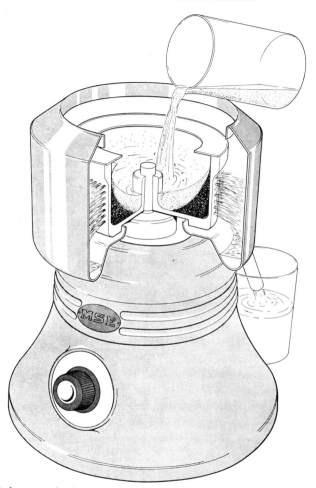

Fig. 8.1. Laboratory basket centrifuge. The basket is revolving around a vertical axis and its cylindrical outer surface is perforated to allow the liquid to escape and lined on the inside with a porous plastic lining. Basket centrifuges are available in sizes ranging from laboratory models with a few liters capacity up to very large centrifuges with basket capacities of several hundred liters. The picture was prepared by MSE, London.

dex G-25. The amount of gel should be sufficient to form a cake that does not completely fill the space in the basket that is intended for the solids. The speed of the centrifuge is then raised until the centripetal acceleration at the periphery is 1,000 g. The centrifuge is run at this speed until no more liquid leaves it, indicating that all the liquid in the interstitial space has been removed from the cake. The gel forms an even layer around the inner surface of the basket. At this point the speed of the centrifuge is decreased until the centripetal acceleration corresponds to 60 g. The sample is then applied simply by pouring it directly onto the central part of the basket (fig. 8.1). The volume of the sample should be 15–20% of the volume of the gel layer along the periphery. The centrifuge is left running at the same rate for about 10 min, during which the solution progresses through the gel layer. The speed is then increased to 1,000 g and the liquid that is spun out is collected. This liquid contains the high molecular weight constituents. Nearly quantitative yields have been obtained. The volume eluted is practically the same as that applied. The salts can be removed from the gel cake by reducing the speed to 60 g and washing with distilled water to wash away the salts. After washing a new cycle can be started. With coarse grade material, the salts are best removed by stopping the centrifuge and resuspending the gel in distilled water. It should be added that when the centrifuge is stopped the cake cracks, and it is therefore necessary to make a new suspension from the gel once the centrifuge has been brought to standstill.

TABLE 8.1

Grades of Sephadex G-25 suited for centrifuge separation at different relative viscosities

Relative sample viscosity (20 °C)	Grade of gel material
1–50	Superfine
5–200	Fine
50–700	Medium
200–2,000	Coarse

Subject index p. 391

Different particle size should be used for different viscosities. Table 8.1 gives the sieve fractions of Sephadex G-25 to be used for solutions of different viscosity.

A method similar to that described may be applied using ordinary laboratory centrifuges, swing-out bucket heads and filter inserts (Flodin 1962a, p. 31; Determann 1967). In this case, the gel slurry is pipetted into the filter insert in the centrifuge tube. After the void volume has been spun out (Determann 1967 indicates 20 min at 1,300 rpm in a centrifuge with 8.3 cm distance between the filter and the centrifuge axis in work with Sephadex G-25 fine) the sample is carefully added to the gel cake. During the following centrifugation, the substances of high molecular weight collect in the tube, while the low molecular weight components are retained in the gel cake.

8.2. *Chromatography with mixed solvents*

Because of their hydrophilic character many of the gel materials intended for ordinary gel chromatography are well suited as supports in classical straight phase partition chromatography. Gels have been used in such partition chromatography for the purification of peptides, antibiotics and nucleic acids (Tanaka et al. 1962; Wells and Dittmer 1963; Schmidt-Kastner 1964; Zeleznick 1964; Yamashiro 1964). This application does not, however, fall within the scope of this treatise, and the reader is referred to standard textbooks on the subject.

In this connection it is worth-while mentioning that when mixed solvents are used, the composition of the liquid in the gel and in the interstitial space may be different, even if the mixed solvent does not in itself produce a two phase system. The separation result will thus be influenced by the difference in composition of the liquids in the gel and the interstitial volume, when mixed eluants are used.

8.3. *Zone precipitation*

The different mobility of salts and of proteins on gel beds can be used for separation of proteins by a method described by Porath (1962).

Unfortunately the technique has attracted very little attention, although it may be valuable for many applications.

The method is based on the reversible precipitation of proteins that occurs when the concentration of a precipitating agent (for instance ammonium sulphate) reaches a certain point. When this precipitation is performed batchwise, the separation that is obtained is usually rather crude. By allowing the precipitation to take place in a gradient of precipitant carried down the chromatographic bed, a considerably sharper fractionation may be obtained. In practice the method is performed in the following way: The precipitating agent that is moving slowly on the bed is applied first. During the application of the precipitating agent the concentration of the solution is decreased, so that a concentration gradient is formed. Immediately after the solution of the precipitating agent has been applied, the solution of the protein is allowed to follow. The column is then eluted with non-precipitating solution. The volume of the solution of the precipitating agent should be calculated so that the front of the precipitating agent zone and the protein zone would reach the outlet at the same time, if the protein were not precipitated. This means that the volume of the solution of precipitating agent is approximately 60% of the column volume, if the proteins are moving in the void volume and the precipitating agent penetrates completely into the gel. The process is illustrated in fig. 8.2.

The proteins overtake the precipitating agent, and finally reach a concentration of precipitant that makes them come out of solution. As the gradient progresses, the proteins precipitate and redissolve, moving through the column at the rate of the gradient. Each substance will be eluted at a precipitant concentration just below its minimum solubility, and will be separated accordingly.

The disadvantages with zone precipitation are that the precipitated particles may to a certain extent be carried along with the stream of liquid, impeding resolution, and that the concentration of precipitant at which precipitation occurs is not absolutely defined (the solubility of the protein decreases gradually and the precipitation and redissolution are fairly slow processes).

Subject index p. 391

Porath (1962) used zone precipitation to fractionate the serum proteins that were eluted in the third peak in chromatography of serum on Sephadex (see fig. 6.5). In this experiment he obtained a separation of the substances into three different fractions. The first fraction contained albumin, ferritin and some α_1-globulin, the second α_1-,

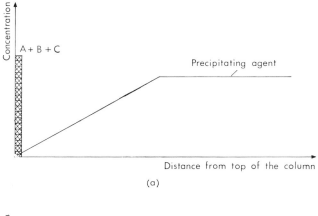

(a)

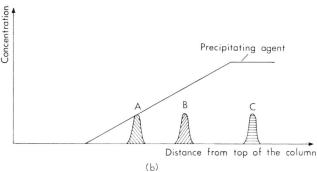

(b)

Fig. 8.2. The principle of zone precipitation. Three substances are applied simultaneously to a column after a gradient of a precipitating agent has been established. They all move faster than the precipitating agent until they reach the concentrations at which they precipitate. A and B precipitate and redissolve, thereby moving at the rate of the gradient. Substance C is not precipitated by the agent and moves through the column at its original rate. From Porath (1962).

α_2- and β-globulins while the third peak contained another two globulin fractions. The precipitant used in the experiment was ammonium sulphate and the analysis of the proteins was performed by paper electrophoresis.

8.4. Zone electrophoresis

In the development of Sephadex, Flodin originally intended to use the material as supporting medium for column electrophoresis. The medium was found to give good results. The energy dissipation in the column is higher than with other supporting materials for column electrophoresis, as the gel particles (and not only the liquid in the interstitial space) conduct the current. On the other hand, sharp and well-defined zones result. The electro-osmotic flow is very low and the protein adsorption is negligible. The material is very easy to handle and can be used in columns, troughs and on thin layers (Gelotte et al. 1962; Dose and Krause 1962; Vendrely et al. 1964; Loontiens and De Bruyne 1963).

As the laboratory technique is similar to other types of electrophoresis and as electrophoresis does not fall within the scope of this treatise, the reader is referred to standard textbooks on the subject.

8.5. Concentration

In certain instances protein solutions have been concentrated by swelling gels in the solutions. The gels take up the liquid and the low molecular weight substances, leaving the proteins in the solution. This concentration will thus not involve any considerable change in the ionic environment, as would an evaporation step (Flodin et al. 1960). The degree of concentration that can be achieved is limited to $2 \times$ to $3 \times$ for each step.

The concentration step is very fast, an important feature in work with substances with a limited stability. It can be used for concentration of both large and small quantities of liquid with a limited amount of equipment. To separate the gel from the protein solution, only a basket centrifuge (in the treatment of larger quantities) or a laboratory centrifuge with swing-out head and filtration inserts (for smaller quantities) are required. In these respects, this method is superior to membrane concentration methods. On the other hand, some work is required to wash and dry the gel after the concentration. For test-tube scale concentration, where only a few grams are used, it is, however, hardly worth the work to wash and dry the gel instead of throwing it away. If somewhat diminished yields can be tolerated, a filter can be used instead of a centrifuge.

In particular, this concentration method can be useful for the concentration of very dilute protein solutions. Kibukamusoke and Wilks (1965) have used the method for concentration of urine prior to electrophoresis. In this way they have been able to study the proteins in urine in tropical disorders. Another case, where the starting protein concentration is low, is in the case of preparation of extracellular enzymes. Pettersson et al. (1963) used concentration with Sephadex as initial step in their preparation of the extracellular cellulase from the basidiomycete *Polyporus versicolor*. They concentrated 85 l of fermentation broth to 315 ml without appreciable losses of activity. Another case where concentration with dry gel is advantageous is when it is essential that the composition of the solution remain unchanged in the concentration step. Painter and McVicar (1963) used Sephadex G-25 for concentration of fibrolysin activated in glycerol, prior to injection. In a separate experiment they confirmed that the change in the composition of the water–glycerol solution was negligible during the concentration process. In one step they achieved a three-fold concentration with 96 % yield of fibrolysin activity.

8.6. *Salt gradient elution*

Beling (1963) developed a technique for purification and enrichment of urinary conjugated oestrogens that is worth mentioning separately. The technique has been used for clinical analysis of oestrogens and has found a widespread use.

The procedure used is the following: The urine is applied to the column and eluted with distilled water. At the high salinity of the urine the oestrogens are strongly retarded. In distilled water the retardation is, however, much less. The difference has been explained as an ion exclusion effect at the lower ionic strength. The retardation of the oestrogens at high ionic strength is so strong that they move slower than the salt zone. At the rear part of the salt zone where the salt concentration is decreasing, the oestrogens are accumulated at the ionic strength where their velocity corresponds to the velocity of the salt zone. The oestrogens are eluted in two sharp bands, considerably narrower than the original urine sample. The chromatographic run in this case causes concentration and focusing of the oestrogens by the influence of the salt gradient.

CHAPTER 9

Some notes on the mechanism of gel chromatography

A very naive interpretation of the mechanism of gel chromatography was given in § 1.2. The starting point for this discussion was the assumption that the molecules in the bed are transported in a random manner. During one interval a given molecule passes into the interstitial liquid and travels at the same rate as the molecules that cannot penetrate into the gel phase, i.e. with the rate of flow of the interstitial liquid. During other intervals the molecule penetrates into the gel. Although the molecule is still in perpetual thermal movement it is statistically stationary as there is no bulk flow through the gel. On the average the molecule thus travels down the bed at a rate that is proportional to that part of the time which it spends in the interstitial volume. As this average for a given molecule over a long period of time can be shown to be equal to the average over a large population of molecules at a given moment, the average rate at which the molecule travels down the bed is related in a simple way to the partition coefficient of the molecular species in question between the stationary gel phase and the interstitial liquid phase. One simple way of deriving the relationship between the elution volume and the partition coefficient is the following: The fraction of the molecules present in the void volume at a given moment is $V_0/(V_0 + KV_s)$. From the above discussion it can be concluded that this is also proportional to the rate of travel of the molecular species. The elution volume is inversely proportional to the rate of travel. As the elution volume for molecules that are completely excluded is V_0 (this can be found by a simple geometrical consideration), the elution volume for a substance with partition coefficient K will be

$$V_e = \frac{V_0(V_0 + KV_s)}{V_0} = V_0 + KV_s. \qquad (9.1)$$

The variables in the above derivation were defined in § 2.2 and § 2.4. This is the equation of Martin and Synge (1941) and Consden et al. (1944) for the elution volumes in partition chromatography, formulated in the way that is most common in gel chromatographic work.

This simple derivation can be verified by the equations of transport for chromatographic processes that also give more detailed information on the process. A discussion of these problems is however far outside the scope of this treatise, particularly as an excellent discussion on the subject can be found in Giddings (1965). It should be pointed out, however, that this relationship does not rest on any assumptions regarding the mechanisms governing the distribution between the stationary and the moving phases as has been assumed sometimes in the literature (Ohasi et al. 1966). It is also irrelevant whether the whole gel phase or only the inbibed liquid in the gel phase is considered to be V_s, as long as the partition coefficient is defined correspondingly.

As stressed in § 1.2, one of the unique characteristics of gel chromatography is the close correlation between molecular size and elution volume. This can thus be referred to a correlation between the partition coefficients and the molecular sizes. Before going into a discussion about this some other parameters appearing in the chromatographic equations of transport should, however, be discussed.

In partition chromatography, the restricted rate of diffusion between stationary phase, the longitudinal diffusion in the bed and the eddy diffusion are the factors causing zone spreading. Longitudinal diffusion is of minor importance under the conditions of ordinary gel chromatography. The most important factor, eddy diffusion, is caused by the irregularities in the flow that are caused by the particles in the bed: a solute molecule in a fast streampath will travel a longer distance than one in a slow streampath. This is a general phenomenon in chromatography and no particular discussion is required in the case of gel chromatography.

Although usually of less importance than eddy diffusion, the restricted rate of diffusion is important in many cases as far as can be judged. In ordinary partition chromatography with considerable surface energy in the surface between the phases, the restrictions to diffusion can be separated into three parts: diffusion in the stationary phase, diffusion in the moving phase, and restricted migration through the phase border. In gel chromatography, the third factor is unimportant, as there seem to be no restrictions to passage through the border. The diffusion in the free solution can be measured by conventional methods. The diffusion in the gel is more difficult to determine. Flodin (1962a) assumed the diffusion coefficient inside the gel grains to be equal to the diffusion coefficient in free solution. As the molecules are thought to be hindered sterically in other ways, their rate of diffusion is probably also influenced by the presence of the gel matrix. Morris (1966) found the rate of electrophoretic migration in thin-layer gel electrophoresis to be proportional to the partition coefficients obtained in gel chromatography in beds packed with the same gels. It seems reasonable therefore to assume that the diffusion coefficient is approximately proportional to the partition coefficient also.

Although the relationship between zone broadening and flow rate indicates that eddy diffusion rather than restricted rate of diffusion between gel and free liquid is responsible for the major zone broadening, the restricted rate of diffusion may acquire more importance in chromatography of very large macromolecules and virus.

One of the most striking features of gel chromatography that has caused most speculation is the very close correlation between molecular size and elution behaviour. One interesting consequence of this is that gel chromatography may throw some light on the structure of gels. This subject is not quite unimportant as large parts of living organisms consist of gels, and very little is known about the way the molecules are arranged in these ill-defined mixtures of unpleasant consistency.

It should be noted in this connection that it is in no way unique to find a relationship between molecular size and partition coefficient. It has been known for very long time that for a homologous series of substances, the distribution is more one-sided the more the molecular weight increases. An attempt to predict quantitatively the effect was made by Brönsted (1931). The only assumption necessary to derive an equation for the effect that is reasonably accurate was that each link in the polymer chain interacts in the same way with the environment as the other links. The contribution from each link to the difference in Gibbs free energy for the molecule in the two phases is then the same. From this the following relationship can be derived:

$$K = \exp\,(\text{const.} \times \text{M}). \tag{9.2}$$

This equation predicts, in accordance with empirical observations that for molecules of high molecular weight, the equilibria tend to be shifted more and more in favour of the one phase or the other, while substances of lower molecular weight are more evenly distributed. The equation was found to represent the behaviour of many polymers in simple two phase systems very well. The correlation between partition coefficient and molecular weight was rediscovered for chromatographic applications by Martin (1949). Bate-Smith and Westall (1950) found that the correlation could be applied – with restrictions – for many chromatographic systems. In chromatographic contexts, the logarithm of $(V_e/V_0 - 1)$, is called R_m. This parameter that differs from log K only by a constant is thus linearly related to the molecular weight of the solute. This has been used for determination of molecular weights, particularly in gas chromatography. To obtain distributions of macromolecules that are not entirely shifted in favour of one of the phases these should be chemically similar so that the contribution from each link in the molecule to the distribution is low, corresponding to low values of the constant in eq. (9.2). Such systems where the phases are similar are for instance the aqueous two phase systems of Albertsson (1960), where both phases are aqueous with small amounts of macromolecules dissolved to create phase separation. In these systems, low molecular weight components distribute evenly while the distribution of the macromolecules can be regulated by changing the composition of the system.

The tendency of macromolecules to distribute almost entirely to one of the phases is also one of the reasons for the difficulty in finding suitable chromatographic systems for proteins. If the molecules are confined to the mobile phase, they are eluted unfractionated in the void volume. If, on the other hand, they are completely taken up by the stationary phase, they will remain on the bed – equally unfractionated.

One of the reasons for the good results obtained with gels as stationary phases is that the gels are chemically very similar to the eluant. The low molecular weight substances are therefore usually evenly distributed between the phases, while the distribution of the macromolecules can be changed by changing the content of dry substance and the structure of the gel matrix.

The equation of Brönsted (9.2) can be used to explain the relationship between molecular weight and partition coefficient for substances of very similar character, for which the constant in the equation can be assumed to have the same value. In gel chromatography it was found however that the effects are of about the same order of magnitude for substances of very different character: dextrans, proteins of different kinds, nucleic acids, inorganic phosphoric acids, synthetic polymers. The constant in eq. (9.2) is of approximately the same magnitude for all these substances. For all these diverse groups of substances, the equilibrium is shifted in favour of the free liquid when the molecular weight is increased. This indicates that the distribution is governed mainly by some factor of a very general nature, influencing all these substances in approximately the same way.

The first attempt to give an explanation to this phenomenon was that of Flodin (1962a). He considers the partition of the solute between the gel and the liquid to be entirely governed by steric factors. The gel matrix chains form a net-work of varying density. Large molecules can only penetrate into regions where the meshes in the net are large. Small molecules, on the other hand, find their way into more tightly knit regions of the net-work closer to the cross-links. In this way, large molecules can only penetrate into a limited part of the gel, the permitted region. The partition coefficient corresponds to the part of the whole space that is a permitted region. The later theoretical discussions have largely been concerned with different models of the gel structure to explain the mesh width distribution that would give the proportions of permitted volume found empirically. Some of the models presented have very little chemical reality and serve only to give an equation that corresponds to the data measured empirically. Others are more closely related to known facts about the structure of gels.

Porath (1963) found that the molecular weight dependence in gel chromatography can be simulated by a model where the liquid in the gel is separated into conically shaped pores. The model is simple and easy to understand. The equation obtained is, however, somewhat too complicated to be useful practically. It is interesting to note that a correction term has been introduced for the water of hydration of the walls that cannot be exchanged for solute. Squire (1964) gives an expression that is based on the assumption that the pore size distribution corresponds to that produced by equal amounts of cones, cylinders and crevices. This approach yields an extremely large and complicated equation. Agneray (1965) uses a model where the gel matrix has been assumed to be a three-dimensional net-work, rather than the structure of pores used by Porath and by Squire. Although it seems somewhat more realistic from this point of view, the assumption that the chains of the matrix follow the edges of cubes in a cubical matrix somewhat oversimplifies the situation.

An attractive approach to the treatment of the steric effects was used by Laurent and Killander (1964). The model that they use is that the molecule is a sphere of a given radius, while the net-work is described as infinitely long straight rods that are randomly located in space. Ogston (1958) calculated the fraction of the space that is available to a sphere with radius r_s if straight cylindrical rods with radius r_r are distributed in the space in a random fashion with an average density of L length units of rod per volume unit of space. The special case

Subject index p. 391

where the rods were of infinite length was used by Laurent and Killander. The formula for the free space in this model,

$$K_{av} = \exp\left(-\pi L(r_s + r_r)^2\right), \tag{9.3}$$

was found to fit well with experimental data for microreticular gel types if L and r_r were calculated from the dimensions of the gel matrix chains known from other experiments. It should be remarked in this connection however that in Ogston's derivation, no correction is made for the fact that two gel matrix chains cannot exist simultaneously at the same point. For the highly swollen gels used by Laurent and Killander, as well as for the original discussion by Ogston about the activity of one macromolecule in solution in the presence of another, this correction is, however, small. For the macroreticular gel types, Laurent (1967) was able to extend his treatment by the assumption that the chains aggregate to form thicker fibres.

Most molecules are not spherical. As the original derivation by Ogston was valid only for spherical molecules, an extension of the formula was desired. The derivation of Ogston can easily be extended to other molecular forms as well. Thus it can easily be shown that a body with a surface that is everywhere positively curved can be accommodated in a fraction

$$K_{av} = \exp\left(-\frac{LA}{4}\right) \tag{9.4}$$

of a space without interacting with lines of average density L length units per unit volume, randomly distributed in this space. A is the surface area of the body. The derivation can be extended to bodies of more irregular shape. For these cases, the simple surface area appearing in eq. (9.4) is substituted by an expression giving the 'effective' surface area exposed outwards. It can easily be seen that for the case of a sphere the expression of Ogston (9.3) is obtained from (9.4). The extension of eq. (9.4) to the case with rods of finite thickness instead of lines is trivial.

Laurent and Killander, like other authors, have used the Stoke's radius as measure of the size of molecules of irregular shape. Although there is no direct theoretical justification for this in the case of gel chromatography, Stoke's radius is a very commonly used parameter to characterize molecular size and very good correlations have been obtained (see also Sigel and Monty 1965, 1966).

Hohn and Pollmann (1963) and Ackers (1967) have used very similar approaches to the question of the mesh size distribution. Without discussing the structure of the gel they make an assumption regarding the form of the relationship between the molecular size and the volume available to the molecule. Hohn and Pollmann assume that K_d is related to the molecular weight by a Boltzmann distribution. Their equation:

$$K_d = k_1 \exp\left(-\frac{Mk_2}{M_1}\right), \tag{9.5}$$

where M_1 is the molecular weight of the monomer and k_1 and k_2 are constants, was found to fit well for oligonucleotides. The similarities between the expressions (9.3), (9.5) and (9.2) are easy to understand considering the statistical assumptions underlying them.

Ackers assumed that the volume of the domains in the gel, where molecules of a certain radius could just reach, could be described by a normal distribution. He demonstrates very good linear relationships between the error function complement of K_d and the molecular radius (probably the Stoke's radius).

The approaches used by Hohn and Pollmann and by Ackers are in a way quite attractive as they make no definite assumptions regarding the detailed structure of the gel, but only an assumption regarding the statistics of the mesh size. On the other hand they have the disadvantage that they do not give much information about the gel.

All experimental evidence bears out the assumption that sterical hindrance in the gels is the major factor governing the partitioning of substances between gel and free liquid. The correlation between the elution behaviour and the molecular weight alone does not prove the dominating importance of the sterical hindrance as this could be explained for instance by the difference in osmotic pressure inside and outside the gel (Ginzburg and Cohen 1964, see also below). One clear indication of the steric basis for the separation in gel chromatography is given by the changes in elution behaviour that follow steric changes such as denaturation of proteins (see for instance Přistoupil 1965; Přistoupil and Ulrych 1967). Other more indirect evidence also indicates a dominating influence of the steric effects. One of these is the temperature dependence of the chromatographic behaviour. The steric effect corresponds thermodynamically to an entropy effect. If the entropy effect dominates and the enthalpy effect is small, the partition coefficient will have very little temperature dependence. For proteins, this has also been found to be the case (see for instance Kirret et al. 1966). Low molecular weight substances on tightly cross-linked gels on the other hand in some instances show considerable temperature effects (Marsden 1965). The substances that gave the most pronounced temperature effects also behaved abnormally in other ways, indicating marked interaction with the gel matrix.

Although the steric effects are the most important ones, arguments of a general physico-chemical character indicate that other factors may be involved also. One factor that has not been discussed is the influence of the elastic properties of the gel matrix (the 'osmotic pressure' in the gel). Although this quantity is difficult to measure and only rather coarse estimates of its magnitudes can be made, the pressures in the gels for chromatographic use seem to be more than sufficient to influence the partition coefficient of molecules with as high molar volumes as proteins. The pressures in ordinary gels for gel chromatography are considerably lower than those in resin ion-exchanger gels, where the pressures are in the range of hundreds of atmospheres, (an 8 % cross-linked resin in the hydrogen form, containing at saturation 12 moles of water per gram equivalent, has a swelling pressure of 160 atm; Boyd and Soldano 1953). A pressure of 0.5 atm is, however, sufficient to change the partition coefficient of albumin approximately by a factor of 2. In this calculation, it has been assumed that the process can be described only as the entrance of the protein into the gel from the outside liquid. A more correct description would include an unknown number of water molecules passing out from the gel simultaneously. Thus, ΔV for the process and the swelling pressures of the gels are not known, and the influence on the partitioning of the substances remains to be determined. In any case the osmotic effect must be assumed to influence the partitioning in gel chromatography, as it does in ionexchanger chromatography, see for instance Myers and Boyd (1956). Ginzburg and Cohen (1964) have, however, probably stressed the importance of the swelling pressure too strongly when they assume it to be the only factor governing the partitioning. As the influence of the elastic effects of the gel is proportional to the molar volumes of the molecules, it is difficult to distinguish it from the steric – both types of effects tend to exclude the molecules increasingly with increase in molecular size.

Other effects influencing the distribution of solutes between the gel phase and the free solution are the effects of electric charges of solutes. It was found very early that the results obtained at low ionic strength were anomalous. This was attributed to the presence of small amounts of charged groups (mainly carboxyl groups) in the gels. Although the gels have been improved, the effects have remained to a large extent. Some interesting observations on these effects were given by Hohn and Schaller (1967). When they chromatographed oligonucleotides, they found good agreement with (9.5) at all ionic strengths; the remarkable feature was that the oligonucleotides were increasingly excluded from the gel (and thus the parameters in (9.5) were changed) when the ionic strength was decreased. The exclusion of the oligonucleotides at low ionic strength obviously was caused by electrostatic forces, but nevertheless the solute behaviour was found to follow (9.5), designed to explain a steric mechanism. It should be pointed out that (9.2), derived without any assumptions about the mechanism, is almost identical to (9.5); this illustrates that a relationship of this kind does not necessarily indicate a steric mechanism. The phenomenon that substances are increasingly excluded from gels at decreased ionic strength has been observed in other connections. In their article Hohn and Schaller write: 'It is known that charged molecules penetrate membranes only

Subject index p. 391

if the ionic strength is sufficiently high. Similarly diffusion of charged molecules into the pores of dextran gels is not possible in distilled water but is enhanced by a rise of the buffer concentration.'

Three types of electrical mechanisms may influence the penetration of charged substances into gels. The mechanism that has been discussed earlier in connection with gel chromatography is the ion-exchanger effect. The gels contain low concentrations of carboxyl or sulphate groups and may act as very weak cation exchangers. This is, however, not sufficient to explain the effects observed. Thus, effects of qualitatively the same type (tailing etc.) can be observed with charged macromolecules irrespective of the sign of the charge. Two other types of effects should be taken into account to give a more complete picture.

The activity of a charged solute depends on the dielectric properties of the environment. The dielectric properties of the gel are somewhat different from those of the surrounding liquid. This effect should be relatively independent of the ionic strength (or at least less dependent than the ion-exchanger effect and the Donnan effect to be described). When low molecular weight ions are added to the system, they distribute relatively evenly between the gel and the liquid and will thus influence their electrical properties in roughly the same way.

If a charged macromolecule with low molecular weight counterions comes in contact with a gel phase where the macroion cannot penetrate, the low molecular weight counterions will nevertheless have a certain tendency to pass into the gel. A Donnan potential thus builds up between the gel and the liquid, balancing the tendency of the counterions to penetrate. This type of Donnan effect will be observed whenever the ions in the liquid have differing tendencies to penetrate into the gel. This will evidently influence the chromatographic behaviour of solutes, and it seems probable that with modern gel types with very low content of fixed charged groups, the Donnan effects are responsible for a large proportion of the anomalous effects observed at low ionic strength. Like the ion-exchange effect, the Donnan effect decreases rapidly on increase of the ionic strength. It should be pointed out that this Donnan effect is somewhat different from that usually discussed in connection with ion exchangers which is caused by the fixed charged groups in the gels and the mobile counterions.

Although this discussion has been intended to demonstrate that some caution is necessary in the interpretation of data from gel chromatography, some conclusions can undoubtedly be drawn.

The effects of electric charges, except for the effects of the dielectric properties of the gel, can be minimized by the choice of suitable buffers with sufficient ionic strength. This has also been illustrated by most of the experiments used as examples in the previous chapters. In analytical experiments, the ionic strength has usually been increased by the addition of some neutral salt, often NaCl. This should be sufficient in most cases to reduce the electric effects so much that they can be neglected.

If it is assumed that the gels are microreticular, the model used by Laurent and Killander indicates that the steric effects are sufficient to account for the effects observed. In their model they have, however, not taken the difference in the affinity of the solute to the solvent and to the gel matrix into account. It is, however, known that water is no theta solvent for dextran, and also in most other cases the solute can be assumed to have greater affinity for the solvent than for the matrix. In that case, the solute molecules would not too frequently penetrate into the layer of liquid immediately surrounding the matrix (or, spend less time in the layer). This would correspond to the hydrated layer in the model by Porath. Such a layer would further reduce the space available to the molecule. If the elastic effects are added to this, it is found that a random net-work of the type described by Laurent and Killander would be too effective in excluding the molecules and would have a fractionation range of lower molecular size than actually observed. This can be explained by assuming that not only the macroreticular gels but also the microreticular gels have a structure that is more heterogeneous than indicated by the random model. A gel with domains where the density of gel matrix is high, alternating with domains with lower density of gel matrix, would give fractionation ranges at higher molecular weight, as the high molecular weight solutes would have the opportunity to enter the domains with low gel matrix density. The domains with high matrix density would then be responsible for the rigidity of the gel. The structure of the microreticular gels would thus be to a certain extent macroreticular, and the distinction between the types would be one of degree. The domains would have to be larger than those proposed by Flodin (the region around one cross-link). The fact that gels can be produced that are intermediate between the macroreticular and the microreticular gels (Fawcett and Morris 1966) also indicates that the distinction between the types may be one of degree.

The fact that the affinity of most of the molecules for the gel matrix is considerably lower than the affinity for the liquid and that the gel matrix is therefore for practical purposes shielded by a hydration layer is probably the reason why gels that are chemically so different have chromatographic properties that are so similar. It would also explain why differences in the chemical structure of the solutes make so little difference in their chromatographic characteristics: the affinity of the solute for the water surrounding the gel matrix chains can be expected to be fairly similar to that for the water in the interstitial spaces. Some speculations have been made about regular arrangement of the water around the gel matrix chains in iceberg structures. It has been argued that the mechanism of the retardation of aromatic compounds would be formation of $C–T$ complexes between the iceberg structures and the aromatic nuclei (Porath 1967; Eaker and Porath 1967).

In conclusion, it is worth mentioning that all authors who have constructed different models of the gel chromatographic process and derived relationships between molecular structure and elution volume from these models (Porath 1963; Squire 1964; Ackers 1964; Agneray 1965; Laurent and Killander 1964; Hohn and Pollman 1963; Ackers 1967) obtain excellent correlations between the relationships they derive and empirical data. From this, the main conclusion seems to be that the range that is covered by the measurements is so small and the experimental errors so large that almost any equation with two parameters that can be adjusted to obtain best correlation will give a satisfactory agreement with empirical data (most of the equations seem to have two parameters free).

The equations mentioned have two purposes. One is to serve as mathematical backbone for the molecular weight determination procedure. In § 2.5, some arguments were given for the use of a semilogarithmic plot between molecular weight and a variable linearly correlated to the elution volume. For this purpose, it is essential that the exact shape of the curve relating the molecular size and the elution volume be determined. The other important task is to elucidate the mechanism of the separation and the structure of the gels. In many cases, close correlations to linearity have been given as arguments for the use of one approach or another. As indicated above linear correlations can be obtained with most types of approaches used. The mere existence of a linear relation thus is of limited value. What may give more detailed information in this field are comparisons of the fractionation ranges that are obtained from models where the general physico-chemical properties of the systems have been considered with the fractionation ranges actually obtained.

Molecular weight determination has been developed into a useful tool for protein chemists; the first purpose of the studies of the relationship between molecular parameters and elution volume thus seems to have arrived at a relatively mature stage where the future developments will mainly be on the technical side rather than on the theoretical. The second purpose, that of elucidating the structure of the gels and the mechanisms of gel–solute interaction, is still at a preliminary stage, and much remains to be done before a clear picture has been obtained.

Acknowledgements

I wish to express my sincere thanks to Dr. T. S. Work for correcting the English in my manuscript and for many suggestions and much encouragement in the course of preparation of this book. His participation has considerably improved the result, and the correspondence with Dr. Work has also been very pleasant personally.

Subject index p. 391

I also wish to thank all my colleagues at Pharmacia Fine Chemicals, who have contributed with discussions and comments. Particularly, I would like to thank Dr. B. Gelotte, Dr. G. Lüben and Mr. B. Söderqvist for reading the manuscript and giving their comments and Miss A.-B. Krantz for carrying out analytical measurements used in the book, particularly those in fig. 5.6.

I wish to thank the various authors, suppliers and publishers, mentioned in the figure legends, for permission to reproduce their published work.

Miss D. Wall and Mrs. E. Wallin have written clear copies of my manuscript and thereby made it legible.

Manufacturers and suppliers of materials required in gel chromatography

TABLE I.1 Manufacturers of material	Gel material (table I.2)	Chromatographic columns (table I.3)	Photometric monitors (table I.4)	Other monitors (table I.5)	Fraction collectors	Metering pumps	Recycling valves	Other valves and connecting nipples	Complete chromatographic systems	Automatic analyzers
Ace Glass Corp., Northwest Boulevard, Vineland, N.J. 08360, USA		×								
American Instruments, 8030 Georgia Avenue, Silver Spring, Md 20910, USA			×			×				×
Baird & Tatlock Ltd., Chadwell Heath, Essex, England					×	×				
Barber Colman Co., 1300 Rock St., Rockford, Ill. 61101, USA				×						
Beaumarais Instrument Co. Ltd., Beaumarais, Anglesey, England					×					
Beckman Instruments Inc., Fullerton, Calif. 92634, USA			×		×				×	×
Bender & Hobein GmbH, 75 Karlsruhe, Kaiserstrasse 12, Germany		×								
Bio-Rad Laboratories, 32nd & Griffin Avenue, Richmond, Calif. 94804, USA	×									
Buchler Instruments, 1327 16th St., Fort Lee, N.J. 07024, USA					×	×				
Bühler Laboratoriumsgeräte, 74 Tübingen, Germany						×				
Canal Industrial Corporation, 5635 Fisher Lane, Rockville, Md 20852, USA			×		×					
Chromatography Corporation of America, Box 362, Carpenterville, Ill. 60160, USA		×	×		×					

TABLE I.1 Manufacturers of material	Gel material (table I.2)	Chromatographic columns (table I.3)	Photometric monitors (table I.4)	Other monitors (table I.5)	Fraction collectors	Metering pumps	Recycling valves	Other valves and connecting nipples	Complete chromatographic systems	Automatic analyzers
Chromatronix Inc., 2743 Eighth Street, Berkely, Calif. 94710, USA		×				×	×	×		
E-C Apparatus Corporation, University City, Philadelphia, Pa 19104, USA				×						
Carlo Erba, Via Carlo Imbonati 24, 20159 Milano, Italy				×						
Fischer and Porter, 295 Warminster Road, Warminster, Pa 18974, USA		×						×		
The Fluorocarbon Company, 1754 South Clementine, Anaheim, Calif. 92803, USA								×		
Gallenkamp & Co., Ltd., Technico House, Christopher Street, London E.C. 2, England					×					
Gilford Instrument Laboratories, Oberlin, Ohio 44074, USA			×							
Gilson Medical Electronics, 3000 W Beltline, Middleton, Wisc. 53562, USA			×		×					
Glass Engineering Co. Inc., 3121 White Oak Drive, Houston, Texas 77007, USA	×							×		
Rudolph Grave AB, Fack S-171 20, Solna 1, Sweden					×					
Hitachi Ltd., No. 4, 1-chome, Marunouchi, Chiyoda-Ku, Tokyo, Japan			×						×	
Holter Co., 3rd and Mill Streets, Bridgeport, Penn, USA						×				

Subject index p. 391

TABLE I.1
Manufacturers of material

	Gel material (table I.2)	Chromatographic columns (table I.3)	Photometric monitors (table I.4)	Other monitors (table I.5)	Fraction collectors	Metering pumps	Recycling valves	Other valves and connecting nipples	Complete chromatographic systems	Automatic analyzers
Instrumentation Specialties Co. Inc., 5624 Seward Ave., Lincoln, Nebr. 68507, USA			×		×					
Japan Electron Optics Laboratory Co. Ltd., New Tokyo Bldg. Marunouchi, Chiyoda-Ku, Tokyo, Japan									×	
Kontes Glass Co., Spruce Street, Vineland, N.J. 08360, USA		×								
LKB-Produkter AB, Box 76, S-161 25 Stockholm-Bromma 1, Sweden		×	×	×	×	×	×	×	×	
Litex, P.O. Box 7, Glostrup, Denmark	×									
Metaloglass Inc., 466 Blue Hill Ave., Boston, Mass. 02121, USA		×			×					
Nester Faust Manufacturing Corp., 2401 Ogletown Road, Newark, Del. 19711, USA				×						
Ole Dich Co., Avedoereholmen 13, Hvidovre, Denmark						×				
Perkin-Elmer, No. 4, 1-chome, Marunouchi, Chiyoda-Ku, Tokyo, Japan			×	×					×	
Pharmacia Fine Chemicals AB, Box 604 S-751 25 Uppsala 1, Sweden	×	×								
W. G. Pye & Co. Ltd., Cambridge, England				×						
Quickfit & Quartz Ltd., Stone, Staffordshire, England						×				

TABLE I.I
Manufacturers of material

	Gel material (table I.2)	Chromatographic columns (table I.3)	Photometric monitors (table I.4)	Other monitors (table I.5)	Fraction collectors	Metering pumps	Recycling valves	Other valves and connecting nipples	Complete chromatographic systems	Automatic analyzers
H. Reeve Angel & Co. Ltd., 14 New Bridge Street, London E.C. 4, England		×								
Seravac Laboratories (Pty.) Ltd., Moneyrow Green, Holyport, Maidenhead, Berkshire, England	×									
Shandon Scientific Co. Ltd., 65 Pound Lane, Willesden, London N.W. 10, England					×					
Sigmamotor, 3 N Main Street, Middleport, N.Y. 14105, USA						×				
Stålprodukter, Byggmästaregatan 3, S-754 35 Uppsala, Sweden					×	×				
Technicon Chromatography, Ardsley, N.Y. 10502, USA					×	×			×	×
Vanguard Instruments, 441 Washington Ave., New Haven, Conn. 06473, USA			×		×					
Vitatron N.V., 23 Spoorstraat, Dieren, Holland			×							
Warner-Chillcott Instruments, 200 S Garrard, Richmond, Calif. 94804, USA					×					×
Waters Associates, 61 Fountain Street, Framingham, Mass. 01701, USA	×			×		×			×	
Watson Marlow Ltd, Marlow, Bucks., England					×					
Wright Scientific Ltd., Cardigan Rd., London NW6		×								

Subject index p. 391

Centrifugal filter holders: Gelman Instrument Company, Box 1448, Ann Arbor, Michigan 48106, USA

Column for determination of protein in spinal fluid according to Patrick and Thiers (1963): Boch & Holm, Sölvgade 34–38, Copenhagen K, Denmark

Rayon Filter Paper (Filtex): Texilon Manufacturing Corp. AB, Nybrokajen 7, S-111 48 Stockholm C, Sweden

Basket centrifuges for the centrifuge separation technique: Measuring and Scientific Equipment Ltd., 25–28 Buckingham Gate, London S. W. 1, England

Porous plastics sheets (Vyon) for lining of basket centrifuges: Porous Plastics Ltd., Dagenham Dock, Essex, England.

TABLE I.2
Gel materials

Supplier	Product name	Chemical nature	Solvent	Molecular weight ranges covered
Bio-Rad Laboratories	Bio-Gel P	Poyacrylamide gels	Aqueous	0–500,000
	Bio-Glas	Glass	Aqueous	
	Bio-Beads S	Polystyrene	Organic	0–2,700
	Bio-Gel A	Agarose	Aqueous	10,000–150 millions
Litex	Gelarose	Agarose	Aqueous	
Pharmacia Fine Chemicals AB	Sephadex Ⓡ	Dextran	Aqueous	0–500,000
	Sephadex LH-20	Substituted dextran	Polar organic	0–5,000
	Sepharose Ⓡ	Agarose	Aqueous	500,000–25 millions
Seravac Laboratories	Sagavac	Agarose	Aqueous	10,000–150 millions
Waters Associates Inc.	Styragel Ⓡ	Polystyrene	Organic	0–40 millions
	Aquapak	Polystyrene	Aqueous	
	Porasil	Silica	Aqueous	<250,000

TABLE I.3.   Chromatographic columns

Supplier	Designation	Column diameter (cm)	Column length (cm)	Bed support material	Tube material	Intended for solvents	Other features
Ace Glass Inc.				Porous polyethylene, porous teflon	Glass	Aqueous	
Bender & Hobein		2–9	20–70	Stainless steel	Glass	Aqueous, organic	Equipped with plungers
Chromatography Corp. of America		0.5–5	20–160			Aqueous, organic	
Chromatronix	LC	0.9, 2.4, 4.8	31, 55, 103	Porous teflon	Glass	Aqueous, organic	Equipped with plungers
Fischer & Porter Co.	Lab-Crest	0.5–5	15–120	Fritted glass	Glass	Aqueous, organic	15 mm ∅ column with plungers and porous teflon bed support
Glass Engineering Co.	Glenco	0.5, 1.0, 2.4, 5.0	30, 60, 110	Fritted glass, porous polyethylene, porous teflon	Glass	Aqueous, organic	
Kontes Glass Co.	Chromaflex ®	1.0, 1.5, 2.5, 4.0	30, 60, 90, 120	Coarse fritted glass	Glass	Aqueous, organic	Equipped with plungers

Table 1. 3 continued

Supplier	Designation	Column diameter (cm)	Column length (cm)	Bed support material	Tube material	Intended for solvents	Other features
LKB-Produkter AB	LKB 4900	3.2, 7.0	55–100	Porous Vyon	Glass, Plexiglass	Aqueous, non-aromatic organic	Equipped with plungers
Metaloglass Inc.		3.2,	70, 100	Porous teflon	Plexiglass	Aqueous	Equipped with plungers
		1.9–5.0		Porous teflon	Glass	Aqueous, organic	Equipped with plungers
Pharmacia Fine Chemicals AB	K 9	0.9	15, 30, 45	Nylon fabric	Plexiglass	Aqueous	
	K 15, K 25,	1.5, 2.5	30, 45, 100	Nylon fabric	Glass	Aqueous	K 25 plunger optional
	K 50, K 100	5.0, 10.0	100	Nylon fabric	Glass	Aqueous	Equipped with plungers
	SR 25	2.5	45, 100	Teflon fabric	Glass	Aqueous, organic	Equipped with plungers
Reeve-Angel & Co	PC	1.0, 1.5, 2.5	20, 45, 100	Porous polyethylene	Glass	Aqueous	Equipped with plungers
Wright Scientific Ltd.		1.5–9.0	30, 60, 90	Porous plastics (not specified)	Plexiglass	Aqueous	

TABLE I.4

Photometric monitors

Supplier	Trade name	Wavelength or wavelength range (nm)	Special features
American Instruments			
Beckman-Spinco	Spectromonitor, model 135 A	220–750	10-channel recorder recording at 3 wavelengths as well as pH, conductivity, temp.
Canal Industrial Corporation	S, SA, D, DA	254	
Chromatography Corporation	7.300	210–340	
Gilford Instrument Laboratories Inc.	2000	185–800 $200 <$	Facilities for simultaneous monitoring of four separate columns
Gilson Medical Electronics	VV-254 VV-2651F VV-2801F	254 265 280	
Hitachi Ltd.	034	220–700	Recording at three wavelengths

Table I. 4 continued

Supplier	Trade name	Wavelength or wavelength range (nm)	Special features
Instrumentation Specialties Co.	VA 2	254, 280	
LKB-Produkter AB	Uvicord I Uvicord II	254 254, 280	
Perkin Elmer, see Hitachi			
Vanguard Instruments	1056	200–400	
Vitatron N.V.	UFD	254, 282, 313, 334, 360–700	Unit for scanning of paper chromatograms etc. available

TABLE I.5

Other monitors (not radio monitors)

Manufacturer	Type or model	Characteristics
Barber-Colman Co.	5400	Flame ionization detector with continuous chain conveyor, mainly for organic solvents, no organic buffers
Carlo Erba		Flame ionization detector
E-C Apparatus Corporation	EC 211	Refractive index monitor for primarily aqueous systems
Japan Electron Optics Laboratory Co. Ltd.	JLC-2A	Complete chromatographic system including absorption–desorption detector
LKB-Produkter AB	Conductolyzer	Conductivity monitor
Nester-Faust Manufacturing Corp.	404	Refractive index monitor
W. G. Pye & Co Ltd.		Argon ionization detector with stainless steel wire conveyor, mainly for organic solvents, no organic buffers; flame ionization detector with stainless steel wire conveyor
Waters Associates	R 4	Refractive index monitor

Analytical procedures to be applied to effluents from gel chromatographic columns

II.1. Protein determination

II.1.1. Direct spectrophotometric determination

The most common analytical procedure to make a rapid estimate of the protein concentration in a solution is to measure the light absorption at 280 nm. The light absorption at this wavelength is produced by the amino acids phenylalanine, tyrosine and tryptophan in the proteins. The absorbancy index of different proteins varies; in general it is in the range $0.5 - 1$ cm^{2}mg^{-1} for proteins not carrying chromophoric prosthetic groups. Many substances interfere with this determination; particularly nucleic acids absorb strongly at this wavelength although their absorption maximum is located at 260 nm. If nucleic acids might be present and interfere, the light absorption should be measured both at 260 and at 280 nm. In the presence of nucleic acids the protein concentration can be approximately estimated by the formula:

$$c_{\text{protein}} = 1.45 \ A_{280} - 0.74 \ A_{260},$$

giving the protein concentration in mg/ml (see for instance J. S. Fruton and S. Simmonds, General Biochemistry, second ed., 1959, p. 74).

The advantage of the spectrophotometric method for protein determination is that it is rapid, simple to perform and non-destructive. It is thus well suited for continuous monitoring (see § 4.4.3.2). The disadvantages are that the content of the aromatic amino acids varies

 Subject index p. 391

considerably from one protein to another, giving the proteins different absorbancy indices and that the determination is unspecific and aromatic substances and many other compounds interfere with the determination. The sensitivity is rather limited – about 10–20 µg/ml is the lower limit that can be detected with ordinary spectrophotometers with 1-cm cells. The sensitivity increases if the measurements are performed in the far ultraviolet, where the absorbancy index of proteins is higher. Approximately a ten-fold gain in sensitivity is achieved, if the absorbancy is measured at 220 nm instead of 280 nm (see for instance R. L. Patrick and R. E. Thiers, 1963, Clin. Chem. 9, 283). As the peptide bonds are responsible for a major part of the light absorption of proteins in this part of the spectrum, the variation of the absorbancy index between different proteins is claimed to be less pronounced at 220 nm than at 280 nm. These advantages are, however, partly offset by the difficulties connected with measurements in the far ultraviolet region of the spectrum and by the very large number of substances interfering with the measurement.

II.1.2. Protein determination by the Folin–Lowry method

The principle of the method is that a copper–tartrate complex is allowed to react with the protein in alkaline solution. The protein–copper complex can reduce phosphomolybdate to form a blue substance with a broad absorption peak around 750 nm. The procedure proposed by O.H. Lowry, N. R. Rosebrough, A. L. Farr et al., 1951, J. Biol. Chem. *193*, 265 is the following (only the procedure for proteins already in solution will be described, as this is of most interest in gel chromatography).

Reagents:

Reagent A: 2% Na_2CO_3 in 0.10 M NaOH

Reagent B: 0.5% $CuSO_4 \cdot 5H_2O$ in 1% sodium or potassium tartrate

Reagent C: 1 ml of reagent B mixed with 50 ml of reagent A.

The solution is unstable and should be discarded after one day.

Reagent E: Commercially available Folin–Ciocalteu reagent diluted to make it 1 N in acid. The commercial reagent is approximately 1.8 N, and the degree of dilution to make it 1 N is determined by titrating the commercial reagent with NaOH using phenolphtalein as indicator.

Procedure for the determination:

To a 0.2-ml sample of the protein solution, containing up to 100 µg of protein (lower limit for the determination about 5 µg), 1 ml of reagent C is added. After mixing, the solution is allowed to stand for 10 min or more at room temperature. 0.10 ml of reagent E is added and mixed rapidly. The rapid mixing is important as reagent E is unstable at alkaline pH and is otherwise destroyed before it has had time to react with the protein–copper complex. The primary reaction product is slowly converted to the blue end product, and the reaction mixture should be allowed to stand for 30 min to give a constant spectrophotometric reading. This time can be shortened by immersing the test tubes into warm water (35 °C, H. P. Rieder 1959, Clin. Chim. Acta 4, 733). The solutions are read spectrophotometrically at 750 nm, and the concentrations determined from a calibration curve (the absorbancy is not proportional to the concentration in the upper concentration range). If the concentrations of protein are high, the solutions may be read at 500 nm, where the absorbancy is lower.

The advantages of the Folin-Lowry reaction are that the determination is very sensitive (10–20 times as sensitive as the direct photometric method) and easy to perform. Its main disadvantages are that it is not equally sensitive for different proteins, although the differences are less pronounced than in the direct spectrophotometric method, and that many substances interfere with it. H. A. Zondag and G. L. Van Boetzelaer 1960, Clin. Chim. Acta 5, 155 indicate that in addition to the aromatic amino acids and phenols, salicylic acid derivatives and antibiotics also interfere, in most cases seriously. They propose that a 'sample blank' is prepared by precipitating the proteins in the sample to correct for interfering substances. Although the procedure is simple to perform, careful work is necessary for good results; particularly, glassware used must be absolutely clean and all precautions taken to prevent contamination (see for instance H. P. Rieder 1959, Clin. Chim. Acta 4, 733).

II.1.3. Other methods for protein determination

The classical method for protein determination is the *Kjeldahl titration*. The principle for this method is that the protein is digested in acid medium with a suitable catalyst. In this digestion, the nitrogen in the protein is converted to ammonium ions. After the digestion is completed, NaOH is added to make the solution strongly alkaline and the ammonia set free is distilled into a receiver, where it can subsequently be determined by titration. This method is considered to be the most reliable method for protein determination, if properly carried out. The sensitivity is approximately the same for all proteins as most protein nitrogen is present in the amide bonds. Most substances containing nitrogen interfere with the determination, and it is advisable to separate them from the protein before the determination (for instance by precipitating the protein with trichloroacetic acid before the determination). The sensitivity of the method is low and the procedure is time-consuming and laborious, and the method cannot be recommended for routine protein determination in column effluents.

In the *nephelometric* or turbidimetric method for protein determination, advantage is taken of the fact that proteins can be precipitated in the form of very tiny particles which keep floating in water uniformly dispersed for long periods of time and which scatter light strongly. The precipitation is usually brought about by sulphosalicylic acid, and the turbidity can be determined by ordinary spectrophotometry. The method is sensitive and easy to perform; on the other hand it may be difficult to produce a sufficiently uniform particle size to get absolutely reproducible results.

The *biuret* reaction is based on the formation of a coloured complex between copper and protein in alkaline solution. The complex has an absorption maximum around 550 nm. The reaction is very insensitive (the direct spectrophotometric method is about 10 times as sensitive). On the other hand the sensitivity varies relatively little between different protein species and the reaction is fairly specific and easy to perform.

The *volumetric* and *gravimetric* methods are so insensitive and time-wasting that they are hardly worth mentioning.

A comparison between the different methods can be found in M. Eggstein and F. H. Kreutz 1955, Klin. Wochschr. *33*, 879. This article also gives references to the original articles where the different methods have been described.

II.2.   Determination of polysaccharides and sugars

II.2.1.   General

Non-conjugated polysaccharides and sugars do not contain any chromophoric groups in the visible or in the available part of the ultraviolet spectrum, and they consequently do not lend themselves to direct spectrophotometric determination. The only physico-chemical property that can be used for determination of polysaccharides and sugars directly without carrying out any chemical reactions with the substances is the optical activity. Polarimetric measurements are, however, very unspecific, as most substances of biological origin show optical activity. In addition, continuous monitoring of the effluent from columns is hardly practical in the case of polysaccharides and sugars. To reduce the interference from proteins, A. Grönvall and B. Ingelman 1945, Acta Physiol. Scand. *9*, 1, precipitated these with trichloroacetic acid.

The spectrophotometric methods for determination of poly-saccharides are all based on hydrolysis of the polysaccharides to yield sugars that can subsequently be measured by specific reactions. With these reactions it is thus impossible to distinguish between poly-saccharides and sugars unless they have been separated previously (see § 6.2.1).

The reactions for determination of sugars are generally based on the production of furfural or furfural derivatives when the sugars are heated in strongly acid solutions (F. Bandow 1937, Biochem. Z. *294*, 124). The furfural or the furfural derivative reacts with various substances to give coloured products that can be used for determination of the sugars. The most common reagents in these tests are

Subject index p. 391

anthrone and o-toluidine, but several other reagents have been used (orcinol, cysteine, thioglycolic acid). A survey of methods permitting different types of sugars to be differentiated is given by Z. Dische 1955, in D. Glick (ed.), Methods of Biochemical Analysis 2, 313.

Some methods for determination of polysaccharides in the presence of sugars have been developed. They are based on precipitation of the polysaccharide, and as they are very insensitive (the lower limit is in the mg-range, while the colour reactions mentioned above do generally reach into the µg-range), they are not extensively used but they may be interesting, if the very high sensitivity of the spectrophotometric methods is not required.

Conjugated polysaccharides are usually conveniently determined by the reactions of the non-sugar groups (sulphate group, amino group).

II.2.2. Anthrone reaction

The anthrone reaction, first described by R. Dreywood 1946, Ind. Eng. Chem. Anal. Ed. 18, 499, can be performed in two ways. The heat required for production of furfural is either produced when the reagent in concentrated sulphuric acid and the aqueous sample are mixed, or supplied from the outside under controlled conditions. The latter method gives considerably better results. The procedure described by T. A. Scott and E. H. Melvin 1953, Anal. Chem. 25, 1656 is reliable. It is carried out in the following way:

Reagent: 2 g of anthrone per liter H_2SO_4

The stability is limited to about 1 month at 4 °C, or some days at room temperature.

Procedure:

2 parts of reagent are added to a test tube standing in a cold water bath. 1 part of sample (containing optimally 20–40 µg of sugars per ml) is added so that it forms a layer on top of the anthrone reagent. The sample and the reagent are then mixed with the tube immersed in the cold water to dissipate the heat of mixing. The tubes are then placed in a 90 °C water bath for 16 min. After the solution has been cooled in the cold water bath its absorbancy at 625 nm is measured.

The method can easily be adapted for automatic analyzers. The colour in the anthrone reaction develops much more rapidly for pentoses and methyl pentoses than for hexoses. The procedure can therefore be made specific for pentoses by cooling the reaction mixture very carefully during mixing and by heating to 40 °C for 10 min only (C. P. Tsiganos and H. Muir 1966, Anal. Biochem. *17*, 495).

II.2.3. Precipitation methods for polysaccharides

As for proteins a nephelometric (or turbidimetric) method can be used for determination of polysaccharides. L. Jacobsson and H. Hansen 1952, Scand. J. Clin. Lab. Invest. *4*, 352, first removed interfering proteins with trichloroacetic acid. The solution was then mixed with ethanol and the turbidity caused by the precipitation of the polysaccharide measured spectrophotometrically.

Another method based on a precipitation of the polysaccharides has been described by H. C. Hint and G. Thorsen 1947, Acta Chem. Scand. *1*, 808. In this method the polysaccharides are precipitated by copper in alkaline solution and the excess copper determined spectrophotometrically.

II.3. Nucleic acid determination

Nucleic acids are generally more difficult to determine than proteins or carbohydrates. The most common method for detecting nucleic acids is the spectrophotometric one. The bases in the nucleic acids are aromatic, giving rise to strong light absorption in the ultraviolet, with an absorption maximum around 260 nm. Spectrophotometry is a detection method of relatively limited specificity. As the absorption maxima of proteins and nucleic acids fall at different wavelengths the specificity can be increased by measuring at two or more wavelengths. The method was discussed in § 4.4.3.2 and in app. II.1.1.

The chemical reactions for nucleic acids are generally based on hydrolysis of the nucleic acid and specific reactions of one of the products – base, phosphate or sugar moiety. The most common methods are based on reactions of the sugars. This was discussed in app. II.2. W. C. Schneider 1945, J. Biol. Chem. *161*, 293, describes a method for nucleic acid determination whereby DNA and RNA can be distinguished.

One method for the detection of nucleic acids that is becoming increasingly popular is the incorporation of radioactive phosphorous and subsequent determination of the radioactivity. This determination can be carried out continuously with a radiation monitor. The incorporation of radioactive phosphate is particularly simple in nucleic acids from microorganisms, tissue cultures and viruses grown on microorganisms and tissue cultures, as in these cases the radioactive phosphorous can be included in the growth medium. The separation of the nucleic acids and the other substances into which the phosphorus has been incorporated usually does not cause any difficulties. In most cases they separate from each other during the extraction procedure or in the column without any special precautions.

A comprehensive survey of the methods for chemical determination of nucleic acids has been given by H. N. Munro and A. Fleck 1966, in D. Glick (ed.), Methods of Biochemical Analysis *14*, 113, while the microbiological methods have been reviewed by H. K. Miller 1958, in D. Glick (ed.), Methods of Biochemical Analysis *6*, 31.

II.4. Determination of oxidizable material

In many cases it is useful to have a very unspecific reaction to get a general idea of the content of organic material in the fractions. The best reactions for this purpose are those based on the oxidation of the substances. One such that has proved to be simple and reliable, although not too sensitive, is the dichromate oxidation reaction described by J. H. Bragdon 1951, J. Biol. Chem. *190*, 513. The principle of the method is that the material to be determined is oxidized by dichromate in sulphuric acid solution. The chromium formed is determined by spectrophotometry. In the original version the method was developed for determination of lipids, and therefore it starts with saponification of the esterified lipids. This is hardly necessary in routine determination of oxidizable material. The following simplified procedure has been found suitable for general purposes:

Reagent: 1 g $Na_2Cr_2O_7 \cdot 2H_2O$ is dissolved in 200 ml distilled water. 200 ml concentrated H_2SO_4 are slowly added under constant stirring. Procedure:

a. Aqueous solutions. 5 ml reagent is added to 1 ml sample. After thorough mixing, the mixture is heated for 15 min in a boiling-water bath. After cooling, the absorbancy at 610 nm is measured in a 1-cm cell.

b. Solutions in volatile organic solvents. A 1-ml sample is placed in a boiling-water bath for 1 hr to boil the solvent away completely and subsequently in an oven at 110°C for $\frac{1}{2}$ hr. 1 ml water and 5 ml reagent are added and the sample is treated as under *a*.

Subject index p. 391

Staining of thin-layer gel chromatograms

III.1. General

As mentioned in § 7.6, the substances separated by thin-layer gel chromatography can be stained on the plate, but the most common and most convenient practice is to stain them on a paper replica. This staining is similar to all staining on paper irrespective of the separation method used. The number of staining methods for paper chromatography and paper electrophoresis is very large. Also staining methods developed for ordinary thin-layer chromatography and for gel electrophoresis can in most cases be used. Here only a few staining methods for the substances most commonly studied in gel chromatography will be mentioned. A more complete survey of the staining methods can be found in standard text books on paper chromatography, paper electrophoresis, thin-layer chromatography and gel electrophoresis, for instance, I. M. Hais and K. Macek 1963, Paper Chromatography, Publishing House of the Czechoslovak Academy of Sciences, Prague. This work also includes a section on specific staining methods for enzymes, based on their enzyme activity. These can in all probability be adapted to use on the wet thin-layer plate as well. A comparison between staining methods for proteins and lipids can be found in E. Hecht 1966, Clin. Chim. Acta *13*, 506.

The methods used to stain proteins, lipids and polysaccharides are very similar to those used for histological staining of the same substances. They are of a rather general nature, and can often be used with very small modifications for staining on the plate and on paper. (See also appendix to the companion volume on immunochemical techniques by Clausen.)

III.2. Protein staining

Proteins are usually stained with acidic organic dyes that become firmly bound to proteins while they can be washed away from the supporting matrix. The staining is very reproducible and simple to perform, and the colour is permanent. The most popular stains are Bromophenol blue and Amidoblack 10B. The protein staining procedures given below for paper replica staining are variations of the standard procedures in protein chemistry. The staining procedure for dried Sephadex thin-layer plates is given to illustrate that essentially the same staining procedure can be used as on paper, if the water content in the staining bath and the rinsing baths is kept so low that the Sephadex grains swell only to a limited extent.

Paper replica protein staining with Amidoblack 10B
Staining bath: 450 ml methanol or ethanol, 450 ml water, 100 ml glacial acetic acid, 0.6 g Amidoblack 10B.
Rinsing bath: 1 % acetic acid in water, or tap water.
Procedure: Immerse the dried paper into the staining bath for 15 min, rinse in three successive rinsing baths (about 30 min each). After this treatment the proteins should appear as dark blue spots on pure white background.

Thin-layer plate protein staining with Amidoblack 10B: According to H. Determann 1967, Gelchromatographie, Springer-Verlag, Berlin.
Staining bath: 750 ml methanol, 200 ml water, 50 ml glacial acetic acid, Amidoblack 10B (saturated solution).
Rinsing bath: 750 ml methanol, 200 ml water, 50 ml glacial acetic acid.
Procedure: The dried plates are pretreated in the rinsing bath (10 min), immersed in the staining bath (5 hr) and rinsed in rinsing bath (2 hr). The proteins appear as blue spots on clear background.

Paper replica protein staining with Bromophenol blue: According to I. M. Hais and K. Macek, loc cit.

Staining bath: 1% Bromophenol blue in ethanol saturated with mercuric chloride.

Rinsing bath: 0.5% acetic acid in water.

Procedure: Immerse the dried paper into the staining bath for 5 min, rinse in 5 successive rinsing baths (about 5 min each). The protein spots appear as yellow to green spots on pure white background. The spots turn clear blue, if the paper is exposed to ammonia vapour before it has dried completely.

III.3. Lipid staining

For lipids in general the histological stains Sudan black or Sudan red are commonly used. They can be used to detect lipoproteins as well as free lipids. The staining is obtained when the lipophilic stain 'dissolves' in the lipids on the chromatogram. In the following procedure two dyes, Sudan black and Ciba blue, are used together:

Paper replica lipid staining with Sudan black and Ciba blue: according to Ch. Wunderly and S. Piller 1954, Klin Wochschr. *32*, 425.

Staining bath: 40 mg Sudan black and 40 mg Ciba blue are dissolved in 120 ml warm ethanol. After 10 min, 10 ml 4% sodium carbonate are added. The solution is filtered warm and kept in a 65 °C water bath. The solution is unstable and should be used for staining immediately.

Rinsing bath: 50% ethanol in water.

Procedure: The dried paper is immersed in the warm staining bath for 9 min, and rinsed in 3 rinsing baths, 30 min to 1 hr each.

III.4. Carbohydrate staining

It is difficult to give a general procedure for staining of sugars and polysaccharides on paper, as the substances are surrounded by polysaccharides in the form of cellulose fibres. The simple sugars can be detected with staining methods for some specific group in the sugar. They can also be detected with weak oxidant as the sugars are much more rapidly oxidized than the cellulose. Such reagents are for instance ammoniacal silver nitrate solution or alkaline triphenyltetrazolium solution. Some reactants based on the production of furfural derivatives (see appendix II.2) may also be used.

In many cases polysaccharides may also be detected, as they are more easily hydrolyzed or oxidized than cellulose. The following staining method is based on the oxidation of the polysaccharides with periodic acid to yield aldehydes that can be detected with Schiff's reagent:

Paper replica polysaccharide staining with Schiff's reagent: according to E. Köiw and A. Grönwall 1952, Scand. J. Clin. Lab. Invest. *4*, 244.
Reagents:
Periodic acid solution: 1.2 g periodic acid, 30 ml distilled water, 15 ml 0.2 M NaAc, 100 ml ethanol. The solution is unstable and should be discarded after a few days.
Reducing solution: 5 g potassium iodide, 5 g sodium thiosulfate, 100 ml distilled water, 150 ml ethanol are added under stirring, followed by 2.5 ml 2 M HCl. The solution is unstable and should be used immediately.
Schiff's reagent: 2 g basic fuchsin in 400 ml boiling distilled water, filtered at 50 °C, 10 ml 2 M HCl and 4 g potassium metabisulfite are added. After cooling, stand in dark overnight and afterwards decolourize with 1 g active carbon and filter. 2 M HCl is added until a spot drying on a glass plate does not turn red (at least 10 ml). To be kept in a cool, dark place.
Sulfite rinsing bath: 100 ml distilled water, 1 ml conc. HCl, 0.4 g potassium metabisulfite.
Procedure: The dried paper is immersed 5 min in the periodic acid solution and rinsed in 70% ethanol. After 5–8 min in the reducing solution the paper is again rinsed generously with 70% ethanol. Thereafter the paper is treated for 25–40 min with the Schiff's reagent. After 3 baths of sulfite rinse water, the water is removed with ethanol and the paper dried. The carbohydrates form violet-red spots. The paper is only faintly stained.

Subject index p. 391

Flow dynamics in Sephadex beds

At very low operating pressures the flow rate per unit column cross sectional area is directly proportional to the pressure drop per unit bed length. This is expressed in Darcy's law:

$$q = -K \frac{dp}{dx}, \qquad (IV.1)$$

where q is the flow rate per unit cross-sectional area, p the pressure caused by the flow and x the distance along the column. K is a proportionality constant, depending on the properties of the liquid and the packing material.

The resistance to the flow in the column is for practical purposes entirely a result of the viscosity of the liquid. The flow in the bed is, at least in laboratory columns for gel chromatography, laminar and the constant K in Darcy's law is inversely proportional to the viscosity of the liquid:

$$K = \frac{K_0}{\eta}. \qquad (IV.2)$$

K_0, the specific permeability, depends on the properties of the packing material (particle size distribution and particle form). Simple capillary models for the flow in the bed indicate that K_0 should be proportional to the particle diameter squared, and this is verified by the equation of Kozeny and Carman, which is an attempt to derive the absolute value of K_0.

378

Darcy's law is valid up to the highest pressures in practical use for the gel types Sephadex G-10 up to Sephadex G-50. The softer gel types Sephadex G-75 up to Sephadex G-200 deviate strongly from Darcy's law at rather low pressures due to the packing of the bed, and the flow rate passes through a maximum, whereupon it decreases on further increase of the operating pressure (see § 5.9).

The flow dynamics in the Sephadex beds can be approximately determined from the diagrams IV.1 to IV.3.

Diagram IV.1 is based on the proportionality between K_0 and d^2. The proportionality constant has been determined empirically and is in good agreement with the Kozeny–Carman equation. To facilitate the use of the diagram the dry particle size has been used as entrance variable. The dry particle sizes of the sieve fractions that can be had commercially are: Coarse 170 μ, Medium 100 μ, Fine 50 μ, Superfine 30 μ (the values are harmonic means). In the calculation of K_0, the bed height has been expressed in cm, the flow rate in cm. hr^{-1}, the viscosity as the viscosity relative to water (dimensionless) and the operating pressure in cm water head.

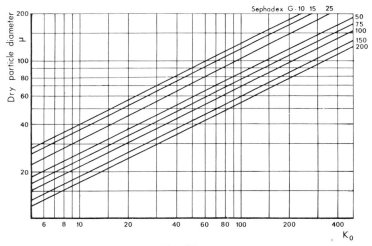

Fig. IV. 1

Subject index p. 391

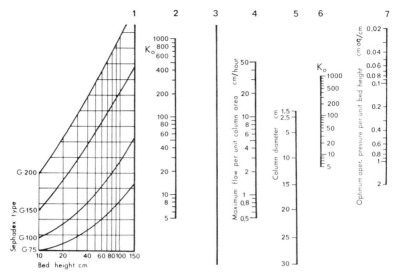

Fig. IV. 2

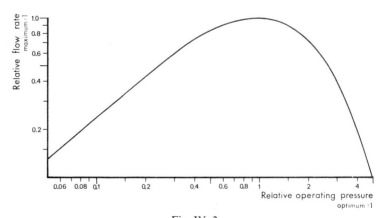

Fig. IV. 3

The value of K_0 obtained from diagram IV.1 can be directly inserted in to eqs. (IV.2) and (IV.1) for the gel types Sephadex G-10 up to Sephadex G-50. For the remaining gel types, the optimum conditions are obtained from diagram IV.2. This diagram is based on empirical relationships for the flow dynamics of these gel types. The diagram is used in the following way: The column bed height is sought on the horizontal axis at the lower left. Via the appropriate curve, the corresponding point is found on axis 1. This point and the value of K_0 from diagram IV.1 inserted on axis 2 together give a point on axis 3. This point and the column diameter on axis 5 give the maximum flow rate per unit column cross-section area on axis 4. The maximum flow rate on axis 4 and K_0 on axis 6 give the optimum operating pressure on axis 7. Note that axis 4, 6 and 7 work together passing over axis 5. Diagram IV.2 is valid for water at 20 °C. An increase of the viscosity of the eluant causes a corresponding decrease of the flow rate.

From diagram IV.3, the flow rates at pressures other than the optimum operating pressure can be obtained. On the vertical axis, the flow relative to the maximum flow obtained in diagram IV.2 is given, the horizontal axis gives the operating pressure relative to the optimum pressure obtained in diagram IV.2.

The flow rates obtained from the diagrams have been determined after about 1 week stabilization of the bed. After 24 hours, the flow rate is usually about 30 % higher. The flow rate continues to decrease slowly even after 1 week stabilization, and after about 1 month it is about 30 % lower than that obtained from the diagrams. Finally it should be stressed that the flow properties depend strongly on the packing and handling of the bed, and that this may cause variations of 50 % or more from the values obtained from the diagrams.

Surveys of the flow dynamics in chromatographic beds can be found in P. C. Carman 1956, Flow of gases through porous media, Academic Press, N.Y.; E. A. Scheidegger 1957, Physics of flow through porous media, Macmillan, N.Y.; and in J. C. Giddings 1965, Dynamics of chromatography part I, Marcel Dekker, N.Y.

The diagrams presented in this appendix were constructed by P. Tibbling, Pharmacia Fine Chemicals, Uppsala, Sweden.

Subject index p. 391

References

ACKERS, G. K. (1964) Biochemistry 3, 723

ACKERS, G. K. (1967) J. Biol. Chem. 242, 3237

ACKERS, G. K. and T. E. THOMPSON (1965) Proc. Natl. Acad. Sci. (Wash.) 53, 342

ADAMS, H. E., K. FARHAT and B. L. JOHNSON (1966) Ind. Eng. Chem. Prod. Res. Devel. 5, 126

AGNERAY, J. (1965) Etude Théorique de la Chromatographie de Filtration sur Gels. (Inaugural dissertation, University of Lille)

AGOSTONI, A., C. VERGANI and B. LOMANTO (1967) J. Lab. Clin. Med. 69, 522

ALBERTSSON, P.-Å. (1960) Partition of Cell Particles and Macromolecules (Wiley, New York)

ALTGELD, K. H. (1965a) Makromol. Chem. 88, 75

ALTGELD, K. H. (1965b) J. Appl. Polymer Sci. 9, 3389

ANDREWS, P. (1962) Nature 196, 36

ANDREWS, P. (1964) Biochem. J. 91, 222

ANDREWS, P. (1965) Biochem. J. 96, 595

ANDREWS, P., R. C. BRAY, P. EDWARDS et al. (1964) Biochem. J. 93, 627

ANFINSEN, C. B. and E. HABER (1961) J. Biol. Chem. 236, 1361

ANSEL, H. C. (1967) J. Pharm. Sci. 56, 616

ANSEL, H. C. and D. E. CADWALLADER (1964) J. Pharm. Sci. 53, 169

ARAKI, C. (1937) J. Chem. Soc. Japan 58, 1338

ARAKI, C. (1956) Bull. Chem. Soc. Japan 29, 543

ARNHEIM Jr., N., G. T. COCKS and A. C. WILSON (1967) Science 157, 568

AROND, L. H. and H. P. FRANK (1954) J. Phys. Chem. 58, 953

AURICCHIO, F. and C. B. BRUNI (1964) Biochem. Z. 340, 321

AURICCHIO, F. and C. B. BRUNI (1966) Biochem. J. 98, 290

BAGDASARIAN, M., N. A. MATHESON, R. L. M. SYNGE et al. (1964) Biochem. J. 91, 91

BATCHELOR, F. R., J. M. DEWDNEY, J. G. FEINBERG et al. (1967) Lancet *i*, 1175

BATE-SMITH, E. C. and R. G. WESTALL (1950) Biochim. Biophys. Acta *4*, 427

BATLLE, A. M. DEL C. (1967) J. Chromatog. *28*, 82

BATSON, H. C., M. JAYNE and M. BROWN (1950) J. Lab. Clin. Med. *35*, 297

BECKER, W. and E. PFEIL (1966) Biochem. Z. *346*, 301

BELING, C. G. (1963) Acta Endocrinol. suppl. 79

BENGTSSON, S. and L. PHILIPSON (1964) Biochim. Biophys. Acta *79*, 399

BENNICH, H. (1961) Biochim. Biophys. Acta *51*, 265

BLUNDELL, D. J., A. KELLER, I. M. WARD et al. (1966) J. Polymer Sci. *4 part B* 781

BOYD, G. E. and B. A. SOLDANO (1953) Z. Electrochem. *57*, 162

BRIGHTON, W. D. (1966) J. Clin. Pathol. *19*, 456

BRÖNSTED, J. N. (1931) Z. Physikal. Chem. *Bodenstein-Festband*, 257

BURDON, D. W. and J. L. WHITBY (1967) Brit. Med. J. *2*, 153

BURSTEIN, M. and J. SAMAILLE (1958) Clin. Chim. Acta *3*, 320

CARNEGIE, P. R. (1965a) Nature *206*, 1128

CARNEGIE, P. R. (1965b) Biochem. J. *95*, 9 P.

CARNEGIE, P. R. and G. PACHECO (1964) Proc. Soc. Exptl. Biol. Med. *117*, 137

ČECH, M. (1962) Virology *18*, 487

CHERSI, A. (1964) Sci. Tools *11*, 1

CONSDEN, R., A. H. GORDON and A. J. P. MARTIN (1944) Biochem. J. *38*, 224

CRISP, L. R. and J. M. E. DE BROSKE (1952) Rev. Sci. Instr. *23*, 381

CRUFT, H. J. (1961) Biochim. Biophys. Acta *54*, 609

CURTAIN, C. C. (1961) J. Histochem. Cytochem. *9*, 484

CURZON, G. (1966) Biochem. J. *100*, 295

DAISLEY, K. W. (1961) Nature *191*, 868

DANIELS, F. and R. A. ALBERTY (1961) Physical chemistry, 2nd ed. (Wiley, New York)

DAVIDSON, W. D., M. A. SACKNER and M. H. DAVIDSON (1963) J. Lab. Clin. Med. *62*, 501

DAVISSON, E. O., H. M. POWELL, J. O. McFARLANE et al. (1956) J. Lab. Clin. Med. *47*, 8

DAVOREN, P. R. (1962) Biochim. Biophys. Acta *63*, 150

DE LALLA, O. F. and J. W. GOFMAN (1954) Methods Biochem. Anal. *1*, 459

DE KONING, P. J. (1962) Neth. Milk Dairy J. *16*, 210

DETERMANN, H. (1964) Angew. Chem. *76*, 635; Angew. Chem. Intern. Ed. Engl. *3*, 608

DETERMANN, H. (1967) Gelchromatographie (Springer-Verlag, Berlin)

DETERMANN, H. and W. MICHEL (1965) Z. Anal. Chem. *212*, 211

DETERMANN, H., G. LÜBEN and T. WIELAND (1964) Makromol. Chem. *73*, 168

DOSE, K. and G. KRAUSE (1962) Naturwissenschaften *49*, 349

DOWNEY, W. K. and P. ANDREWS (1965) Biochem. J. *94*, 642

DRIEDGER, A. A., L. D. JOHNSON and A. M. MARKO (1967) Anal. Biochem. *18*, 177

DUFFEY, D., B. CHANCE and G. CZERLINSKI (1966) Biochemistry 5, 3514

EAKER, D. and J. PORATH (1967) Separation Sci. 2, 507

EKMAN, K. H. and J. J. LINDBERG (1966) Paper Timber (Helsinki) 48, 241

EMNÉUS, A. (1968) J. Chromatog. 32, 243

ENGLANDER, S. W. (1963) Biochemistry 2, 798

ENKVIST, T., C. MAJANI and T. TYLLI (1966) Acta Polytech. Scand., Chem. Met. Ser. 53 (Helsinki)

EPSTEIN, C. J. and C. B. ANFINSEN (1963) Biochemistry 2, 461

ERNST, B. and H. SCHILL (1965) Acta Biol. Med. Ger. 15, 527

FAIRCLOUGH JR., G. F. and J. S. FRUTON (1966) Biochemistry 5, 673

FASOLD, H., G. GUNDLACH and F. TURBA (1961) In: E. Heftmann (ed.) Chromatography (Reinhold, New York) p. 406

FAWCETT, J. S. and C. J. O. R. MORRIS (1966) Separation Sci. 1, 9

FEINBERG, J. G. (1967) British patent 1,078,847

FLEISCHMAN, J. B. (1967) Biochemistry 6, 1311

FLODIN, P. (1961) J. Chromatog. 5, 103

FLODIN, P. (1962a) Dextran gels and their applications in gel filtration (Uppsala)

FLODIN, P. (1962b) US patent 3,208,994

FLODIN, P. and K. ASPBERG (1961) Biological structure and function, Vol. 1 (Academic Press, New York) p. 345

FLODIN, P. and B. INGELMAN (1959) US patent 3,042,667

FLODIN, P., B. GELOTTE and J. PORATH (1960) Nature 188, 493

FOTHERGILL, J. E. and R. C. NAIRN (1961) Nature 192, 1073

FRANKLAND, B. T. B., M. D. HOLLENBERG, D. B. HOPE et al. (1966) Brit. J. Pharmacol. 26, 502

FRANZINI, C. (1966) Clin. Chim. Acta 14, 576

FRESCO, J. R. (1967) Chem. Eng. News 17, July, 34

GAMBLE, L. W., L. WESTERMAN and E. A. KNIPP (1965) Rubber Chem. Technol. 38, 823

GELOTTE, B. (1960) J. Chromatog. 3, 330

GELOTTE, B. and A. EMNÉUS (1966) Chem. Ing.-Tech. 38, 445

GELOTTE, B., P. FLODIN and J. KILLANDER (1962) Arch. Biochem. Suppl. 1, 319

GELOTTE, B. and J. PORATH (1967) In: E. Heftmann (ed.) Chromatography, 2nd. ed. (Reinhold, New York) p. 343

GEORGE, W. and K. W. WALTON (1961) Nature 192, 1188

GIDDINGS, J. C. (1965) Dynamics of Chromatography. Part I. Principles and theory (Dekker, New York)

GIDDINGS, J. C. (1967) Anal. Chem. 39, 1027

GIERER, A. and G. SCHRAMM (1956) Z. Naturforsch. 11B, 138

GIMLETTE, T. M. D. (1967a) J. Clin. Pathol. 20, 170

GIMLETTE, T. M. D. (1967b) J. Clin. Pathol. 20, 175

GINZBURG, B. Z. and D. COHEN (1964) Trans. Farad. Soc. 60, 185

GIVOL, D., S. FUCHS and M. SELA (1962) Biochim. Biophys. Acta *63*, 222

GOLDSTEIN, G., I. S. SLIZYS and M. W. CHASE (1961) J. Exptl. Med. *114*, 89

GRANT, G. H. and P. H. EVERALL (1965) J. Clin. Pathol. *18*, 654

GRANATH, K. A. (1964) In: New Biochemical Separations (Van Nostrand, London) p. 112

GRANATH, K. A. and P. FLODIN (1961) Makromol. Chem. *48*, 160

GRANATH, K. A. and B. E. KVIST (1967) J. Chromatog. *28*, 69

GRAUL, E. H. and W. STUMPF (1963) Deut. Med. Wochschr. *88*, 1886

GREENWOOD, F. C., W. M. HUNTER and J. S. GLOVER (1963) Biochem. J. *89*, 114

GRÖNWALL, A. and B. INGELMAN (1945) Acta Physiol. Scand. *9*, 1

GROSS, M., B. SKOCZYLAS and W. TURSKI (1965) Anal. Biochem. *11*, 10

HAAHTI, E. and T. NIKKARI (1963) Acta Chem. Scand. *17*, 2565

HAGLUND, H. (1967) Sci. Tools *14*, 17

HALLER, W. (1965) Nature *206*, 693

HAMILTON, P. B. (1958) Anal. Chem. *30*, 914

HAMOLSKY, M. W., M. STEIN and A. S. FREEDBERG (1957) J. Clin. Endocrinol. Metab. *17*, 33

HANSON, L. Å., B. G. JOHANSSON and L. RYMO (1966a) Clin. Chim. Acta *14*, 391

HANSON, L. Å., P. ROOS and L. RYMO (1966b) Nature *212*, 948

HARBOE, N. M. G. and A. DRIVSHOLM (1963) Protides Biol. Fluids *11*, 450

HARRISON, J. F. and B. E. NORTHAM (1966) Clin. Chim. Acta *14*, 679

HESS, M. and R. F. KRATZ (1966) J. Polymer Sci. *4 part A 2*, 731

HJERTÉN, S. (1961) Biochim. Biophys. Acta *53*, 514

HJERTÉN, S. (1962a) Arch. Biochem. Biophys. *Suppl. 1*, 147

HJERTÉN, S. (1962b) Arch. Biochem. Biophys. *99*, 466

HJERTÉN, S. (1962c) Biochim. Biophys. Acta *62*, 445

HJERTÉN, S. (1964) Biochim. Biophys. Acta *79*, 393

HJERTÉN, S. and R. MOSBACH (1962) Anal. Biochem. *3*, 109

HOCMAN, G. (1966) J. Chromatog. *21*, 413

HOCMAN, G., M. KUTKA, V. LIČKO et al. (1966) Clin. Chim. Acta *13*, 775

HODGSON, R. and P. SEWELL (1965) J. Med. Lab. Tech. *22*, 130

HOHN, Th. and W. POLLMANN (1963) Z. Naturforsch. *18B*, 919

HOHN, Th. and H. SCHALLER (1967) Biochim. Biophys. Acta *138*, 466

HORINO, M., S. Y. YU and H. T. BLUMENTHAL (1966) Diabetes *15*, 812

HUMMEL, J. P. and W. J. DREYER (1962) Biochim. Biophys. Acta *63*, 530

HUNTER, W. M. and F. C. GREENWOOD (1962) Nature *194*, 495

HVID-HANSEN, H. (1966) Scand. J. Clin. Lab. Invest. *18*, 240

INGELMAN, B. and M. S. HALLING (1949) Arkiv Kemi *1*, 61

IVATSUBO, M. and A. CURDEL (1963) Compt. Rend. *256*, 5224

JACOBSSON, L. (1962) Clin. Chim. Acta *7*, 180

JACOBSSON, L. and G. WIDSTRÖM (1962) Scand. J. Clin. Lab. Invest. *14*, 285

JASPERSEN, H.-P. (1963) Schweiz. Apotheker-Ztg. *101*, 480

JEANES, A. (1966) Encyclopedia of Polymer Science and Technology, Vol. 4, p. 805

JOHANSSON, B. G. and L. RYMO (1962) Acta Chem. Scand. *16*, 2067

JOHANSSON, B. G. and L. RYMO (1964) Acta Chem. Scand. *18*, 217

JOHANSSON, B. G. and L. RYMO (1966) 14 annual colloquium on the Protides of the Biological Fluids, Brugge, Belgium, 1966

JONES, G. D., J. ZOMLEFER and K. HAWKINS (1944) J. Org. Chem. *9*, 500

OJUSTRA, M., B. SÖDERQVIST and L. FISCHER (1967) J. Chromatog. *28*, 21

KÁVAI, M., S. JUSUPOVA and B. CSABA (1966) Acta Microbiol. Acad. Sci. Hung. *13*, 215

KELLETT, G. L. (1967) Lab. Pract. *16*, 857

KEMP, E. and I. RUBIN (1964) Acta Chem. Scand. *18*, 2403

KIBUKAMUSOKE, J. W. and N. E. WILKS (1965) Lancet *i*, 301

KILLANDER, J. (1963) Acta Soc. Med. Upsaliensis *68*, 230

KILLANDER, J. (1964a) Separation of Immunoglobulins and some other Plasma Proteins by Gel Filtration, Dissertation (Almqvist and Wiksell, Uppsala, 1964)

KILLANDER, J. (1964b) Biochim. Biophys. Acta *93*, 1

KILLANDER, J., S. BENGTSSON and L. PHILIPSON (1964) Proc. Soc. Exptl. Biol. Med. *115*, 861

KILLANDER, J. and L. PHILIPSON (1964) Acta Pathol. Microbiol. Scand. *61*, 127

KILLANDER, J., L. PHILIPSON and S. WINBLAD (1965) Acta Pathol. Microbiol. Scand. *65*, 587

KILLANDER, J., J. PONTÉN and L. RODÉN (1961) Nature *192*, 182

KIRBY, K. S. (1956) Biochem. J. *64*, 405

KIRRET, O., I. ARRO and H. HEINLO (1966) Trans. Acad. Sci. Estonian SSR *15*, 414

KISLIUK, R. L. (1960) Biochim. Biophys. Acta *40*, 531

KNUDSEN, P. J. and J. KOEFOED (1961) Nature *191*, 1306

KUBÍN, M. (1965a) Collection Czechoslov. Chem. Commun. *30*, 1104

KUBÍN, M. (1965b) Collection Czechoslov. Chem. Commun. *30*, 2900

KUN, K. A. and R. KUNIN (1964) J. Polymer Sci. *B2*, 587

KYLE, R. A. and W. F. McGUCKIN (1966) J. Lab. Clin. Med. *67*, 344

LACHMANN, P. J. (1964) Immunology *7*, 507

LARGIER, J. F. and A. POLSON (1964) Biochim. Biophys. Acta *79*, 626

LAURENT, T. C. (1967) Biochim. Biophys. Acta *136*, 199

LAURENT, T. C. and K. A. GRANATH (1967) Biochim. Biophys. Acta *136*, 191

LAURENT, T. C. and J. KILLANDER (1964) J. Chromatog. *14*, 317

LEA, D. J. and A. H. SEHON (1962) Can. J. Chem. *40*, 159

LEACH, A. A. and P. C. O'SHEA (1965) J. Chromatog. *17*, 245

LINDBERG, J. J., K. PENTTINEN and C. MAJANI (1965) Suomen Kemistilehti *B 38*, 95

LINDNER, E. B., A. ELMQVIST and J. PORATH (1959) Nature *184*, 1565

LIONETTI, F. J., C. R. VALERI, J. C. BOND et al. (1963) J. Lab. Clin. Med. *64*, 519

LIPP, W. (1961) J. Histochem. Cytochem. *9*, 458

LISSITZKY, S. and J. BISMUTH (1963) Clin. Chim. Acta *8*, 269

LISSITZKY, S., J. BISMUTH and M. ROLLAND (1962) Clin. Chim. Acta *7*, 183

LISSITZKY, S., J. BISMUTH and C. SIMON (1963) Nature *199*, 1002

LOONTIENS, F. G. and C. K. DE BRUYNE (1963) Naturwissenschaften *50*, 614

MAKOWETZ, E., K. MÜLLER and H. SPITZY (1966) Microchem. J. *10*, 194

MANIPOL, V. and H. SPITZY (1962) Intern. J. Appl. Radiation Isotopes *13*, 647

MARGOLIS, S. and R. G. LANGDON (1966) J. Biol. Chem. *241*, 469

MARSDEN, N. V. B. (1965) Ann. N.Y. Acad. Sci. *125*, 428

MARTIN, A. J. P. (1949) Biochem. Soc. Symposia *3*, 4

MARTIN, A. J. P. and R. L. M. SYNGE (1941) Biochem. J. *35*, 1358

MATHEKA, H.-D. and G. WITTMANN (1961) Zbl. Bakt. *182*, 169

MOORE, J. C. (1964) J. Polymer Sci. *A2*, 835

MORRIS, C. J. O. R. (1964) J. Chromatog. *16*, 167

MORRIS, C. J. O. R. (1966) 14 annual colloquium on the Protides of the Biological Fluids, Brugge, Belgium, 1966

MORRIS, C. J. O. R. and P. MORRIS (1964) Separation Methods in Biochemistry (Sir Isaac Pitman and Sons Ltd., London)

MUNSON, T. O., M. J. DILWORTH and R. H. BURRIS (1965) Biochim. Biophys. Acta *104*, 278

MYERS, G. E. and G. E. BOYD (1956) J. Phys. Chem. *60*, 521

MÜLLER, K. (1967) Clin. Chim. Acta *17*, 21

MÜNZEL, K. (1959) Pharm. Acta Helv. *34*, 453

NEELY, W. B. (1960) Advan. Carbohydrate Chem. *15*, 341

NUMA, S., E. RINGELMANN and F. LYNEN (1964) Biochem. Z. *340*, 228

NYSTRÖM, E. and J. SJÖVALL (1965a) Anal. Biochem. *12*, 235

NYSTRÖM, E. and J. SJÖVALL (1965b) J. Chromatog. *17*, 574

NYSTRÖM, E. and J. SJÖVALL (1966a) J. Chromatog. *24*, 208

NYSTRÖM, E. and J. SJÖVALL (1966b) J. Chromatog. *24*, 212

ÖBERG, B. and L. PHILIPSON (1967) Arch. Biochem. Biophys. *119*, 504

OGSTON, A. G. (1958) Trans. Faraday Soc. *54*, 1754

OHASHI, S., N. YOZA and Y. UENO (1966) J. Chromatog. *24*, 300

OHNO, S. and M. MORRISON (1966) Science *154*, 1034

ONCLEY, J. L., K. W. WALTON and D. G. CORNWELL (1957) J. Am. Chem. Soc. *79*, 4666

ÖSTLING, G. (1960) Acta Soc. Med. Upsaliensis *65*, 222

PAINTER, R. H. and G. A. McVICAR (1963) Can. J. Biochem. *41*, 2269

PATRICK, R. L. and R. E. THIERS (1963) Clin. Chem. *9*, 283

PEARSON MURPHY, B. E. and C. J. PATTEE (1964) J. Clin. Endocrinol. Metab. *24*, 187

PEART, W. S., A. M. LLOYD, G. N. THATCHER et al. (1966) Biochem. J. *99*, 708

PECKHAM, W. D. (1967) J. Biol. Chem. *242*, 190

PEDERSEN, K. O. (1962) Arch. Biochem. Biophys. *suppl. 1*, 157

PETTERSSON, G., E. B. COWLING and J. PORATH (1963) Biochim. Biophys. Acta *67*, 1

PFLEIDERER, G. and F. AURICCHIO (1964) Biochem. Biophys. Res. Commun. *16*, 53

PHILIP, B. A., P. HERBERT and J. W. HOLLINGWORTH (1966) Proc. Soc. Exptl. Biol. Med. *123*, 576

PICKETT, H. E., M. J. R. CANTOW and J. F. JOHNSON (1966) J. Appl. Polymer Sci. *10*, 917

POLSON, A. (1961) Biochim. Biophys. Acta *50*, 565

PORATH, J. (1962) Nature *196*, 47

PORATH, J. (1963) J. Appl. Chem. *6*, 233

PORATH, J. (1967) Lab. Pract. *16*, 838

PORATH, J. and H. BENNICH (1962) Arch. Biochem. Biophys., *suppl. 1*, 152

PORATH, J. and P. FLODIN (1959) Nature *183*, 1657

POTTER, D. G. and J. L. GUY (1964) Proc. Soc. Exptl. Biol. Med. *116*, 658

PRELLWITZ, W. and C.-H. HAMMAR (1966) Klin. Wochschr. *44*, 989

PŘISTOUPIL, T. I. (1965) J. Chromatog. *19*, 64

PŘISTOUPIL, T. I. and S. ULRYCH (1967) J. Chromatog. *28*, 49

RABINOWITZ, J. L., B. SHAPIRO and P. JOHNSON (1963) J. Nucl. Med. *4*, 139

RATCLIFF, A. P. and J. HARDWICKE (1964) J. Clin. Pathol. *17*, 676

REISFELD, R. A., U. J. LEWIS, N. G. BRINK et al. (1962) Endocrinology *71*, 559

REITH, W. S. and B. L. BROWN (1966) Biochem. J. *100*, 10P

RICKETTS, C. R. (1961) Progr. Org. Chem. *5*, 73

RINDERKNECHT, H. (1962) Nature *193*, 167

RIVERA, J. V., E. TORO-GOYCO and M. L. MATOS (1965) Am. J. Med. Sci. *249*, 371

ROBERTS, G. P. (1966) J. Chromatog. *22*, 90

ROSKES, S. D. and T. E. THOMPSON (1963) Clin. Chim. Acta *8*, 489

RUSSEL, B., T. H. MEAD and A. POLSON (1964) Biochim. Biophys. Acta *86*, 169

SAMUELSSON, E.-G., A. EMNÉUS and B. HALLSTRÖM (1967a) Svenska Mejeritidn. *59: 89*, 3

SAMUELSSON, E.-G., P. TIBBLING and S. HOLM (1967b) Food Technol. *21:11*, 121

SCHANE, H. P. (1965) Anal. Biochem. *11*, 371

SCHMIDT-KASTNER, G. (1964) Naturwissenschaften *51*, 38

SHAPIRO, B. and J. L. RABINOWITZ (1962) J. Nucl. Med. *3*, 417

SHEPHERD, G. R. and D. F. PETERSEN (1962) J. Chromatog. *9*, 445

SIEGEL, L. M. and K. J. MONTY (1965) Biochem. Biophys. Res. Commun. *19*, 494,

SIEGEL, L. M. and K. J. MONTY (1966) Biochim. Biophys. Acta *112*, 346

SJÖVALL, J. and R. VIHKO (1966a) Acta Chem. Scand. *20*, 1419

SJÖVALL, J. and R. VIHKO (1966b) Steroids 7, 447

SMITH, W. B., S. A. MAY and C. W. KIM (1966) J. Polymer Sci. 4 part A-2, 365

SPITZY, H., H. SKRUBE and K. MÜLLER (1961) Microchim. Acta 1961, 296

SQUIRE, P. G. (1964) Arch. Biochem. Biophys. 107, 471

STEERE, R. L. (1963) Science 140, 1089

STEERE, R. L. and G. K. ACKERS (1962) Nature 194, 114

STEWART, G. T. (1967) Lancet i, 1177

STICKLAND, R. G. (1965) Anal. Biochem. 10, 108

STONEHILL, E. H. and M. E. BALIS (1965) Anal. Biochem. 10, 486

STUMPF, W. and E. H. GRAUL (1963) Med. Klin. 58, 192

SUN, K. and A. H. SEHON (1965) Can. J. Chem. 43, 969

SUSSKIND, H. and W. BECKER (1966) Nature 212, 1564

SVENSSON, H. (1966) J. Chromatog. 25, 266

SYNGE, R. L. M. and M. A. YOUNGSON (1961) Biochem. J. 78, 31P

TANAKA, K., H. H. RICHARDS and G. L. CANTONI (1962) Biochim. Biophys. Acta 61, 846

TOKUMARU, T. (1962) J. Immunol. 89, 195

TORO-GOYCO, E., M. MARTINEZ-MALDONADO and M. MATOS (1966) Proc. Soc. Exptl. Biol. Med. 122, 301

TUNG, L. H. (1966a) J. Appl. Polymer Sci. 10, 1271

TUNG, L. H. (1966b) J. Appl. Polymer Sci. 10, 375

TUNG, L. H., J. C. MOORE and G. W. KNIGHT (1966) J. Appl. Polymer Sci. 10, 1261

VAUGHAN, M. F. (1960) Nature 188, 55

VENDRELY, R., Y. COIRAULT and A. VANDERPLANCKE (1964) Compt. Rend. 258, 6399

VESTERBERG, O. and H. SVENSSON (1966) Acta Chem. Scand. 20, 820

VIHKO, R. (1966) Acta Endocr. 52, suppl. 109, 15

VON ZEIPEL, G. and H. AM ENDE (1966) Acta Pathol. Microbiol. Scand. 68, 445

WALLHÄUSSER, K. H. and H. SCHMIDT (1967) Sterilisation, Desinfektion, Konservierung, Chemotherapie (Thieme, Stuttgart)

WALTON, K. W. and P. J. SCOTT (1964) J. Clin. Pathol. 17, 627

WARREN, B. and M. DOLINSKY (1966) Proc. Soc. Exptl. Biol. Med. 123, 911

WELLS, M. A. and J. C. DITTMER (1963) Biochemistry 2, 1259

WHITAKER, J. R. (1963) Anal. Chem. 35, 1950

WIELAND, TH., G. LÜBEN and H. DETERMANN (1962) Experientia 18, 430

WIEME, R. J. (1965) Agar Gel Electrophoresis (Elsevier, Amsterdam)

WILK, M., J. ROCHLITZ and H. BENDE (1966) J. Chromatog. 24, 414

WILLIAMSON, J. and A. C. ALLISON (1967) Lancet ii, 123

WINZOR, D. J. (1966) Arch. Biochem. Biophys. 113, 421

WINZOR, D. J. and L. W. NICHOL (1965) Biochim. Biophys. Acta 104, 1

WIRTH, K., U. ULLMAN, K. BRAND et al. (1965) Klin. Wochschr. 43, 528

WOOD, H. G., H. LOCHMÜLLER, C. RIEPERTINGER et al. (1963) Biochem. Z. *337*, 247

YAMASHIRO, D. (1964) Nature *201*, 76

ZELEZNICK, L. D. (1964) J. Chromatog. *14*, 139

ZWAAN, J. and A. F. VAN DAM (1961) Acta Histochem. (Jena) *11*, 306

Subject index

IMMUNOCHEMICAL TECHNIQUES FOR THE IDENTIFICATION AND ESTIMATION OF MACROMOLECULES

J. Clausen

The Neurochemical Institute
58 Rådmandsgade
Copenhagen

Contents

Preface

The aim of this manual is to present practical advice on application of the rapidly expanding mass of data on immunochemistry, and more specifically to examine the possibilities of employing immunological microtechniques in biochemical analyses. The terminology in immunochemistry and protein chemistry has been bewildering (Grabar 1963) and no official names of immunoglobulins and antigens have been agreed upon. However, where it has been possible, widely accepted terminologies have been employed, e.g. in naming the immunoglobulin system, the World Health Organization terminology has been used throughout the manual, although this terminology has not been generally accepted in all laboratories working in the field of immunochemistry (WHO 1964).

It is not the object of this manual to present an entire and comprehensive work in the field of immunochemistry, competing with the classical work of Kabat and Mayer (1961), but rather to describe the practical application of immunochemical analysis for laboratory use and especially to stress for the reader the possible errors and misinterpretations.

There are certain omissions; for instance the immunochemical microtechniques employing corpuscular systems, such as coated erythrocytes and latex particles, have not been included in the present manual as it is the intention of the editors to cover this field in a separate volume.

It is a pleasure to participate in creating this series of 'Laboratory Manuals' in collaboration with Drs. T. S. and E. Work.

J. CLAUSEN

CHAPTER 1

Introduction

1.1. The antigen-antibody reaction

Since the initial discovery of infectious agents and of the acquired defense reactions towards these agents (Pasteur 1876; Von Behring and Kitasato 1890; Koch 1891; Metchnikoff 1892), followed by the demonstration of the presence of specific serum factors neutralizing the infectious agents (Ehrlich and Morgenroth 1900), immunochemistry has developed into a well-defined physicochemical discipline. This development was initiated by the discovery of the blood group antigens (Landsteiner and Van der Scheer 1928) and further advanced by the discovery of precipitating antibodies (Kraus 1897). The discovery of the precipitin reaction arose from the demonstration of the precipitate formed when cell-free filtrates of typhoid cultures were mixed with the corresponding antiserum. This technique was made quantitative by Heidelberger and Kendall (1935), thus permitting detection of less than 0.1 μg antigen in solution. During recent years, precipitation reactions in which antigens and antibodies diffuse through and react in semi-solid matrices (e.g. agar gel) have become essential tools in biochemical analysis. These techniques generally fall into three distinct categories, simple diffusion, double diffusion and immunoelectrophoresis. Before describing them in detail, some understanding is required of the physicochemical factors involved.

 Subject index p. 557

1.1.1. Physicochemical aspects of the antigen–antibody reaction

As early as 1902 Arrhenius and Madsen described how the antigen–antibody reaction may be treated on the basis of the law of mass action: the combination of antibody (Ab) and antigen (Ag) was considered as a reversible bimolecular reaction:

$$Ab + Ag \underset{k_2}{\overset{k_1}{\rightleftarrows}} AbAg \tag{1.1}$$

where k_1 and k_2 are the rate-constants of the forward and backward reactions. According to the law of mass action, the following relationship holds:

$$\frac{(AbAg)}{(Ab) \times (Ag)} = \frac{k_1}{k_2} = K \tag{1.2}$$

where (Ab), (Ag) and (AbAg) represent the concentration of reactants and products and K is the equilibrium or association constant. The determination of the value K for any particular antigen–antibody reaction at different temperatures is necessary for determination of thermodynamic constants. The thermodynamic data indicate the nature of the bonds established between the two reactants (see p. 408).

The quantitative nature of antigen–antibody reaction was first exploited by Heidelberger and Kendall (1929, 1935) who found that it is possible to isolate and estimate the immunoprecipitate formed by adding increasing amounts of an antigen to a fixed amount of antibody. The amount of the precipitated complex increases with rising quantities of antigen up to a certain point. This region of increasing precipitation is referred to as the interval, or zone, of antibody excess. Above this point there is no further increase in precipitated complex as long as some degree of equivalence exists between the two reactants (zone of equivalence). With increasing quantities of added antigen, a so-called zone of inhibition of complex formation is reached (antigen excess); here, there is a progressive decrease in amount of antigen–antibody complex precipitated (fig. 1.1).

These results led to the postulate that the formation of immuno-

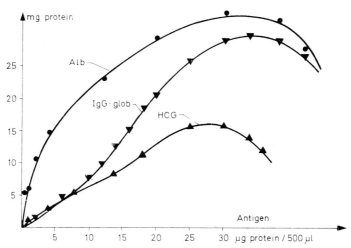

Fig. 1.1. Precipitation curves of three protein antigens. The three curves illustrate the immunoprecipitation from free buffer solution of human albumin (Alb), IgG globulin (IgG glob) and human chorionic gonadotropin (HCG) with corresponding specific antibodies. *Abscissa*: μg of protein present per 500 μl antigen solution. *Ordinate*: mg protein precipitated by corresponding specific antisera per 100 ml solution (for detail see the text).

precipitates is based on a series of bimolecular reactions following the law of mass action:

$$Ab + Ag \rightleftharpoons Ab - Ag$$

$$Ab - Ag + Ab \rightleftharpoons (Ab)_2 - Ag \text{ (antibody excess)}$$

or $\qquad Ab - Ag + Ab - Ag \rightleftharpoons (Ab)_2 - (Ag)_2 \text{ etc.} \qquad (1.3)$

Using light-scattering and fluorescence-quenching measurements, Tengerdy and Small (1966) recently showed that the primary Ab–Ag complex is established within 10 seconds, while equilibrium dialysis has demonstrated that the final polymerized antigen–antibody complex is formed during the first half hour (Hughes-Jones et al. 1963). Heidelberger's basic concept was further modified by Eisen and Keston (1949) who demonstrated the existence of polyvalent binding sites on the antigen. The antibody–antigen reaction may be considered similar to the binding of drugs to e.g. serum albumin (Klotz 1946; Clausen 1966b).

The antibody–antigen reaction shows temperature dependence of the rate of association of the two reactants between about 0 to 40 °C. Various investigators have found Q_{10} values varying from about 2 (Burnet et al. 1937) to about 1.4. Values intermediate between these extremes may be the most correct. Jerne and Skovsted (1953) demonstrated that the reaction was maximal at a low salt concentration. Finally, the antigen–antibody reaction is dependent on pH, showing an optimum at 7.0 (Kleinschmidt and Boyer 1952). The immunoprecipitate is soluble below pH 4.5 and above pH 10.0.

From a physicochemical point of view the antigen–antibody reaction is characterized by small changes in the thermodynamic constants. Thus, the change in Gibbs' free energy ΔG^0 seems of the order of -9 kcal/mol. The change in entropy ΔS^0 is positive and the change in enthalphy ΔH^0 is about -9 kcal/mol (Wurmser and Filitti-Wurmser 1957; Karush 1958; see also the survey by Schultze 1962). These values are of the same order as the changes in the thermodynamic constants for binding of drugs to serum albumin (Klotz 1946; Clausen 1966b).

The small changes in the thermodynamic constants and the positive entropy change may be partly related to displacement of water from the antibody site and to conformational changes of the reactants after establishment of the antigen–antibody complex. These changes may be related to formation of hydrophobic bonds (Scheraga 1963).

The physicochemical event during the antigen–antibody reaction depends on the type (horse or rabbit) of antibody used. The antigen–antibody complex formed is usually characterized by being soluble in excess of antigen and also, in the case of horse type antibody only, in excess of antibody.

A more detailed description of the antigen–antibody reaction based on physicochemical studies is not the object of this book; the interested reader is referred to Goldberg (1952) and Singer and Campbell (1952).

1.2. Antigen–antibody reaction in gels

Early in this century Bechhold (1905) discovered that immunochemical reactions could also be performed in gels. The 'gel diffusion' method was further developed by Arrhenius (1907) who showed that it could fractionate antigen mixtures such as tetanus and diphtheria toxins in complex with their corresponding antibodies. Qualitative methods for identification of antigens and antibodies were introduced by Nicolle et al. (1920). Both Petrie (1932) and Sia and Chung (1932) further developed the gel method as a means of identification of bacterial antigens. Later, Maegraith (1933) and Hanks (1935) suggested gel diffusion as a microanalytical tool for demonstration of the antigenic composition of unknown samples.

In 1946 Oudin elaborated the physicochemical and mathematical basis for employing the diffusion in gels of a single antigen and/or antibody for quantitative purposes. The basic work of Oudin (1946; review, 1952) was extended and modified by Ouchterlony (1949) and Elek (1948). In 1953 Grabar and Williams described 'immunoelectrophoresis' which combined the electrophoretic separation of proteins in agar gel with a subsequent antigen–antibody reaction performed by immunodiffusion in the same agar gel. Although the basic principle of this method had been independently developed by Poulik (1952) who combined filter paper electrophoresis with agar gel immunodiffusion, the recent expansion in analytical immunochemistry was initiated by the work of Grabar and Williams. On the basis of their method, Scheidegger (1955) developed his micro-immunoelectrophoretic method which made it possible to separate and identify a large number of antigens in a volume of about 1.5 μl.

Electrophoresis combined with the antigen–antibody reaction was also the basis for the development in recent years of radio-immuno-chemical techniques (Berson and Yalow 1961; Berson et al. 1964). These techniques have provided the impetus for development of ultra-micro-methods for estimation of proteins and peptide hormones in biological fluids.

Gel diffusion reactions are dependent on the high water content (often as high as 99%) of the gelatinous supporting media. This permits the antigens and antibodies to migrate through the gel by diffusion (or be accelerated by an electric field) almost independently of the supporting medium, provided that the diameter of the reactants is less than the width of the microstructure of the gels (Wieme 1957, 1959). Under these conditions the free diffusion of both antigens and antibodies conforms to laws of gaseous diffusion and thus follows Fick's law:

$$dx/dt = D d^2 c/dt^2, \qquad (1.4)$$

where c represents the concentration of diffusing agent and t the diffusion time, x the distance of diffusion, and D the coefficient of diffusion.

Gel immunodiffusion techniques are based on the fact that the diffusion of reactants creates concentration gradients in the gel. As a result, concentration ratios of antigen/antibody suitable for immuno-precipitation occur in fairly narrow zones in which the precipitates will be visible as opaque lines in the transparent gels. In the single diffusion test, a single concentration gradient is established. A relatively low concentration of the antiserum is mixed with agar, allowed to set in a half-filled glass tube and antigen in considerable excess is then layered on the gelled antiserum. As the antigen begins to diffuse through the agar it becomes dilute enough to form a precipitation line with the anti-body; but as antigen continues to diffuse and its concentration builds up, the initial precipitate redissolves in the antigen excess. Thus, the precipitation front advances along with, but slightly behind, the front of diffusing antigen and creates an image of a slowly migrating preci-pitate (cf. fig 2.1).

On the basis of Fick's law, it is possible mathematically to elaborate an equation for the correlation between the distance of diffusion and the concentration of one of the reactants (Oudin 1952). Assuming that the initial antigen concentration is c_0, the concentration c at the distance x is expressed by using Fick's law:

$$c = c_0[1 - 2\pi^{-\frac{1}{2}} \int_0^{y} e^{-y^2} dy], \qquad (1.5)$$

where $y = \frac{1}{2}x(Dt)^{-\frac{1}{2}}$, and

$$\varphi(y) = 2\pi^{-\frac{1}{2}}\int_0^y e^{-y^2}dy = \mathrm{erf}(y),$$

the function of statistical error. The $\varphi(y)$ can be developed on the basis of Taylor's formula to:

$$\varphi(y) = 2\pi^{-\frac{1}{2}}\left(y - \frac{y^3}{1!3} + \frac{y^5}{2!5} - \ldots\right).$$

This, introduced into (1.5), gives by logarithmic calculation the Oudin equation:

$$x = -K \log_e(c/c_0), \tag{1.6}$$

where $K = (\pi Dt)^{\frac{1}{2}}$ (higher orders of y are neglected).

This approximate equation predicts a linear relationship between the distance of diffusion and the logarithm of the concentration of the diffusing reactants. The distance of migration x between the meniscus and the leading edge is proportional to the square root of the diffusion time t:

$$x = K_1\sqrt{t}, \tag{1.7}$$

x is also proportional to the logarithm of the antigen concentration and to the reciprocal value of the antibody concentration:

$$x = K_2 \log_e C_{Ag} + K_3, \tag{1.8}$$

$$x = K_4 \log_e(1/C_{Ab}) + K_5. \tag{1.9}$$

(K_1 to K_5 are a series of constants.) These equations have been confirmed experimentally, and it is now established that during immuno-diffusion in gels containing a specific antibody, the corresponding antigen, in the presence of other antigens or antibodies, gives rise to only one precipitate whose distance of migration at a certain time is proportional to the logarithm of the antigen concentration. Because the precipitate is soluble in excess of antigen, the precipitation line moves away from the point of entry of antigen (fig. 2.1) and the antilogarithm of the distance moved by the boundary of the precipitate at a fixed diffusion time is proportional to the amount of antigen present. Migrating precipitates are only obtained when the initial concentration of antigen exceeds that of the antibody in the gel.

Similar equations are valid for diffusion of antibody in a gel which contains the antigen in a homogenous solution (fig. 2.1 and pp. 426–429). In double diffusion techniques, roughly equivalent amounts of both antigen and antibody diffuse in the gel towards each other and two concentration gradients are established. The diffusion of antigen and antibody still follow Fick's law; however, the mathematical treatment is more complicated and the precipitate does not move if the systems are balanced. The reader is referred to Ouchterlony (1962, 1967).

1.3. Antibodies; the immunoglobulins

Biologically, antibodies are defined as proteins formed when an animal is immunized with an antigen. The WHO committee (WHO 1964) defined immunoglobulins as 'Proteins of animal origin endowed with known antibody specificity, and certain proteins related to them by chemical structure and hence antigenic specificity. Related proteins for which antibody activity has not been demonstrated are included – for example myeloma proteins, Bence–Jones proteins and naturally occurring subunits of immunoglobulins... Immunoglobulins do not

TABLE 1.1

Nomenclature of immunoglobulins

WHO nomenclature *	Synonyms
IgG	γ–G, γ_2, γ_{ss}, $7S\gamma$, $6.6S_\gamma$–globulin
IgA	γ–A, γ_1–A, β_{2A}, β_x–globulin
IgM	γ–M, γ_1M, β_{2M}, β_2C, $19S_\gamma$–globulin
IgD	γ D
IgE	Reaginic antibodies
IgND **	Reaginic antibodies
γL	γU, γ–microglobulin

 * Bull. World Health Organ. (1964) *30*, 447 and (1968) in press.
** Not officially accepted.

TABLE 1.2

Some physiochemical and biological properties of certain immuglobulins

Immuno-globulin type	Molec-ular weight	Sedimen-tation constant ($S_{20}w$)	Carbohy-drate content	Concentration * in normal human serum (mg/100 ml)	Some biological * properties
IgG	160,000	6 to 7 (6.8)	2.9	756–2210	Main serum immunoglobulin
IgA	160,000 and polymers	7, 10, 13	7.5	50.8–379	Main immunoglo-bulin of secretions Contains allergic antibodies
IgM	1,000,000 and polymers	19, 30–150	10.9	20.6–279	Increases in the initial immunolo-gical response Anti-carbohydrate antibodies (in horses)
IgD	About 160,000			1.0–55.7	
IgND†				$105–1394 \times 10^{-6}$	Allergic antibodies
IgE†	About 160,000	7.7			Allergic antibodies

* From Johansson (1967).

** From Tomasi and Zigelbaum (1963).

† These two immunoglobulins are identical (cf. Johansson et al. 1968).

include the components of the complement system.' Thus only three criteria are needed to include a component into the groups of immuno-globulins viz. (1) that it is a protein (2) it comes from an animal source and (3) it has conformational structures in common with the other members. Antibodies are characterized by certain physico-chemical and biological properties. Salting-out procedures combined with column chromatography or Sephadex filtration have made it possible to isolate from most animal species five main classes of antibodies now usually called IgA, IgG, IgM, IgD and IgE (IgND) (table 1.1). These differ physicochemically and immunologically (table 1.2). In practice, it is necessary to remember these differences, especially differences in molecular weights. Thus IgM (and some IgA molecules) are such large molecules that they cannot freely diffuse through the micelle-structure of agar gel.

IgG constitutes more than 83 % of the total immunoglobulin content of normal human serum (table 1.2). Because of this fact, and the tendency of the other immunoglobulins (IgA and IgM) to polymerize, it is mainly the IgG which participitates in immunochemical reactions in gels.

The structures of immunoglobulins IgG, IgA and IgM have been elucidated after splitting the purified globulins into subunits with papain and pepsin (Porter 1959, 1967; Fleischman's review 1966). The subunit structure was revealed by reductive alkylation, followed by starch gel electrophoresis in 8 M urea at acid pH (Edelman and Poulik 1961). There are two light chains (L-chains) and two heavy chains (H-chains) which are interconnected in pairs through disulfide (fig. 1.2) and hydrogen bonds. The peripheral part of the two H-chains may be split by digestion with papain, pepsin and trypsin. The papain fragment Fc retains the ability to fix to cell surfaces and to pass through the placenta; other parts of the molecule (papain fragment Fab) do not have these properties, but have the antibody-combining site. These

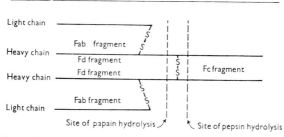

Fig. 1.2. Polypeptide structure of IgG. The nomenclature of the fragments is that recommended by the World Health Organization (1964). From Porter (1967).

studies thus demonstrate that the antibody site and the site for fixation to cell surfaces are of different topographic localization in the molecule. Recently, the affinity labelling method (Singer and Doolittle 1966) suggests that parts of both H- and L-chains are in fact localized in the antibody combining site. However, other studies seem to indicate that H-chain contributes most to the antibody site (Fleischmann 1966).

X-ray analysis indicated that the IgG globulin molecule is a cylinder $240 \times 57 \times 19$ Å (Edelman and Gally 1964; Kratzky et al. 1955). The antibody combining site of this cylinder was measured by Kabat (1957) by the dextran–antidextran reaction using progressively smaller dextran molecules. In this way it was shown that an oligosaccharide of only five glucose units was sufficient to liberate about 98 % of maximal free energy during fixation of antibody, but one glucose molecule alone could only give rise to 39 % of the maximal value. From these data and similar data obtained by the reaction between other oligosaccharides and antibodies, the maximum size of the antibody site was estimated to be $34 \times 12 \times 7$ Å. Recently, electron microscopy has made it possible to photograph the immunoglobulins directly. Thus, Valentine and Green (1967) showed that the IgG globulin had the physical form of a Y with two long and one very short arm. Chesebro et al. (1968) photographed the IgM molecule and found it to be a flexible, spider-like particle with five appendages joining a central ring.

The subunit structures of H- and L-chains have also been shown to be present in IgA, IgD, IgE and IgM (Putnam et al. 1964; Ishizaka et al. 1967b). However, differences in the subunit structure occur and these are summarized in table 1.3. Only one type of H-chain is present in

TABLE 1.3

Subunits of immunoglobulins

	H-chains	L-chains	Subunit formula
IgG	γ	κ or λ	κγγκ or λγγλ
IgA	α	κ or λ	κααικ or λααλ
IgM	μ	κ or λ	κμμκ or λμμλ
IgD	δ	κ or λ	κδδκ or λδδλ

Subject index p. 557

each immunoglobulin, but the type is specific for each globulin. On the other hand, two types of L-chains (kappa and lambda, WHO nomenclature 1964) are present in all immunoglobulins (Cohen 1963). About 60% of the immunoglobulins in normal human serum contain κ chains and 40% have λ L-chains. Recent studies indicate that, although the main parts of the heavy and light chains from different monospecific IgG globulins are identical in amino-acid sequence, some regions of the two chain types exhibit variations in amino-acid pattern (Appella and Ein 1967; Porter 1967; Putnam et al. 1967; Waxdale et al. 1967). An immunoglobulin subunit consisting of two L-chains normally found in plasma and urine is IgU; it also occurs in Bence–Jones proteins (Berggård 1961; Fleischman 1966).

The IgD and IgE globulins have recently been demonstrated in human serum (Ishizaka et al. 1967a, b; Johansson 1967). The IgE (IgND) globulins contain reaginic antibodies; IgE especially, contains the antibodies against ragweed pollen extract (antigen E), and it also carries the antibodies of asthma patients (Johanson 1967; Stanworth et al. 1967).

It is essential in understanding immunological reactions to grasp the fact that a particular preparation of antibody globulin, even that from a single animal immunized with a 'single antigen' is a mixture of closely similar molecules and not a preparation of identical molecules. This is explained by the fact that most 'pure' antigens contain multiple sites (or chemical groups) every one of which gives rise to specific antibody formation. The IgG globulin can be separated into two main fractions by column chromatography on DEAE cellulose (Fahey and Horbett 1959), the slow- and fast-migrating IgG globulins. These two fractions show different immunological specificity towards certain antigens; thus the complement consuming (fixing) activity is related to the slow, and not to the fast-migrating IgG globulins (Murphy et al. 1965).

The worker in the field of immunochemistry should remember the structures of the three main types of immunoglobulins, because the presence of both kappa and lambda L-chains in all three main classes of immunoglobulins explains the partial immunolagical relationships

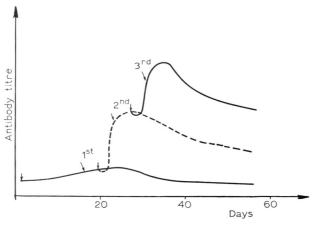

Fig. 1.3. The relationship between antibody titre and time after immunization. At the arrows, doses of antigen are given. The first, second and third responses are indicated. The increase in antibody titre of initial immunization is small and delayed. The second and third responses are fast and pronounced. Soon after the second and third injections there is a small temporary decrease in antibody titre, caused by a neutralization of antibody.

between IgG, IgA and IgM in reactions with antibodies against these immunoglobulins. This can give rise to difficulties during work with specific antibodies against these immunoglobulins, because anti-IgG, anti-IgA and anti-IgM have some common antibodies directed toward the L-chains. Only after absorption of antisera with L-chain antigen, may strictly specific antisera against H-chains (type γ, α or μ) be obtained. This applies for instance in studies on paraproteins in human and animal pathology and on immunoglobulin structure in animals.

During active immunization (fig. 1.3) the IgM globulin is the one to respond to the primary introduction of antigen to the body (Murphy et al. 1966) especially when carbohydrates are injected (Robbins et al. 1965). During long-term immunization, the antibody is mainly of the IgG globulin type. The IgA globulin fraction has been claimed to contain 'allergic' antibodies giving rise to the positive Praunitz–Küzner reaction. However, recent studies by Ishizaka et al. (1967a, b) and

Johansson (1967) have shown IgE globulins to be carriers of reaginic antibody activity (table 1.2); other recent studies suggest that the IgA globulin is the immunoglobulin of secretions, thus it is present in products of the salivary, bronchial and intestinal glands (Tomasi and Zigelbaum 1963; review by Schultze and Heremans 1966).

During tissue destruction or infection with pneumococci, an increase occurs in the serum content of a specific globulin with γ-mobility, the so-called C-reactive protein (CRP). CRP precipitates the C-polysaccharide of the pneumococcus (Tillet and Francis 1930) but seems to differ from the immunoglobulins by requiring calcium ions for its precipitation. This precipitation is inhibited by organic phosphate monoesters (Gotschlich and Edelman 1967). CRP consists of 6 subunits held together to form aggregates having a molecular weight of 144,000 (Gotschlich and Edelman 1965).

1.4. Antigens

The natural antigens may be proteins, nucleic acids, carbohydrates, lipids or combinations of these. An antigen may be defined as any agent giving rise to antibody formation specific for that agent when transferred to a living cell-system containing cells of the immunologically competent type (Burnet 1959). Other substances (haptens) may induce antibody formation only when combined in complex with macromolecules, as for instance peptides and some oligosaccharides. Different antigens show different specificity and reactivity in the antigen–antibody reaction – depending on the type of antigen.

1.4.1. Polysaccharide antigens

Some polysaccharide antigens show a highly specific reaction, so specific that it is possible to use the antigen–antibody reaction chemically for identification of carbohydrates and glycosidic bonds in different carbohydrate antigens (Heidelberger et al. 1946; Heidelberger and Wolfram 1954). Acid mucopolysaccharides such as chondroitin-4- and -6-sulphate, dermatan sulphate, heparin and keratosulphate, however, do not act as good antigens (Gibian 1959), probably owing to the widespread occurrence of these substances in all animal species (immune tolerance).

1.4.2. Glycopeptide antigens

The glycopeptide blood-group antigens have been extensively studied (Kabat 1956; Morgan 1956). They also show a high specificity in the antigen–antibody reaction and have carbohydrate determinant groups. The identification of end-groups in these substances has been carried out by means of strictly specific antisera against carbohydrates with known chemical structure. Using inhibition of precipitation reactions to identify the end-group it has been possible to prove that fucose, O-α-N-acetyl-D-galactosyl aminoyl-(1-3)-D-galactose and O-α-galactosyl-(1-6)-N-acetyl-glucosamine are end-group determinants of H-, A- and B-substances respectively (see reviews, Boyd 1962; Kabat and Mayer 1961).

1.4.3. Glycoprotein antigens

Glycoprotein antigens are encountered among tissue and serum proteins. They consist of a protein and a polysaccharide moiety both of which may contribute to the antigenic properties.

N-acetyl-neuraminic acid (NANA) is often found to be a part of the carbohydrate moiety, as in seromucoid, α-1-(S-3.5)-glycoprotein and several other serum proteins (Schultze 1957). The NANA has been localized as a biological determinant group of these proteins, but it does not contribute to the immunological properties. Because of its acidic nature, NANA contributes a negative charge to the electrophoretic mobility. The enzyme neuraminidase from *Vibrio cholerae* splits NANA from the glycoprotein without affecting the rest of the antigen molecule; this causes a decrease in the electrophoretic mobility without change in serological reactivity (Schultze and Schwick 1957).

1.4.4. Lipopolysaccharide and lipoprotein antigens

Lipopolysaccharide antigens (O-somatic antigens) are the main thermostable surface antigens of Gram-negative bacteria. The poly-

Subject index p. 557

saccharide moiety is responsible for the antigenic specificity and has been the basis for the serological and chemical classification of Salmonellae and *Escherichia coli* into chemotypes (review, Lüderitz et al. 1966; Work 1967). Chemically, these lipopolysaccharide and lipoprotein antigens are characterized by poor solubility and high molecular weight, causing difficulties in the practical performance and interpretation of their immunochemical reactions.

In human cell membranes three similar types of lipopolysaccharides occur. They all belong to the group of amino-sugar containing sphingoglycolipids: hematoside, globoside and ganglioside. The first two substances exhibit blood group specificity (review, Hakomori 1965) and are strong antigenic substances of low solubility. The Wasserman hapten (antigen) seems to be mainly a phospholipid, cardiolipin, which consists of fatty acid- and phosphate-esters of glycerol (Schultze 1961). Cardiolipin is the only non-carbohydrate-containing lipid shown to possess a strong haptenic property (Inoue et al. 1965). When this component is mixed with non-antigenic substances such as cholesterol and lecithin then its activity in the complement binding antigen-antibody reaction is strikingly increased.

Lipopolysaccharides and lipoprotein antigens are able to combine with many proteins, e.g. albumin or antibodies. This often gives rise to precipitates through false immunochemical reactions. They also can often cause unspecific consumption of complement in the complement binding reaction (Inoue et al. 1965).

1.4.5. Protein antigens

Protein antigens are analogous to carbohydrate antigens in that both reveal high immunochemical specificity, but the structure of their antigenic determinants is still largely unknown (Crumpton 1965). Endgroups differ to some extent in different animal species (survey, Schultze 1961). However, most proteins (enzymes) are common to a range of related animal species, and in different stages of the phylogenetic development the active sites and function of many proteins and enzymes seem to be identical (Cinader 1963). Therefore, some antigenic groups in protein antigens are common for proteins with identical functions in different animal species. Specific antibodies against a certain protein antigen will therefore be able to precipitate the proteins with similar function present in different animal species (Clausen and Heremans 1960). These facts must be remembered in working with gel-diffusion, since antibody from one animal may precipitate antigens in the antibody-containing serum from another animal.

As the active sites of some proteins conferring specific functions are preserved through different stages of phylogenetic development, Cinader (1963) pointed out that it should not be possible to produce antibodies against these sites. However, after immunochemical reactions between enzymes and anti-enzymes (antisera to enzymes), the enzymic activity is often found to be partially or totally absent. This may be due either to masking of the enzymic site, or to conformational changes at this site, both caused by coupling of the antibody to other areas of the antigen molecule.

1.4.6. Virus antigens

Virus antigens are usually protein or nucleoprotein in nature (Schuster et al. 1956; Schäfer 1958). Nucleoprotein antigens are rarely investigated by means of gel-diffusion. They will not be further commented on in this manual.

Guide to further reading

Comprehensive textbooks covering all aspects of antigens, antibodies and the antigen-antibody reaction do not exist. However, the student especially interested in physicochemical aspects is referred to:

Boyd, W.: Introduction to Immunochemical Specificity, Interscience Publ., New York, 1962.

Day, E. D.: Foundations of Immunochemistry, Williams and Williams Publ., Baltimore, 1966.

Kabat, E. A. and M. M. Mayer: Experimental Immunochemistry, Charles C Thomas Publ., Springfield, Ill., 1961.

Subject index p. 557

The reader interested in biological and clinical aspects is referred to:

Gell, P. G. H. and R. R. A. Coombs: Clinical aspects of Immunology, Blackwell Publ., Oxford, 1964.

Humphrey, J. H. and R. G. White: Immunology for Students of Medicine, Blackwell Publ., Oxford, 1964.

The reader interested in the structure and synthesis of antibodies is referred to:

Frisch, L. (ed.): Cold Spring Harbor Symposia on Quantitative Biology Vol. XXXII: Antibodies. Cold Spring Harbor L.I., N.Y., 1967.

CHAPTER 2

Immunodiffusion in gels

During the process of gelation of agar, a micelle structure is formed. Molecules with a molecular weight below 200,000 can pass relatively freely through the micelles; but those of a larger size, such as fibrinogen, α-2-lipoprotein, α-2-macroglobulin and IgM-globulin are retarded because of friction between the surface of the protein molecules and the channels of the micelles (Wieme 1959).

The immunoprecipitates formed between antigen and antibody during the phase of immunodiffusion are usually of a molecular size above 200,000 and cannot diffuse further or be washed out of the gel once they have been formed. On the other hand, un-reacted antigen and antibodies may easily be washed out if they have a molecular weight below 200,000. This is the basis for the identification of immunoprecipitates with protein stains in both immunodiffusion and immunoelectrophoresis.

2.1. Diffusion in one dimension

2.1.1. Single (simple) diffusion in one dimension (Oudin's technique)

The process of diffusion of an antigen in an antibody-containing gel, or of an antibody in an antigen-containing gel (fig. 2.1) is in agreement with Fick's law (see p. 410). The experimental technique based on this fact (single diffusion) was first described in detail by Oudin (1946). It may be used for qualitative evaluation of mixtures of antigens, but its main application has been in the field of quantitative estimation of protein

  Subject index p. 557

antigens in biological fluids (see review by Oudin 1952; Störiko 1965).
The Oudin technique is based on the fact that in gels, proteins are
physicochemically independent of each other (Oudin 1952; Buchanan-
Davidson and Oudin 1958) and so the diffusion of mixtures of antigens
into an antibody-containing gel will produce independent precipitates
from each antigen–antibody pair.

It is not possible to apply this method to polyvalent reactants. Thus,
the diffusion of a complex antigen mixture into a gel containing a
polyvalent antiserum will give rise to multiple precipitin lines partially
overlapping each other. However, using a mono-specific antiserum, the
corresponding antigen can easily be identified in different samples by
the presence or absence of an immunoprecipitate in the gel. With specific antisera it is also possible to reveal specific antigenic groups in
similar proteins of different biological origin, thus for instance, the
allotypic groups in serum protein antigens (Oudin 1956).

Since the distance of diffusion after a certain time is proportional
to the logarithm of the concentration of the antigen in question, this
technique may be used for quantitative purposes by comparing the
distance of migration of the test sample of antigen with migration of
the same antigen at known concentration, the same antibody concentration being used throughout. However, the mathematical equations outlined are valid only if the other antigens present are non-
related antigens. If the sample contains two or more related antigens,
the relationship between the length of diffusion and the concentration
of the reactants is more complex (Buchanan-Davidson and Oudin 1958).

In practice (see pp. 411–412, 451–453) quantitative results are in all
cases based upon determination of distances or areas of diffusion (vide
infra). The diffusion time (t) determines the migration distance of the
precipitate (x) according to the equation: $x = k_1 \sqrt{t}$, k_1 a constant.
Details of the use of this technique are described in appendix 8.

2.1.2. Single radial diffusion (Petrie plate technique)

In single radial diffusion one of the components in the antigen–antibody
system (usually the antibody) is incorporated in an agar-gel spread on
a flat surface, whereas the other component is applied in a hole in the

gel and allowed to diffuse radially. Ring-shaped precipitation bands will form and migrate concentrically around the holes; after some time the migration ceases, owing to the fact that the amount of antigen applied in the holes is not in such excess over the antibody in the gel as in the case of the Oudin tube technique.

After a certain time at a fixed temperature, the areas covered by the immunoprecipitates are examined either directly or after staining with protein stains (Mancini et al. 1965). This technique was originally developed by Petrie (1932) for qualitative comparative purposes; if two antigens applied in neighbouring wells are immunologically identical, a complete fusion of the boundaries of the zones containing immunoprecipitates occurs. In cases of non-identity, the rings around each well are not influenced by the neighbouring rings. Where there is partial antigenic relationship, the rings coalesce.

This method was developed by Mancini et al. (1964) for quantitative purposes. The authors demonstrated empirically that a straight-line relationship exists between the antigen concentration and the area or diameter of the terminal immunoprecipitate, provided the diffusion is allowed to proceed until all the antigen has been combined: $S_w + S_p = S_0 + KC_{Ag}$, where S_w is the area of the well, S_p the area of the immuno-precipitate, S_0 the intersection with the abscissa. A rectilinear relationship was found over a wide range of antigen concentration. A series of dilutions of standard antigen solution is set up as a reference on the test plate. This method has recently been used widely (review Schwick and Störiko 1965; Störiko 1965; Becker et al. 1968) for estimation of serum proteins, but it is a relatively slow technique compared with the Laurell electrophoresis in antibody-containing gel (p. 437). The method is not limited to proteins with low isoelectric point as is the Laurell technique which does not allow determination of immunoglobulins possessing a low electrophoretic mobility (vide infra). Details of the use of this technique are described in appendix 9.

Subject index p. 557

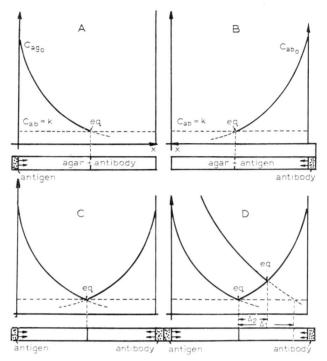

Fig. 2.1. Single and double immunodiffusion. The relationship between the concentration of an antigen or an antibody diffusing from a lateral well through an agar gel and the distance of migration at a certain time (Oudin 1952). *Abscissa*: distance from the trough. *Ordinate*: concentration (*C*) of the diffusing reactant (antigen: ag, antibody: ab) at a certain time. The point of equivalence is indicated by eq. *A*: diffusion curve for an antigen diffusing through agar gel mixed with corresponding specific antibody; *B*: diffusion curve for an antibody diffusing through agar gel mixed with the corresponding antigen; *C* and *D*: diffusion curves in double diffusion of both antigen and antibody through an intermediate block of agar; *D*: shows the change in the point of equivalence between the two reactants with change in antigen concentration. The ordinate on the right represents the concentration of antibody. The curve on the right represents the diffusion curve of specific antibody in the intermediate agar block. The ordinate on the left represents antigen concentration. The two diffusion curves on the left represent curves corresponding to two different concentrations of antigen applied in the lateral antigen well. (*Continued on page 427.*)

2.2. Double diffusion

2.2.1. Double diffusion in one dimension

This method was developed from the Oudin technique by Oakley and Fulthorpe (1953). It involves the presence of antigen and antibody compartments situated in a glass tube on each side of the common gel compartment. After application of the reactants in their respective compartments, the antigen and the antibody will diffuse towards each other in the common gel. A precipitate will be formed at the place of equivalence. The mathematical basis of this method has been mentioned previously (pp. 410–411). Comparison of single linear diffusion with double diffusion (fig. 2.1) shows that the distance travelled under identical experimental conditions is greater in the former method. This means that single diffusion determines antigens more accurately than double diffusion. The method has the same range of application as the Oudin technique (Ouchterlony 1962).

2.2.2. Double diffusion in two dimensions

This method, which was developed simultaneously by Ouchterlony (1949) and Elek (1948), involves the use of agar plates with wells for both antigens and antibodies. The two reactants diffuse into the gel,

---

The change in point of equivalence with increased concentration of antigen is shown as Δ_2. Had this been a single diffusion experiment (e.g. A), the point of equivalence for the right hand curve would have been more to the right; its change in position with change in antigen concentration is indicated as Δ_1. From these changes in position of point of equivalence in single and double diffusion, it is seen that single diffusion gives a more pronounced change in the point of equivalence with change in antigen concentration than does double diffusion. This argues for superiority of single diffusion over double diffusion in quantitative estimation of antigen or antibody. The dotted lines continuing the diffusion curves, indicate that the exact shape and the mathematical equation explaining these extremities are unknown because of the unknown consumption of the reactants at the point of equivalence.

Subject index p. 557

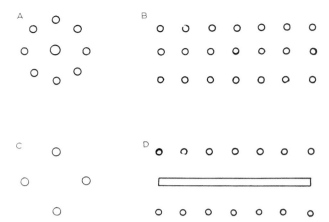

Fig. 2.2. Examples of basic set-ups for double immunodiffusion. *A*: The circular well method; *B*: the (quantitative) agar plate method; *C*: quadrangular set up; *D*: the basin set-up.

in which the immunoprecipitates are formed at the point of equivalence for each antigen–antibody pair. Each precipitate acts as an immuno-specific barrier for the particular pair of reactants and prevents their further diffusion, but does not hinder diffusion of other reactants. Thus, if the concentrations of antigen and antibody are reasonably balanced, the precipitate does not migrate, but grows peripherally in lines or arcs at constant angles to the line joining the two wells. In an unbalanced mixture, the excess of one reactant might give rise to migrating or multiple precipitates through alternate solubilization and reprecipitation.

Petrie dishes or microscope slides may be used; the wells are situated either circularly around a central hole, in triangles or quadrangles, or alongside a central trough (figs. 2.2 and 2.3). The method is simple to carry out and is widely used for examination of antigenic compositions of unknown samples as well as for the evaluation of the antigenic relationship between different protein antigens. The method may also be applied to a semi-quantitative evaluation of the titre of one of the reactants compared with known concentrations in other wells (Fein-

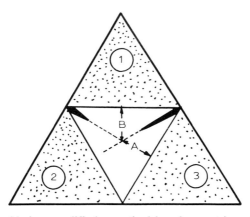

Fig. 2.3. The double immunodiffusion method based upon triangular plate technique for qualitative and quantitative analysis. (1) Antibody reservoir; (2) reservoir for standard (reference) antigen; (3) reservoir for unknown (sample) antigen; the distances A and B are a function of the distances travelled by the end point of the immunoprecipitate formed by the unknown reactant and the standard indicator respectively. The ratio $A:B$ is called the diffusivity ratio. This ratio is linearly related to the logarithm of concentration of the unknown sample (see p. 453).

berg 1959). By applying serial dilutions of samples in circularly placed wells, the immunoprecipitates around each well will fuse with each other. The end point of this immunoprecipitate indirectly defines the antigen concentration as the reciprocal value of the dilution of the antigen present in the corresponding well. As shown in fig. 2.1 a direct quantitative estimation of one of the reactants is possible by measurement of the distance of immunodiffusion at a certain time, but since the distance is small, it is not recommended for accuracy. Full instructions for double diffusion using the Ouchterlony technique are given in appendix 11.

2.3. Determination of diffusion constants

During immunodiffusion (double diffusion) the point of first appearance of the precipitate along the axis joining the two wells depends on

Subject index p. 557

the diffusion coefficient of the two reactants, expressed by the equation: $x_{Ag}/x_{Ab} = \sqrt{(D_{Ag}/D_{Ab})}$, where x_{Ag} and x_{Ab} are the migration distances from the antigen and the antibody well respectively, and D refers to the diffusion coefficient of the two reactants (Polson 1958).

This equation has been used to estimate the diffusion coefficients of the antigen or antibody (Van Oss and Heck 1961). In a two-dimensional double diffusion, the initial precipitate will be formed medially at a certain point between the two wells and will extend as an arc with a radius determined by the distances from the two wells $r = X_{Ab} \cdot X_{Ag}/(X_{Ab} - X_{Ag})$. The ratio between the two migration distances is proportional to the square root of the ratio between the two diffusion coefficients as indicated above. The diffusion coefficient of one of the reactants can be determined on the basis of this equation by knowledge of the diffusion coefficient of the other reactant and by estimation of the position of the precipitate in the gel between the respective wells when the two reactants are present in equivalent proportions (Preer 1956). Thus, the diffusion coefficient for hemocyanins, poliomyelitis virus, diphtheria antitoxin and the turnip yellow mosaic virus have been estimated by this method.

Another experimental set-up with two rectangular troughs placed at right angles has been recommended by Ouchterlony (1962) and by Allison and Humphrey (1959). If the two reactants are employed in equivalent amounts, the precipitin arc is a straight line and the angle (α) between the antigen well and the precipitin arc depends only on the diffusion coefficients: $tg(\alpha) = D_{Ag}/D_{Ab}$. Working with one reactant with a known diffusion coefficient, it is possible to determine the diffusion coefficient of the other.

2.4. Immunoelectrophoresis

2.4.1. General principles

Immunoelectrophoresis consists of a combination of electrophoresis and radial immunodiffusion in gels. It is based on the fact that in agar gel, the movement of molecules in an electric field is similar to that in a liquid medium, with the advantage that free diffusion during and after electrophoresis is lessened. The constituents of a mixture are then defined both by their electrophoretic mobilities and by their antigenic specificities.

IMMUNOELECTROPHORESIS

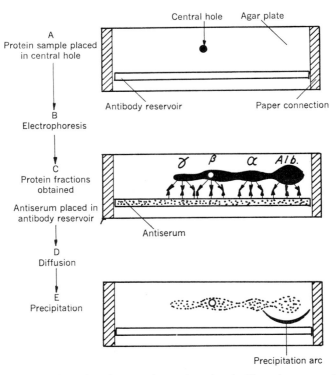

Fig. 2.4. Method for micro-immunoelectrophoresis. *A*: The microscope slide is covered with buffered agar gel. The central hole (for insertion of the antigen) is dug out of the agar gel. *B*: Electrophoresis is performed for $1\frac{1}{2}$ h (10 v/cm). *C*: The electrophoretic pattern is obtained; antiserum solution is placed in the antibody reservoir which is dug out of gel after electrophoresis. *D*: Diffusion is allowed to proceed in a moist chamber. *E*: As the result of diffusion, antigen–antibody reactions occur between corresponding fractions, and precipitation arcs or lines appear; these are specific for each antigen. The precipitation arc for albumin is illustrated here (Clausen 1960a).

This technique may be performed on a macro scale, as originally demonstrated by Grabar and Williams (1953) and Poulik (1952, 1958), or as a micromethod (Scheidegger 1955). The principle of this technique is illustrated in fig. 2.4. The antigen sample is applied to a hole placed in the middle of a glass plate coated with buffered gel. Electrophoresis separates the antigen mixture into various zones. A longitudinal trough parallel to the long edge of the plate is then made in the gel and is filled with antiserum against the antigen mixture. A double diffusion takes place; the antiserum diffuses into the gel and the antigens diffuse radially in all directions from the electrophoretic zones. The antigens eventually meet the antibodies and precipitates are formed at equivalence points; the number of precipitates formed corresponds to the number of independent antigens present (fig. 2.4, 2.5). Because of the previous electrophoretic separation the precipitates are dispersed in a characteristic system of arcs with precipitation lines located alongside the electrophoretic zones.

Two- and three-dimensional immunoelectrophoresis or one-dimensional electrophoresis combined with two-dimensional chromato-immunodiffusion have been suggested (Blanc 1959, 1961; Peeters and Vuylsteke 1960).

Caption for page 433.

Fig. 2.5. Micro-immunoelectrophoresis of normal human serum. Serum was placed in the two holes, and after electrophoresis precipitation pattern was developed with a horse antiserum against pooled normal human serum (placed in central trough). The main precipitation arcs are marked. *Experimental conditions – Antigen*: 1.5 μl normal human serum (6.5 g protein/100 ml) have been applied in the two antigen wells. *Electrophoresis*: 10 V/cm for 70 min, buffer: 0.05 M veronal buffer, pH 8.6. *Antiserum*: 80 μl polyvalent antiserum from a horse against normal pooled human serum is applied in central trough. *Immunodiffusion*: 16 hr at 24 °C. *Staining*: After washing by standing for two days in 0.9 % (w/v) aqueous NaCl and for 1 hr in distilled water, the slide is dried in open air and stained for protein with Amido Black (appendix 18). *Photography*: See appendix 17.

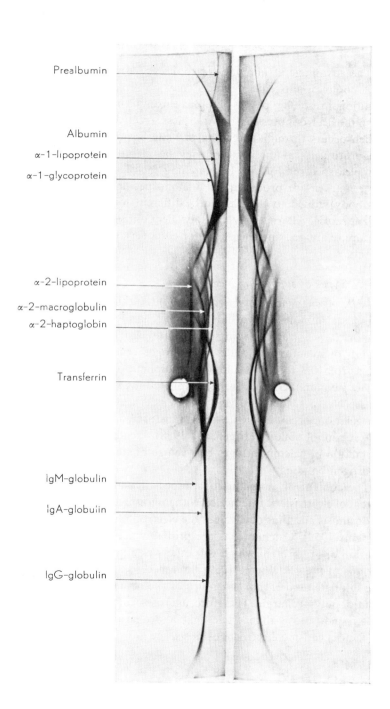

Prealbumin

Albumin
α-1-lipoprotein
α-1-glycoprotein

α-2-lipoprotein
α-2-macroglobulin
α-2-haptoglobin

Transferrin

IgM-globulin

IgA-globulin

IgG-globulin

The advantage of immunoelectrophoresis over immunodiffusion is that complex antigenic mixtures may be separated because of the additional resolving power obtained through the electrophoretic step. Immunoelectrophoresis is, however, less sensitive owing to the dilution which occurs through spreading of materials during electrophoresis.

Constituents in the mixture may be identified serologically in a complex spectrum of arcs by matching each individual arc by means of a marker arc produced by a monospecific reactant (antigen or antibody) added to the plate in a different location from the polyvalent serum. Alternatively the polyvalent antiserum may be absorbed by a pure antigen and then used for comparison with the unabsorbed serum.

2.4.2. Types of supporting media

2.4.2.1. Agar (agarose and agaro-pectin) (Araki 1937)

Agar is a mixture of two linear polysaccharides, agarose and agaro-pectin. It is extracted from seaweeds (algae); chemically it consists mainly of galactose molecules linked together at C-1 and -3, and contains from 0.3 to 3.7% sulphur as sulphate (one sulphate per 8–50 galactose units). Ordinarily, the sulphate ions are combined with such ions as Na^+, K^+, Ca^{++} and Mg^{++}. These salts are thought to be necessary for gelation, because when agar is transformed to its acid form at pH 2.0, it cannot solidify (Jirgensons 1958). Gelation depends partly on formation of calcium bridges between sulphate groups and partly on hydrogen bonding.

The content of inorganic ions, especially sulphate, determines the extent of electrostatic interaction with migrating colloids and of electro-endosmosis and thus determines the electrophoretic properties of agar (Wieme 1959). Calcium ions are probably necessary for optimal migration of lipoprotein which will otherwise interact with the sulphate groups of the gel (Wieme 1959; Laurell 1966). Agaro-pectin contains the sulphate (and carboxyl) groups of the agar, whereas agarose is a neutral polysaccharide. Therefore, agarose produces a less pronounced electroendosmosis than crude agar and agaro-pectin (for discussion of factors causing electroendosmosis, see Gordon 1968).

Agarose may be isolated as described by Araki (1937, 1956) and Hjertén (1962) (appendix 6). The use of an agarose gel instead of an ordinary agar gel has advantages as the gel is free from ionized groups and does not cause pronounced electroendosmosis or interaction with certain basic proteins such as lysozyme (Uriel et al. 1964). Agarose is more resistant to acids than agaro-pectin and therefore electrophoresis may be carried out at lower pH. On the other hand, the complicated preparation of agarose may limit its use (see appendix 6); it is available commercially, but it is relatively expensive.

2.4.2.2. Cellulose acetate

Immunoelectrophoresis can also be performed on cellulose acetate paper (Kohn 1958, 1959, 1962, 1968; Lomanto and Vergani 1967). The technique suffers from difficulties involved in applying the antiserum evenly on the paper. It is therefore not recommended for the beginner in the field of immunochemistry. The difficulty is not encountered in the agar technique where the application of antiserum merely consists of filling the antibody trough with antiserum. On the other hand, the cellulose acetate easily sucks up buffered solutions of antisera and may be recommended for radial immunodiffusion (see appendix 9) and electrophoresis of antigens in an antibody-containing medium (Laurell technique, p. 437) (Vergani et al. 1967). Cellulose acetate has also been used in combination with thin-layer gel filtration for immuno-chemical detection of serum proteins. The serum proteins are first separated by thin-layer gel filtration on Sephadex G 200. The cellulose acetate foil is applied onto the Sephadex surface on which the proteins have been separated. Strips of filter paper soaked with antiserum are placed parallel to either side of the cellulose membrane. By allowing immunodiffusion to develop for 48 hours, twelve different serum protein antigens have been described (Agostoni et al. 1967).

2.4.2.3. Starch gel

Horizontal or vertical starch gel electrophoresis (Smithies 1955, 1959) of protein antigens may be followed by diffusion in gel by cutting the electrophoretic starch gel vertically in two halves. One half is stained for proteins and the other half is placed in a melted agar buffer solution. After gelling, an antibody trough is made in the gel in the anode–cathode direction, and an antiserum is applied in this trough. The antigen separated in the starch gel will now diffuse into the agar gel and meet the corresponding antibody and thus create multiple precipitation lines. This method is laborious, because the electrophoresis and immunodiffusion cannot be performed in one step. However, starch gel electrophoresis has a higher resolving power for the antigen mixture than agar has. Horizontal starch gel electrophoresis may produce 18 electrophoretic zones in separation of serum proteins, whereas agar gel electrophoresis results in only seven.

It has been possible to separate and analyse subunits of proteins by starch gel electrophoresis (Poulik 1964a, b). By reductive alkylation followed by starch gel electrophoresis in 8 M urea (formate buffer) the L- and H-chains of immunoglobulins are separated (pp. 415–416).

2.4.2.4. *Polyacrylamide gel*

Immunoelectrophoresis may be performed in an acrylamide gel (Antoine 1962; Keutel 1964). Polymerized acrylamide, a linear polymer gel is an adequate inert supporting medium for electrophoresis. Although the electrophoresis can be completed within twenty minutes, immunodiffusion time is more than three times longer than in agar gel (Keutel 1964). The acrylamide immunoelectrophoresis is preferred when the samples distort agar gel during electrophoretic separation, where extreme acid or alkaline conditions are required or where antigens are to be enzymically detected. (For factors governing separation in acrylamide the companion volume by Gordon (1968) should be consulted.)

2.4.2.5. *Fibrin–agar*

Fibrin–agar electrophoresis is mainly used in studies of proteolytic enzymes, their activators and inhibitors. Such studies involve characterization of a number of the individual steps in the catalytic processes, for example blood coagulation, by examination of the reaction products (Heimburger and Schwick 1962; Schwick 1967). The method is based on the combination of immunoelectrophoresis and the classical test of fibrinolysis performed by means of the fibrin-plate technique (Astrup and Müllertz 1952). By mixing agar with buffer, fibrinogen and calcium ions followed by appropriate heating, a medium is obtained which possesses the electrophoretic properties of the agar and the substrate properties required for proteolytic digestion. After electrophoretic separation and incubation, every electrophoretic zone containing a proteinase will appear as a clear zone of lysis. By cutting out troughs for antisera, precipitation lines corresponding to the antigenic proteinases may appear. The troughs may also be used for application of an activator or inhibitor of proteinase function. An electrophoretic zone containing a proenzyme of a proteinase may, during diffusion towards the trough containing the activator, cause the formation of a clear zone of digested fibrin as a sign of the activation of the proenzyme. Combined with immunodiffusion on the second half of the slide, this method offers possibilities for localization of enzymes and proenzymes belonging to the group of proteinases. Similarly, it is possible to demonstrate anti-proteinase activity (Heide and Haupt 1964).

2.4.3. *Electrophoresis in antibody-containing media* (*Laurell technique*)

In this technique, the antigen–antibody reaction occurs during the electrophoresis of an antigen mixture in an antibody containing medium (Bussard 1959; Ressler 1960a, b). Both antigen and antibody move according to their electrophoretic mobilities, and they also react together, resulting in flame-shaped precipitin zones of antigen–antibody complexes (fig. 2.6). Under the influence of the electric field, unbound antigen within the peak of the flame-shaped precipitate migrates into the precipitate which redissolves in the excess antigen. Thus, the leading edge of the flame is gradually displaced in the direction the antigen is migrating. The amount of antigen within the leading boundary edge is successively diminished because of the formation of soluble antigen–antibody complexes. When the antigen is diminished to equivalence with the antibody, the antibody–antigen complex can no longer be dissolved and a stable precipitate will form at the leading edge, which

Subject index p. 557

is thereafter stationary. The distance finally travelled by the peak depends on the relative excess of antigen over antibody and can be used as a measure of the amount of antigen present. Every precipitin band featured as a flame represents an individual antigen. By absorbing the antibody with pure antigens prior to the migration it is possible to identify the pattern (Ressler 1960a). Greater resolution can be obtained if, prior to the electrophoresis in the agar gel containing antiserum, the proteins are separated by starch gel electrophoresis; a number of precipitates of albumin and ceruloplasmin have thus been obtained (Ressler 1960a, b). Electrophoresis in an antibody-containing medium may thus be applied to studies of antigenic sites.

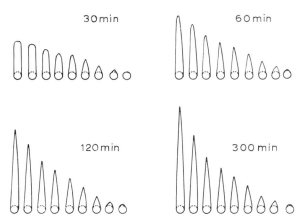

Fig. 2.6. Electrophoresis of serum albumin in antibody-containing agarose gel. Serum albumin dilutions run for 30, 60, 120 and 300 min in agarose gel containing 2.5% rabbit anti-albumin serum. Amount of albumin in each series from left to right: 5, 3.75, 2.5, 2.0, 1.5, 1.0, 0.5, 0.25, and 0.125 µg. (From Laurell 1966).

The electrophoresis of an antigen mixture in an antibody-containing agar gel has been used one-dimensionally or two-dimensionally. The techniques (see fig. 2.6, Laurell's method) have been used for quantitative estimation of antigens in solutions containing from 500 to 12.5 µg/ml (Clarke and Freeman 1967; Laurell 1966) provided the isoelectric point of the antigen differs from that of the antibody. Systematic studies of the migration rate in an agarose medium containing the antibody (Laurell 1966) revealed empirically that within a certain time (2 to 10 hr) a rectilinear relationship between final migration distance of the leading edge and the amount of antigen may be established. This method is appropriate for estimation of serum proteins or other antigens in different biological fluids (vide infra) and is described in appendix 13. The migration rate of the antigens must be faster than that of the IgG globulin.

Subject index p. 557

CHAPTER 3

Antisera

The result of active immunization depends on the type of antigen, the dose and whether the immunization is primary or secondary. Jerne (1951) studied these factors in detail and demonstrated that it was possible to evaluate the result of immunization quantitatively by estimation of the concentration and avidity of antibodies in immune sera. The avidity of an antibody is defined on the basis of the avidity constant k_1, which is identical with the association constant of the primary reaction

$$\overset{k_1}{Ag + Ab \rightleftharpoons Ag\ Ab \rightleftharpoons (Ag-Ab-)_n}.$$

A very low value of k_1 will be reflected by a ready dissociation of the immune complex. The avidity is thus estimated quantitatively by estimation of k_1. The k_1 of a certain antiserum can be calculated from the estimation of initial free amount of Ab after the formation of the primary Ag–Ab complex. The experimental system consisted simply of a certain amount of antigen to which the immune serum was added in different dilutions (Jerne 1951). Jerne's studies indicated that, after the primary response to antibody, the titre increased slowly and slightly (cf. fig. 1.3). The avidity of antibodies of the primary response was low (low k_1 value) but increased during the succeeding weeks after immunization. The antibodies obtained after secondary immunization revealed high avidity. Maximal concentration of antibody is obtained about 8 days after the secondary or later injections.

Rabbit antisera showed higher avidity than other antisera. No difference in avidity could be demonstrated between young and old animals.

3.1. Preparation and choice of antigen

Polyvalent as well as specific monovalent antisera are commercially obtainable. However, these antisera are expensive and are often diluted to a low titre. It may therefore be wise for laboratory workers in the field of immunochemistry to prepare their own antisera; for this, suitable antigens must be available.

When preparing antisera against biological fluids, the fluid ought to have a concentration of protein or other macromolecular antigens of about 5% (w/v). With biological fluids of low antigen content, e.g. tissue culture media, urine or cerebrospinal fluids, a preliminary concentration step is needed. This may be performed by lyophilization, pressure or vacuum dialysis, or dialysis against a suitable macromolecular colloid such as polyvinyl-pyrrolidone (PVP) or carbowax of high molecular weight (see appendix 3).

Theoretically it should not be necessary to concentrate an antigen solution because animals have a high sensitivity to antigenic stimulation. However, in the author's hand, only by working with antigen mixtures of about 5% (w/v) protein (antigen) solutions could maximal response to immunization be obtained. This may be because highly diluted colloids are present in solutions in the monomeric forms. These forms are washed more rapidly into the blood stream from the injection site than the polymeric concentrated solutions which tend to be retained at the site of injection. An additional advantage of concentrating the antigen solution when producing polyvalent antisera is that even trace amounts of antigens may become potent in provoking antibody synthesis.

Preparation of polyvalent antisera against organ antigens is limited by three factors. First, the lipid content of the organs may mask certain protein antigens to a degree which makes it impossible to provoke antibody formation. To avoid this difficulty, the antigens of the organ may be unmasked either by repeated freezing and thawing (Van Alten and LaVelle 1966) or by removal of the lipids, for instance by Folch's procedure (Folch et al. 1951) or by acetone extraction (Laterre and Heremans 1963). These procedures for removal of lipid may cause protein denaturation with possible alteration of antigenic specificity. The second difficulty in preparing antiserum against organ antigens is the auto-immune reaction in the recipient animal provoked by the introduction of antigens possessing partial immunological identity with proteins from corresponding organs in the recipient animal. This auto-immune reaction may cause the death of the animal, by for instance, nephritis or allergic encephalomyelitis. Thirdly, antigenic similarities between different animal species may give rise to immune-tolerance towards some antigens, thus causing an unsuccessful immune response. In order to avoid this, another animal species may be chosen (Dray 1960).

In order to prepare *specific antisera* against given proteins, the proteins must be absolutely pure. The purification is performed as described in the manuals of this series covering fractionation of proteins by gel electrophoresis (Gordon 1968), gel filtration (Fischer 1968) or chromatography (Peterson 1969). It is necessary to show immunological purity of a concentrated sample (5 % w/v) of the preparation in question, prior to immunization, for instance by means of immuno-electrophoresis (double trough, p. 458) using a polyvalent antibody preferably against the original mixture of antigens. Every step during the preparation of the immunologically pure antigen must be controlled for purity, but even using strict criteria for purity, it is not always possible to produce an absolutely pure antigen in practice. It must be stressed that only immunological criteria for purity can be used. Thus, for instance, characterization by means of different electrophoretic procedures is not sufficient, because an electrophoretic zone may cover antigens with identical electrophoretic mobility, but different immunological properties. Conversely, the presence of multiple electrophoretic bands will not necessarily indicate heterogeneity, because several proteins exist in electrophoretically distinguishable forms: IgA globulin, haptoglobin, α-1-glycoprotein and Gc-globulin (Hirschfeld 1962; Schmid and Benette 1961; Schultze et al. 1962).

3.2. Preparation of antiserum

It is well known that injection of 'pure' protein antigens into a number of animals of the same species will not cause the same immune response in all of them. Some animals may form only one specific antibody; others may form antibodies against other antigens. This 'polyvalent' response to a 'pure' antigen may be explained by adsorption of a few foreign antigen molecules onto it. It is therefore largely a question of luck as to whether a particular animal will produce only one antibody. This is the reason for immunizing several animals at the same time, hoping that at least one of them may respond by producing a specific antiserum.

Many different species of animal may be used for antibody production, for instance horse, goat, sheep, duck, hen, rabbit and guinea pig. Horses are expensive, but the horse type of antibody is characterized by forming well-defined precipitation arcs because its antigen–antibody complex is soluble in excess of both antigen and antibody. However, horse antibody may easily give rise to multiple immunoprecipitates under unbalanced or unstable conditions (see pp. 499, 500–502). In order to avoid these effects, rabbit antisera may be preferred. For the purpose of making specific antisera, rabbits are also convenient because they are inexpensive and so it is possible to use larger groups of animals from which those containing only the specific antibody with optimal titre may be selected. Rabbit-type antibodies are also present in goats and guinea pigs and most other species mentioned above.

In some immunochemical studies, double immunochemical reactions have to be used (the double antibody precipitation, pp. 492 and 505) (Schalch and Parker 1964). In these methods, two specific antibodies are necessary for determination of proteins and peptide hormones. The complex of protein hormone and rabbit anti-hormone can be separated from the nonreacted protein hormone by means of a specific anti-rabbit IgG globulin antiserum. Under such circumstances and in cases where the immunization schedules are unsuccessful in rabbits, other species such as goat, sheep, duck or hen should be used for immunization. The antibody response may be increased, in certain cases, by going from

Subject index p. 557

mammals to birds. In practice, birds, especially hens, produce good antibodies but their antisera are not directly applicable in immunochemical reactions, because the sera are hyperlipaemic. Avian antibodies are to some extent different in their properties from mammalian antibodies, thus, in free buffer solutions their precipitating power seems maximal at salt concentrations about 10 times that normally used for mammalian antisera (Crowle 1961). However, this is not the case during immunodiffusion in agar gels (Crowle 1961). In cases of avian antisera where the lipid content disturbs the immunochemical reactions, the serum may be cleared by flotation or by a specific complex formation combined with flotation in solutions of the organic sulphate derivatives, heparin or dextran sulphate (Burstein 1956; Oncley et al. 1957).

Several schedules for antigen injection have been suggested by different authors. Many of these are intended to decrease the immunization time by daily intravenous injections of antigens. These methods, however, seem inappropriate because the daily injections consume large amounts of antigen, which is often undesirable, especially when making specific antibodies, e.g. against certain protein hormones. Also, daily injections of protein antigens may saturate the reticuloendothelial system (Sweet et al. 1965). They may even give rise to decreased antibody response and secondary amyloidosis (Teilum 1956) and cause decreased resistance of the animal.

In the author's opinion, it is wisest not to be too impatient in provoking antibody response by abandoning the classical extended immunization schedules (see appendix 2).

3.3. Use of adjuvants

Not all macromolecules are equally effective antigens and it is often difficult to elicit any significant antibody response by injection of a pure antigen. Various local irritants and other adjuvants have been introduced, which overcome this difficulty to some extent. Thus, tapioca, nucleic acids, potassium aluminum hydroxide and various mineral oils emulsified with mycobacteria as for instance, *Mycobacte-*

rium butyricum and *M. smegmatis* (cf. appendix 1) or *Haemophilus pertussis* and *Corynebacterium parvum* have been used. Adjuvants containing the last two bacterias are available commercially.

The antigen is generally mixed with the adjuvant and injected subcutaneously. The exact mechanism of operation of these adjuvants is unknown (Schultze 1961), but in all probability the adjuvants induce local inflammation with proliferation of macrophages and bring macrophages into immediate contact with the antigen. Recent studies have shown that immuno-competent lymphocytes do not take up injected foreign antigens. However, the foreign antigens seem to be taken up by macrophages which can hereafter produce a stimulating factor (RNA) giving rise to proliferation of lymphocytes and the formation of antibodies (Ada 1966; Raska and Cohen 1968). As an adjuvant causes proliferation of macrophages, it seems probable that the increasing amounts of macrophages will give rise to the formation of higher amounts of the stimulating factor, initiating formation of more lymphocytes and antibodies. Full instructions for use of Freund's adjuvant are given in appendix 1.

3.4. *Absorption of antisera*

In order to avoid the complicated and time-consuming procedures for isolation of a pure protein, mono- or oligospecific antisera against certain antigens may be prepared by certain 'tricks'. It is not possible in this manual to cover all variables but some advice may be given. Newborn sera from man and certain animals lack some of the proteins present in adult sera, for instance haptoglobin and IgA globulin (see the survey by Hitzig 1963). Thus, by absorbing a polyvalent antiserum against adult human serum with foetal serum in a dilution series (from 1:1 to 1:200) it is possible by means of immunoelectrophoresis to choose the dilution giving an antiserum specific against haptoglobin and IgA. Sera from patients genetically lacking albumin, α- or β-lipoprotein, IgG, IgA, β-1-AC, haptoglobin, etc., may be used similarly to prepare the corresponding antisera. Early in the lactation period, human milk contains no IgG globulins, but an immunoglobulin closely

Subject index p. 557

related to IgA (Hanson 1961). Therefore, an anti-human milk anti-serum does not contain antibodies against the gamma chain of IgG. This antiserum may be used specifically against IgA after absorption with newborn serum.

Normal cerebrospinal fluid and urine contain only traces of α-2-macroglobulin and α-2-lipoprotein. These biological fluids added in a series of experiments in increasing amounts to polyvalent antiserum against human serum may give a specific antiserum against these two macro-globulins.

Inulin added to serum causes precipitation of β-1-C (third part of complement). This precipitate can be used for preparing a specific antiserum (Brummerstedt-Hansen 1967).

CHAPTER 4

Techniques of immunodiffusion

4.1. Choice of method and its limitations

Immunodiffusion may be used for qualitative or quantitative examination of a single or a limited number of antigens (or antibodies). Complex mixtures cannot be analysed in one operation, as in techniques using immunodiffusion combined with electrophoresis, because of the possibility of overlap of multiple immunoprecipitates. This overlap may hinder a detailed study of individual precipitates.

In order to study antigens qualitatively or semiquantitatively the method and pattern of choice are determined beforehand by the purpose itself (vide infra). For quantitative studies using monovalent antisera, single diffusion methods are superior to double diffusion because they give rise to greater distances of diffusion (cf. fig. 2.1, p. 426–427). On the other hand, methods in which both reactants are applied in holes use less material than the more wasteful single diffusion methods utilising agar mixed with one of the reactants. Double diffusion tests are on the whole easier for inexperienced workers to set up and interpret than single diffusion tests; they are also less susceptible to artifact formation, e.g. through changes of temperature. Double diffusion tests are usually more sensitive because of the concentrating effect imposed by the precipitate barrier, and they are more versatile. For these reasons, double diffusion tests are more widely used than single diffusion methods. Micro methods are preferable to the macro tests, being more economical in material, space and time.

In immunochemical studies of high molecular weight components,

447

such as IgM, α-2-M, higher polymers of IgA immunoglobulin and other antigens with a molecular weight above 200,000, diffusion is not free, owing to the limiting action of the micellar structure of the gel; the resulting retardation of movement often gives rise to striated patterns. In these cases gel diffusion can only be used with caution for quantitative studies.

4.2. Choice of antiserum

In immunodiffusion using horse-type antisera, the precipitates are sharp because the antigen-antibody complex is soluble in excess of both reactants. With rabbit-type antisera the zone of immunoprecipitate shows a sharp contour only at the side facing the antigen well. Facing the antibody well, the precipitate is blurred because the precipitate in that case is insoluble in excess of antibody. Only the boundary of the precipitate toward the antigen well can thus be used as marker for estimation of the distance of immunodiffusion. The blurring may create some difficulties in interpretation of the precipitation lines formed, especially in studies resulting in spur phenomena. The rabbit type antibody does not dissolve precipitates already formed, therefore this antiserum may be used in search for minor impurities in certain preparations of proteins and in the study of antigens only present in trace amounts in a sample.

However, horse antiserum, under certain conditions, induces Liesegang's phenomenon (periodic precipitates) more easily than rabbit-type antiserum. Indeed, Crowle (1961) says that, to his knowledge, no well-documented proof is at present available that Liesegang's phenomenon develops at all with rabbit type antiserum. Finally, it must be emphasized that in experiments using antisera from different species on the same agar plate, as used sometimes in double diffusion (Clausen and Heremans 1960), crosswise absorption of the two antisera must be carried out to avoid false precipitation phenomena caused by antigenic similarities between serum proteins from different animal species.

4.3. Choice of amount of antigen

Immunodiffusion techniques represent almost the only method of examining the composition of tissue antigens, particularly those from
insoluble subcellular particulate fractions. Partial solubilization of
these fractions can result from homogenisation in the presence of
detergents (Triton-X-100, sodium deoxycholate or Lubrol W) (Perlman
et al. 1964). However, antigens thus obtained must be used with caution,
because lipids will also be present in the mixture, and during diffusion
lipids may react spontaneously with serum proteins to give 'false'
precipitates which resemble immunoprecipitates. Colloidal suspensions
of membranes can be made by using the X-press (Ebedo 1960); a
frozen tissue homogenate is forced through a small opening and the
crystal structure of the ice changes; this change is associated with the
development of an internal pressure of about 25 tons and causes
tissue disruption (Dammacco and Clausen 1966).

Extracts of tissues or microorganisms containing mixtures of proteins, lipids and carbohydrate are impossible to standardise with regard to individual components. In order to produce the maximum number of immunoprecipitates, a suitable antigen/antiserum ratio must be
chosen; this is in order to avoid either overlapping of immunoprecipitates or such an excess of one reactant that some antigens are not
precipitated in the gel phase. This ratio may be found by trials using
both reactants successively in a series of dilutions. Thus, for instance,
the antigen mixture, in a dilution series ($0-^1/_{20}$ or more) is reacted
with undiluted antiserum; in another series undiluted antigen mixture
is reacted with a dilution series of the antiserum. In this way, different
proportions of antigen and antibody are related and the correct ratio
can be judged from examination of the resulting precipitates.

The concentration of individual antigens should be kept as constant
as possible when examining (for example) successive changes in a given
biological fluid. However, the use of identical volumes of the fluid or
of identical amounts of total proteins or carbohydrates provides
acceptable alternatives for obtaining proper reproducibility. For
example, the same volumes of equally concentrated human cerebros-

pinal fluid have been used to bring out changes in antigens normally present in trace amounts (Clausen et al. 1964).

4.4. Choice of hole patterns in double diffusion

The most usual set-up is that with the antigen (or antibody) wells (1.5 to 5.0 µl vol.) arranged circularly around a central antibody (antigen) well with the holes about 1 cm from each other (figs. 2.2.A p. 428, and 4.1; see also Ouchterlony 1962, 1967). The antigen samples may also be applied in wells arranged parallel to a longitudinal antibody trough (1 mm broad) (fig. 2.2.D). This set-up is useful both for qualitative and quantitative purposes and is especially useful for

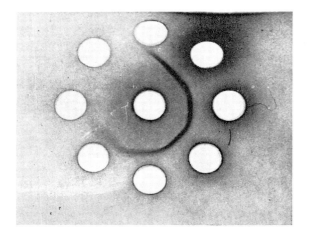

g. 4.1. Semi-quantitative estimation of antibody activity of a myeloma serum ainst Cowan's type I *Staphylococcus aureus*. The antibody activity of the serum rresponds to a dilution factor of 1:16. *Experimental condition – Antibody*: Outer ːlls: clockwise from the right ('one o'clock'), a constant amount (5 µl) of progressive lutions (undiluted, 1:1, 1:2, 1:4, 1:8, 1:16, 1:32 and 1:64) of the myeloma serum .2 g/100 ml). *Antigen*: Center well: 1.5 µl extract of Cowan's type I *Staphylococcus reus* made by disintegration of the bacteria in the X-press of Edebo (1960) ʼammacco and Clausen 1965). *Immunodiffusion*: 16 hr. *Staining* as in fig. 2.5.

the demonstration of the presence or absence of a certain antigen in different samples. However, the method cannot be used for revealing spur phenomena (pp. 467–469, fig. 6.1) because spurs can only be seen in cases where main precipitates meet each other at angles.

There are many other patterns for demonstrating the four types of reaction patterns described by Ouchterlony (see pp. 467–469). Besides the Ouchterlony schemes, triangular plastic chambers divided into a four compartment system may be used (fig. 2.3); this method is convenient for detailed studies of spur phenomena (Jennings and Malone 1957).

4.5. Quantitative methods

The choice of an agar gel method for estimation of antigens or antibodies depends on the accuracy required, the specificity and the amount of antigen or antibody to be estimated (Schwick 1964; Störiko 1965). For semiquantitative purposes, immunoelectrophoresis or Ouchterlony double diffusion methods, using serial dilutions of the sample in question, may be used. To estimate mμg quantities of protein hormones, radio-immuno assay (p. 486) may be the tool of choice. For estimations of protein antigens present in the sample in higher concentrations, the Oudin technique, the Mancini method or the Laurell method of immunoelectrophoresis may be chosen.

4.5.1. Single diffusion techniques

As mentioned previously, the Oudin technique (see pp. 411–412 and 424, and appendix 8) for quantitative estimation of antigens is the method which has been applied in studies of the mathematical and physicochemical background of immunodiffusion. Oudin's equations (p. 411) are the basis of the quantitative estimation of an antigen when mixed with other antigens. The method depends on a specific antiserum being available. It is possible to estimate the distance of migration after one to two days of incubation at constant temperature. Performed as the microtube gel precipitin technique the diffusion time is minimal and not more than 20 μl of each reactant is necessary (El-Marsafy and Abdel-

Gawad 1962). A serious drawback of this method is that it is rather sensitive to changes in temperature which give rise to formation of multiple precipitates; however, these artifacts usually remain stationary. The diffusion rate can also be affected by the use of inappropriate antigen/antibody ratios.

The Mancini method (see p. 427 and appendix 9, p. 517) has also been used for quantitative estimation of serum proteins. Under certain conditions, the area or diameter of the precipitate formed during immunodiffusion of an antigen in the single radial diffusion method is rectilinearly related to the concentration of antigen. This method is more sensitive than the Oudin technique, as it is possible to estimate down to 0.0025 μg of antigen. However, the length of time required for high-molecular-weight antigens to complete their diffusion may be a drawback. The time required for the precipitate to become stationary and for obtaining a sufficient area covered by the immunoprecipitate depends on the antigen in question. The time is only a few hours for low-molecular-weight components such as Bence–Jones proteins, but several weeks for higher molecular weight units (see the survey by Schultze and Heremans 1966).

4.5.2. (Semi-)quantitative estimation of antigens by double diffusion

A single antigen may be semi-quantitatively estimated by Ouchterlony double diffusion methods applying an antibody of standardized titre in the central well and a series of diluted samples in the radial wells (figs. 2.2.A and 4.1); the dilutions are best applied from one o'clock clockwise around the central well. In all cases a standard solution of known antigen content must be included. After a certain time, the immunoprecipitate developed around one well will fuse with the next precipitate and so on, as long as the titre of the antigen in question is sufficiently high. Below a certain limit, the point of equivalence between the two reactants is situated in the antigen well (e.g. well 6 in fig. 4.1). The reciprocal value of the dilution of the sample corresponding to that particular well indicates arbitrarily the amount of antigen present in the original sample. A similar set-up may be arranged by making a longitudinal trough for the antibody and applying the diluted sample in antigen wells placed parallel to the antibody trough (fig. 2.2. D) (review Crowle 1961; Ouchterlony 1962, 1967).

Another variation of the double diffusion method which may be used also directly for quantitative estimation of antigens (Darcy 1960, 1961) is the triangular plate technique of Jennings and Malone (1957). Buffered agar is poured into a triangular plate and when set, equal areas of the three corners are cut out. One corner is filled with the standard antiserum, another with a standard antigen solution and the third with the unknown sample (fig. 2.3). After immunodiffusion, the intersection of the continuation of the immunoprecipitate of the unknown sample and the standard antigen solution is determined. The perpendicular distances of this intersection to the antigen (A) and antibody (B) reservoirs are measured. The ratio of these distances A/B, called the diffusivity, has been shown to be linearly related to the logarithm of the concentration (C_u) of the unknown sample:

$$A/B = \pm K. \log C_u + r_0,$$

where r_0 refers to a constant.

This direct method is said to estimate protein antigens with an error of about 5%.

CHAPTER 5

Techniques of immunoelectrophoresis

Immunoelectrophoresis involves two distinct and separate operations. In the first step, suitable holes are cut in a buffered agar plate, filled with antigen and the proteins of the antigen sample are spread lengthwise through the agar by electrophoresis. After completion of this step, a suitable trough is made in the agar parallel to, but well separated from, the track of electrophoretic separation. This trough is filled with antibody which is then allowed to diffuse towards the antigen under controlled conditions. Precipitates are deposited as arcs between the antibody trough and the antigen track.

5.1. Choice of buffers

The buffers used in the gel have an influence on electrophoretic mobility and on the position of the immunoprecipitate. The pH of the buffer must be chosen with the isoelectric point of the antigen in mind, it being desirable usually to work at a pH slightly above the isoelectric point (see Gordon 1968), so that the proteins have a negative charge and do not react with the agar. A pH of 8.2–8.4 is usually used for serum.

As stated previously, immunological reactions take place only between pH of about 4.5 and 9.0. In studies of antigens with different isoelectric points, it is important to remember this fact. Thus, glycoproteins with low isoelectric points should be separated at pH between 3.5 and 4.5; however, the subsequent antigen–antibody reaction cannot be performed at this acid pH. Therefore, another buffer must be introduced into the gel prior to immunodiffusion. To do this, an appropriate buffer, with a pH of about 6.5 is placed in the antibody trough prior to the application of antiserum. In this way, a zone of diffusing buffer neutralizes the acid electrophoretic medium prior to immunodiffusion and antigen–antibody reaction. The ionic strength is also of great importance in gel electrophoresis; if it is too high, heating is liable to occur, while too low a buffer concentration does not keep the pH constant during the passage of current. Unless cooling is used, the ionic strength should not exceed 0.05.

Specific properties of certain buffer ions may also influence electrophoretic mobility. Thus, borate chelates with carbohydrates in glycoproteins and glycolipids, creating negatively-charged complexes and liberation of protons. This may be used for localization and identification of certain carbohydrate-containing proteins or lipoproteins. Citrate or succinate may chelate metal ions and change the mobility of proteins.

The buffer must also be chosen with regard to the other biochemical factors studied after immunodiffusion; thus, not all buffer solutions can be used in studies of enzyme activity because certain inorganic ions may be potent inhibitors or accelerators of the enzymes.

Some natural polyelectrolytes or inorganic ions may change the electrophoretic mobility of certain proteins; thus, at pH 8.6, hyaluronic acid forms a complex with albumin, possessing a slower migration rate than free albumin; the complex formations seem pH-dependent (Pigman et al. 1961).

5.2. Choice of method

5.2.1. General considerations

Two basic methods are available, i.e. the original macro technique (Grabar and Williams 1953) and the micro technique on microscope slides (Scheidegger 1955). The macro technique is time-consuming, taking up to 14 days for immunodiffusion; furthermore, it requires a large amount of antiserum and is therefore not used as a routine meth-

od. However, for some purposes the macro technique is more convenient; it is especially useful for revealing weak precipitation lines.
In studies of the binding capacities of proteins for drugs and hormones,
weakly binding proteins giving rise to weak precipitation lines may be
revealed by radioactive labelling. The macro method should also be
used for the demonstration of enzyme activities of individual antigens,
using conventional agar or fibrin agar. For other purposes, particularly
in routine work, micro techniques are preferable. Here the times of
electrophoresis (1–1.5 hr) and diffusion (16 hr) are relatively short and
only 100 µl of antiserum and 1–3 µl of antigen are used.

The separating power of micro-immunoelectrophoresis may be enhanced by carrying out the electrophoresis below light petroleum
ether (Wieme 1959; fig. 5.1). This enables a constant temperature to be
maintained, since heating of the electrophoretic slide during the run
will cause evaporation of the petroleum ether, with consequent cooling.
A field strength up to 20 V/cm can be used, because of the cooling
process; this is higher than is possible in ordinary gel electrophoresis
(5 to 7 V/cm). The higher field strength results in enhanced separation and

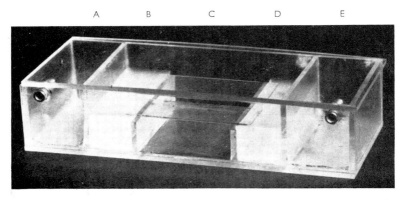

Fig. 5.1. A chamber for agar gel micro electrophoresis. A: Anode vessel for buffer
$(3.2 \times 4.0 \times 7.5$ cm); B: anode vessel for agar buffer $(2.5 \times 2.2 \times 7.5$ cm); C: central
reservoir for petroleum ether $(6.8 \times 2.2 \times 7.5$ cm); D: cathode vessel for agar buffer
(dimensions as B); E: cathode vessel for buffer (dimensions as A). The walls between
A and B and D and E have holes $(4 \times 1$ cm) to provide electrical connections.

faster movement of fractions. Thus, by electrophoresis of cerebrospinal fluid and urinary colloids, the γ-globulin area may optimally be split into eight zones within 24 min, contrasting with only one homogenous zone obtained by conventional agar gel electrophoresis (Wieme 1959). However, this improved method needs additional care in the preparation of the agar slides because of the higher currents.

5.2.2. Choice of type of pattern

As a general rule, the antigen samples are applied in circular holes. However, when using the Wieme technique with its higher resolving power, the antigen is placed in rectangular holes in order to avoid overlapping of adjacent fractions.

5.2.2.1. Comparison of antigenic composition of two or more samples

As a standard set-up (fig. 5.2.A) two holes containing the two samples are placed on each side of the antibody trough. The number of lines, their shape and distances from the trough may thus be compared. Two holes may, however, also be placed on the same side, equidistant from the trough, so demonstrating fusion of lines (fig. 5.2.B). This method is limited to studies of samples containing only a few antigens, otherwise the picture will be too complicated to interpret. Two antigens may also be compared by using a set-up with one hole and two troughs, one on each side of the hole (fig. 5.2.C). After electrophoresis of one of the antigen solutions, one of the two troughs is filled with the antibody; the other trough is filled with the other antigen solution. The diffusion through the gel of this antigen solution will give rise to formation of immunoprecipitates, where the antigen meets the antibody from the opposite trough. This precipitate is formed parallel to the troughs; however, at electrophoretic loci of common antigens the immunoprecipitate will fuse with the corresponding deflecting antigen–antibody complex focused around the electrophoretic locus. This method is also limited to samples containing only a few antigens, or to cases where identification of immunoprecipitates can be performed by applying pure antigen in the remaining trough. In a series of experiments, the set-up C is used when unabsorbed antiserum is applied in the one

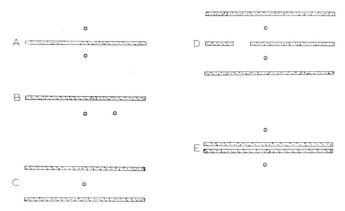

Fig. 5.2. Different arrangement of wells and antibody troughs for immuno-electrophoresis. *A*: Conventional set-up for comparison of two different antigen mixtures; *B*: another set-up for comparison of two different antigens; *C*: set-up for the comparison of two different antisera, or for absorption experiments; *D*: set-up for the combined diffusion method (cf. fig. 5.3); *E*: set-up for comparison of two different antigens or antibodies, when the antibodies originate from two different animal species.

trough and absorbed antiserum in the other. The absorption with a certain pure antigen will cause the corresponding antibodies to be inactivated. After immunodiffusion, the lack of immunoprecipitates may indicate antigens in common.

5.2.2.2. Comparison of composition of antibodies in different antisera
This comparison may be performed by the set-up C, consisting of one trough on each side of the hole or just by means of one hole and one trough. The fig. 5.2.C set-up is appropriate when two antisera, containing antibodies against the same antigen solution are to be compared or controlled for antibodies during immunization. The fig. 5.2.A set-up may be used for simple control of antibody composition of an antiserum. Working with antisera of different animal origin, the double trough system as well as the combined immunodiffusion system (fig. 5.2.D; see next section) cannot be used without crosswise

absorption of respective antisera with normal serum from other animals, because serum proteins from one animal species may show some antigenic properties in common with the other animal species. Without absorption, the two antisera would react with each other as well as with the antigen solution in question. A set-up which avoids the necessity for absorption of the antisera is shown in fig. 5.2.E; two troughs are placed medially neighbouring each other at a distance of 1 mm. The antigen wells are placed laterally to each trough; in this manner no mutual reaction between the two antisera may disturb the immunoelectrophoretic pattern.

5.2.2.3. Comparison of one or two antigen solutions with two antisera
A combination of immunoelectrophoresis and Ouchterlony double diffusion (known as combined immunodiffusion) is useful for identifying complex mixtures (Clausen and Heremans 1960). The agar gel contains two holes for antigen solutions and three troughs; one trough is placed laterally to each hole and one midway between them (fig. 5.2.D). The latter trough is cut out in sections, thus leaving a bridge of agar connecting the two antigen areas. The bridge is in the area where the antigens to be examined are expected to occur. After electrophoresis, antisera against the respective antigens are placed in each of the lateral troughs and a mixture of the two antisera in the intermediate interrupted trough. Immunodiffusion of antigens to the lateral troughs will reveal the optimal number of immunoprecipitates, the medially diffusing antigens will cause precipitation lines to fuse with those antigens of the other antigenic zone which are in common in the two solutions (fig. 5.3). The fusion may show total or partial immunological identity of the two antigen solutions. This method may be used to correlate different antisera and antigen solutions for instance, from different biological fluids or from different animal species.

5.3. Antigen

The choice of type and amount of antigen preparation is governed by the same factors as in immunodiffusion and is discussed on p. 449.

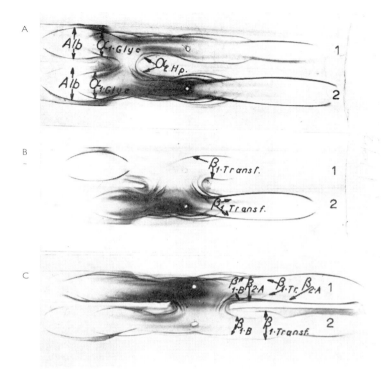

Fig. 5 3. The combined diffusion method of immunoelectrophoresis. Identification of the serum proteins found in concentrated normal cerebrospinal fluid by means of the immunoelectrophoretic tracings of normal human serum.

A: Identification of the serum proteins in the albumin and α-area. The intermediate agar bridge remains in the α-1-area. (1) Immunoelectrophoresis of normal cerebrospinal fluid, concentrated 100 times. (2) Immunoelectrophoresis of normal human serum.

B: Identification of the serum proteins in the α-2- and β-1-area. The intermediate agar bridge remains in the α-2-area. (1) Immunoelectrophoresis of normal concentrated cerebrospinal fluid. (2) Immunoelectrophoresis of normal human serum.

C: Identification of the serum proteins in the β-2-area. (1) Immunoelectrophoresis of normal human serum. (2) Immunoelectrophoresis of normal cerebrospinal fluid concentrated 100 times.

Corresponding precipitation lines are similarly identified. In all experiments the three antibody reservoirs have been filled with horse anti-human antiserum (Clausen 1960). Experimental conditions: as in fig. 2.5.

When working with tissues, a tissue block may be incorporated directly in the agar prior to electrophoresis (Wieme 1959). More often, homogenates or different types of extracts are used.

The location of the precipitate in gel diffusion is influenced by the concentration of the antibody as well as of the antigen (pp. 426–427). For routine analysis, therefore, a standard reference antigen solution of known concentration should always be included. For instance, in order to cover the biological variations in studies of the antigen composition of different samples of a biological fluid, a 'normal' sample obtained by pooling 10 or more normal samples, should be used as a standard. The standard is run on the same slide and against the same antiserum used for the unknown sample. The standard immunoelectrophoretic pattern in these cases may consist of two antigen wells cut equidistant from the antibody trough (fig. 5.2.A). In this set-up the amount of an antigen may be roughly estimated from the location of the apex of the corresponding immunoprecipitate and the standard precipitate relative to the common antibody trough. As mentioned previously (p. 426; fig. 2.1), an increased amount of antigen in the sample will cause the point of optimal precipitation to be placed closer to the antibody trough.

In conclusion, in order to evaluate an immunoelectrophoretic slide, the individual arcs of the precipitation pattern produced by the sample and by the reference standard arcs are compared as follows:

1. the electrophoretic position of the precipitate;
2. the distance from the apex of the precipitin arc to the antiserum trough;
3. the length of the precipitation line;
4. the shape of the precipitate;
5. the sharpness and thickness of the precipitate; and
6. the interaction with other precipitates or the presence of double humped or multi-humped precipitate arcs (eventually fusion with other lines).

Subject index p. 557

5.4. Reference markers

In a systematic study of the migration rate of serum proteins, Tizelius (1937) found that at alkaline pH the serum proteins arrange themselves into four main classes of electrophoretic zones called albumin, α-, β- and γ-globulins. This splitting into mobility intervals was greatest at alkaline pH farthest away from the iso-electric point of the (serum) proteins (below 6.8); but above pH 8.6 denaturation of the proteins may occur. Therefore, pH 8.6 was chosen as basis for the designation of albumin, α-, β- and γ-globulin mobility in free electrophoresis. This nomenclature is still in use even in zone electrophoresis of serum proteins. Electrophoresis of serum proteins in solid supporting media also causes a separation into at least four main zones. However, in this case the electrophoretic mobility is influenced by the supporting material and reference markers must be used in order to define the mobility.

In order to characterize the antigens by means of their relative electrophoretic mobility, standard marker with known electrophoretic mobility must be used (Wieme 1959; Grabar et al. 1960; Grabar and Burtin 1964). Albumin and dextran are suitable markers, possessing the relative mobilities $M_r = 1.00$ and 0.00 respectively. Zero mobility does not correspond to the application point because of electroendosmosis; dextran, an inert non-ionised polymer with a molecular weight between 100,000 and 150,000 will mark the point of zero mobility. Practically, the relative electrophoretic mobility of a certain antigen is estimated by applying a standard sample of 5 % (w/v) albumin + dextran in a hole beside the antigen well (appendix 16).

The relative electrophoretic mobility of every immunoprecipitate shaped like a circle or an ellipse is measured from the apex of the arc, i.e. the point of the arc closest to the antibody trough. By measuring the distance (x) from the zone of zero mobility (dextran spot) to the apex and the distance from the dextran spot to the albumin (a), it is possible to calculate the relative electrophoretic mobility $(M_r = x/a)$ assuming a straight-line relationship between M_r value and distance from zero mobility. The relative electrophoretic mobility is usually, but not invariably, a well-defined characteristic of the antigen in question in a given buffer.

5.5. Steps in electrophoresis and diffusion (appendix 12)

5.5.1. The electrophoretic stage

The power applied in ordinary micro-immunoelectrophoresis is about 5–10 V/cm without cooling. When some method of cooling the gel is used, up to 20 V/cm can be applied. It is unwise to apply a higher voltage because of a pronounced heating of the electrophoretic medium, which may cause denaturation of proteins and melting of the agar gel. Initially, it may even be necessary to apply a lower voltage and after some minutes to increase the power to maximally 10 V/cm; this is to eliminate the danger that the buffer solution, because of electro-endosmosis, may be forced out of the holes, thereby washing out the antigen.

5.5.2. Diffusion stage

After electrophoresis the troughs are cut and filled with antisera. The slides are now placed in a moist chamber and kept at a constant temperature. During incubation, antigens and antibodies will diffuse in all directions and therefore also towards each other; precipitates are formed at the points of equivalence. After completion of the diffusion and formation of immunoprecipitates, the antigen–antibody reaction is stopped and unreacted proteins are removed by washing the slides in 0.9 aqueous NaCl.

It may be advantageous to perform immunodiffusion steps between 30 and 40 °C; in this range, immunoprecipitation occurs more rapidly, but sometimes less completely than at 0 °C. At elevated temperatures, there should be strict temperature control, because slight changes in temperatures during immunodiffusion may give rise to false precipitation phenomenon and Liesegang's phenomenon (Wilson 1958; Crowle 1961). In large-scale immunochemical experiments it is therefore unwise to carry out the immunodiffusion at elevated temperature and room temperature is preferable. In any case, not all antigen–antibody reactions are enhanced at elevated temperatures. Some specific precipitates form only in the cold and may even disappear on warming (Ritsman et al. 1960). Sometimes more complete precipitation may be obtained at lower temperatures of 0 to 4 °C (Crowle 1961) but in general a constant temperature about 18–24 °C is safe to use.

The incubation time during immunodiffusion depends on the type of technique used. In macro-immunoelectrophoresis, it may be 4 to 14 days; during that period, the plates should be examined daily and photographed at intervals to obtain the best result as the precipitin lines do not all appear simultaneously. With micro techniques, diffusion time is shortened to 12–16 hr because of the shorter distance of diffusion.

5.6. Quantitative methods

5.6.1. Electrophoresis prior to immunoprecipitation

In immunoelectrophoresis of different samples it is possible to evaluate the amount of an antigen semi-quantitatively by measurement of the distances of a certain precipitation arc from the antibody trough. A standard mixture of antigen is applied to a well on the opposite side of the antibody trough. In this way, the distance from the antibody trough of every immunoprecipitate developed may be compared with that of a standard immunoprecipitate, provided suitable standard antigens are available. A rough evaluation of the antigen content of the unknown sample may thus be obtained.

A technique of immunoelectrophoresis may be used like the one which depends on a principle similar to that of the single radial diffusion method for quantitative estimation of main immunoprecipitates; Alfonso (1964) and Bogdanikowa et al. (1966) have used it. In immunoelectrophoresis of an antigen mixture with a set-up with a central well and two troughs, one on each side, these authors showed that the areas of main immunoprecipitates depend linearly on the amount of the corresponding antigen present in the electrophoretic locus.

Instead of achieving precipitation by permitting diffusion of antibody from a trough, antibody may instead be applied uniformly over the agar gel after completion of the electrophoretic separation. When this is done, the process becomes akin to the single radial diffusion methods of Mancini (pp. 425 and 452), Wilson (1964), Fahey and McKelvey (1965).

5.6.2. Electrophoresis in a medium containing antibodies (Laurell 1966)

Electrophoresis of an antigen solution in an antibody-containing agarose medium (p. 434) or in cellulose acetate sprayed with antibody (Kohn 1967) gives rise to a precipitate moving on the leading edge of the migrating surplus of antigen (fig. 2.6). The distance of migration at a certain time under defined experimental conditions is rectilinearly dependent on the antigen concentration. Because of the electrophoretic migration of the antigen, this method may be carried out with high-molecular-weight components within 2–10 hr. It is therefore useful, as a means of rapidly determining the antigen content of several samples. The sensitivity of the method is similar to that of the Oudin technique (about 0.5 μg of antigen). (For experimental details, see appendix 13). As with the other agar gel techniques, it is not absolutely necessary to have a strictly specific antiserum, because it is possible to differentiate between main immunoprecipitates and minor precipitates originating from antibody impurities.

Subject index p. 557

CHAPTER 6

Visualization and interpretation of precipitates in gels

6.1. Direct identification and interpretation of immunoprecipitates

Visual recording of results on untreated slides is possible by directly inspecting the immunoprecipitates in the slides on a black background, using a slit lamp. Negative or positive photographic prints of the slides, (stained or unstained) can be produced by using specially constructed photographic boxes (see appendix 17.3). In order to facilitate interpretation of results, the immunoprecipitates may be developed by staining (appendix 18–27). Prior to the staining, immunodiffusion must be stopped by washing the slides in 0.9 % aqueous NaCl. This washing is also necessary as a preparatory step in the staining of the immunoprecipitates with specific stains, as it removes unreacted proteins.

6.1.1. Identification by absorption of antisera

Absorption of specific or polyvalent antisera with immunologically pure antigen solutions (see appendix 4) may be used in all gel diffusion methods for identification of precipitates. The absorption process will cause removal of the antibodies corresponding to the antigen in question. The precipitin patterns against unabsorbed and absorbed antisera are compared; the loss of a zone of precipitation from the absorbed antiserum reveals the identity of the antibody. However, the absorption process must be used with caution, as will be discussed in chapter 7.

6.1.2. Morphology of precipitates

If the two antigen reactants are present in equivalent amounts, the arc formed during the antigen–antibody reaction will be sharp and roughly symmetrical, and will not change its position during the subsequent diffusion of the two reactants. If however, the systems are unbalanced, asymmetric arcs are formed, lines migrate and are duplicated, or false spurs develop (see pp. 500–502). The shape of the precipitates, formed during double diffusion from circular wells, has been studied by Korngold and Van Leeuwen (1957). These authors showed that the precipitin arc will curve in such a manner that its concavity is on the side of the reactant with the lower diffusion coefficient, i.e. with the higher molecular weight. When the antigen and antibody have the same diffusion coefficient (e.g. when immunoglobulins IgG and IgA are antigens), the result will be a straight line.

6.1.2.1. Double diffusion

Working with a three-component system consisting of two antigen samples diffusing in a gel each from one well and the antibody sample from a third well, Ouchterlony (1949, 1962, 1967) described four types of pattern and variations thereof (fig. 6.1). The patterns are the result of the extension of the precipitation areas from their initial sites between the wells into the central areas. During this extension, changes in the regularity of the lines may occur if there are serological relationships between the antigens which result in interaction between the precipitate lines.

Reaction type I: the socalled 'reaction of complete identity' or 'the reaction of complete fusion of lines'. When two antigens are completely identical or when they have a number of antigenic groups in common and the antiserum well contains only antibodies towards these common antigens, the precipitation lines deviate and fuse completely in the central area. Sometimes a weak spur phenomenon may develop because of large excess of antigen or antibodies (an unbalanced system). Also, slowly precipitating complexes giving rise to diffusion of immunocomplexes may cause false spurs.

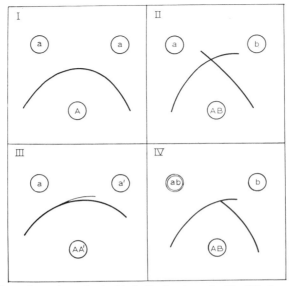

Fig. 6.1. Type of reactions obtainable in Ouchterlony double diffusion. *I*: Reaction type I. Basic precipitation pattern. The two upper wells (a) contain identical antigens: the lower well (A) contains the corresponding antibody (A). A complete fusion of lines is obtained.

II: Reaction type II. a and b are two non-related antigens. The antibody well contains the two corresponding antibodies (A and B). An intersection of the two lines of precipitation is obtained.

III: Reaction type III. Comparison of two serologically related antigens (a and a'). These two antigens diffuse against the antibodies (A and A') in the lower well. A spur is obtained corresponding to the precipitation of the antigenic groups specific to one of the antigens (a).

IV: Reaction type IV. Comparison of a single (b) and a multideterminant (a−b) antigen, diffusing against corresponding antibodies applied in the lower well. A spur will appear caused by a determinant carried by one of the antigens .

Reaction type II: the so-called 'reaction of non-identity' or the 'absence of deviation of the lines'. In this case the two precipitation arcs intersect. The antiserum well contains separate antibodies against both antigens and there is no serological relationship between the antibodies.

Reaction type III: the so-called 'reaction of partial identity' or 'partial fusion of lines' (Jennings 1959; Jennings and Kaplan 1960). This reaction occurs when the two antigens share a number of antigenic groups, but also possess group characteristics of their own; it indicates a serological relationship between antigens that are not identical. If the antiserum well contains antibodies against all antigenic groups, a strongly curved precipitation line develops as a result of partial fusion of the two lines. From the curved arc small spurs develop opposite an antibody well; if only one of the antigens contains antigenic groups specific to itself, the spur develops opposite the corresponding well. For description of different types of spurs, see Ouchterlony (1967).

Reaction type IV: the so-called 'reaction of inhibition' or 'the interference by inhibition without deviation or fusion phenomenon'. This pattern is formed when multivalent antigens or single antigens possessing different determinant groups are used. The immuno-complex in that case is determined by the antigenic type of the diffusing edge of the common antigen, and the spur by the antigenic determinants carried only by one of the antigens. The shape and site of the precipitate depends on the initial concentration of the reactants and their diffusion coefficients.

A similar pattern may be obtained by working with two antibody wells, one with antibody containing two combining sites, the other one with a monospecific antibody, with multideterminant antigens applied in the third well.

6.1.2.2. *Immunoelectrophoresis*
The shape of the precipitates in immunoelectrophoresis is influenced both by the electrophoretic mobility of the antigens (Hirschfeld 1960) and by the fact that double diffusion in two dimensions has taken place. Interpretation of the morphology of precipitates in general is similar in principle to that applied in the case of double diffusion in two dimensions; fusion, deviation and spur phenomena all occur under appropriate conditions. Electrophoretically homogenous antigens will migrate in the gel as a zone in which the distribution of the individual molecules follow a Gaussian distribution. In that case, a more or less

circular precipitation zone is formed. On the other hand, substances with identical antigenic properties but possessing different electrophoretic mobilities will produce immunoprecipitates located in accordance with the electrophoretic mobilities. Thus, immunoglobulins precipitated by the corresponding antibodies develop as protracted lines extending from the slow γ-area ($M_r = 0.00$) towards the α-2-area ($M_r = 0.50$). This indicates a family of globulins with identical immunological (antigenic) properties, but different electrophoretic mobilities.

Double-humped arcs indicate the presence of an antigen with two main electrophoretic mobilities, but with identical or with partially identical immunological properties. Immunoelectrophoretic studies of biological fluids have revealed double-humped arcs for the transferrin of cerebrospinal fluid (fig. 6.2) and for the β-1-AC globulin (the third part of the complement) present in serum stored for more than a few days (Pette and Stupp 1960; Clausen 1960a, b, Clausen and Munkner 1961b; Müller-Eberhard et al. 1960; Müller-Eberhard and Nilsson 1960; Lundh 1965).
Uriel and Grabar (1956) demonstrated two fast-moving lipoproteins in immunoelectrophoresis, one, present in fresh serum, possessing an electrophoretic mobility of an α-1-globulin, and one present in stored serum with pre-albumin mobility. This change during storage was later shown to be caused by a lipase (Schultze and Schwick 1957).

The electrophoretic mobility may thus be used to indicate successive changes in the composition of stored antigens. In studies comparing two or more immunoelectrophoretic patterns, the electrophoretic mobility of an antigen cannot be used solely as a criterion of identity of different antigens precipitated in different patterns, since, besides that mentioned above, in groups of individuals the electrophoretic mobility of the so-called group-specific proteins may differ from one group to another (allotypia). The differences in migration rate of antigens with identical immunological properties, seems to be genetically determined (Heide 1960; Schultze 1962; Hirschfeld 1962; Nerstrøm and Skafte Jensen 1963).

The shape of the immunoprecipitate can be an indicator of the conformational state of the protein antigen and can show whether the

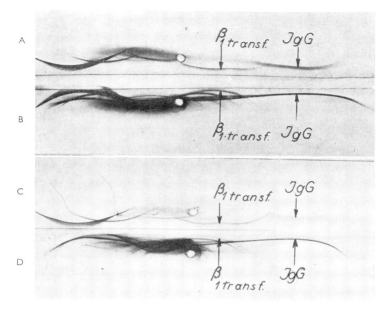

Fig. 6.2. Micro-immunoelectrophoretic pattern of pathological cerebrospinal fluids (CSF) compared with that of normal human serum (Clausen 1960b). Horse antihuman antiserum (80 µl) in troughs. In the wells the following samples are placed: *A*: 1.5 µl CSF, concentrated by vacuum dialysis 50 times, from a patient with multiple sclerosis in slow progression; *B* and *D*: 1.5 µl normal human serum; *C*: 1.5 µl CSF, concentrated 50 times, from a patient with epilepsy. From comparison of the CSF and serum patterns, it is seen that CSF transferrin is double-humped. *Experimental conditions*: see text to fig. 2.5.

protein is native, denatured or split into subfractions by proteolytic digestion. Endopeptidases may split proteins into subfractions which may have different electrophoretic mobilities, but possess the antigenic sites of the original protein antigens. After immunodiffusion every subfraction will therefore give rise to an immunoprecipitate. However, because of the immunological similarities, the immunoprecipitates may fuse, causing double-humped or multiple-humped precipitates (fig. 6.3). Similar changes are encountered during denaturation of proteins by

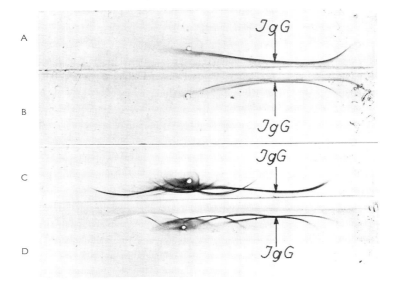

Fig. 6.3. Demonstration of proteolytic digestion of a normal human serum sample caused by bacterial contamination. *A* and *C*: 1.5 μl normal serum; *B* and *D*:1.5 μl contaminated serum. The antibody trough between *A* and *B* is filled with 80 μl specific anti IgG globulin; that between *C* and *D* is filled with 80 μl horse antiserum against pooled normal human serum. The patterns in *B* and *D* demonstrate the IgG-globulin precipitate splitting into two crossing arcs. One of these arcs is double-humped, thus demonstrating precipitation of an antigen with two main electrophoretic mobilities, but with identical immunological properties. *Experimental conditions* as in fig. 2.5.

chemical treatment, for example, during iodination, if more than two molecules of iodine have been introduced into one molecule of protein in which case the corresponding immunoprecipitate is double-humped, shows asymmetric arcs or a striated pattern in the gel. Also hydrazine treatment is known to change the mobility of a β-1-C in human serum (Bammer 1964).

As mentioned on pp. 437–439, immunoelectrophoresis in an antibody-containing agar gel is based on the migration in the electric field of the zone of excess of antigen through the gel (Ressler 1960 a, b). The migration rate of the precipitin arcs through the gel ahead of the zone of antigen excess depends on the properties of the antigen. The migration of certain proteins can indicate additional antigenic sites especially in proteins where allotypic forms exist (Oudin 1956). Multiple precipitation arcs develop, e.g. in electrophoresis of serumprotein antigens migrating in an agar medium containing polyvalent antiserum.

6.2. Staining gels for proteins, lipids and carbohydrates

In order to visualize better the precipitation arcs in the dried gel, the pattern may be stained with an appropriate stain. A protein stain is usually used (appendix 18), as it will always stain because of the presence of protein in the antibody of the immunoprecipitate. For special purposes, staining reactions based upon other chemical or enzymic properties may be used (vide infra). After staining, the slides are de-stained and dried.

Not all staining procedures are specific, thus protein stains do not exclusively characterize the antigens as proteins because the antibodies present in precipitate also take up the stain. Some antigens may, however, be specifically characterized by means of their content of lipids. By staining the slide with lipid stain (appendix 19), the lipoproteins precipitated by their corresponding antibodies take up the stain. In order to characterize the pattern further, the slides may subsequently be stained for proteins with light green. Thus, a double stained pattern appears with lipoproteins stained red or black (see appendix 20) and proteins stained green.

Immunoprecipitates may also be characterized chemically by their content of carbohydrates. The carbohydrate stains are not completely specific because of the presence of carbohydrates in the immunoglobulins (see table 1.2). However, the relatively high content of carbohydrates in glycoproteins may give rise to a more prominent stain than that caused by immunoglobulins.

Methods of staining carbohydrates (appendix 21) are similar to those used in histochemistry. One procedure is based upon the oxida-

Subject index p. 557

tion of diol-components by means of periodic acid followed by the Schiff stain (Malaprade 1928; McManus 1946; Hotchkiss 1948). Only carbohydrates with at least two adjacent secondary alcohol groups are stained. Fortunately, the agarose and agaro-pectin of the agar are not stained because they contain 1.3 glycosidic bonds (Jirgenson 1958) with ester-binding of sulphate groups to other hydroxyl groups.

Another colour reaction for carbohydrates is based upon the oxidation of p-phenylenediamine with hydrogen peroxide catalyzed by aldehydes (Woker 1914). Uriel (1958) indicates that this is preferable as it is more specific and less laborious than the periodic acid-Schiff reaction. In this staining procedure for demonstrating carbohydrates, the aldehydes formed by the periodic acid oxidation of carbohydrates catalyse the formation of indophenol blue.

Finally, carbohydrates may be demonstrated by transformation into arylhydrazones of the aldehydes liberated by periodic acid oxidation. These hydrazones react secondarily with diazonium salts producing the corresponding formazan derivatives (Uriel and Grabar 1961). This procedure has been used for demonstration of carbohydrates in glycoproteins separated by agar-electrophoresis.

Chemical reactions make it possible to demonstrate other chemical groups of antigens in agar gel. Thus, acetal phosphatides may be revealed by hydrolysis yielding a glycerol and an aldehyde. The latter component may be detected by the aldehyde reagents used in carbohydrate staining procedures (vide supra) (survey by Grabar and Burtin 1964).

In order to demonstrate nucleoproteins, the slide may be stained with the reagents of histochemistry (Brachet 1940) where methyl green is used as a selective stain for DNA in chromatin and pyronin G as an RNA stain (review Pearse 1961). These staining reactions depend on electrostatic interaction between the polynucleotide-phosphate groups and positively-charged amino groups in the basic dye. In agar gel the pyronine will however stain both DNA and RNA (Grabar and Burtin 1964). In order to differentiate between these two components, the staining procedure must be performed prior to and after treatment with ribonuclease. Polynucleotides may be revealed in agar gel by the Feulgen reaction which stains only the DNA (Uriel and Avrameas 1961). The deoxyribose phosphate liberated by acid hydrolysis reacts through the potential aldehyde group of the C-1 atom with the fuchsin-sulphuric acid (vide supra). Carbohydrates with a CH_2 group at C-2 are not hydrolyzed by HCl (Pearse 1961).

In order to demonstrate the capacity of certain proteins to bind small molecules specifically, staining procedures locating the transported molecule may be used. Thus, bilirubin may be demonstrated in the agar gel by the Van Den Berg reaction (Van Den Berg and Müller 1916) using diazosulphanilic acid as coupling reagent (Clausen et al. 1965). The copper binding proteins may be selectively stained by the ability of cupric ions to make an intensive blue complex with alizarin blue (Feigl and Caldas 1953; Uriel et al. 1957). The binding capacity may also be elucidated by the combination of immunodiffusion methods with autoradiography (Clausen and Munkner 1960, 1961a, b) (see pp. 483–485).

6.3. Enzymic reactions in gels

As enzymes are proteins, glycoproteins or lipoproteins they precipitate during gel immunodiffusion. The precipitate so formed may be characterized by suitable staining reactions which utilize the enzymic activity of the corresponding antigen. Using such staining methods, it must be remembered that antigen, antibody and substrate form a three-component system (Cinader 1963) and that one of the reactants may compete with the others.

In phylogenetic development, enzymes of similar biological function are encountered in most animal species. Therefore, the active sites of different enzymes with similar biological functions may be chemically identical. This means that normally no antibodies will be created during immunization against the active site of the enzyme molecule. However, other parts of the molecule may change their primary, secondary or tertiary structure during phylogenetic development. These changes explain why it is possible to create antibodies against enzymes.

In practice, immunoprecipitates of enzymes and anti-enzymes may sometimes show no enzymic activity; in other immunoprecipitates, partial or full enzymic activity may be present. The lack of enzyme activity of an immunoprecipitate of an enzyme–anti-enzyme complex has been explained partly by conformational changes in the enzyme molecule after linking to the corresponding antibody, and partly by the fact that the antibody molecule may wholly or partially cover the enzymic site, thus preventing complex formation between enzyme and substrate (Cinader 1963). These facts must always be remembered when trying to characterize immunoelectrophoretic patterns by means of enzymic reactions. Thus, a positive result will indicate enzymic activity in the corresponding antigen, if it is possible to exclude non-enzymic colour reactions (Pearse 1961), but a negative result does not exclude the possibility that the corresponding antigen may have enzymic properties. In the following, some enzymes stainable by enzyme reactions after immunoprecipitation, will be mentioned. The code numbers of 'The Report of the Commission on Enzymes of the International Union of Biochemistry' are indicated behind the name of the enzyme by E.C. followed by a number.

6.3.1. Hydrolases (E.C. 3)

6.3.1.1. Carboxylic esterases (E.C. 3.1.1)

Esterases are demonstrable in immuno-complexes (Uriel 1960, 1964). About 20 enzymes catalyzing the hydrolysis of carboxylic esters at pH optima between 5 and 9 are included in this group (Dixon and Webb 1958). Esterases are found in all cells and in most biological fluids. Their low and overlapping substrate specificities indicate a basic similarity of their active centres. Thus, the inhibition of both aliesterases and cholinesterases by organic phosphorous compounds can be explained by the presence of serine in the active centres of both types. Table 6.1 contains classification of esterases (Augustinsson 1961).

TABLE 6.1

The affinity of esterases for substrates and inhibitors (Augustinsson 1961)

	Aryl-ester-ases (Ar. e.)	Ali-ester-ases (Ali. e.)	Cholin-ester-ases (Ch. e.)
Substrates			
Aromatic esters	+ + +	+	+
Aliphatic esters	−	+ + +	+ +
Choline esters	−	−	+ + +
Inhibitors			
Organophosphor-ous compounds	−	+ + +	+ + +
Eserine	−	−	+ + +
EDTA	+ + + (Only serum) Ar. e.)	−	−
Activator Ca^{++}	+	−	−

+ + + Pronounced affinity; + + affinity; + slight affinity; − no affinity. More exact values in terms of inhibitor constants for different inhibitors can be obtained from the data of Pearse (1961).

Subject index p. 557

Cholinesterases show high hydrolysis rates of choline esters. They are inhibited by 10^{-5} M eserine. Two sub-types can be differentiated, e.g. acetylcholinesterase which is inhibited by the inhibitor 62C47 (Wellcome, Pearse 1961) and cholinesterase which hydrolyses cholinesters of carboxylic acid other than acetic acid and is inhibited by iso-OMPA (tetra-isopropyl-pyrophosphoramide).

Aliesterases hydrolyse many aliphatic esters. They are resistant to 10^{-5} M eserine. Aliesterases are the main esterases in plasma of lower vertebrates, but are absent from the plasma of man.

Arylesterases are more or less resistant to organophosphorous compounds and to eserine. They are stabilized and activated by calcium ions and are inactivated by chelating agents, for instance EDTA. Heavy metals as Hg^{++}, Ag^+, Cu^{++} are strong inhibitors, and the SH group seems of importance for the activity because SH-reagents (e.g. p-hydroxy-mercuri-benzoate) inhibit the enzymes. In human plasma, there is an arylesterase moving fast on electrophoresis, close to albumin.

Esterases may be visualized in agar gel by means of β-naphthyl-acetate or indoxyl acetate (appendix 25). β-Naphthol is liberated from β-naphthylacetate by the enzyme and can be visualized by coupling to an azo-reagent. In the method presented in appendix 25, the azo-reagent is present in the substrate solution and couples with the liberated naphthol directly at the reaction sites where the azo dye is precipitated. Thus the following chemical reactions give rise to the formation of an azo dye.

Other coupling reagents can be used (Uriel 1964); in the indoxyl-acetate method, hydrolysis of indoxylacetate by the esterase gives rise to free indoxyl which through catalysis by Cu^{++} ions is oxidized to insoluble indigo:

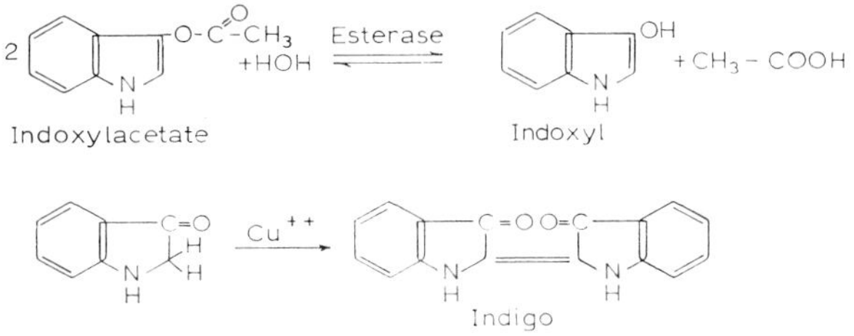

Comparison of the results obtained by the diazo reaction and the indigo method shows that the serum esterases have certain substrate specificities. Thus, the arylesterase with albumin mobility is not developed by the indigo method.

The formazan method permits the tracing of choline esterases by their action on acetyl thiocholine (Köelle and Friedenvald 1949; Uriel 1964). The liberated thiocholine reduces a tetrazolium salt yielding a blue formazan derivative which is insoluble. This is a similar principle to that used for detecting dehydrogenases (p. 482).

6.3.1.2. Phosphatases (E.C. 3.1.3)

Acid phosphatases act by catalyzing the hydrolysis of monoesters of orthophosphoric acid at acid pH. Multiple forms of these enzymes exist in human tissue extracts (Gerhardt et al. 1963). Thus, in human brain, two phosphatases with α- and β-mobilities can be detected by electrophoresis. One of the acid phosphatases isolated from human serum is a low-molecular-weight protein with isoelectric point at pH 4.5; in dilute solutions it undergoes a rapid inactivation influenced by temperature (Fishman 1960).

The phosphatases can be visualized by a coupling reaction similar to one used in the demonstration of esterases. Thus, naphthylphosphate is hydrolysed at pH 4.5 by acid phosphatase with liberation of naphthol which can be coupled to an azo-reagent (see appendix 26).

Alkaline phosphatases catalyse the hydrolysis of monoesters of orthophosphoric acid at alkaline pH (maximum between 9.2 and 9.6).

The enzymes are activated by Mg^{++}, Zn^{++}, Cu^{++} and inhibited by cyanide, cysteine, phosphate and arsenate. Phosphatases of different cellular origins have different immunological properties; thus, an antiserum against intestinal phosphatase does not precipitate phosphatases from other organs (Nisselbaum et al. 1961). Multiple forms of alkaline phosphatase exist in serum, where 13–29 % of the total activity is precipitated by an antiserum against intestinal phosphatase and 40–59 % by antiserum against bone phosphatase.

Alkaline phosphatases of biological fluids, e.g. from the intestinal tract still exhibit enzymic activity after immunoprecipitation (Schlamowitz 1954; Moog and Angeletti 1962). A part of alkaline phosphatase activity of tissue is bound to particulate fractions (Clausen and Formby 1968). Its activity can be liberated by solubilization of these membranous complexes with butanol, leaving the phosphatase activity in the aqueous phase (Börnig et al. 1967). The naphthol liberated from naphthol esters by the enzymes can be directly visualized in the gel by ultraviolet scanning (Moss et al. 1961).

6.3.1.3. Proteolytic enzymes (E.C. 3.4)

The method of location of proteolytic enzymes has already been mentioned in the chapter concerning fibrin–agar immunoelectrophoresis (see p. 436 and appendix 14, p. 525).

6.3.1.4. Amylases (E.C. 3.2.1.1 and E.C. 3.2.1.2) and other glycoside hydrolases (E.C. 3.2.1.1)

Amylases are defined as hydrolases causing the hydrolysis of starch (amylose and amylopectin). During the hydrolysis, maltose and maltotriose are formed. Amylases, possessing different electrophoretic mobilities, antigenic and inhibitory properties can be visualized in agar gel either by means of a contact method where the agar slide is sandwiched to an agar plate containing starch as substrate, or by direct dipping of the slide in a starch solution (appendix 27, p. 539). During incubation, hydrolysis of starch occurs at loci corresponding to each amylase isoenzyme. By applying an iodine solution to the starch–agar gel or the agar, a blue colour will develop in all parts where amylase has not been present. Amylases with different electrophoretic mobilities can be differentiated by means of inorganic ion inhibition. Thus, the β-amylases are inhibited by copper ions (Cu⁺⁺) and α-amylases on the other hand need calcium ions (Ca⁺⁺) in order to be active and stable. Thus, by correlating the electrophoretic patterns with and without copper sulphate in the substrate, β-amylases may be identified; and by correlating the results of electrophoresis with and without a calcium precipitating agent, e.g. sodium hexa-meta-phosphate, the α-amylases may be identified. The α- and β-amylases of germinating barley give rise to individual immuno-precipitates still showing amylase activity (Grabar and Daussant 1965; Frydenberg and Nielsen 1965).

Enzymes other than amylases splitting the glycosidic bonds of simple and complex polysaccharides can also be traced by special staining reactions (cf. appendix 27 p. 539).

6.3.2. Oxidoreductases (E.C. 1)

6.3.2.1. Oxidases (appendix 22) (E.C. 1.4)

The serum protein ceruloplasmin, which can oxidize catecholamines and other phenols, has been demonstrated after immunodiffusion of serum by the oxidation of p-phenylenediamine. The oxidation product is a quinoid component named Brandovsky's base which is insoluble in water (Uriel 1964; Peares 1961).

6.3.2.2. Peroxidases (appendix 23) (E.C. 1.9 and E.C. 1.11)

Peroxidases may be visualized in agar gel by the NADI reagent, although the specificity of this reaction is low. (NADI is the abbreviation for the two reagents used for the staining procedure, namely α-naphthol and dimethyl-p-phenylenediamine.) Peroxidases, in the presence of H_2O_2, catalyse the oxidation of dimethyl-p-phenylene-diamine and α-naph-thol, coupling them together to form an indophenol.

Peroxidases may also be demonstrated in agar gel by the simple benzidine reaction. The reaction depends on the oxidation of benzidine by the peroxidase system to a blue or brown component. First two molecules of benzidine are linked together following dehydrogenation forming the blue component. During the next step, the blue compound is reduced to a brownish high molecular polymer of a quinoid structure.

6.3.2.3. *Dehydrogenases with NAD+ and NADP+ as acceptor* (*appendix 24*) (*E.C. 1.1.1*)

The location of dehydrogenases in immunoprecipitates is not always possible because the combination of immunoprecipitation with the dehydrogenase reaction involves a four-component system consisting of enzyme (antigen), antibody, substrate and coenzyme. The antibody may easily cover either the coenzyme or the substrate site (Cinader 1963). More than 70% of glutamic dehydrogenase activity is neutralised by anti-glutamic dehydrogenase in free buffer solutions (Bollet et al. 1962) and more than 60% of lactate dehydrogenase activity by anti-lactate dehydrogenase (Mansour et al. 1954). However, in certain cases, the antigen–antibody complex precipitated in agar gel still has enzyme activity; thus after immunodiffusion, the antigen–antibody complex formed between lactate dehydrogenase isoenzymes and the corresponding antibodies still contains some dehydrogenase activity (Avreameas and Rajewsky 1963; Kaplan and White 1963). Lactate dehydrogenase activity is detected after immunoprecipitation by the transfer of hydrogen from lactate, via the reduced coenzyme and phenazine methosulphate to tetrazolium, which is thereby reduced to an insoluble coloured formazan (Pearse 1961; Wilkinson 1965; Clausen and Øvlisen 1965).

6.4. Fluorescent techniques (appendix 28)

Fluorescent methods may be used to demonstrate different character-istics of antigens. Thus, fluorescent reagents such as fluorescein or rhodamine in the form of fluorescein-isothiocyanate and -isocyanate and Lissamine rhodamine sulphonyl chloride may be coupled to amino groups of immunoglobulins. The fluorescence of the rhodamine–immu-noglobulin complex is as intense as the fluorescence of the original reagent and the immunoglobulin still has the ability to precipitate immunologically in immunodiffusion. The precipitation arcs exhibit a typical emission fluorescence when exposed to visible or ultra-violet light since agar gel is transparent with only minimal absorption of ultraviolet or visible light (survey by Nairn 1964).

Fluorescent coupled proteins may be used in a manner similar to the isotopically labelled immunoglobulins, mentioned below, but they can also be used in histologic studies (survey Nairn 1964). In this way, minor quantities of antigens not visible by ordinary protein staining can be detected (Francq et al. 1959). Fluorescent methods have advantages over normal staining procedures (Neurath 1965). Thus, the use of fluorescent labelled antibodies in precipitation reactions may increase the sensitivity of the method more than fifty times. Fluorescent substances (drugs or coenzymes) attached to an antigen can also be detected in immunoprecipitates in gels.

6.5. Isotopic methods

Radioactive isotopes may be used in immunoelectrophoresis and in other gel-diffusion methods for the identification of precipitates. They have been used in (1) demonstration of binding function of proteins; (2) elucidation of protein synthesis; (3) control of purity; (4) elucida-tion of the conformational changes of proteins leading to denaturation, e.g. during processes of labelling of proteins used for turn-over studies; and (5) estimation of $m\mu g$ amounts of protein (see radio-immuno-electrophoresis, ch. 7).

Electrophoresis in agarose gel, in contrast to that on paper or starch gel avoids serious absorption of labelled material to the supporting medium because of the high water content and lack of ionized groups of agarose. The washing procedure eliminates non-reacting antigens and antibodies, leaving radioactivity only in precipitates representing bound antigens.

In order to study the binding function of, for example, serum proteins, an appropriate amount of serum is mixed with the labelled drug

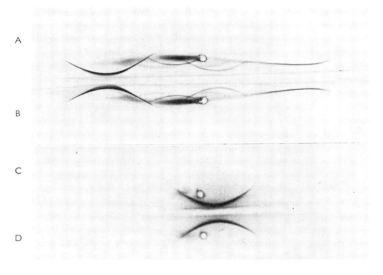

Fig. 6.4. Immunoelectrophoresis combined with autoradiography (Clausen and Munkner 1961a). Normal human serum was incubated with ^{59}Fe. Horse anti-human antiserum (80 µl) is in the troughs; in wells A and C 1.5 µl serum is incubated with 320 µg/100 ml ^{59}Fe. Wells B and D show 1.5 µl serum incubated with 640 µg%^{59}Fe. A and B developed as normal immunoelectrophoresis. C and D developed as an autoradiogram. Experimental conditions: *Incubation procedures*: The incubation with iron was performed at three different concentrations: A and C, to 25 µl of normal human serum were added 10 µl of water and 0.5 µl of ^{59}FeCl solution with an activity of 0.03 µC corresponding to 0.008 µg ^{59}Fe. Total Fe added was 320 µg/100 ml; B and D: to 25 µl of serum and 10 µg of water were added 1 µl of ^{59}FeCl$_3$ with an activity of 0.126 µC corresponding to 0.016 µg ^{59}Fe. Total Fe added was 640 µg/100 ml. *Immunoelectrophoresis*: See text to fig. 2.5. *Autoradiography*: Exposure to Kodak autoradiographic film for 2 weeks.

in an amount corresponding to conditions normally occuring in vivo. The drug should have a specific activity sufficiently high to be detectable on a photographic plate (ordinary X-ray film or stripping film) placed close to the agar surface during autoradiography (fig. 6.4) (Keutel 1960; Clausen and Munkner 1960, 1961a, b; Deckert 1964; Kallee et al. 1964; Clausen 1966b). The resolving power of the autoradiogram depends on the isotope in use, the thickness of the gel and the emulsion of the photographic film. As is the case with other electrophoretic methods combined with autoradiography, it is of importance to study the binding capacity of proteins by electrophoresis in several different buffers, because the buffer solution may influence binding capacity (Pitt-Rivers and Tata 1959).

Two different types of photographic film may be used for detection of radioactivity, ordinary X-ray film or stripping film. X-ray film is convenient for most autoradiography of immunoelectrophoretic slides and is suitable for ^{14}C, ^{35}S, ^{131}I and ^{125}I. Stripping film is a technique where the photographic emulsion is poured directly onto the object to be autoradiographed; it is thus possible to locate tritium which cannot be located with ordinary film as its gel layer of the film absorbs too much radioactivity. The duration of exposure depends on radioactivity, thickness of agar gel and film, geometry and hardness of radiation. Several identical slides should be used and the photographic film exposed different lengths of time (Clausen 1966b). Autoradiography is used, not only for studies of the transport function of antigens (vide supra) but also in studies of purity of proteins. Labelling of the tyrosine residue in proteins in vitro by ^{125}I or ^{131}I (appendices 29, 30) makes it possible to trace protein impurities by autoradiography.

In order to study protein synthesis in tissue culture, C^{14}-labelled amino acids may be added to the culture and will be incorporated into certain proteins (Abdel-Samie et al. 1960; Hochwald et al. 1961; Van Furth et al. 1966). By addition of different carrier proteins, and immunoelectrophoresis of the medium or the cell homogenates, it is possible by autoradiography to demonstrate which of the proteins are radioactive. A specific identification of protein synthesized in different cells may thus be achieved.

Subject index p. 557

CHAPTER 7

Radio-immunochemical techniques

Radio-immunoelectrophoresis was originally developed for the quantitative estimation of proteins and peptide hormones (Yalow and Berson 1960, 1966; Grodsky and Forsham 1960). While the original immunoelectrophoretic method of Grabar and Williams (1953) was based upon an electrophoretic separation of the antigens prior to the immunochemical reaction, radio-immunoelectrophoresis uses the opposite principle. A solution of antigen–antibody complex is formed under conditions of antigen excess and then separated electrophoretically from the free antigen (Berson et al. 1964). With specific antisera against small antigen molecules, the antigen–antibody complex will always be soluble in antigen excess. Electrophoresis of the antigen–antibody complex will give rise to a zone containing antigen as well as several zones containing antigen–antibody complexes. These zones may possess electrophoretic mobilities from the anodic α-1-area to the slow γ-area depending on the proportion between the two reactants (Bennington 1960).

The antigen–antibody complex may also be separated from the unreacted antigen by ion-exchange chromatography (Lazarus and Young 1966), gel filtration (Haber et al. 1965, see companion volume by Fischer 1968), adsorption onto charcoal (Herbert et al. 1965), double antibody precipitation (p. 505, cf. appendix 30) (Schalch and Parker 1964) or by specific adsorption of free peptide hormone onto certain sorts of plastic (p. 493), talcum powder and precipitated silica (Yalow and Berson 1966).

For the estimation of protein or peptide hormones in biological fluids, the tyrosine present in the protein or peptide is labelled with ^{131}I or ^{125}I. The labelled hormone can still react normally with the corresponding antibody as long as the amount of iodine is below approximately one iodine atom per protein molecule (Garratt 1964; Yalow and Berson 1966). Mixing a known amount of non-labelled hormone (H) with a certain amount of ^{131}I- (or ^{125}I-) labelled hormone and the corresponding specific antiserum (AH), the labelled hormone (^{131}IH) will compete with the non-labelled hormone for the anti-hormone $^{131}IH + AH \rightleftarrows AH - ^{131}IH$; $H + AH \rightleftarrows AH - H$. Both labelled and unlabelled hormone will reversibly equilibrate with the specific antiserum. After equilibration, the labelled as well as unlabelled hormone bound to the corresponding specific antiserum is separated from the free hormone by suitable means. By determination of radioactivity of the two isolated products, it is possible to determine the amount of labelled hormone present in these two fractions. The distribution of radioactivity between the two fractions is dependent on the amount of unlabelled hormone present in the mixture. A standard curve expressing the relationship between the ratio of the radioactivity of the bound versus the free fraction (B/F ratio) as a function of the dilution of non-labelled standard peptide hormone, will make it possible from the experimentally determined bound/free (B/F) ratio to determine the amount of hormone present in an unknown sample (see appendices 29 and 30).

7.1. Radio-immunoelectrophoresis of peptide hormones

One of the important applications of radio-immunoelectrophoresis is for assay of peptide hormones in blood, serum and in organ secretions. The method requires (1) a sample of the pure hormone; (2) a mild method for iodination with radioactive iodine such that the antigenic specificity of the hormone is unaltered by iodination; (3) a specific antiserum to the hormone; and (4) a method of separation of antigen–antibody complex from free hormone. The equipment necessary depends on factors such as the price of the apparatus, the number of samples to be determined and the isotope in use. Two iodine isotopes are available viz. [125]I and [131]I. [125]I is a pure gamma-ray emitter possessing an energy of 35 keV (100%) and a half life of 60 days. By electron capture it is transformed to $^{125}_{52}$Te. The relatively long half life is appropriate in immunochemical studies of high cost hormones, but the relatively weak gamma-emission needs scintillation systems with a wellcounter in order to obtain acceptable counts. [131]I radiates gamma-rays with 82% of the order of 364 keV and beta-rays with 87% of the order of 610 keV. It is transformed to $^{131}_{54}$Xe. The half life, eight days, limits its use for many purposes, but the relatively high emission energies make it easy to use, especially in studies using radioactive scanning of paper electrophoretic strips.

Two methods exist for the introduction of labelled iodine into proteins with high specific activity, viz. the methods of McFarlane (1963) and Hunter and Greenwood (1962), (cf. appendices 29 and 30). The methods are both based upon the transformation of the radio-active iodide to a higher oxidation level. In the McFarlane method this is accomplished by the formation of labelled ICl (for detail see also Helmkamp et al. 1967 a,b) which at alkaline pH is transformed to labelled HOI. The labelled HOI at an alkaline pH, which facilitates the ionisation of the tyrosyl residues of the protein, introduces the labelled 'positive' iodine in the tyrosine molecules (Brunfeldt 1967). In the method of Greenwood et al. (1963) the oxidation of labelled iodide is directed towards the formation of iodine. This is accomplished by ClO^- formed from chloramine T under conditions where 90% of the radioactivity in statu nascendi can be incorporated into the protein. In order to avoid superiodination the process is stopped after one minute reaction time by adding the reducing agent sodium disulphite or the more stable compound sodium dithionite ($Na_2S_2O_5$). In order to control the iodination all steps must be carefully standardized and the final product must be checked for immunological and biological reactivity (Brunfeldt et al. 1968). In some experiments for the esti-mation of hormones, even an iodination as low as 0.2 atoms iodine per molecule must be preferred (Arquilla et al. 1968).

Essentially, the radioimmunochemical determination of an antigen involves mixing antibody (in bovine serum albumin as diluent) with excess of radioactive antigen and, after sufficient time to allow complete reaction, the antibody-bound hormone is separated from the free hormone by electrophoresis. The ratio of radioactivity in

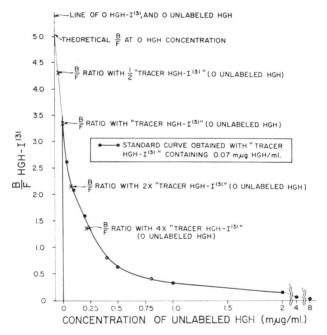

Fig. 7.1. Standard curve for the determination of human growth hormone (HGH). The B/F ratio of HGH is related in this figure both to the concentration of labelled hormone (in case of absence of unlabelled hormone) $(- \times - \times -)$ and to the concentration of unlabelled hormone $(- \cdot - \cdot -)$. All mixtures for the standard curve contained the same concentration of 'tracer HGH$-^{131}$I', estimated at 0.070 mμg. HGH/ml from the yield obtained in the labelling procedure. Other mixtures were prepared with one-half, twice and four times this concentration of HGH$-^{131}$I but without added unlabelled hormone. The B/F ratios for mixtures containing only labelled HGH are plotted as $- \times - \times -$ at concentrations corresponding to 0.035 mμg/ml, 0.070 mμg/ml, 0.140 mμg/ml and 0.280 mμg/ml respectively. If the estimated concentration of HGH$-^{131}$I had been exactly correct, the two curves would have been identical. (From Berson et al. 1964.)

the two zones gives a measure of the ratio (B/F) of bound to free hormone (see fig. 7.1). This ratio is of course altered if non-radioactive hormone is mixed with the radioactive hormone and the change in the B/F ratio is a measure of the amount of non-radioactive hormone added. The method is calibrated by adding known quantities of purified hormone, thereby producing a standard curve (fig. 7.1) which can be used to estimate the amount of hormone present in any 'unknown'.

In preparing an antiserum for hormone assay it must be remembered that even when all animals are of the same species and are immunized by the same schedule, the resulting antisera may vary greatly and one serum can easily be 100-fold more active than another (Berson et al. 1964). It is desirable therefore, that a fairly large number of animals should be immunized. Even a few ml of a good antiserum will be sufficient for a million assays (or more, since a dilution between one thousand and one million will be necessary before use). In order to select a suitable antiserum, it is necessary to carry out trials in which various dilutions of antiserum are mixed with radioactive hormone. The method of doing this is described in appendix 29.

Besides the quality and avidity of the antiserum, other factors also determine the sensitivity of the radio-immunoassay. The lower the specific activity of the labelled hormone preparation, the higher will be the amount of labelled hormone required to provide the desired radioactivity. On the other hand, highly labelled hormone may be denatured and react inefficiently with the antibody. In assaying the insulin concentration in serum, it has been found that serum contains a factor damaging the labelled hormone probably by reduction of the disulfide linkages. In order to avoid such damage, it may be necessary to dilute the serum sample about 20 times (Berson et al. 1964).

After selecting the optimal batch of labelled hormone and the optimal antiserum of adequate dilution, a series of dilutions of the purified hormone is made ranging from 0 to about 20 mμg of hormone per ml. The labelled hormone is diluted until an adequate concentration is reached; this can be very low, for example, labelled human growth hormone is diluted so much that the amount of labelled hormone added to the reaction mixture is about 0.1 mμg per ml.

7.1.1. Difficulties

In using radio-immunoelectrophoresis for quantitative estimation of peptide hormones, it is necessary to have pure samples of the hormone which must be immunologically identical with the hormone in the unknown sample; the specificity of the antiserum is less important. Certain pure hormones, such as insulin, are available commercially; for hormones not available commercially, purification may be a laborious task. For techniques of purification of hormones, the reader is referred to the companion manuals describing gel electrophoresis (Gordon 1968), gel filtration (Fischer 1968) and column chromatography (Peterson 1969). Here, it can only be stressed that it is essential to work with immunologically pure hormones, and that every step of purification should be checked by immunoelectrophoresis and gel diffusion.

It is also wise to carry out control experiments on the final preparation of radioactive hormone by immunoelectrophoresis. Denatured hormone may give rise to a changed immunoelectrophoretic pattern, for instance instead of symmetrical precipitation arcs, double-humped precipitates or a typical tailing phenomenon may be seen. Minor conformational changes in the hormone may, however, only be revealed by estimation of the biological half life of the hormone by turn-over studies in steady state conditions.

The necessity of preparing immunologically pure hormones, followed by a labelling of the hormone with radioactive iodine under strictly defined conditions may be troublesome in a routine method. The labelling must maximally cause incorporation of maximally 1 iodine atom per molecule of hormone.

A hazard in studying hormone levels in biological fluids of patients treated with these hormones is that antihormone antibodies binding the foreign hormones may give rise to incorrect B/F ratio. Thus, the γ-globulin fraction of diabetic patients binds pig- and/or calf-insulin (Deckert 1964), and in patients treated with growth hormone, the

Subject index p. 557

γ-globulin fraction contains anti-growth antibodies (Prader 1966). These antibodies occur even in cases of treatment with autologous hormones (Prader 1966). This antibody formation may be explained by a slight denaturation of the hormone during the isolation procedure. Full instructions for performance of insulin and growth hormone assay using ^{131}I-labelled hormone and a suitable antibody are given in appendices 29 and 30.

7.2. Double antibody precipitation

In estimation of hormones, the precipitin reaction in free buffer solution may replace radio-immunoelectrophoresis in separating an antibody-bound hormone from the free hormone (Schalch and Parker 1964). This is achieved by means of an antibody directed against the one to which the hormone is linked. The antibody-bound hormone can be separated from the free hormone by centrifugation or by filtration (see appendix 30). This method, the so-called double antibody technique, requires the production of two different antibodies, first an anti-hormone globulin and then an anti-globulin. The latter antiserum need not be completely specific; it may be made by immunization of an animal species different from that in which the anti-hormone antiserum is made, using as an antigen the 1.8 M ammonium sulphate precipitate (pH 6.8) of whole serum from the first animal species. This method is suitable in assaying protein hormones of high molecular weight, where the migration rate of the hormone–anti-hormone complex is too low for the purposes of electrophoresis.

7.3. Solid-phase radio-immunochemical techniques

Like other proteins, antibodies (Ab) are able to couple covalently through their free terminal NH_2-residues with reagents reactive towards such groups, e.g. reagents containing isothiocyanate or thiophosgene (Mahler and Cordes 1966). These reagents are attached to a solid phase (SP), i.e. a thiophosgene derivative can be coupled to Sephadex or an isothiocyanate derivative can be bound to the graft co-polymer, of styrene and polytetrafluoroethylene (Catt et al. 1966; Wide 1967). Thereby it is possible to prepare insoluble but still reactive antibodies.

Chemically the synthesis of these stable complexes requires several steps. Thus the synthesis of antibody linked Sephadex requires (Axen and Porath 1966; Wide and Porath 1966): (1) preparation of *p*-nitrophenoxy–hydroxy–propylether of Sephadex; (2) reduction of this component to the amino-derivative; (3) conversion to the isothiocyanate derivative; (4) coupling with the antibody. Recent studies (Catt and Tregar 1967) have, however, revealed that certain plastics (polystyrene and polypropylene) bind antibodies by strong adsorptive forces. This binding is so resistant to chemical treatment, that the complexes can be directly used in solid phase radio-immunochemistry. The antibody-containing solid phase when swelled in water, shows the ability to bind antigen irreversibly:

$$SP-[\quad]-Ab+Ag \rightarrow SP-[\quad]-Ab-Ag.$$

This ability offers the possibility for quantitative estimation of protein hormones in biological fluids using labelled hormones. A defined amount of solid-phase antibody is added to either a non-labelled standard solution of the protein hormone or to an unknown sample, i.e. serum. The antigen (hormone) binds to the solid phase antibody. By adding, after washing, a labelled hormone of known specific activity, the radioactivity left on the solid phase indirectly indicates the amount of hormone present in the sample (Catt et al. 1966).

This method is in use in some laboratories for quantitative estimation of protein hormones, but from the literature it is too early to evaluate its advantages and disadvantages over the other radio-immunochemical techniques.

Subject index p. 557

Difficulties and artifacts arising in gel diffusion and in immunoelectrophoresis

The quality of the results obtained by immunodiffusion in gels depends primarily on the technical skill of the person performing the immuno-diffusion experiments. As already mentioned, several factors not directly connected with the physicochemical properties of the two reactants used in the immunodiffusion are of importance.

8.1. Antibody–antigen ratio

During studies of the qualitative composition of antibody or antigen mixtures, it is important (for instance, in immunoelectrophoretic or immunodiffusion studies of the amounts and composition of one of the reactants) to use a constant amount of one reactant during all experiments, although it is normally not possible to assess the absolute concentration of all its individual components. It is important to use the optimal ratio of antibody to antigen so that balanced systems are obtained in immunoelectrophoresis or in double immunodiffusion. Too low a concentration of antigen may cause the precipitate to be located in the antigen well in double diffusion experiments, and too high a concentration may push the position of equivalence into the antibody well. Other results of unbalanced systems are multiple precipi-tates, Liesegang lines or false spurs.

8.2. Position of immunoprecipitates

As already mentioned (pp. 426–427) the distance of the immunoprecipitate (at a certain time) from the diffusion centers, i.e. the wells in immunodiffusion and electrophoretic locus and trough in immunoelectrophoresis, is dependent on concentration of reactants. Therefore, the distance from one of the diffusion centers may be used as a measure of the concentration of the corresponding reactant, provided that the concentration of the other reactant is kept fixed.

However, the distance of diffusion cannot always be used directly as an indication of the concentration of one of the reactants. That is the case when the molecular weight of one reactant exceeds 200,000; under these circumstances there is retardation since there is no free diffusion in the gel of the reactants (p. 423). When there is a pronounced electrostatic interaction between the antigen, for example lysozyme (Uriel et al. 1964) and the few ionized groups present in the agar gel, precipitation of the antigen in the gel may occur, which may hinder the immunodiffusion. The interaction may be avoided by using agarose which does not possess ionized groups (see also Süllman 1964; Engel 1966). Such interactions may be the cause of artificial precipitation phenomena developed during immunodiffusion of antigen extracts obtained from mammalian tissue by means of buffers containing detergents (pp. 420 and 449).

Other cases where the distance is not proportional to concentration occur in unbalanced systems where excess of one reactant may cause false or migrating precipitation zones. In considering reactions of nonidentity in the Ouchterlony double diffusion plate technique (type II, p. 468), it is important to realise that the undisturbed crossing lines might be missed if the lines have a limited extension or grow in directions which made crossing unlikely on the plate.

8.3. Variation in agar

As mentioned (p. 434), different batches of agar may give rise to different results during immunodiffusion. To avoid this, the agar must be as pure as possible. Commercially purified agar such as Noble agar, is usually satisfactory for immunochemical studies, but there may be differences in electrophoretic mobility of some antigens when using different sources of purified agar. Thus, for instance, the electrophoretic mobility of the high molecular weight α-2-lipoprotein is higher in Behringwerke Reinagar than in Difco Special Noble agar.

8.4. Effect of molecular size on electrophoretic mobility

Mobility is not always characteristic for a particular antigen. Thus, it is possible to split from an antigen certain groups which do not possess immunological properties and thereby cause changes in the electrophoretic mobility without influencing the immunological properties. The effects of loss of the sialic acid residue from glycoproteins and fatty acids from lipoproteins have already been discussed (pp. 419 and 470). It must be emphasised that for many reasons, the immunochemical reactions of lipoproteins are difficult to interpret (cf. pp. 420, 449 and 498). The electrophoretic mobility of glycoproteins may be changed by the removal of carbohydrate residues other than sialic acid, as in the case with part of the transferrin of the cerebrospinal fluid (Parker and Bearn 1962; Parker et al. 1963).

Certain pathological sera, especially those containing paraproteins and cryoglobulins (see the survey by Schultze and Heremans 1966) contain aggregated proteins. These complexes may consist of polymerized IgA, IgM, IgG or complexes of these with other serum proteins, e.g. IgA complexed with albumin or haptoglobin and IgM complexed with IgG. These complexes migrate slowly in agar. However, addition of neutralized cystein or even distilled water (Heremans 1960) to the sample prior to electrophoresis may cause partial or total disaggregation of the complexes. The electrophoretic migration is then enhanced and individual abnormal precipitates may be revealed (Clausen 1963). Even normally occurring serum proteins, possessing a molecular weight above 200,000, such as IgM, are highly retarded in the agar gel (p. 423), also α-2-macroglobulin, α-2-lipoprotein and fibrinogen exhibit relatively low electrophoretic mobilities. All four high-molecular components are therefore localized near the central antigen well in immunoelectrophoresis.

Physical factors may also change the electrophoretic mobility. Thus, exposure of proteins to X-ray or radioactive irradiation may split the proteins into subunits with different electrophoretic mobilities, but with similar immunological properties (Grabar et al. 1955). This may give rise to artifacts in tracer studies.

8.5. Antigens

As already mentioned, immunologically pure protein antigens cannot be made easily by chemical fractionation of biological fluids. Some impurities may adhere to the protein in question. This absorption is of special importance when the antigen is used in highly concentrated solutions for absorption purposes. Furthermore, when dealing with certain antigens showing only partial immunological identity, for instance the immunoglobulins, having the L-chains in common, absorption procedures must be used with care. Thus, in studies of immunoglobulins in biological fluids, absorption with antibodies prepared by immunization with IgG globulin isolated by column chromatography will give rise to absorption of not only IgG but also of IgM and IgA, due to the light-chain antigens in common (p. 415). In handling cross-reacting antigens and their antibodies, the absorption technique may be useful in the sense that after absorbing antibodies against one immunoglobulin with another immunoglobulin, the solution will contain antibodies strictly specific against the immunological group not in common (e.g. anti-H-chains will not precipitate but the anti-light-chains will be removed; see table 1.3).

The opposite procedure, where an antigen solution prior to immuno-diffusion or immunoelectrophoresis may be absorbed with an antibody solution, has serious drawbacks. For example, the absorption with an antiserum obtained from an animal other than that which provides the antiserum used directly in the antibody trough may cause precipitation between the two antisera because of antigenic similarities between antigens from different animal species. Moreover, precipitation

Subject index p. 557

phenomena in the gel may be caused by surplus of antigen or antibody in an unbalanced system (Ouchterlony 1962). Unexpected results are related mainly to the physicochemical and biological properties of antigens and their concentrations.

Factors related to the molecular size have already been mentioned (p. 423). These factors are especially critical during work with solubilized antigenic particulate fractions. Triton-X-100, sodium deoxycholate or Lubrol W (Perlmann et al. 1964; Lundkvist and Perlmann 1967) solutions of antigens of particulate fractions may form non-immune precipitates probably by interaction with the agar gel. The agar gel diffusion is very slow for these antigens; they often precipitate close to the antigen well and it may be difficult to interpret the results. We have to set against this the fact that agar gel immunodiffusion has so far been the only tool for demonstrating antigenic differences between the plasma membrane, microsomes and the nuclear membrane, all of which are best extracted by detergents.

The concentration of the antigen is also of importance (see p. 426) since in unbalanced systems the precipitates may not be visible in the diffusion areas. The way the antigen has been stored may also influence the final result. Bacterial contamination of the sample may introduce proteolytic enzymes or neuraminidase. In the former case, subfractions of the original antigen may precipitate instead of the original antigen itself; with the latter the electrophoretic mobility of glycoproteins will be lowered. Therefore, bacteriostatic agents must be added to the antigen solution if it has to be stored for a long time. Even freezing may introduce errors. Thus, freezing and thawing of a protein dissolved in a phosphate buffer may introduce changes in the protein molecule, because it may create an acid eutectic mixture of the salt, as has been observed during storage of lactate dehydrogenase isoenzymes (Chilson et al. 1965). No general advice can be given for the handling and storage of either the antigen solution or the antiserum which will be applicable in every case.

Consideration should also be given to the possibility of bi-or multi-specific antigens, i.e. the reactive colloid particles having determinant groups of two or more specificities. There is also the possibility that antibodies may be bi-specific, i.e. carrying two serologically different reactive sites. It is thus essential during studies of multivalent antigens and antibodies, always to use balanced immuno-systems.

8.6. Antisera

As already emphasised, it is not possible to obtain antisera of equal titres from different animals. It is not even possible to be certain that an injection of a so-called pure antigen in different animals will always give rise to formation of only one specific antibody. Therefore, during protracted immunochemical studies, the same batch of antibody must always be used or the composition of the different antisera must be known. An immunoelectrophoretic analysis where two or more troughs are filled with different antisera and used on the same slides laterally to the central antigen well will allow comparison of the amount, shape and intensity of the precipitation arcs of the different antisera. Only by such strict controls is it possible to maintain exact biological reproducibility. Although horse antiserum gives rise to sharp precipitation lines which are easier to interpret in gels than the immunoprecipitates developed with the rabbit type antisera, horse antiserum may under some circumstances (see below) cause a false spur phenomenon or multiple precipitation lines.

8.7. Various artifacts

8.7.1. Interaction of antigens with non-antibody substances

Under certain conditions false precipitation due to non-immune phenomena occurs in agar gel (Berenbaum et al. 1962). This is especially the case in analysis of lipid or lipoprotein antigens with low water solubility. Thus, albumin may flocculate in the agar gel during interaction with β-lipoprotein of serum giving rise to non-immune precipitation arcs similar to those caused by antigen–antibody reactions. Proteolytic enzymes of tissue extracts may cause non-immune precipitate formation during immunodiffusion (Niece and Barrett 1963). Also lipoproteins of low water solubility may well be solubilized by extraction

Subject index p. 557

with detergents; being high-molecular-weight colloids, lipoproteins will flocculate spontaneously during diffusion in agar gel not containing the detergent in question, and thus produce turbid areas resembling immunoprecipitate arcs (Clausen, unpublished data). They even flocculate in precipitates when they meet normal serum proteins, i.e. normal gammaglobulins. However, the opposite may also be the case, i.e. that detergents inhibit antigen–antibody reaction. This has been found in cases of pure protein antigens reacting with the corresponding antibody (Weetall and Bozicevich 1967).

Even though the antibody–antigen reaction of blood group substances is immunologically specific, these substances may participate in an unspecific immunochemical-like reaction with a protein of non-immunoglobulin nature present in specific plant proteins extractable from different types of beans (Boyd 1962; Hossaini 1966). The lima bean proteins, lectins, evidently have a conformational structure which enables them to be linked specifically to certain blood group antigens. This is a typical example of an unspecific immunochemical reaction. Although the reaction between blood group substances and lectins is a non-immunoglobulin reaction, it is specific and can be used practically for differentiation between different blood group antigens. The lectin-reaction demonstrates that, without a critical physicochemical study of the protein linked to the antigen (subunit analysis), one cannot always be sure that the basis for an immunochemical-like precipitation is a reaction between an antigen and the corresponding antibody (p. 502).

8.7.2. *Artifacts in double immunodiffusion techniques*

Duplication of immunoprecipitates occurs mainly as mentioned (p. 449) during work with horse antibody (Crowle 1961). This type of antibody may form multiple immunoprecipitates, if a disproportional amount of either antigen or antibody diffuses towards the other one, or if the immunodiffusion is not performed at a constant temperature (Crowle 1961; Ouchterlony 1962). It is also possible in a slowly precipitating system that a soluble complex of the two reactants might diffuse beyond the barrier of the immunoprecipitate and cause a second line of precipitation (Burtin 1954; Korngold and Van Leeuwen 1957). Finally, duplication of lines may be caused by the presence of different determinants attached to the same antigen molecule (Jennings and Kaplan 1960).

The spur phenomena developed during double immunodiffusion, do not always involve serological relationship between the antigens in question (Augustin 1959). So-called bispecific antibodies capable of precipitating either of two unrelated antigens can produce spurs (Ouchterlony 1962, 1967). When two unrelated antigens are tested in a mixture towards two antibody-containing immune sera made against these two unrelated antigens, spur phenomena may also develop (Ouchterlony 1962). Sometimes false spur patterns may be obtained with an antigen mixture in one of the wells and for instance, only one antigen in the other well. If the first well contains a specific antigen not present in the second, a precipitin band may happen to develop overlapping the precipitin band of the antigenic groups in common for the two wells, thus simulating a spur phenomenon. To avoid misinterpretation of spur phenomenon, the samples must be studied in different degrees of dilution or after crosswise absorption.

If one antigen solution is much more concentrated than the other related antigen during double diffusion experiments with horse antibody, the line formed by the more concentrated antigen solution will migrate towards the antibody well more rapidly than that produced by the weaker antigen solution and so break the original loop of fusion unevenly, producing a false spur phenomenon. Various artifacts can develop through recharging wells with antigen during immunodiffusion.

As mentioned (p. 426), the site of the immunoprecipitate depends on the initial concentration of the reactants and their diffusion coefficient. Balanced systems produce stable precipitation lines; unbalanced systems may produce migrating precipitates and eventually multiplication of lines. Established precipitates may dissolve in an excess of antigen and for certain immunosystems (e.g. horse antibodies) in an excess of antibody as well. A precipitate settled in the gel usually acts as a barrier for the specific reactants taking part in the precipitation; but this is not invariably the case, as demonstrated by the false spur phenomenon frequently occurring in unbalanced systems. These false spurs are subsequently gradually dissolved and thus differ from the true spurs which grow in length.

8.7.3. *Abnormal binding of antigens to antibodies*

As mentioned in chapter 1, the antibody site of immunoglobulins is localized in Porter's papain fragment Fab, i.e. the site consists of both H- and L-chains. However, in some cases, antigens seem to fix to papain fragment Fc. The biological and practical implications of this ability have not been elucidated. Thus, myeloma sera seem to exhibit low antibody titres against pneumococcal and streptococcal antigens but normal 'antibody' titre against the A-antigen from staphylococci (Dammacco and Clausen 1965). This compares with the widespread occurrence of immunoglobulins precipitating the A-antigen in normal human individuals (Jensen 1959) and led Forsgren and Löfquist (1966, 1967), and Gustavson et al. (1967) to the demonstration that the A-antigen precipitates the Fc but not the Fab papain fragments, i.e. pure H-chains bind the A-antigen. In gel diffusion systems, the complex formation between antigen and antibody, tied at the Fc fragment, cannot be distinguished from ordinary antigen–antibody reactions. The practical and biological implications of this finding are not yet understood, but the papain cleavage of immunoglobulins precipitating a certain antigen, followed by studies of the ability of the fragments to link the antigen, may be used to differentiate between binding of antigen to antibody site (Fab) and binding to the Fc fragment. On the other hand, isolated A-antigen may be used for separation and isolation of pure Fab and Fc fragments.

CHAPTER 9

Immunochemical reactions in free buffer systems

Immunochemical reactions in free buffer solutions have been used for the quantitative estimation of small amounts of specific poly-saccharides and other antigens (Heidelberger and Kendall 1929, 1935) and for estimation of albumin and globulins in serum and in other biological fluids (Kabat et al. 1948; Goettsch and Kendall 1935; Goettsch and Reeves 1936; Goettsch and Lyttle 1940; Kendall 1938).

Between 1945 and 1960, the Heidelberger–Kendall technique was replaced by the qualitative and quantitative immunochemical gel techniques mentioned in previous chapters. Recently, however, the method is being utilized more and more, either for preparative purposes or combined with tracer techniques, for quantitative estimation of mμg amounts of antigens (peptide hormones).

9.1. Qualitative and structural analysis of antigens

The precipitin reaction may be used to bring out qualitatively and quantitatively the structural constituents of carbohydrate antigens (Markowitz and Heidelberger 1954). By means of specific antisera, Kabat (1960) has succeeded in elucidating the antigenic structure of dextran (see p. 415) and the determinant end groups of the blood group substances (review Kabat and Mayer 1961). Using strictly specific antisera towards different bacterial polysaccharide moieties, it is possible to estimate the carbohydrate content of polysaccharides. This may be performed by analysing specific precipitates for two or

Subject index p. 557

more distinctive constituents of a given antigen preparation. It is thus possible to estimate fructose, mannose, galactose, galactosamine and other carbohydrates in micro amounts of the immunoprecipitate.

The draw-back of an immunochemical analysis combined with chemical assay for carbohydrates is that the sensitivity of the chemical methods determines the lower limit for the amount of precipitate required for the analysis. It is sometimes necessary to introduce correction factors because the carbohydrates of the antibodies may contribute to the colour reaction.

The quantitative precipitin method may also be used for preparative analysis of the lipid constituents of lipoprotein. Although it has been shown that the ability of antibodies to precipitate certain lipoproteins, i.e. lipovitelline, may vary depending on some uncontrollable factors (Francis and Wormal 1948, 1950), the antigen–antibody reaction may be used to elucidate the composition of polar lipids in certain lipoprotein antigens. Thus, by combination of the quantitative precipitin reaction with microscale quantitative thin-layer chromatography, Clausen (1966a) was able to demonstrate the relative distribution of the sialic acid-free polar lipids present in the β-lipoprotein of serum and cerebrospinal fluids and further to determine the total amount of this lipoprotein in these two biological fluids.

9.2. Quantitative estimation

9.2.1. Direct precipitation

Working below the point of equivalence between the two reactants, it is possible from the quantitative precipitin curve to estimate the amount of antigen in an unknown sample (Goettsch and Kendall 1935; Goettsch and Reeves 1936; Kendall 1938; Kabat and Mayer 1961). When using this method, it is absolutely necessary that the antibody used is strictly specific against the antigen in question. Furthermore, the solutions of the two reactants must be completely free of microbiological and other cellular contamination because these factors contribute to the nitrogen or to the total protein content of the precipitate formed; because of that and other uncontrollable factors this method is not recommended for either the beginner in the field of immunochemistry or for routine assays.

9.2.2. *The quantitative precipitin reaction combined with tracer technique*

This method has already been described, under the heading 'Double antibody precipitation', on p. 492; cf. appendix 30.

CHAPTER 10

Appendices

Preparation of Freund's adjuvant (Crowle 1961)

This is available commercially.

1. Incomplete type (without mycobacteria) one of two formulas may be used:

   a. 3 parts (by vols) light mineral oil U.S.P.
      1 part Aquaphore, Falba, or anhydrous lanolin
      4 parts phosphate buffer, made by mixing 24 ml 2.2% (w/v)
      KH_2PO_4 with 76 ml 2.2% (w/v) $Na_2HPO_4.2H_2O$
   b. 4 parts n-hexadecane
      1 part glycerol monooleate (Myverol Ⓡ, Distillation Prod. Inc.)
      10 parts phosphate buffer (vide supra).

2. Complete type (with mycobacteria) i.e. incomplete type + mycobacteria. Suspend mycobacteria (either live avirulent tubercle bacilli, heat-killed virulent tubercle bacilli, *Mycobacterium byturicum*, or *M. smegmatis*) in buffer to give a final concentration of 10 mg (wet weight) per ml of water-in-oil emulsion. The same final concentration of the particular antigen can be used.

3. Emulsification. Emulsifier (e.g. glycerol monooleate) is dissolved in oil, and the oil solution is layered upon water. Water-in-oil emulsions are obtained by mixing these two phases together vigorously with a syringe having a large-gauge needle, or by a vibrator, high-speed stirrer, or other such instrument. For example, one can employ a high-speed engraving tool in which is chucked a $2\frac{1}{2}$ inch box nail as impeller. With this nail rotating at high speed (e.g. 15,000 rpm or more) the head is slowly lowered into the mixture, causing emulsification to proceed from top to bottom. The stability of a water-in-oil emulsion can be tested by dropping some onto the surface of cold water; the drop should remain intact.

Preparation of antisera

Immunization

Immunization may be performed as a micro or macro technique. In the micro technique about 10–50 μl of 5 % (w/v) antigen solution is applied intradermally in the foot pad of the four legs in rabbits or other animals. The application may most conveniently be performed by means of a Hamilton syringe. This method saves antigen, but is laborious because of difficulties in handling the animal. Furthermore, the food pad injection is painful to the animal. In the macro technique about 250–500 μl of 5 % (w/v) antigen solution is injected subcutaneously into an animal the size of a rabbit.

1. Long-term immunization is performed by injecting 5 times either intradermally or subcutaneously, the antigen amounts indicated above, every third week. The first injection is accompanied by a subcutaneous injection of 0.5 ml Freund's complete adjuvant (see appendix 1) (Freund's adjuvant excites the reticuloendothelial system in its antigenic response). Eight days after the last injection the animal is bled (cf. fig. 1.3).

2. Short-term immunization is achieved by injecting about 200–500 μl of 5 % antigen solution intravenously every second day for about three weeks. The first injection is accompanied by subcutaneous injection of 0.5 ml Freund's complete adjuvant. Eight days from the last injection the animal is bled.

The latter method seems undesirable because of the large consumption of antigen and because the animal cannot be used for longer periods due to development of secondary amyloidosis.

Bleeding

In rabbits, bleeding is performed from an ear vein. After irritation of the ear with benzene or xylene, the border vein of the ear is punctured by a needle. In goats and larger animals the blood can be drawn by a 2-mm cannula inserted into the jugular vein. The jugular vein is easily seen below a stasis of the neck. In guinea pigs, birds and smaller animals the blood is taken by heart puncture. The puncture is performed by forcing a 1-mm cannula on a syringe through the frontal and left side of the thorax between the fourth and fifth rib. Blood will appear in the syringe when the heart cavity is reached.

In order to bleed rabbits or to handle them during injection in the foot pad, different types of apparatus have been used. The simplest for both procedures is a wooden board measuring $100 \times 30 \times 1$ cm, fixed in a $60°$ position; a triangular

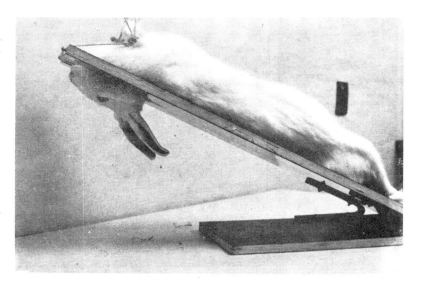

Fig. 10.1. Simple equipment for fixing rabbit for bleeding from the ear or by heart puncture. The wooden plate, $100 \times 30 \times 1$ cm, is fixed at $60°$ to a vertical plate and equipped with four screws. The rabbit is placed on the upper part of the plate, with the neck between the cutting and the head below the plate, fixing the body to the plate. The extremities may be tied to the screws.

portion is cut from the top (fig. 10.1). The board is covered by plastic and equipped with four screws at top and bottom. The rabbit is placed on its back on the board with the neck in the triangular gap and the head below the board, thus fixing the body. The legs are tied to the screws. The animal does not move and is not harmed when placed as described; it is easy to inject and bleed. Bleeding from the ear may also be performed by holding the rabbit's body in a closed box equipped with a hole for the neck allowing the head to be outside the box.

In large-scale experiments where the investigator intends to use several batches of antisera, it is wise to save the immunized animals. One bleeding of a large rabbit produces 40 to 50 ml whole blood. On the day of bleeding, the animal can be immunized again and bled again 8 days later. Thereafter, the animal should go without treatment for about 4 weeks to recover. The antibody titre can then easily be restored by a single injection of antigen.

The author has had animals (rabbits and goats) bled nearly every month for more than one year. One must be aware that sometimes the titre will decrease after 8 to 10 injections probably because of secondary amyloidosis. When that happens, the animal should be killed.

Preparation of serum from whole blood

After clotting, e.g. after 30 min settling, serum is obtained from whole blood by centrifugation (2000 g for 10 min). In order to avoid loss of serum included in the clot, it is advisable to loosen the clot from the glass surface before centrifugation by turning a wooden stick around in the glass near the glass wall.

In the case of heart puncture it may be wise to have 100 μl 3.2% citrate in the syringe in order to avoid coagulation. Prior to centrifugation, recalcification can be obtained by adding 100 μl 3.2% $CaCl_2$. The coagulation is thus initiated by mixing and is completed by standing for 30 min.

Storage of antisera

The antisera may be stored without preservatives in closed ampoules either after lyophilization or deep frozen at $-20\,°C$. Sera may be frozen and thawed several times without damage to the antibodies. However, during freezing, eutectic mixtures with low pH may be produced (see p. 498), thus giving rise to acid denaturation or conformational changes in the antibody molecule. To avoid contamination with microorganisms it is wise to distribute small amounts in closed ampoules and to add, e.g., 0.1% (w/v) NaN_3 (not stable) or 0.01% (w/v) merthiolate. When using preservatives in immunochemical reagents one should always remember that the anti-bacterial agent may have undesirable effects such as toxicity or inhibition of enzyme activity. Thus, NaN_3 inhibits oxidase activity of ceruloplasmin (Uriel 1960, 1964). NaN_3 also causes lung oedema when injected in antigen used for immunization experiments.

Subject index p. 557

APPENDIX 3

Concentration of protein solutions (antigens and antibodies)

Increase of antibody titre

Sometimes antisera are obtained possessing a rather low titre. The titre may be increased by salting out the immunoglobulins at 2.0 M $(NH_4)SO_4$ (pH 6.8). The precipitate is isolated by centrifugation, washed three times with 2.0 M $(NH_4)SO_4$ and finally dissolved in 0.1 M $NaHCO_3$ in a volume 4 to 10 times lower than the original volume of the antiserum.

Alternatively the antiserum can be lyophilized and redissolved in a smaller volume or submitted to pressure or vacuum dialysis, or other concentration procedures mentioned below. The degree of concentration may be evaluated from the final volume or from the total protein content prior to and after dialysis.

Dialysis against a macromolecular colloid solution

The protein solution may be concentrated by dialysis against a high molecular weight, inert substance, e.g. polyvinylpyrrolidone (PVP) or polyethyleneglycol (carbowax). The dialysis membranes must possess a pore size allowing colloids with a molecular weight below 10,000 to pass. These membranes are commercially available, but may be prepared from cellulose acetate. The macro-molecular colloids used in the dialysis such as PVP or carbowax, are prepared as approximately 40% (w/v) solutions in distilled water or suitable buffers. A certain volume of the sample to be dialyzed is transferred to a dialysis bag and the bag is placed in the cold PVP or carbowax solution and kept at 4 °C. A micromodification of this principle has been developed by Colover (1960). Usually after dialysis for about 16 hours, the sample is concentrated sufficiently.

Pressure dialysis

Pressure dialysis may be performed at 4 atm of N_2 in commercially available chambers (Fig. 10.2). The N_2 pressure is applied on the sample, forcing water and salts through the dialysis membrane, supported from below by a porous stainless steel shield.

Vacuum dialysis

Vacuum dialysis may be performed in commercially available suction flasks (fig. 10.3) connected to a suction pump. The dialysis bag, formed as a cone and connected to a glass neck, is placed in buffer in the flask to be evacuated. This method

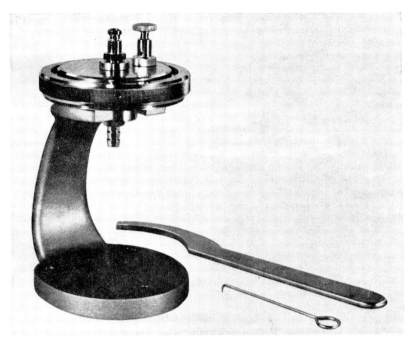

Fig. 10.2. Procedure of pressure dialysis (courtesy of Membranfilter Gesellschaft, Göttingen, Germany). The apparatus for pressure dialysis consists of a steel chamber whose upper and lower parts are screwed together, but separated by means of porous steel plate on which the membrane is supported. The upper half of the chamber contains a known volume of the sample; below this is placed a beaker to collect the fluid pressed through the membrane. The upper chamber is connected through high pressure cable with reduction valve of a nitrogen cylinder. Hereafter a pressure of about 5 atm is applied. After 4–6 hr pressure dialysis a certain amount of fluid is pressed through the membrane. The pressure dialysis is stopped, the upper chamber is removed; the remaining fluid on the membrane is sucked up.

Subject index p. 557

will concentrate a 10-ml sample 100 times within 3 hr. Also ordinary dialysis membranes tied to a conical glass tube may be placed in a suction flask. The glass tube is connected with the open air through a rubber tube. A slight vacuum may cause concentration of the sample applied in the bag. In the author's hand, vacuum dialysis is better than the other methods because dialysis against PVP or carbowax will give rise to contamination of the sample with low-molecular-weight fragments of these substances, and because pressure dialysis and lyophilization needs expensive equipment.

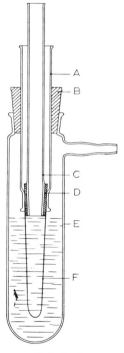

Fig. 10.3. Apparatus for vacuum dialysis (courtesy Membranfilter Gesellschaft, Göttingen, Germany). The outer glass mantle A is equipped with a ground joint articulating through the teflon cone D with the internal glass tube C. Between these two the dialysis membrane F is fixed around the teflon cone D. The solution to be concentrated is placed in F. During dialysis, the outer chamber E is filled with buffer. The glass shaft to which the dialysis membrane is fixed, is fastened to the upper rubber cork B during vacuum suction.

Concentration by evaporation

A protein solution may be concentrated by lyophilization in commercially available apparatuses. However, for the concentration of most proteins not possessing enzymic activities, a hand hair-drier, running with warm air, can be hung 0.5 to 1.0 m from the dialysis bag; the air flow causes the water outside the dialysis bag to evaporate, cooling the inside of the bag. After two to four hours, 5 to 15 ml protein solution will be concentrated about 100 times (Bürgi 1967).

APPENDIX 4

Specific absorption of antisera

The absorption is performed in a dilution series where the antiserum is absorbed with a 1% (w/v) antigen solution added in the proportion $1:1$, $2:1$, $4:1$, $8:1$ and more. After mixing the solution of antigen and antibody, the mixture stands for 0.5 hr at 37 °C. It may then be applied directly to the reservoir for the antibody. However. in order to avoid the accumulation in the trough of the immunoprecipitate formed during the absorption process, the immunoprecipitate may be removed by centrifugation. The serum selected for further use is that which shows complete loss of the unwanted antibody after adding the minimum quantity of antigen.

APPENDIX 5

Purification of agar

Agar may be purified for immunoelectrophoretic or immunodiffusion work, by two different methods, depending on whether a raw agar or a pre-purified type is used.

1. Pre-purified agar. The type of agar used for bacteriological purposes is mixed with distilled water to give a 4% (w/v) solution; after adjusting the pH to 7.0 by dropwise addition of 1.0 N sodium hydroxide or hydrochloric acid, the suspension is heated in a water bath at 90 °C. When the mixture is completely dissolved and homogenous, the solution is poured into a glass container to give a layer about 2–3 mm thick. After gelation, blocks about 5×5 mm are cut with a knife. The agar blocks are washed for 2 days in 100 times their volume of distilled water, the water being changed at least 5 times.

2. Raw agar. Although agar may be obtained from different localities in the world, only that originating from the coastlines of Japan and America, Korea or New Zealand, is suitable for gel diffusion and immunoelectrophoresis, and then only after removal of excess inorganic ions after extensive washing.

Subject index p. 557

To purify Japanese agar as directly imported, it is washed in tap water and dissolved by heating to 90 °C in distilled water at a 10 % (w/v) solution. 10 g of calcium chloride (anhydrous) is added to every 100 g of agar to precipitate impurities. The agar is filtered through gauze or glass wool and then congealed and the cloudy bottom layer is discarded. The agar is cut into small blocks and placed in a single layer on gauze. The blocks are extracted for 3 days in running tap water, and then for 2 days in about 5 changes of distilled water (1000 times the volume of the blocks). The agar is melted again and filtered through a gauze. The volume and dry weight are measured. The purified agar is dissolved in saline or an appropriate buffer and bacteriostatic agent and stored for future use.

APPENDIX 6

Preparation of agarose (Hjertén 1962)

Agaro-pectin is a sulphated acid mucopolysaccharide and is therefore precipitated by tertiary ammonium compounds such as cetylpyridinium chloride; non-ionized agarose is not precipitated. Therefore, agarose can be isolated from ordinary agar by removal of agaro-pectin with cetylpyridinium chloride. The precipitation of the agaro-pectin by cetylpyridinium chloride must be performed at a temperature above 45 °C, which is the approximate gelling temperature of agar. The precipitate is removed by centrifugation and the excess of cetylpyridinium chloride is removed by washing and adsorption on Fuller's earth. After freezing and subsequent thawing, residues of salts, etc., can be squeezed out. The agarose gel is dehydrated by freeze-drying or by precipitation with alcohol. Details of the preparation are as follows.

Precipitation with cetylpyridinium chloride

800 ml of 0.02 M sodium citrate is heated to boiling in an Erlenmeyer flask; agar (32 g) is cautiously added with stirring. The heating is continued until all agar has dissolved. Cetylpyridinium chloride (12 g in 400 ml 0.02 M sodium citrate) at 100 °C is added slowly, with stirring, to the hot agar solution. A precipitate is immediately formed. The stoppered Erlenmeyer flask is left for 30 min at 65 °C, in an oven containing also the rotor and tubes of the centrifuge to be used for separating the precipitate. The centrifuge is at room temperature before the run; centrifugation of the mixture for 30 min at 9000 rev/min (13,000 g) gives a sediment sharply demarcated from the supernatant (agarose) which is in general in the form of a stiff gel when the centrifugation has been finished. If the centrifuge tubes used are made of semi-transparent plastic such as polyethylene, it is easy to locate the boundary between the gel and the sediment and to remove the upper gel layer. Centrifuges, giving a maximal centrifugal force considerably lower than 13,000 g can also be used with a longer centrifugation time.

To remove excess of cetylpyridinium chloride and sodium chloride, the agarose gel is broken into small pieces and transferred to a 6-l beaker filled with distilled water. The suspension is stirred for 0.5 hr with a motor-driven stirrer, after which the gel particles are allowed to sediment and the supernatant liquid is decanted. Four further washes, the last involving stirring overnight, are recommended. Finally, the gel particles are washed several times on a coarse glass filter. The washed gel is then transferred to a beaker and liquified by heating, with stirring to prevent the gel from getting burnt at the bottom of the beaker. In doing so, a rich stable foam appears. Treated Fuller's earth (see below) in the form of a slurry at 65 °C is added in portions until the foam has almost entirely disappeared, indicating that the last traces of the cetylpyridinium ion have been adsorbed. The Fuller's earth with adsorbed cetylpyridinium ions is then spun down in warm centrifuge tubes placed in a warm rotor and under the same experimental conditions as those used for removal of the cetylpyridinium chloride precipitated. Impurities are removed by decantation and washing as described above.

Dehydration

The gel particles are liquified by heating. The solution is allowed to gel at room temperature, is frozen and then thawed. Water with residues of salts, etc. is squeezed out by 4–5 washings on a coarse glass filter. The gel is dehydrated by freeze-drying or by precipitation with 5 volumes alcohol. The yield is about 15 g agarose.

Pre-treatment of Fuller's earth

The absorbent is shaken with 10 vols 1 % (w/v) sodium acetate for 30 min and then allowed to settle for 1 h or centrifuged at slow speed for a short time. The suspension is decanted from the deposit. The deposit is processed again; once more in sodium acetate, then in 25 % (w/v) saturation of sodium chloride and finally, three times in distilled water.

APPENDIX 7

Preparation of agar gel for immunodiffusion or immunoelectrophoresis

The gels are usually prepared at a concentration below 2 % (w/v). A purified agar, or agarose, must be used. For immunodiffusion experiments the gel may be mixed with NaCl (final concentration 0.85 % w/v) or a buffer. For immunoelectrophoresis, buffers are used usually at a final concentration of 0.05 M. 700 ml buffer (0.05 M) is placed in a Roux flask in a boiling water bath. The flask is loosely stoppered by a volumetric flask of 5 ml, placed upside down in the neck. When the buffer is hot, it is mixed with 7 g of agar (either dried, or as a gel in water, appendix 4) and during the next 40 min (time must be standardized to ensure identical slides) the flask is repeatedly taken out and *shaken* thoroughly; after 40 min it is inspected. The molten agar must be absolutely clear, otherwise grains will appear on the slides. If it is not clear, heating should be continued. If stored agar gel is used, it is melted with an equal volume of 0.1 M buffer. After complete solubilization the agar is mixed with a bacteriostatic agent (0.1 % w/v sodium azide or 0.01 % merthiolate) and either poured directly on slides or stored in stoppered test tubes or 50- to 100-ml bottles at 4 °C.

During storage the agar gel must not be allowed to dry out or freeze, otherwise the micelle structure will be broken. During melting of the stored gel before pouring, the flask must be heated in such a way as to avoid evaporation of water. The water content of the agar is decreased when the same batch of agar is stored and melted several times. The author found it convenient to heat the agar gel in small beakers which are dipped in the water below the rings in an electrical thermostated water bath. Thus, the melting is performed in an atmosphere saturated with water vapour. During melting, the temperature must not exceed 100 °C or be maintained for too long a time at this temperature, as prolonged heating causes partial destruction of gel structures and the appearance of brownish decomposition products.

The melted agar is poured onto prepared slides or plates (appendix 10).

APPENDIX 8

Simple linear immunodiffusion (Oudin technique)

A. Reagents

1. A specific antiserum.
2. Pure agar (Noble or purified agar as in appendix 5).
3. Immunologically pure antigen (for preparation of standard antigen solutions in 0.9 % w/v NaCl).

B. Preparation of agar tubes

A 1 % (w/v) agar solution dissolved and melted in $^1/_{15}$ M phosphate buffer pH 7.5, containing 0.9 (w/v) NaCl, is cooled slowly in a water bath to 48 °C. One part of agar is mixed with two parts of an appropriate dilution of specific antiserum, also at 48 °C. The warm mixture is poured by a warm pipette into pre-warmed glass tubes (100 × 2.5 mm) to a height of 2.5 cm. The tubes are stored in a refrigerator at 4 °C. In order to find the optimal dilution of the antiserum, initial experiments must be performed using tubes containing antiserum diluted with buffer 1/2, 1/5, 1/10, 1/20 and 1/40; at each dilution, five tubes are prepared. The dilution producing the best standard curve (see below) is selected.

C. Loading of tubes with antigens

A dilution series of a standard solution of immunologically pure protein antigen, or the unknown sample, is placed above the gel (about 2 μl). After a fixed immuno-diffusion time of 24 to 72 hr with the tube placed vertically at a constant temperature (22 °C), the migration distance measured from the meniscus of the gel to the meniscus of the immunoprecipitate is measured in millimeters.

Within a certain concentration of the standard solution, the distance of migration x is proportional to the logarithm of antigen concentration $x = K_2 \log C_{Ag} + K_3$ (form. 1.8). For the standard curve the length of diffusion should be plotted as a function of the amount of protein antigen in a logarithmic coordinate system. The length of diffusion may be evaluated with a standard deviation of about $\pm$ 0.1 mm by a telescope lens.

D. Precautions

1. Care must be taken that immunodiffusion is not disturbed by formation of air bubbles (use a Hamilton syringe for sample application) or by the gel lifting from the glass surface. 2. The temperature during immunodiffusion must be constant, to within $\pm$ 0.1 °C. 3. Antigen must be in great excess.

APPENDIX 9

1. Single radial immunodiffusion in agar gel (Mancini et al. 1964)

A. Reagents

1. A specific antiserum is diluted with 0.9 % (w/v) aqueous NaCl to an extent giving rise to antigen excess during immunodiffusion (usually 5 to 12 times).
2. 0.1 M sodium barbital buffer pH 8.6.
3. Noble agar or agarose.
4. Immunologically pure antigen in buffer (for preparation of standard antigen solution).

B. Preparation of agar dishes

A 3 % (w/v) agar solution dissolved in barbital buffer and containing as bacteriostatic agent 0.01 % w/v merthiolate, is mixed with a diluted antiserum as described in appendix 8. The agar–antiserum mixture is poured into pre-warmed horizontal Petrie dishes to give a layer 1.0 mm in thickness. The dishes are covered; after the agar has set, holes of 1 mm diameter are made in the gel (see appendix 10.1.1.1). In the holes are placed (with a constriction pipette or a Hamilton syringe) known volumes of the standard solution of antigen in 0.9 % (w/v) NaCl (for instance from 0.2 to 0.5 μg of albumin per μl) and of the unknown solution of antigen. After several days of immunodiffusion when the precipitates have ceased to migrate, the diameter or area of the circles covered by immunoprecipitation is measured; one of these is directly proportional to the amount of antigen. A standard curve is plotted, relating the area or diameter to the amount of standard antigen used. The areas or diameters are measured directly by means of appropriate magnifying equipment. Prior to that, immunoprecipitate areas may be stained with protein stains (appendix 18).

2. Single radial immunodiffusion on cellulose acetate (Vergani et al. 1967)

A. Reagents

1. Antiserum. The monospecific antiserum is diluted with 0.9 % w/v aqueous NaCl to an extent giving rise to antigen excess during immunodiffusion (normally five to twelve times).

2· Antigen. Make a standard series of dilutions of the immunologically pure antigen (i.e. IgG globulin in the interval from 0.1 to 0.7 mg/ml). The dilution is performed with 0.9 % (w/v) aqueous NaCl containing 5 % (w/v) dextran.

B. Procedure

A strip of cellulose acetate (2.5×18 cm, Schleicher and Schüll, Dassel/kr, Germany) stretched on a bridge in a moist chamber of Perspex, is sprayed with 0.02 ml/cm^2 of the diluted antiserum. A glass rod is repeatedly run over the strip until the antiserum is completely absorbed. The strip is left for 30 min at 23 °C in the moist chamber.

1.0 μl of the standard solutions and the test samples are applied 3 cm apart on the strip. The strip is then placed immediately into mineral oil (White Oil 120, Manchester Oil Refinery, England) and left there at 37 °C until diffusion is completed (12 to 48 hr). The strip is then removed from the oil, immersed in a detergent solution, e.g. Teepol (Hopkin and Williams, Chadwell Heath, England) in water (1 % w/v) to wash off oil, for less than 30 sec. The strip is then washed under a strong jet of tapwater. To remove the unreacted reactants the strip is immersed for 5 min at room temperature into a solution of the detergent Haemo-Sol (Meinecke and Co., Baltimore, U.S.A.) (2 g/l). The strip is then placed in a protein staining solution (appendix 18) for 15 min. After de-staining, the strip is laid on a glass plate and can be cleared by immersion in dioxan + isobutanol $(7+3)$ and dried in an oven at 80 °C. The standard curve relating ring diameter of immunoprecipitate to protein content is made. The antigen content of the test sample can now be estimated from the diameter of the immunoprecipitate and the standard curve.

APPENDIX 10

Preparation of agar slides for immunoelectrophoresis and double immunodiffusion

10.1. Micro techniques

10.1.1. Conventional technique

The buffered agar (see appendix 7) is stored at 4 °C in a stoppered flask or bottle. The flask is placed in a boiling water bath until the agar is completely melted. A 10-ml pipette is placed in the flask so that the pipette is at the same temperature as the agar. Microscope slides are degreased successively in 90% (v/v) ethanol, ethanol:ethyl ether (1:1v/v) and ether. They are dried and numbered consecutively in agreement with protocol. The slides are placed on horizontal wooden blocks with their ends free. (A commercially available rack can be used.) With the pipette, each slide is covered, free hand, with 1 ml of fluid agar, avoiding air bubble formation in the agar. If bubbles form, these can be removed by tilting the pipette slightly, at the same time touching the bubbles. After the agar has set on the slides, they are placed in pairs in Petrie dishes containing a few drops of water or some damp cotton wool to avoid drying out of the agar. The dishes are stored at 4 °C until used.

It is especially important that agar should be of equal depth throughout the slide; otherwise, during the electrophoretic separation or the immunodiffusion, irregularities will cause asymmetrical migrations and diffusions. Furthermore, the thickness of the agar gel must not be over 1 mm, otherwise there may be difficulties in washing out the unreacted antigen and antibody and also peeling of the agar gel surface from the slide may occur after drying.

To obtain the highest reproducibility in preparing agar slides for immunoelectrophoresis and gel diffusion, especially when these methods are performed routinely by unskilled assistants, it is wise to use special casting racks made of plastic which are commercially available. Equipment for cutting wells and troughs is also available commercially. For ordinary purposes, it is unnecessary to use the commercial equipment for casting and cutting, as similar equipment may be made cheaply by the investigator; after some practice, slides may be covered by an even layer of agar without the aid of a casting rack.

10.1.1.1. Cutting the pattern in gels for micro-immunoelectrophoresis and immunodiffusion. The cutting for immunodiffusion or immunoelectrophoresis may be made by free hand or by means of templates. The template technique is based upon the use of plastic or metal cutting and sucking devices for making appropriate wells and troughs (Heremans 1960; Crowle and Leaker 1962). Templates for immunoelectrophoretic analysis are commercially available. They are, however, expensive and the necessary equipment may well be home-made with advantage. Working with only a few slides it may be sufficient to place the agar plate on white paper on which wells and troughs are drawn. It is then possible to trace the pattern (vide infra).

The holes on the slides can be made by a syringe needle, 1 mm in diameter, square cut and ground at the end. By forcing the needle through the gel and applying continuous suction by mouth through a rubber tube it is possible to make a hole with a capacity of about 1.5 μl. In the macro procedure the holes may be made by means of forcing metal cylinders (e.g. cork borer) of an appropriate diameter into the gel.

10.1.2. Wieme technique (1959)

Preliminary coating of slides: numbered microscope slides are defatted by rubbing with an ethanol–ether mixture (vide supra) and laid out, touching each other and with clear surfaces up on a horizontal surface. They are now coated with a uniformly thick layer (1 mm) of melted agar 1 % (w/v) in *distilled water* applying the agar quickly from a large pipette. The agar is dried into a thin film that adheres firmly to the glass surface by placing the slides at 40 to 50 °C.

Pouring of the electrophoresis layer: glass vessels with flat bottoms and of a size suitable for a number of slides ($15 \times 15 \times 3$ cm will hold two rows of five slides each), are placed firmly on a horizontal surface. They are filled to a depth of about 1 cm with buffered agar gel. When the gel has solidified an absolutely flat and horizontal surface is thus obtained. From now on the vessels must not be moved. The coated slides are laid out on the solid gel surface, and an exact amount of warm buffered agar is poured over them, calculated to cover each slide with a layer exactly 1.0 mm thick. When the gel is solid, the vessels are covered with tightly fitting lids and stored at $+4$ °C. The structure of the gel and the electroendosmotic flow during the electrophoretic run will not be stabilized until the slides have been stored for at least 24 hr at $+4$ °C. They will keep for about five days. The coated slides may be cut out from the agar with a knife and are ready for use.

10.1.2.1. Cutting the pattern.

In the Wieme technique, a slit for the antigen is made by carefully inserting into the gel a piece of hard, thin filter paper (0.5×1.0 cm). (The paper may be Schleicher and Schüll, Dassel, No. 1) Thereby a slit of 0.5×10 mm width in the agar is made. The length may conveniently be about 10 mm. This operation requires some training; too deep an insertion will distort the shape of the application slit or give rise to capillary suction of the sample into a space between the underside of the agar and the glass surface. After a short training however, an operator will be able to make up to eight perfect electrophoreses every half hour (two on each slide). The filter paper will stick in the agar, sucking buffer from the slit thus produced; it is removed after about 20 seconds. The application slit is filled dropwise from a drawn out capillary tube, a Hamilton syringe or a constriction pipette, which may be calibrated. When separating protein fractions by salt fractionation, preliminary dialysis against the buffer is necessary. The slit will accommodate between 4 and 8 µl. It may be filled twice. Two or even three slits may be placed on the same slide, thus making possible a parallel run of a reference mixture for determination of relative electrophoretic mobilities possible. By applying the slit laterally, an area of agar gel will be left large enough to prepare a longitudinal trough for antibody after the electrophoretic run.

The antibody troughs (cut after the electrophoretic step) may be made by means of a knife and a ruler, but the cutting of two completely parallel lines may be difficult. Therefore, it is more convenient either to use a drawing pen or a trough cutter made by two razor blades screwed together in a plastic or wooden holder with a distance of about 1 mm between the blades. The distance may be varied by means of spacers of different thickness. The cutter is guided by a plastic frame which holds the agar slide and has two pillars on each side of a recess for the agar gel slide. Thus, by driving the razor blade holder towards the surface of the agar gel, the position of the trough will be determined by the guide pillars and a standard trough will be cut without damage to the gel. It is important not to make the antibody trough by removing the agar from the slide prior to the electrophoretic run, because this may cause irregular electrophoretic separation.

10.2. Macro technique

Preparation of plates and pattern for macro-immunoelectrophoresis (Grabar technique): Cover horizontally placed defatted glass plates (e.g. 9×17 cm) with a 2 mm thick agar layer. After gel formation, holes and troughs are made. The holes (1.0 cm) are conveniently made by forcing a cork borer through the gel. The troughs (15×0.5 cm) are made with a ruler and a knife.

APPENDIX 11

Double immunodiffusion (Ouchterlony technique)

In double immunodiffusion, unbalanced systems may easily be developed. In order to avoid this, initial trials to fix a balanced proportion between antigen and antibody must be made. This is done by performing the double immunodiffusion in two series, e.g. one with fixed amount (or volume) of the antigen diffusing against a series of antibody dilutions (e.g. undiluted, diluted 1:1, 1:2, 1:4, 1:8, 1:16 with saline) and *vice versa*. On this basis, artificial duplication of lines, for instance, can

Subject index p. 557

be avoided and detailed morphological studies of spur phenomena can be performed with the reactants in optimal proportion.

The interpretation of the results is mentioned in the text (pp. 467–469). As in immunoelectrophoresis, the results obtained must always be referred to properly by indicating the amount and volume of both reactants, the mutual distance of wells or between wells and troughs, the time of diffusion, the temperature and the staining technique.

Micro technique

Microscope slides are covered with melted agar buffer as described in appendix 7. Place the agar slide on a white paper containing a drawing in India ink of the pattern desired (cf. fig. 2.2). The holes are sucked out with a 1 mm flat ground injection needle. Troughs 1 mm wide are made with a drawing pen. The pattern may also be made with commercially available templates. Reactants are poured in respective holes or troughs. The application of the reagents is standardized as much as possible in amount and volume; during application of the circular well technique (cf. fig. 2.2.A) the antiserum is filled in the central well and the antigen samples or a series of antigen dilutions are filled from 1 o'clock clockwise around the wells 1 cm apart and 0.5 to 1 cm from the antibody well.

Immunodiffusion, washing and staining procedures are as described in appendices 12 and 17.

Macro technique

The macro plates are prepared as described in appendix 7. The desired pattern is made as indicated above. The wells can be punched out by means of a cork borer. The troughs can be made with a large drawing pen.

Application of samples, standardization and staining are performed as described above. However, as in macro-immunoelectrophoresis, diffusion time must be extended to 4–10 days with daily inspections of the slide. The washing procedure must also be extended by several days because of the thicker agar layer (cf. appendix 7).

APPENDIX 12

Techniques for immunoelectrophoresis

12.1. Electrophoretic step

12.1.1. Micro scale
As already mentioned in appendix 10, it is possible to use the Wieme technique not only for conventional agar electrophoresis, but also for immunoelectrophoresis.

The pattern is made as described previously. After filling the transverse slit with antigen solution the agar slide is turned around so that the agar surface is downwards, and the slide is placed in the middle compartment of the electrophoresis box (cf. fig. 5.1). The anode and cathode chambers are filled with buffers; the middle one is filled to a level above the glass surface of the slide with light petrol ether (boiling point 40 °C). Electrophoresis is performed for 24 min with a power of 20 V/cm.

In ordinary microscale immunoelectrophoresis the slides prepared by the micro procedure (Scheidegger 1955) allow the electrophoretic separation of proteins with isoelectric point below 6.8 within $1\frac{1}{2}$ hr at 5–10 V/cm, at pH 8.6. The electrophoretic stage may be performed in a custom-built or a commercially available apparatus, allowing from one to 18 slides to electrophorese simultaneously. A home-made box for electrophoresis may be prepared from a plastic box used for storing material in refrigerators, e.g. $20 \times 20 \times 5$ cm. The box is equipped with platinum electrodes and with two transverse plastic boards in the middle of the box 5 cm from each other. These boards support the slides, and divide the box into anode and cathode compartments. The plastic boards are fixed to bottom and side of the box by dissolving a part of the corresponding edges of the boards in chloroform; slight pressure and heating will water-proof the board and fix it to the box.

Filter paper soaked in buffer and laid on both ends of the slides or frame connects the buffer solution in the anode and cathode compartments with the agar surface.

12.1.2. Macro scale

The electrophoretic step of the macro scale procedure can be performed in the custom-built plastic boxes mentioned above. The anode and cathode vessels, filled with 0.05 M veronal buffer (pH 8.6) are connected with the agar plate by means of filter paper strips. The plate is electrophoresed at 7 V/cm for about 4 to 6 hr. The migration rate may be evaluated by illuminating the slide along the lateral part, whereby the electrophoretic zones appear as shadows. The fastest migrating fraction ought to reach 2 cm from the anodic edge of the slide.

12.2. Immunodiffusion

12.2.1. Micro scale

The application of antiserum for immunoelectrophoresis can best be performed by means of ordinary constriction pipettes. It is wise to apply a defined volume of antiserum (80–100 μl in the micro method). As already mentioned, the trough for antiserum is not made until after electrophoretic separation. The immunodiffusion must be performed in a moist chamber, i.e. the electrophoretic box, at constant temperature for 16 hr. Thereafter the precipitates may be inspected directly or the pattern may be washed, dried and stained.

Subject index p. 557

12.2.2. *Macro scale*

The immunodiffusion step must continue in the electrophoretic chamber (constant temperature) for at least four days, with daily inspection of the precipitin lines formed. The washing of the plates must continue for at least four days in order to wash out all unreacted reactants. Prior to drying and staining, the macroplates are sealed with 1 % agar dissolved in distilled water.

In summary it must be stressed that every result of immunoelectrophoresis must be given on the basis of a strictly standardized experimental technique, recording nature of sample (antigen), volume or amount, antibody volume, also, if possible, antibody titre, specification of electrophoresis and immunodiffusion. Only in this way can reproducible data be obtained.

APPENDIX 13

Immunoelectrophoresis in an antibody-containing medium for quantitative estimation of antigens (Laurell 1966)

1 % (w/v) agarose in a barbital buffer (ionic strength 0.07, 2 mM calcium lactate, pH 8.6) is melted in boiling water and cooled to 45 °C. The desired amount of antiserum is added and carefully mixed. A mould is prepared from plate glass rectangles 1 cm wide and 1.5 mm thick, two placed along the short edges and one along the long edge of a plate ($150 \times 90 \times 3$ mm). A similar plate is then placed on top and the whole held together by spring paper clips. The mould is warmed, placed with its open edge uppermost and filled with the agarose–antiserum mixture at a temperature of 40–45 °C through a pipette moved along the opening. No leakage will occur if the corners of the mould have been properly fitted together. The mould is left for at least 30 min to cool to room temperature. The paper clips are removed. The mould is placed flat on a bench and the top glass plate is carefully pushed off. This is facilitated by placing the long edge against a 4 mm thick stop plate to prevent the intermediate strips from following the sliding cover plate.

Holes (3–3.5 mm diameter) are cut in the agarose gel along a line 2 cm from, and parallel with, one of the long edges. The distance between the centers of adjacent holes must be at least 8 mm. The holes are filled with 10 µl of antigen solution. 24 samples can be run on each gel. Dilutions of a standard antigen are used for calibration.

A cooling system, for instance that used in high voltage electrophoresis, may be used to cool the gels during electrophoresis.

The glass plate with the strips still in position is placed on the cooled surface (4 °C) of the cooling system and connected with the electrode vessel by agarose sheets (3 mm thick) or linen bridges. The agarose sheets (2 cm $\times$ 3 mm) are cut out of an agarose plate by a double-bladed knife and used as conducting bridges. Electrophoresis is run at 10 V/cm for 2 to 10 hr, depending on the charge and a-mount of antigen applied in relation to antibody concentration (see 'Comments' below) and on desired exactness of the estimation of the peak height.

The gels on the glass plates are placed in 0.2 M NaCl until the following day, then dried and stained in the usual way. The height of the various peaks e.g. the maximal migration distance of the boundary of antigen excess (see pp. 438 and 465) can be measured directly under darkfield illumination, with an error not exceeding 0.2 mm, if the peak heights are between 2 and 5 cm. A standard curve is constructed, plotting concentration of standard antigen against peak height. If the electrophore-sis has been allowed to continue until all the antigen excess has been consumed and the precipitin arcs are stationary, the relationship is linear and only two antigen concentrations are needed as standard for calibration. In shorter experiments, a series of concentrations of the standard must be used covering the desired con-centration range.

APPENDIX 14

Fibrin–agar micro electrophoresis (Heimburger and Schwick 1962; Schwick 1967)

Preparation of fibrin–agar slides

A 1.5 % (w/v) purified agar solution in 0.05 M sodium diethyl barbiturate buffer pH 8.2 is melted and cooled to 50–55 °C. 9 parts of this melted agar solution are mixed with two parts of a solution of ox or calf fibrinogen 0.4 % (w/v) in diethyl barbituric acid buffer pH 8.2 at 50–55 °C and 1 part 0.1 N $Ca(H_2PO_4)_2$. After thorough mixing of the three solutions, 3 ml of the mixture is pipetted on the upper side of defatted slides. After gelation, the slides are activated (fibrinogen is transformed to fibrin) in a moist chamber at 40 °C for 60 min. The moist chamber may be made by using Petrie dishes equipped with wet filter paper. The activated slides may be stored for not more than 24 hr at 4 °C prior to use.

The hole pattern is similar to that used for the ordinary immunoelectrophoresis (appendix 10) and the sample to be separated (1.5 μl) is placed by means of a constriction pipette in holes made by a ground injection needle.

Electrophoresis

The electrophoresis is performed as ordinary immunoelectrophoresis at about 6 V/cm for 45 min.

Subject index p. 557

Development of pattern

After the electrophoresis, the troughs are cut and filled with 40–100 μl of either an appropriate antiserum or with a proteolytic enzyme or proenzyme, or an activator of a proteolytic enzyme. Then the slides are placed in a moist chamber at 37 °C for 15 hr. Precipitated proteolytic enzymes present in certain electrophoretic loci cause a lysis of the fibrin in the zones corresponding to the area around the precipitate.

When a proteolytic enzyme is applied in the trough, after diffusion, the whole plate shows lysis with the exception of electrophoretic loci and precipitates containing inhibitors of the enzyme.

APPENDIX 15

Buffers

The buffer selected for the agar slides and tanks depends on physicochemical aspects of the electrophoretic system and/or enzymological and affinity properties of the sample to be studied.

Physicochemical aspects of the electrophoretic system

The buffer must be selected to give optimal buffer capacity at the *p*H chosen. From the known *p*K values of the buffer components and from the required *p*H it is not possible to calculate the exact amounts of the buffer components because of the salt effect. The *p*H must therefore be finally adjusted with acids or bases to the required value. Instead of making the buffers on the basis of calculations, it is often more convenient to obtain the composition from tables, e.g. made on the basis of the titration curve of the buffer (vide infra).

Choice of ionic strength of buffers is important. A primary function of buffers is the maintenance of a constant *p*H, if the concentration is too low variations in *p*H may occur. If it is too high, however, heating is excessive at the desirable current densities. Electrophoretic mobility is lower the higher the ionic strength, and *vice versa* (see Gordon 1968). Therefore in studies of slowly migrating antigens a buffer of low ionic strength is preferable. The best range is 0.025–0.05 M.

Ionic strength may also influence solubility of antigens and antibodies. Generally speaking, increasing ionic strength decreases solubility. However, this is a rule with many exceptions.

Enzymological and/or affinity properties of the sample

Many organic and inorganic ions are inhibitors of enzymes. Therefore in immuno-chemical studies on enzymes, the buffer must be selected with regard to known inhibitors. Similarly, the components of the buffer may displace drugs from the binding sites of certain proteins. Thus, e.g. borate may chelate carbohydrates in glycoproteins. This may displace drugs from binding sites. Therefore the binding capacity of a drug must be studied in different buffer systems or the binding must always be defined in relationship to the buffer system used.

Buffers for agar gel electrophoresis

Buffer solutions commonly employed are in the *p*H range of 7.6 to 8.6 with ionic strength between 0.05 and 0.025. For routine work one of the following buffers may be used.

(1) Veronal, barbital or barbitone buffer:

pH 8.4 (0.05 M)

Sodium diethyl barbiturate (sodium veronal)	42.5 g
HCl, N	58.0 ml
Distilled water	to 5.0 liters

This buffer, made from Na-diethyl barbiturate, is easily prepared because this component is soluble in water. Barbiturate buffers made from the less soluble diethyl barbituric acid are difficult to prepare.

Any of the following buffers may be used in electrophoresis; they should be diluted if necessary to a final concentration of 0.05 M or less.

(2) Citrate–phosphate 0.1 M, pH 3.0–7.2; x ml 0.2 M $Na_2HPO_4 + 0.1$ M citric acid to 100 ml

pH	3.0	3.2	3.4	3.6	3.8	4.0	4.2	4.4	4.6	4.8	5.0
x	20.6	24.7	28.5	32.2	35.5	38.6	41.4	44.0	46.7	49.3	51.5

pH	5.2	5.4	5.6	5.8	6.0	6.2	6.4	6.6	6.8	7.0	7.2
x	53.6	55.8	58.0	60.5	63.2	66.1	69.3	72.8	77.2	82.4	86.9

(3) Phosphate 0.1 M, pH 5.7–8.0; x ml 0.2 M $Na_2HPO_4 + 0.2$ M NaH_2PO_4 to 100 ml + 100 ml water

pH	5.7	5.8	5.9	6.0	6.1	6.2	6.3	6.4	6.5	6.6	6.7	6.8
x	6.5	8.0	10.0	12.3	15.0	18.5	22.5	26.5	31.5	37.5	43.5	49.0

pH	6.9	7.0	7.1	7.2	7.3	7.4	7.5	7.6	7.7	7.8	7.9	8.0
x	55.0	61.0	67.0	72.0	77.0	81.0	84.0	87.0	90.5	91.5	93.0	94.7

Subject index p. 557

(4) Veronal, barbiturate HCl 0.1 M, pH 7.0–8.6; x ml 0.1 M HCl+0.1 M sodium diethylbarbiturate to 100 ml.

pH	7.0	7.2	7.4	7.6	7.8	8.0	8.2	8.4	8.6
x	46.4	44.6	41.8	38.4	33.8	28.4	23.1	17.9	12.9

(5) Tris, 0.05 M, pH 7.2–8.6; 50 ml 0.2 M tris (hydroxymethyl) aminomethane+x ml 0.2 M HCl+water to 200 ml.

pH	7.2	7.4	7.6	7.8	8.0	8.2	8.4	8.6
x	44.2	41.4	38.4	32.5	26.8	21.9	16.5	12.2

(6) Glycine–NaOH 0.1 M, pH 8.6–12.8; x ml 0.1 M NaOH+0.1 M glycine to 100 ml

pH	8.6	8.8	9.0	9.2	9.4	9.6	9.8	10.0	10.2	10.4	10.6
x	5.8	8.6	12.4	17.0	22.3	28.0	33.8	38.3	41.0	44.8	46.7
pH	10.8	11.0	i1.2	11.4	11.6	11.8	12.0	12.2	12.4	12.6	12.8
x	48.0	48.9	49.8	50.6	51.4	52.6	54.4	57.4	61.8	70.0	81.0

APPENDIX 16

Reference markers for immunoelectrophoresis

The only unambiguous way of characterizing proteins and enzymes after electro-phoretic separation is the determination of their relative electrophoretic mobilities. Use of the older nomenclature of albumin alpha, beta and gamma areas will give a gross picture only, whereas correlation between close lying protein and enzyme fractions should be possible with a precision of at least $\frac{1}{2}$ mm. A reference solution of the following composition is run alongside the sample on the same slide (Wieme 1959):

> Human albumin, immunologically pure (Behringwerke), 3g/100 ml 10 ml
> Dextran, MW, 100,000 to 150,000, 3g/100 ml   10 ml
> Buffer (0.05 M)   1 ml

After the electrophoretic run the side of the agar gel containing the dextran and albumin is cut from the remaining part of the gel and fixed in 96% ethanol. The centers of the white spots corresponding to the dextran and albumin are marked by sucking out holes in the gel. Alternatively, the dextran may be stained by alkaline $KMnO_4$, followed by decolouration with potassium metabisulphite (De Boer et al. 1967). After immunodiffusion and washing out surplus non-reacting antigen and antibody, the gel strip containing the standard marker is placed again on the slide in the original position. The combined gels are dried. It is now possible to estimate the relative electrophoretic mobility (see pp. 462).

(see pp. 462)

APPENDIX 17

Washing, drying, photographing and storing of completed slides or plates

17.1. Washing of agar

After immunodiffusion or immunoelectrophoresis, the agar is washed free of non-reacted antigen and antibody in 0.9 % (w/v) aqueous NaCl. Slides may be washed in various types of commercially available apparatuses of more or less ingenious construction, or in glass boxes used for storing food in household refrigerators. These are available 8 cm in width (the length of the slides) and slides placed in rows across the container will be supported by the walls of the box about 1 cm above the bottom; 0.9 % (w/v) aqueous NaCl poured into the box will thus flow around every slide. It is not necessary to agitate or change the saline during the washing procedure. On the contrary it is best to leave the slides undisturbed in the washing fluid because streaming and moving of the container may cause the agar to float and lift off the glass surface. The washing of slides must be continued for at least 2 days. Insufficient washing will later, during the staining stage, give rise to a general staining of protein (antibody and antigen) widely dispersed in the agar. Working with the macro-technique, the plates must be washed prior to staining for at least 4 days.

After washing, NaCl is washed out in de-ionized or distilled water for about 3 hr. After desalting, the agar on micro–immunoelectrophoretic slides is cut at each end of the slide so that the agar beyond the ends of the trough is removed. It is then possible to move the agar strips gently towards each other, thus eliminating the trough. This is necessary to avoid irregular retraction of the agar gel during drying of the slide, which can cause distortion of the immunoprecipitates. Working with the macro method of immunoelectrophoresis it is more convenient to avoid retraction phenomena by filling the antibody reservoir and the antigen wells with melted agar (1 % w/v) dissolved in de-ionized water.

17.2. Drying of agar slides

The slides may be dried in an oven at 40° or simply by letting them stand in open air until the next day. Some authors recommend combining the de-salting and the drying procedures by applying a filter paper on the surface of the gel. However, it does not seem possible to decrease the drying period more than indicated above.

Subject index p. 557

17.3. Photography of results

(Aa Aarsøe, leader of the Department of Photographic Reproduction, University Hospital, Rigshospitalet, Copenhagen, personal communication, 1968):

Distinct photographic copies of stained immunoprecipitates developed in agar are made by a two step procedure: first, a primary copy of the slide in natural size, followed by a secondary magnification to the desired size:

Step 1: The slide is placed with the agar surface downward, facing a white paper, thus avoiding shadows during exposure. The slide and paper are placed between four photographic lamps, two on each side, and the exposure is made with a camera, Laborator 138, Durst, Bolzano, Italy. The film used is Kodak, professional plane film (9×12 cm). The exposure is performed with objective lens 1/156–135 regulating the level of the camera above the slide to give a copy in natural size. The film is developed with Agfa F-A-T-developer for 8 min at 21 °C.

Step 2: The natural copy is magnified in an ordinary magnification apparatus using ordinary Kodak magnification paper of great hardness.

Fig. 2.5 shows a result obtained with the above procedure. It is also possible to obtain a commercial apparatus for direct copying of wet agar slides.

17.4. Storing of slides

The stained or unstained slides may be stored at room temperature in appropriate boxes such as those ordinarily used for storing microscopic sections. Sometimes the agar layers may peel off, the reason being that the agar layer is too thick; they may sometimes be refixed to the glass surface by swelling in a destaining solution containing glycerol (10% v/v) which softens the agar layer. Usually when peeling starts, however, the slide is lost because of cracking; this process is accelerated by covering the agar with cellulose. It is also convenient to fix the slides with tape to perforated cards or to an index card containing all specifications of the experiment. Special plastic storage frames are commercially available, but they are expensive.

APPENDIX 18

Protein stains

1. Amido black (Wieme 1959) (Blue stain)

Amido black 10 B (Bayer)	0.50 g
mercuric chloride	5.0 g
glacial acetic acid	5.0 ml
distilled water to	100.0 ml

Filter before use. Stain for half an hour and wash in 2 % (v/v) acetic acid for 30 min, 3 times or in running distilled water for 30 min.

2. Light green:

Light green SF 0.5 % (w/v) in 5 % (w/v) trichloroacetic acid. Stain 1 hour. Wash with 5 % (w/v) trichloroacetic acid for 30 min. This method is recommended when double staining proteins and lipids (vide infra).

3. Lissamine green (Wieme 1959)

Lissamine green (B.D.H.)	0.30 g
glacial acetic acid	15.0 ml
distilled water to	100.0 ml

Stain 1 hour. Wash with 2 % (v/v) acetic acid.

4. Thiazine red R (Crowle 1961)

Thiazine red R	0.1 g
1 % glacial acetic acid in distilled water	100.0 ml

Stain for 1 hour. Wash in 70 % (v/v) ethanol containing 1 % (v/v) acetic acid for 20 min.

5. Azocarmine B, for cellulose acetate (Kohn 1958) (red stain)

Azocarmine B	0.05 g
2 % (v/v) glacial acetic acid in distilled water	100.0 ml

Stain 1 hour. Wash in 2 % acetic acid

6. Nigrosin for cellulose acetate (Kohn 1959)

Nigrosin (Geigy) water-soluble	5 mg
2 % glacial acetic acid in distilled water	100 ml

Soak in stain for 1 hour. Wash with 2 % acetic acid. Dry strip between filter paper under pressure.

7. For special protein stains the reader is referred to Crowle (1961).

APPENDIX 19

Lipid stains

1. Sudan Black B (Uriel 1964)

Make a saturated solution of Sudan Black B in 60 % ethanol (v/v) at 37 °C. Cool solution to room temperature and filter. Just before use, filter again and add 0.1 ml of 25 % (w/v) sodium hydroxide for every 50 ml of dye. Stain for a few minutes (micro technique) or for 2 or more hours (macro technique); wash with 50 % ethanol (30 min). This method is preferably applied to dried agar.

2. Oil red O (Uriel 1964)

Make a saturated solution of oil red O in 60 % (v/v) ethanol at 37 °C. Cool solution to room temperature and filter. Filter again just before use. Stain for 30-60 min (micro technique) or for several hours (macro technique). Wash with 50 % (v/v) ethanol (30 min). This method is also preferably applied to dried agar.

3. Nile Blue A (Crowle 1961)

Subject index p. 557

Dissolve 0.1 g Nile Blue A in 100 ml 1 % (v/v) sulphuric acid. Boil for 5 min, cool before using. Stain for 15–20 min (micro technique) and wash with 1 % (v/v) sulphuric acid (30 min). Wash, before drying, with distilled water and then with distilled water containing 1 % (v/v) glycerol.

4. Pre-staining of lipoproteins (after MacDonald and Kissane 1960)

This modification of the lipoprotein staining entails prestaining of the sample before submitting to electrophoresis.

Sudan Black B (Harmann-Leddon Co., Phila.)	0.1 g
ethyl acetate, analytical grade	1.0 ml

Stir at room temperature until the dye is dissolved; dilute with 9 ml of propylene glycol and stir. Keep in darkness. The reagent is added to e.g. human serum at room temperature in the ratio of 1:5 (v/v) and shaken. The serum-dye mixture is allowed to stand for 15 min, centrifuged to remove excess dye and submitted to electrophoresis. The migration of the serum lipoprotein–dye complex is not altered.

APPENDIX 20

Double stains for protein and lipid

1. Proteins are stained blue, lipid red (Uriel 1964)

Bromophenol blue or Amido black 10 B	50 mg
glacial acetic acid	2 ml
60 % (v/v) ethanol–water saturated with oil red O	100 ml

Stain pre-dried agar as required. Wash with 50 % ethanol containing 1 % (v/v) glacial acetic acid (30 min). If bromophenol blue version is used, expose dried slide to ammonia vapor.

2. Proteins are stained blue, lipids black-blue (Uriel 1964)

Azocarmine B	50 mg
glacial acetic acid	2 ml
60 % (v/v) ethanol saturated with Sudan black B	100 ml

Stain pre-dried agar as required. Wash with 50 % ethanol containing 1 % (v/v) glacial acetic acid (30 min).

3. For cellulose acetate strips, proteins are stained red, lipids black (Kohn 1959)

a. Ponceau S	150 mg
trichloroacetic acid	3 g
distilled water	100 ml
b. Nigrosin WS	2.5 mg
glacial acetic acid	2 ml
distilled water	100 ml

Stain first with solution (a), then with solution (b), both for about 30 min; wash in 2 % (v/v) glacial acetic acid for 30 min.

4. Proteins are stained green, lipids red (Crowle 1961)

   a. For proteins

Light green SF	1 g
glacial acetic acid	1.0 ml
distilled water	100 ml

   b. For lipids

Thiazine red R	0.1 g
glacial acetic acid	1.0 ml
distilled water	100 ml

Stain with solution (a), wash with 1% (v/v) acetic acid; stain with solution (b), wash with 1% acetic acid. Staining time for micro method is about 15 min for each stain.

5. For other special double or triple stains the reader is referred to Crowle (1961).

APPENDIX 21

Polysaccharide stains

(To be used on pre-dried agar)

1. Schiff reagent (Crowle 1961)

A. Solutions

   a. Dissolve 1.5 g basic fuchsin in 500 ml boiling distilled water. Filter at 55 °C and cool to 40 °C. Add 25 ml 2 N HCl and 3.75 g $Na_2S_2O_5$, sodium metabisulphite. Agitate to ensure rapid solution. Allow to stand stoppered in refrigerator for 6 hr. Add 1.2 g charcoal. Mix vigorously for 50 sec and filter rapidly, filtration time not exceeding 2–3 min. Store stoppered in refrigerator.

b. Periodic acid	1.0 g
anhydrous sodium acetate	0.82 g
distilled water	100.0 ml
c. Glacial acetic acid	0.54 ml
anhydrous sodium acetate	0.89 g
hydroxylamine hydrochloride	10.0 g
distilled water	100 ml
d. 10% (w/v) $Na_2S_2O_5$	5 ml
2 N hydrochloric acid	5 ml
distilled water	90 ml

Solution d should be made just before it is used. This also serves as the final wash when it contains 20% (v/v) glycerol.

B. Procedure: Soak pre-dried slide in (c) for 15 min. Wash in running water for 15 min. Soak in solution (b) for 10 min. Wash in running water for 10 min. Soak for 3 min in solution (a), diluted immediately before use with an equal volume of distilled water. Wash three times for 2 min each in solution (d). Wash 3 times for 1 hr each in glycerinated solution (d). Dry agar in warm air oven.

2. p-phenylenediamine oxidation reaction (Crowle 1961)
A. Solutions

a.	Periodic acid	1 g
	anhydrous sodium acetate	1.64 g
	50% (v/v) ethanol	100 ml
b.	α-Naphthol	144 mg
	distilled water	100 ml
	dissolve with heat and then cool	
c.	p-Phenylenediamine	108 mg
	distilled water	100 ml
	Prepare immediately before using	
d.	Hydrogen peroxide 10% (v/v)	

B. Procedure: Soak pre-dried agar for 15 min in (a). Wash for 10 min in distilled water. Soak for 5–10 min in fresh mixture of solutions (b)+(c)+(d) in proportion of 5:5:1 (by vols.). Wash for 10 min in running water and finally in distilled water. Air dry in warm oven.

APPENDIX 22

Staining for oxidase activity (including ceruloplasmin)

Preparation of substrate (Uriel 1964; Uriel et al. 1957)

Dissolve 50 mg p-phenylenediamine in 100 ml 0.1 M sodium acetate buffer (pH 5.7). The solution must be used immediately.

Procedure: The incubation for 2 hr at 37 °C is performed as described for esterases (appendix 25). After incubation, the enzymic process is stopped by immersing the slide for 2 hr in an 0.1 M sodium acetate buffer (pH 4.7) using 50% ethanol as solution for the buffer.

The slide with the brown colour developed has to be stored in complete darkness otherwise the entire agar plate will be diffusely developed. Note that sodium azide NaN_3 cannot be used as a bacteriostatic agent in the agar gel because it is a potent inhibitor of ceruloplasmin oxidase activity. On the contrary, sodium azide (1 ml of 0.1 M) added to the substrate (100 ml) in parallel experiment may be used as a control.

APPENDIX 23

Staining for peroxidase activity

(For haemoglobin, free or linked to haptoglobin and for haemin linked to hemo-pexin.)

A. *Benzidine reaction* (Uriel 1964)

1. Staining of haemoglobin: dissolve 1 g benzidine by slow warming in 100 ml methanol. Cool. Mix this solution immediately before use with equal parts of: (1) 1.0 M acetate buffer pH 4.7; (2) 0.1 M NaN_3 (inhibitor of catalase); (3) 3% (v/v) aqueous H_2O_2.

The dried plates are immersed for 15 min in the reaction mixture. The slides are then washed in distilled water for 10 min. The benzidine stained slides are inspected immediately or after drying in an oven (37 °C). The blue colour developed is unstable to light.

2. Staining for haptoglobin: mix the sample prior to immunodiffusion with a fifth volume of 1% (w/v) pure haemoglobin dissolved in 0.05 M phosphate buffer pH 7.0. After immunodiffusion, washing and drying of slides, the pattern is stained by the benzidine reagent described above.

B. *NADI reaction* (Pearse 1961; Uriel 1964)

In order to produce a stable stain for haemoglobin, the NADI reaction can be used: (1) Dissolve 144 mg α-naphthol in 100 ml 0.1 mM ethylenediamine tetra acetic (ED-TA) acid neutralized with 0.1 mM NaOH; (2) Zn-acetate saturated in 50% ethanol; (3) dissolve 216 mg p-phenylenediamine in 100 ml 0.1 mM neutralized EDTA; (4) 0.1 M NaN_3 in 5% (v/v) glacial acetic acid; (5) 3% aqueous H_2O_2.

Soak in reagent (2) for 1 hr. Wash twice in distilled water for 2 hr and dry. Mix the remaining reagents in proportion $1 + 1 + 0.2 + 0.2$ (v/v) and place the dried slides immediately in the reagent mixture for 15 min. Wash in running distilled water for 15 min, dry at 37 °C in an oven.

APPENDIX 24

Staining of lactate dehydrogenase isoenzymes and other NAD- or NADP-dependent dehydrogenases (Clausen and Øvlisen 1965)

Reagents: Stock solutions — all made up in 0.05 M sodium phosphate buffer pH 7.5 and stored at 4° in the dark

Subject index p. 557

(1) 1.0 M Lithium-lactate (659 mg/10 ml) (80% Li-lactate BDH Ltd) + 0.0001 M NaCN (4.9 mg/1000 ml) + 0.05 M MgCl₂ (4.76 mg/10 ml) dissolved in 0.05 M sodium phosphate buffer pH 7.5.

(2) 0.33 mM NAD (nicotinamide adenine dinucleotide) in 0.05 M sodium phosphate buffer pH 7.5 (2.2 mg/10 ml)

(3) 1 mg p-nitro-Blue-Tetrazolium in 1.0 ml buffer (0.05 M)

(4) 1 mg phenazine methosulphate in 1.0 ml buffer (0.05 M)

Staining: Place the unfixed agar slide upside down on two matches in a Petrie dish. Apply with a pipette a mixture consisting of 5.5 ml solution (1) + 2.5 ml of solution (2) + 1.0 ml of solution (3) + 0.25 ml of solution (4). Incubate for 1 hr at 37 °C. Lactate dehydrogenase appears as a blue stain. Fix for 10 min in 5% glacial acetic acid. By replacing Li-lactate with substrates of other NAD or NADP dehydrogenases it may be possible to trace these.

APPENDIX 25

Staining for esterase activity

(Modified after Nachlas and Seligman 1949; Uriel 1964).

25.1. Naphthylacetate method

Stain: Dissolve 10 mg of β-naphthylacetate in 0.5 ml of acetone. Add sodium phosphate buffer, 0.07 M, pH 7.4 to 50 ml; shake well and add 10 mg of Diazo Blue B (Gurr). Shake and filter. Use immediately.

Fixative: 70% ethanol, 5% acetic acid and 25% water by vols.

Procedure: The slides are placed with the agar sides downward in a glass vessel that will accommodate four slides. The slides are placed on matches so the agar is 1–2 mm from the bottom of the vessel. In this way a volume of 25 ml reaction-mixture poured under the slides will suffice for four slides. Incubation time is usually 60 min at 37 °C for tissue extracts and 30 min for serum. The reaction is fast, and the coloured products will be visible within 5 min. During the incubation, a reddish precipitate forms and sediments to the bottom of the container instead of layering on the slides. The reaction is stopped by pouring 40–50 ml of fixative over the slides *in situ*, and letting the vessel stand for 20 min at room temperature. The agar gel cools and hardens and so will not fall off when the slides are carefully lifted out. Dry under filter paper. If the slides are left longer in the fixative, loss of colour will occur. Areas or precipitates with esterase activity are coloured red-violet.

25.2. *Indoxyl acetate method*

Stain: Dissolve 10 mg of indoxylacetate (or better, O-acetyl-5-bromo-indoxyl) in 1 ml of acetone. Add 44 ml of M sodium veronal buffer, pH 8.4, and 5 ml 10^{-1} M cupric acetate. To be used immediately.

Fixative and procedure: as under naphthylacetate method.

APPENDIX 26

Staining for phosphatase activity

A. Acid phosphatase (Burstone 1958; Pearse 1961)

Reagents: 4.0 mg naphthol AS phosphate (the acetate of 2-hydroxy-3-naphthoic acid anilide, ICI Ltd) is dissolved in 0.25 ml dimethyl formamide, the volume is made up to 25 ml with water and an equal volume of Na acetate buffer (0.2 M, pH 5.2) is added. Add 35 mg red violet LB salt (diazotized-5-benzamido-4-chloro-2-tolui-dine) and 2 drops of 10% $MgCl_2$. Filter; the solution remains clear for several hours at room temperature, but cannot be stored for days.

Staining: The incubation method described in appendix 25 is used. Incubate for several hours or overnight at $37\,^{\circ}$C. The reaction can be inhibited by 0.001 M sodium arsanilate or 0.001 M $ZnSO_4$ – (NaF and $CuSO_4$ are alternative inhibitors).

B. Alkaline phosphatase

The procedure is as for acid phosphatase with the exception that the reagents are dissolved in 0.5 M sodium diethyl-barbiturate buffer (pH 8.3). *Results:* The enzyme activities are shown as red or red-violet lines.

An alternative method is that of Seligman (1951): a 20 mg/100 ml (w/v) β-naphthyl-phosphate solution is prepared in a veronal buffer pH 9.1, ionic strength 0.1 M (0.1 M Na-diethyl-barbiturate 950 ml + 0.1 M HCl 50 ml). Just before incubation Diazo Blue is added to the substrate mixture to a concentration of 40 mg/100 ml. *Result:* Enzyme activity is shown as blue lines.

Subject index p. 557

APPENDIX 27

Staining for amylase activity (Grabar and Daussant 1965; Frydenberg and Nielsen 1965) **and glycosidase activities**

Amylase activity:
Reagents

(1) 0.02 M phosphate buffer (*p*H 7.3); dissolve 9.85 g K_2HPO_4 and 4.73 g NaH_2 $PO_4.2H_2O$ in 1.0 liter distilled water.

(2) Agar gel: A solution of 1% DIFCO Special Noble agar in the phosphate buffer is made by heating the mixture at 90 °C until completely solubilized.

(3) Starch agar-gel: Substrate for sandwich technique. Dissolve 1 g of DIFCO Special Noble agar and 0.5 g Smithies hydrolysed starch (Connaught Labs., Toronto) in 100 ml phosphate buffer. Heat at 90 °C until the agar is completely solubilized. 1 ml of the starch-agar is dispersed on a slide. And the starch-agar gel is allowed to dry into a thin film.

(4) Substrate for direct reaction. A 0.4 M phosphate buffer, *p*H 7.0 is made by mixing 199 ml 0.4 M $Na_2HPO_4.12H_2O$ and 63 ml 0.4 M $KH_2PO_4.2H_2O$. 5 g soluble starch (Stärkelöslich-Merch; Damstadt pro analysis) is dissolved in 495 ml of the phosphate buffer and the solution is cooled, with mixing, to 20–25 °C.

(5) Inhibitors. (a) 10^{-3} M $CuSO_4$ solution is used as inhibitor of β-amylases. (b) A 20% (w/v) solution of sodium-hexametaphosphate is used as inhibitor of α-amylases.

(6) Iodine solution. Dissolve 5.5 g of iodine and 11 g of KI in 250 ml water (to be stored in a brown flask). 2 ml of this stock solution is mixed with 250 ml distilled water containing 10 g of KI. This solution is used the same day for staining of the starch substrate.

The enzymic reactions

After immunoelectrophoresis and/or agar gel electrophoresis, the amylases of the sample can be visualized either by means of the sandwich technique or by direct substrate reaction.

(a) *Sandwich technique.* The wet slide is sandwiched to a slide with dried starch agar gel. After 0.5–1 hr, the starch–agar gel slide is stained in the iodine solution. The immunoprecipitate or electrophoretic zones containing the amylase activity will appear on the agar slides as bright zones contrasting to the general blue background caused by the presence of iodine–starch complex. In order to differentiate between α- and β-amylases, six drops of $CuSO_4$ or of sodium-hexameta-phosphate solution are applied on the agar surface prior to the sandwiching. $CuSO_4$ inhibits β-amylase; the sodium-hexameta-phosphate inhibits the α-amylase.

(b) *Direct substrate reaction.* The antibody trough is filled with 1 % melted agar buffer after immunoelectrophoresis. The entire slide is thereafter dipped in the starch solution for $\frac{1}{2}$ hour, then the slide is stained in the iodine solution. In the wet slide, the amylase zones or amylase precipitate appear as bright areas in the blue-stained agar gel. It is necessary to fill the antibody trough with agar prior to the substrate reaction in order to prevent the iodine from penetrating between the glass surface and the agar gel into the zones of amylase activity, thus blurring the amylase fractions and precipitates.

The differentiation between α- and β-amylases is performed as described at (a).

Miscellaneous glycosidases splitting simple and complex polysaccharides:

Enzymes splitting the glycosidic bonds of simple and complex polysaccharides, viz. β-galactosidase, β-glucosidase, β-glucuronidase and β-acetyl aminodeoxy glucosidase, can also be traced by means of a simultaneous coupling azo dye procedure, similar to that used in the demonstration of esterase activity (appendix 25). This coupling can involve the use of 6-bromo-2-naphthol-glycoside as substrate in conjunction with Garnet GBC salt (Raunio 1968).

APPENDIX 28

Labelling of antibodies with fluorescein isocyanate (modified after Kabat and Mayer 1961)

The antibody fraction of serum from an immunized animal is prepurified by precipitation at 2.0 M ammonium sulphate (pH 6.8): dilute the immune serum twice with 0.9 % aqueous NaCl and add a volume of 4.0 M ammonium sulphate which is equal to the final volume. Stand for 18 hr at 22 °C, then centrifuge at 5000 g for 15 min. The precipitate is twice suspended in 2.0 M ammonium sulphate (pH 6.8) and centrifuged; finally dissolved in 0.1 M NaHCO₃, and dialysed against 0.1 M NaHCO₃ for 18 hr. The protein content of the solution is adjusted to 5.0 g/100 ml by addition of 0.1 N NaHCO₃.

To 3.0 ml immunoglobulin fraction is added 10.5 ml 0.9 % aqueous NaCl + 3.0 ml carbonate/bicarbonate buffer, pH 9.2. (Mix: 2.0 ml 0.2 M Na₂CO₃ (21.2 g/l) with 23.0 ml 0.2 M NaHCO₃ (16.8 g/l)) 7.5 mg fluorescein isocyanate dissolved in 1.0 ml dioxane and 0.5 ml acetone is added. After 18 hr stirring at 0 °C the mixture is dialyzed for 18 hr against 10 l 0.9 % NaCl. The diffusate is discarded and the sac contents adjusted to pH 7.0 with 1 N HCl. The neutralized solution is extracted with two vols ethylacetate, the organic phase is discarded and the remaining ethylacetate is removed by suction at a water pump. Finally the conjugated immunoglobulin fraction is freeze-dried and may be stored until use at −10 °C.

As an alternative method of purification, it is simpler to separate the labelled protein by filtration on Bio-Gel or Sephadex G-200 previously equilibrated with 0.1 M NaCl. (See companion volume by Fischer 1968.)

Subject index p. 557

APPENDIX 29

Radio-immunoelectrophoresis for estimation of protein or peptide hormones

1. Preparation of ^{131}I-labelled hormone (Greenwood et al. 1963;Landon et al. 1967). (See also appendix 30.2.)

The reaction is carried out in the rubber-capped vial (10 ml) in which the (^{131}I) iodide sample is packaged. Care is taken that the vial is kept upright in transport by requesting delivery in a 1 inch lead pot. This ensures that the small volume (0.05 ml) of (^{131}I) iodide solution is not spread over the surface of the vial and its cap.

The radioactivity is counted by using a scintillation counter with a well-type sodium iodide crystal with the geometry modified such that 2 mC in 0.05 ml gives approximately 400 counts/second. The lid of the lead castle is removed and the sample in a 1 inch lead pot is placed 3.0 cm above the aperture.

To 50–100 µl of carrier-free Na[131]I (2–3 mC) is added 25 µl of 0.5 M Na phosphate buffer, pH 7.5, followed by hormone (5.0 µl 0.1% (w/v) and fresh chloramine-T (100 µg) in 0.025 ml of 0.05 M phosphate buffer, pH 7.5. After each addition, made by injection through the rubber cap with a micrometer or Hamilton syringe, the contents of the vial are briefly mixed. 2 min after mixing the chloramine-T there is added 0.1 ml of sodium metabisulphite (2.4 mg/ml of 0.05 M phosphate buffer, pH 7.5). This addition prevents any subsequent iodination of Sephadex-gel bed by converting (^{131}I) iodine into (^{131}I) iodide. This residual iodide is diluted with 0.4 ml of carrier KI (10 mg/ml of 0.05 M phosphate buffer). In order to demonstrate that the electrophoretic migration rate of the iodinated hormone has not been affected by the iodination, the reaction mixture is examined by agar gel electrophoresis and immunoelectrophoresis, appropriately combined with autoradiography.

Separation of ^{131}I-labelled hormone from the reaction mixture is carried out by gel filtration on a column (10 × 1 cm; 1 g) of Sephadex G-50 (buffer height above the gel, 3 cm). Equilibration of the gel and elution from it is carried out with 0.07 M barbiturate buffer, pH 8.6. Before the Sephadex column is used, crystalline bovine serum albumin (BSA, 20 mg in 1 ml of buffer) is passed through, followed by a 20-ml wash with the buffer. This 'pre-saturation' of the Sephadex with albumin allows a subsequent recovery of 70% of 3–4 µg of ^{131}I-labelled hormone from the Sephadex.

The elution pattern, determined by counting 1-ml eluates, is reproducible. Routinely, 3 fractions are collected into calibrated counting vials, a non-radioactive fraction (1.5 ml), a protein peak (4.0 ml), and a salt peak. The protein peak is collected into a vial containing 1.0 ml of a mixture of BSA (10 mg/ml) in 0.07 M barbiturate buffer (pH 8.6). The amount of ^{131}I-labelled hormone eluted is calculated from the radioactivity and a sample diluted as required for the immunoassay with 0.07 M barbiturate buffer, pH 8.6, containing BSA 1.0 mg/ml.

The time taken from the mixing of the hormone and (^{131}I) iodide to the loading of the column is about 4 min. Within a further 15 min the ^{131}I-labelled hormone is eluted freed from unchanged (^{131}I) iodide and other low-molecular-weight substances.

2. Radio-immunoassay

Antiserum to the hormone must be prepared first in rabbits or obtained commercially. For radio-immunoassay, varying amounts of samples under assay and of standard hormone (see appendix 30.7 for preparation of standard solutions) are added to 5 ml conical centrifuge tubes and brought to 500 µl with 0.01 M phosphate buffered 0.14 M saline at pH 7.0 containing 1 % BSA (PBS–1 % BSA). To each tube is added 200 µl rabbit anti-hormone serum which has been suitably diluted with normal rabbit serum containing PBS-1 % BSA. In order to keep the antigen–antibody complex in solution; conditions of antigen excess must be used, and the final dilution of antiserum determined by preliminary trials on a dilution series is usually 1:1200 to 1:2,000,000. This reaction mixture is incubated without agitation at 4 °C for 24 h and then 100 µl of suitably diluted labelled hormone is added. The latter is diluted in PBS-0.1 % BSA so that, on the day after preparation 100 µl gave from 40,000 to 60,000 cpm in an automatic gamma-counting system (3 inch crystal). After an additional 24 h of incubation at 4 °C, the γ-globulin-bound hormone is separated from the free hormone by agar gel micro-electro-phoresis or paper electrophoresis of 25 µl samples.

The zones of free and antibody-bound hormone are located by cutting the whole gel into blocks 1 mm broad which are dissolved in 500 µl 1.0 NaOH by heating (80 °C), and their radioactivities are measured. B/F ratio of hormone is calculated and dose–response curves are drawn (see fig. 7.1). Similarly the paper is cut and counted. It is advisable to fix dose–response curves for several antisera in a series of dilutions in order to obtain optimal experimental conditions (see the text).

The electrophoretic stage can also use paper or starch gel as supporting media.

Appendix 30

The double antibody technique for determination of insulin and other protein hormones
(*Hales and Randle, 1963; see procedure 'Data Sheet' no. 5616, The Radiochemical Centre, Amersham, England*)

Reagents

30.1. Insulin binding reagent *
Antisera are prepared to crystalline pig insulin (in guinea pigs) and to guinea pig

---

* With courtesy by The Radiochemical Centre, Amersham, England which supplies iodinated insulin and insulin binding reagent.

Subject index p. 557

serum proteins (in rabbits). After adjusting the concentration of the anti-insulin serum to a level giving rise to antigen excess, i.e. excess of insulin in the reaction mixture, it is diluted in buffer containing ethylenediamine tetra-acetic acid (EDTA) (0.03 M) and mixed with a predetermined amount of the anti-guinea pig precipitating serum (see below). The mixture is allowed to react at 4 °C for 18 hr and is then freeze-dried. When reconstituted to a volume of 8 ml, each vial will contain guinea-pig serum precipitate diluted to 1 in 16,000 and 0.03 M EDTA in in buffer A (see below). This reagent used in the present method will bind approximately 40 % of the standard dose of 250 μμg iodinated insulin.

Store at 2 to 4 °C in the dry state. After reconstitution, storage at −20 °C for three days is permissible, but the material must not be frozen and thawed more than once.

30.2. Iodinated insulin ^{125}I

Iodinated insulin is prepared from specially purified crystalline ox insulin (potency 24.3 international units/mg) by iodination with iodine monochloride; unbound iodine has been removed by gel filtration (appendix 29). Each vial contains 0.1 μg of iodinated insulin dissolved in 1 ml of buffer A. The specific radioactivity at a given time is stated on the label.

The working solution is prepared by adding 0.1 ml of the binding reagent to 3.9 ml of buffer A; 0.1 ml of the diluted mixture will contain 250 μμg of iodinated insulin.

Store the stock solution at −10 to −20 °C. The working solution may be kept at 2 to 4 °C for not more than a week or deep frozen for longer periods. Do not re-freeze after thawing.

30.3. De-ionized water

All solutions should be prepared with de-ionized water, obtained by passing ordinary distilled water through a mixed-bed ion-exchanger. Variations in the quality of ordinary distilled water used for the preparation of buffers may give rise to considerable variations in the amount of insulin bound to the antibody precipitate.

30.4. Buffer A

Phosphate buffer (40 mM, pH 7.4) containing thiomersalate (0.6 mM) and bovine plasma albumin (0.1 % w/v) for dilution of antisera and iodinated insulin. 2 N NaOH to bring to pH 7.4. De-ionized water, to 1 litre. Check pH after making to volume and adjust to pH 7.4 if necessary. Store at 2 to 4 °C.

30.5. Buffer B

Isotonic buffer for dilution of standard insulin or plasma samples.

NaCl	9.0 g
Buffer A, to	1 litre

Store at 2 to 4 °C.

30.6. Buffer C
Buffer of high protein content for washing antibody precipitates,

Horse serum	500 ml
buffer A	500 ml

Store at 2 to 4 °C.

or

Bovine albumin powder	39 g
buffer A, to	1 litre

Store frozen in 200-ml volumes in polyethylene bottles.

30.7. Standard insulin solutions
The following procedure applies to the preparation of standard insulin solutions from the pure solid. (Store solid insulin in a cool, dark place at constant humidity.) *First stock solution (200 μg/ml)*. Avoid condensation of water vapour on the solid protein by allowing the insulin in its container to warm up to room temperature before opening. Weight out accurately about 2 mg insulin into a small tube and add 1 ml of 0.03 M HCl. When solubilization is complete, transfer with washing into a 10-ml volumetric flask and make up to volume, using de-ionized water. Mix thoroughly. With a syringe dispense 0.1-ml volumes into small capped test-tubes. Store deep-frozen. Repeated freezing and thawing of this solution is not recommended.

Second stock solution (2 μg/ml). Allow one of the test-tubes of the first stock solution to thaw, add about 2 ml of buffer B, mix and transfer with the aid of a teat-pipette to a 10-ml graduated vessel. Rinse the test-tube twice more with buffer, add the rinsings to the graduated vessel, make up to 10 ml and mix thoroughly.

This second stock solution may be kept for not more than one week at 2 to 4 °C. Alternatively, it may be dispensed in 0.5 ml volumes and stored deep-frozen, when it will keep for some weeks without noticeable deterioration. Repeated freezing and thawing of this solution is not recommended.

Working standards (to be prepared immediately before use). Prepare an initial working standard containing 20 mμg/ml insulin by diluting 0.5 ml of the second stock solution to 50 ml with buffer B. From this initial standard prepare a series of standards according to the following table:

Standard No.	Initial working standard (ml)	Buffer B (ml)	Final insulin concentration	
			(mμg/ml)	(micro-unit/ml)*
1	0.2	9.8	0.4	10
2	0.2	4.8	0.8	20
3	0.2	1.8	2.0	50
4	1.0	4.0	4.0	100
5	1.0	1.5	8.0	200
6	undiluted	–	20.0	500

* 1 mg = 25 units (approx.).

Procedure

1. Reconstitution of insulin binding reagent

To one bottle of insulin binding reagent add 8 ml of de-ionized water and mix carefully, avoiding foaming. Dispense 0.1- ml volumes with a syringe into precipitin tubes. Each bottle of the reagent is thus sufficient for up to 80 tubes.

Sufficient tubes should be set up for:
(a) 'zeroes', to which no unlabelled insulin is added;
(b) the standard insulin solutions;
(c) the unknowns.

As with other tests of this nature, some form of quality control is desirable in order to detect assays affected by major errors. If a suitable serum is available it can be stored frozen in small aliquots and included in each batch of tests.

At least three tubes should be set up for each determination but additional replicates may be found necessary for adequately precise results. It is advisable to include in each run one or two tubes containing buffer A only (without insulin binding reagent) as controls of washing procedure.

2. Addition of unlabelled insulin

From a syringe add 0.1 ml of insulin-containing solution (standard or unknown) or 0.1 ml of buffer B for the 'zeroes'; use the same syringe throughout, rinsing carefully with each new solution before dispensing. If the insulin content of an unknown is expected to exceed that of the highest standard it should be diluted first in known proportion with buffer B and 0.1 ml of the mixture then taken; mix the contents of each tube, then place the tubes in a refrigerator at 2 to 4 °C for six hours.

3. Addition of labelled insulin

Mix the contents of each tube and add from a syringe 0.1 ml of the working solution of iodinated insulin (250 μμg). Mix again and return the tubes to the refrigerator for 18 hr.

It is convenient at this stage to take samples of the working solution of iodinated insulin for determination of the total radioactivity added to each tube. The method required depends on the type of counter used (see below under 'Determination of radioactivity'); for liquid scintillation counters 0.1 ml of the iodinated insulin and a suitable amount of scintillant should be pipetted into a counting vial, but for the other types of counter 0.1 ml insulin followed by one drop of buffer C is pipetted onto circles of lens tissue supported on suitable planchets (for planchet-type counters) or on pieces of aluminum foil (for well-type crystal scintillation counters). Care should be taken to prevent the fluid overrunning the edges of the lens tissue discs, which should be of the same diameter as the filters used and can be cut from large sheets with a sharp cork borer. The tissues must be allowed to dry before being counted.

4. Filtration

The precipitates in the tubes are collected by micro-filtration through 'Millipore' cellulose acetate membrane filter discs mounted on a 'Millipore' microanalysis filter holder held in a vacuum-filtration flask.

Float sufficient filter discs for a day's use one at a time on the surface of a suitable quantity of buffer C contained in a beaker. Within 10–20 sec all filters become soaked with buffer; they are kept in the buffer until required. Rinse the filter holder with buffer C and assemble with the first disc in place. Keep the tubes in the refrigerator (or on the bench in melting ice) until ready for filtration; they must not be allowed to warm. Buffer C must also be kept cold.

Mix the contents of each tube as before and then deliver to the filter using a teat-pipette; apply suction and wash the tube with two successive portions (approx. 1 ml) of ice-cold buffer C, transferring the washings to the filter. The rate of filtration may decrease after 10–20 samples have been filtered but can be restored to its original value by sucking de-ionized water through the sintered disc of the filter holder. Washing of the filtration apparatus between individual samples is not necessary. It is convenient to use two teat-pipettes for a batch of filtrations, one for transferring buffer C to the precipitin tubes and the other for transferring the assay samples and washes from the precipitin tubes to the filter. After transferring the second wash, this pipette is clean enough to be used for the next sample without further treatment. When filtration of a sample is complete and while the filter is still under vacuum, remove the glass reservoir from the filter and lift the filter disc with the aid of a scalpel blade and forceps.

Subject index p. 557

5. *Determination of radioactivity*

The further treatment of the filter disc depends on the type of counter to be used:
(a) Planchet type (windowless gas-flow and end-window crystal scintillation counters).

Attach the filter discs with rubber solution to unwaxed bottle-top liners. This should be done while the filters are still damp, as otherwise they curl up and fracture during handling. After mounting, dry the discs in covered Petri dishes at 100 °C for 10 min and then for at least another 30 min at 37 °C with the lids partly raised.

(b) Well-type crystal scintillation counters.

Place the filter disc, while still damp, on a 5 cm square of aluminum foil. Fold the foil around the disc and into a pellet; drop the pellet into a test tube of suitable size for the counter. (The foil prevents contamination of the test tube.)

(c) Liquid scintillation counters.

The filters are transferred to empty counting vials and dried for 10 min at 120 °C. The filter is then freed from the surface of the vial if necessary before adding scintillant. Leave at room temperature for one hour before counting.

The filter discs for each sample in the immunoassay, a clean filter for background count-rate determination and the unfiltered samples of iodinated insulin for total count-rate determination should be counted to the desired precision; an accumulated count of 1000 is generally sufficient.

Calculation of results

1. Express the count-rate for each determination in counts per minute. Subtract the background count-rates. Compute the mean count-rates corrected for background for each series of replicates, rejecting any count-rates which are grossly aberrant.

The following are indications of satisfactory operation:

(a) Good agreement between replicates.

(b) Controls (no insulin binding reagent) not more than 5 % of total count (i.e. washing procedure satisfactory).

(c) 'Zero' value (i.e. iodinated insulin bound to antibody precipitate in absence of added unlabelled insulin) in the range 30–50 % of total count. This value is governed by the titre and dilution of the anti-insulin serum used. The titre has been adjusted by the suppliers to give a 'zero' value within this range when used under the conditions described when recently prepared iodinated insulin is used. As this substance ages, the proportion bound decreases so that at the extreme of its useful life this value might fall to 20 %. This does not affect the sensitivity of the determination but results in proportionately lower count rates throughout the assay.

2. Plot on a graph the amount of bound iodinated insulin (as given by the observed count-rate) at each concentration of insulin in the standards and for the 'zero'. The concentration of insulin in each of the unknowns, expressed in terms of the particular species of insulin used as standard, may then be read directly from the graph.

References

ABDEL-SAMIE, U. M., E. BRODA and G. KELLNER (1960) Biochem. J. *75*, 209
ADA, G. L. (1966) Australasian Ann. Med. *15*, 17
AGOSTONI, A., C. VERGANI and B. LOMANTO (1967) J. Lab. Clin. Med. *69*, 522
ALFONSO, E. (1964) Clin. Chim. Acta *10*, 114
ALLISON, A. C. and J. H. HUMPHREY (1959) Nature (Lond.) *183*, 1590
ANTOINE, B. (1962) Science *138*, 977
APPELLA, E. and D. EIN (1967) Proc. Natl. Acad. Sci. *57*, 1449
ARAKI, C. (1937) J. Chem. Soc. Japan *58*, 1338
ARAKI, J. (1956) Bull. Chem. Soc. Japan *29*, 543
ARQUILLA, E., H. OOMS and K. MERCOLA (1968) J. Clin. Invest. *47*, 474
ARRHENIUS, S., and T. MADSEN (1902) In: A. Solomonsen (ed.) Contributions from the University Laboratory for Medical Bacteriology to celebrate the inauguration of the State Serum Institute (Olsen, Copenhagen), ch. 3
ARRHENIUS, S. (1907) Immunochemistry (Macmillan, N.Y.)
ASTRUP, T. and S. MÜLLERTZ (1952) Arch. Biochem. Biophys. *40*, 346
AUGUSTIN, R. (1959) Immunol. *2*, 148
AUGUSTINSSON, K.-B. (1961) Ann. N.Y. Acad. Sci. *94*, 844
AVREAMEAS, S. and K. RAJEWSKY (1963) Nature (Lond.) *201*, 405
AXÉN, R. and J. PORATH (1966) Nature (Lond.) *210*, 367
BAMMER, H. (1964) J. Neurol. Sci. *1*, 129
BECHHOLD, H. (1905) Z. Physik. Chem. *52*, 185
BECKER, W., W. RAPP, H. G. SCHWICK and K. STÖRIKO (1968) Z. Klin. Chem. Klin. Biochem. *3*, 113
BEHRING, E. A. VON and S. KITASATO (1890) Deut. Med. Wochschr. *16*, 1113
BENNINGTON, J. L. (1960) Proc. Soc. Exptl. Biol. Med. *104*, 148
BERENBAUM, M. C., G. M. KITCH and W. A. COPE (1962) Nature (Lond.) *193*, 81
BERGGÅRD, L. (1961) Clin. Chim. Acta *6*, 545
BERSON, S. A., and R. S. YALOW (1961) Nature (Lond.) *191*, 1392
BERSON, A. S., R. S. YALOW, S. M. GLICK and J. ROTH (1964) Metabolism *13*, 10, part 2

BLANC, B. (1959) Bull. Soc. Chim. Biol. *41*, 891

BLANC, B. (1961) In: H. Peeters (ed.) Protides of the biological fluids (Elsevier, Amsterdam) p. 159

BOGDANIKOWA, B., J. DROZD, L. DUBINSKA and T. BOGDANIK (1966) Clin. Chim. Acta *14*, 807

BOLLETT, A. J., J. S. DAVIS and J. O. HURT (1962) J. Exptl. Med. *116*, 109

BÖRNIG, H., J. STÉPAN, A. HORN, R. GIERTLER, G. THIELE and B. VEČEREK (1967) Z. Physiol. Chem. *348*, 1311

BOYD, W. C. (1962) Introduction to immunochemical specificity (Intersci. Publ., N.Y., London)

BRACHET, J. (1940) Compt. Rend. *133*, 88

BRUMMERSTEDT-HANSEN, E. (1957) The serum proteins of the pig (Munksgaard, Copenhagen)

BRUNFELDT, K. (1967) Acta Med. Scand. (Suppl. 476) 53

BRUNFELDT, K., B. A. HANSEN and K. R. JØRGENSEN (1968) Acta Endocrinol. *57*, 307

BUCHANAN-DAVIDSON, D. J. and J. OUDIN (1958) J. Immunol. *81*, 484

BÜRGI, W. (1967) Z. Klin. Chem. Klin. Biochem. *5*, 277

BURNET, M. (1959) The clonal selection theory of acquired immunity (Cambridge Univ. Press)

BURNET, F. M., E. V. KEOGH and D. LUSH (1937) Australian J. Exptl. Biol. Med. Sci. *15*, 231

BURSTEIN, M. (1956) Compt. Rend. *243*, 527

BURSTONE, M. S. (1958) J. Natl. Cancer Inst. *21*, 523

BURTIN, P. (1954) Bull. Soc. Chim. Biol. *36*, 1021

BUSSARD, A. (1959) Biochim. Biophys. Acta *34*, 258

CATT, K., H. D. NIALL and G. W. TREGEAR (1966) Biochem. J. *100*, 31c

CATT, K. and G. TREGAR (1967) Science *158*, 1570

CHESEBRO, B., B. BLOTH and S.-E. SVEHAG (1968) J. Exptl. Med. *127*, 399

CHILSON, O. P., L. A. COSTELLO and N. O. KAPLAN (1965) Biochemistry *4*, 271

CINADER, B. (1963) Ann. N. Y. Acad. Sci. *103*, 495

CLARKE, H. M. G. and T. FREEMAN (1967) In: H. Peeters (ed.) Protides of the biological fluids. XIV Colloquium, Bruges 1966. (Elsevier, Amsterdam) p. 503

CLAUSEN, J. (1960a) World Neurol. *1*, 479

CLAUSEN, J. (1960b) Acta Psychiat. Neurol. Scand. *35*, (Suppl. 148) 11

CLAUSEN, J. (1963) Science Tools *10*, 29

CLAUSEN, J. (1966a) Acta Neurol. Scand. *42*, 153

CLAUSEN, J. (1966b) J. Pharmacol. Exp. Therap. *153*, 167

CLAUSEN, J., S. J. DENCKER and L. SVENNERHOLM (1964) Acta Neurol. Scand. *40*, (Suppl. 10) 89

CLAUSEN, J. and B. FORMBY (1968) Z. Physiol. Chem. *349*, 909

CLAUSEN, J. and J. HEREMANS (1960) J. Immunol. *84*, 128

CLAUSEN, J., I. KRUSE and H. DAM (1965) Scand. J. Clin. Lab. Invest. *17*, 325

CLAUSEN, J. and T. MUNKNER (1960) Proc. Soc. Exptl. Biol. Med. *104*, 40
CLAUSEN, J. and T. MUNKNER (1961) In: H. Peeters (ed.) Protides of the biological fluids. VIII Colloquium, Bruges 1960 (Elsevier, Amsterdam) p. 147
CLAUSEN, J. and T. MUNKNER (1961) Nature (Lond.) *189*, 60
CLAUSEN, J. and B. ØVLISEN (1965) Biochem. J. *97*, 513
COHEN, S. (1963) Biochem. J. *89*, 334
COLOWER, J. (1960) Biochem. J. *78*, 5 P
CROWLE, A. J. (1961) Immunodiffusion (Acad. Press, Inc. N.Y.)
CROWLE, A. J. and D. C. LEAKER (1962) J. Lab. Clin. Med. *59*, 697
CRUMPTON, M. J. (1966) Proc. 2nd FEBS Meeting, Vienna 1965 (Pergamon Press, Oxford) Vol. I p. 61
DAMMACO, F. and J. CLAUSEN (1966) Acta Med. Scand. *179*, 755
DARCY, D. A. (1960) J. Immunol. *3*, 325
DARCY, D. A. (1961) Nature (Lond.) *191*, 1163
DE BOER, W., H. J. HOENDERS, P. A. J. DE BOER and H. A. TOOROP (1967) Clin. Chim. Acta *15*, 533
DECKERT, T. (1964) Insulin antibodies (Thesis, Munksgaard, Copenhagen)
DIXON, M. and E. C. WEBB, (1958) Enzymes (Longmanns Ltd., London)
DRAY, S. (1960) Science *132*, 1313
EDEBO, L. (1960) J. Biochem. Microbiol. Technol. Eng. *2*, 453
EDELMAN, G. M. and M. POULIK (1961) J. Exptl. Med. *113*, 861
EDELMAN, G. M. and J. A. GALLY (1964) Proc. U.S. Natl. Acad. Sci. *51*, 846
EHRLICH, P. and J. MORGENROTH (1900) Dritte Mitteilung, Berl. Klin. Wochschr. *37*, 453
EISEN, H. N. and A. S. KESTON (1949) J. Immunol. *63*, 71
ELEK, S. D. (1948) Brit. Med. J. *1*, 493
EL-MARSAFY, M. K. and Z. ABDEL-GAWAD (1962) Experientia *18*, 240
ENGEL, R. (1966) Deut. Med. Wochschr. *47*, 2125
FAHEY, J. L. and P. HORBETT (1959) J. Biol. Chem. *10*, 234
FAHEY, J. L. and E. M. MCKELVEY (1965) J. Immunol. *94*, 84
FEIGL, F., and A. CALDAS (1953) Anal. Chim. Acta *8*, 117
FEINBERG, J. G. (1959) Feinberg agar gel cutters – data sheet (Shandom Scientific Co., London)
FISHER, L. (1968) This series of manuals to be published
FISHMAN, W. H. (1960) Plasma enzymes, In: Putnam, F. W., The plasma proteins Vol. II (Acad. Press Inc., N.Y.) p. 59
FLEISCHMAN, J. B. (1966) Immunoglobulins, In: Ann. Rev. Biochem. *35*, 835
FOLCH, J., I. ASCOLI, M. LEES, J. A. MEATH, and F. N. LEBARON (1951) J. Biol. Chem. *191*, 833
FORSGREN, A. and J. SJÖQUIST (1966) J. Immunol. *97*, 822
FORSGREN, A. and J. SJÖQUIST (1967) J. Immunol. *99*, 19
FRANCIS, G. E. and A. WORMALL (1948) Biochem. J. *42*, 469

FRANCIS, G. E. and A. WORMALL (1950) Biochem. J. *47*, 380

FRANCQ, J.-.C., A. EYQUEM and P. GRABAR (1959) Rev. Franç. Etudes Clin. Biol. *4*, 821

FRYDENBERG, O. and G. NIELSEN (1965) Hereditas *54*, 123

GARRATT, J. C. (1964) Nature (Lond.) *201*, 1324

GERHARDT, W., J. CLAUSEN, E. CHRISTENSEN and J. RIISHEDE (1963) Acta Neurol. Scand. *39*, 85

GIBIAN, H. (1959) Mucopolysaccharide und Mucopolysaccharidasen. (F. Deuticke, Wien)

GOETTSCH, E. and F. E. KENDALL (1935) J. Biol. Chem. *109*, 221

GOETTSCH, E. and J. D. LYTTLE (1940) J. Clin. Invest. *19*, 9

GOETTSCH, E. and E. B. REEVES (1936) J. Clin. Invest. *15*, 173

GOLDBERG, R. J. (1952) J. Amer. Chem. Soc. *74*, 5715

GORDON, A. H. (1968) This series of manuals to be published

GOTSCHLICH, E. G. and G. M. EDELMAN (1965) Proc. Natl. Acad. Sci. *54*, 588

GOTSCHLICH, E. G. and G. M. EDELMAN (1967) Proc. Natl. Acad. Sci. *57*, 706

GRABAR, P. (1963) Nature (Lond.) *197*, 642

GRABAR, P. and P. BURTIN (1964) Immunoelectrophoretic analysis (Elsevier, Amsterdam) (also: 1960, Analyse immunoélectrophorétique (Masson et Cie., Paris)

GRABAR, P., J. COURÇON, P. L. T. ILBERG, J. F. LOUTIT and J. P. MERRILL (1955) Compt. Rend. *245*, 950

GRABAR, P., J. URIEL and J. COURÇON (1960) Ann. Inst. Pasteur *99*, 13

GRABAR, P. and J. DAUSSANT (1965) Cereal Chem. *41*, 523

GRABAR, P. and C. A. WILLIAMS, Jr. (1953) Biochim. Biophys. Acta *10*, 193

GREENWOOD, F. C., W. M. HUNTER and J. S. GLOVER (1963) Biochem. J. *89*, 114

GRODSKY, G. M. and F. H. FORSHAM (1960) J. Clin. Invest. *39*, 1070

GUSTAVSON, G. T., J. SJÖQUIST and G. STÅLENHEIM (1967) J. Immunol. *98*, 1178

HABER, E., E. B. PAGE and F. F. RICHARDS (1965) Anal. Biochem. *12*, 163

HAKOMORI, S. (1965) In: E. A. Balazs and R. W. Jeanloz (eds.) The amino sugars, Vol. II. A (Acad. Press Inc., N.Y.)

HALES, C. N. and P. J. RANDLE (1963) Biochem. J. *88*, 137

HANKS, J. H. (1935) J. Immunol. *28*, 95

HANSON, L. Å. (1961) Int. Arch. Allergy Appl. Immunol. *18*, 241

HEIDE, K. (1960) Behringwerk-Mitt. *38*, 3

HEIDE, K. and H. HAUPT (1964), Behringwerk-Mitt. *43*, 161

HEIDELBERGER, M. and F. E. KENDALL (1929) J. Exper. Med. *50*, 809

HEIDELBERGER, M. and F. E. KENDALL (1935) J. Exper. Med. *62*, 697

HEIDELBERGER, M. C. MACLEAD, S. F. KAISER and B. ROBINSON (1946) J. Exper. Med. *83*, 303

HEIDELBERGER, M. and M L. WOLFRAM (1954) Federation Proc. *13*, 496

HEIMBURGER, N. and G. SCHWICK (1962) Thromb. Diath. Haemorrhag. *7*, 432

HELMKAMP, R. W., M. A. CONTRERAS and W. F. BALE (1967a) Int. J. Appl. Radiat. Isotopes *18*, 737

HELMKAMP, R. W., M. A. CONTRERAS and M. J. IZZO (1967b) Int. J. Appl. Radiat. Isotopes *18*, 747

HERBERT, V., K. S. LOU, C. H. GOTTLIEB and J. BLEICHER (1965) J. Clin. Endoc. Metab. *25*, 1375

HEREMANS, J. (1960) Les globulins sériques du système gamma (Editions Arscia S.A., Bruxelles)

HIRSCHFELD, J. (1960) Nature (Lond.) *185*, 164

HIRSCHFELD, J. (1962) The Gc system. Immunoelectrophoretic studies of normal human sera with special reference to a new genetically determined system (Gc). Thesis. In Progr. Allergy *6*, 24

HITZIG, W. H. (1963) Die Plasmaproteine in der klinischen Medizin (Springer Verlag, Berlin)

HJERTÉN, S. (1962) Biochim. Biophys. Acta *62*, 445

HOCHWALD, G. M., G. J. THORBECKE and R. ASOFSKY (1961) J. Exper. Med. *114*, 459

HOSSAINI, A. A. (1966) Am. J. Clin. Pathol. *46*, 507

HOTCHKISS, R. D. (1948) Arch. Biochem. *16*, 131

HUGHES-JONES, N. C., B. GARDNER and R. TELFORD (1963) Biochem. J. *88*, 435

HUNTER, W. M. and F. C. GREENWOOD (1962) Biochem. J. *85*, 39P

INOUE, K., S. NOJIMA and T. TOMIZAWA (1965) J. Biochem. *57*, 824

ISHIZAKA, K., T. ISHIZAKA and M. HORNBROOK (1967a) J. Immunol. *97*, 75

ISHIZAKA, K., T. ISHIZAKA and H. HORNBROOK (1967b) J. Immunol. *97*, 840

JENNINGS, R. K. (1959) J. Immunol. *83*, 237

JENNINGS, R. K. and M. A. KAPLAN (1960) Intern. Arch. Allergy Appl. Immunol. *17*, 267

JENNINGS, R. K. and F. MALONE (1957) J. Pathol. Bacteriol. *74*, 81

JENSEN, K. (1959) Undersøgelser over Stafylococcernes antigenstruktur (E. Munksgaard, Copenhagen)

JERNE, N. K., 1951, A study of avidity, in: Communications de Statens Seruminstitut, vol. 41

JERNE, N. K. and L. SKOVSTED (1953) Ann. Inst. Pasteur *84*, 73

JIRGENSON, B. (1958) Organic colloids (Elsevier, Amsterdam) p. 396

JOHANSSON, S. G. O. (1967) Lancet p. 951

JOHANSSON, S. G. O., T. MELLBIN and B. VAHLQUIST (1968) Lancet p. 1118

KABAT, E. A. (1956) Blood group substances (Acad. Press Inc., N.Y.)

KABAT, E. A. (1957) J. Cell. Comp. Physiol. *50*, (Suppl. 1) 79

KABAT, E. A. (1960) Bull. Soc. Chim. Biol. *42*, 1549

KABAT, E. A., M. GLUSMAN and V. KNAUB (1948) Am. J. Med. *4*, 653

KABAT, E. A. and M. M. MAYER (1961) Experimental immunochemistry, 2nd edn. (C. C Thomas, Springfield, Ill.)

KALEE, E., S. DEBIASI, C. KARYPIDIS, K. HEIDE and H. G. SCHWICK (1964) Acta Isotopica 4, 103

KAPLAN, N. O. and S. WHITE (1963) Ann. N. Y. Acad. Sci. 103, 835

KARUSH, F. (1958) Trans. N. Y. Acad. Sci. 20, 581

KENDALL, F. E. (1938) Cold Spring Harbor Symposia on Quantitative Biolcgy 6, 376

KEUTEL, H. J. (1960) Klin. Wochschr. 15, 768

KEUTEL, H. J. (1964) Ann. N. Y. Acad. Sci. 121, 484

KLEINSCHMIDT, W. J. and P. D. BOYER (1952) J. Immunol. 69, 247

KLOTZ, I. M. (1946) J. Am. Chem. Soc. 68, 2899

KOCH, R. (1891) Deut. Med. Wochschr. 17, 101

KÖELLE, G. B. and J. S. FRIEDENWALD (1949) Proc. Soc. Exptl. Biol. Med. 70, 617

KOHN, J. (1958) Clin. Chim. Acta 3, 450

KOHN, J., 1959, In: H. Peeters (ed.) Protides of the biological fluids. VI Colloquium, Bruges 1958 (Elsevier, Amsterdam) p. 74

KOHN, J. (1962) In: H. Peeters (ed.) Protides of the biological fluids. IX Colloquium, Bruges 1961 (Elsevier, Amsterdam) p. 120

KOHN, J. (1967) Exhibition. In: H. Peeters (ed.) Protides of the biological fluids. XIII Colloquium, Bruges 1967 (Elsevier, Amsterdam)

KOHN, J. (1968) Nature (Lond.) 217, 1261

KORNGOLD, L. and G. VAN LEEUWEN (1957) J. Immunol. 78, 172

KRATZKY, O., G. PORAD, A. SEKORA and B. PALETTA (1955) J. Polymer Sci. 16, 163

KRAUS, R. (1897) Wien. Klin. Wochschr. 10, 736

LANDON, J., T. LIVANOU and F. C. GREENWOOD (1967) Biochem. J. 105, 1075

LANDSTEINER, K. and J. VAN DER SCHEER (1928) J. Exptl. Med. 48, 315

LATERRE, E. C. and J. F. HEREMANS (1963) Clin. Chim. Acta 8, 220

LAURELL, C. B. (1966) Analyt. Biochem. 15, 45

LAZARUS, L. and J. D. YOUNG (1966) J. Clin. Endocrinol. Metab. 26, 213

LOMANTO, B. and C. VERGANI (1967) Clin. Chim. Acta 15, 169

LÜDERITZ, O., A. M. STAUB and O. WESTPHAL (1966) Bacteriol. Rev. 30, 193

LUNDH, B. (1965) Acta Univ. Lundensis 27, 1

LUNDKVIST, U. and P. PERLMANN (1967) Immunology 13, 179

MACDONALD, H. J. and J. Q. KISSANE (1960) Analyt. Biochem. 2, 178

MAEGRAITH, B. C. (1933) Brit. J. Exptl. Pathol. 14, 227

MAHLER, H. R. and E. H. CORDES (1966) Biological chemistry (Harper Internat., N. Y.)

MALAPRADE, L. (1928) Compt. Rend. Soc. Biol. (Paris) 186, 625

MANCINI, G., A. O. CARBONERA and J. F. HEREMANS (1965) Immunochemistry 2, 235

MANCINI, G., J. P. VAERMAN, A. O. CARBONERA and J. F. HEREMANS (1964) In: H. Peeters (ed.) Protides of the biological fluids. XI Colloquium, Bruges 1963 (Elsevier, Amsterdam) p. 370

MANSOUR, T. E., E. BEUDING and A. B. STRABITSKY (1954) Brit. J. Pharmacol. *9*, 182

MARKOWITZ, H. and M. HEIDELBERGER (1954) J. Am. Chem. Soc. *76*, 1317

MCFARLANE, A. S. (1963) J. Clin. Invest. *42*, 346

MCMANUS, J. F. A. (1946) Nature (Lond.) *158*, 202

METCHNIKOFF, E. (1892) Leçon sur la pathologie comparû de l'inflammation (G. Masson, Paris)

MOOG, F. and P. U. ANGELETTI (1962) Biochim. Biophys. Acta *60*, 440

MORGAN, W. T. J. (1956) In The Josiah Macy Jr. Foundation Transact. I. Conf. (April 1955, New York)

MOSS, P. W., D. M. CAMPBELL, E. MAGNASTORE-KAKURAS and E. J. KING (1961) Biochem. J. *81*, 441

MÜLLER-EBERHARD, H. J. and U. NILSSON (1960) J. Exptl. Med. *111*, 217

MÜLLER-EBERHARD, H. J., U. NILSSON and T. ARONSSON (1960) J. Exptl. Med. *111*, 201

MURPHY, F. A., OSEBOLD, J. W. and O. AALUND (1965) Arch. Biochem. Biophys. *112*, 126

MURPHY, F. A., J. W. OSEBOLD and O. AALUND (1966) J. Infect. Diseases *116*, 99

NACHLAS, M. M. and A. SELIGMAN (1949) J. Natl. Cancer Inst. *9*, 415

NAIRN, R. C. (1964) Fluorescent protein tracing. 2nd. edn. (Livingstone Ltd., Edinburgh)

NERSTRØM, B. and J. SKAFTE JENSEN (1963) Acta Pathol. Microbiol. Scand. *58*, 257

NEURATH, A. R. (1965) Z. Naturforsch. *20b*, 974

NICOLLE, M., E. CESARI and E. DEBAIN (1920) Ann. Inst. Pasteur *34*, 596

NIECE, J. L. and J. T. BARRETT (1963) Nature (Lond.) *197*, 1021

NISSELBAUM, J. S., M. SCHLAMOWITZ and O. BODANSKY (1961) Ann. N. Y. Acad. Sci. *94*, 970

OAKLEY, C. L. and A. J. FULTHORPE (1953) J. Pathol. Bacteriol. *65*, 49

ONCLEY, J. L., K. W. WALTEN and D. G. CORNWELL (1957) J. Am. Chem. Soc. *72*, 4666

OUCHTERLONY, Ø. (1949) Arkiv Kemi *1*, 43

OUCHTERLONY, Ø. (1962) Diffusion-in-gel methods for immunological analysis. II. Progr. Allergy VI

OUCHTERLONY, Ø. (1967) In: Weir (ed.) Handbook of experimental immunology, p. 655

OUDIN, J. (1946) Compt. Rend. *222*, 115

OUDIN, J. (1952) Methods Med. Res. *5*, 335

OUDIN, J. (1956) Compt. Rend. *242*, 2489

PARKER, W. C. and A. G. BEARN (1962) J. Exptl. Med. *115*, 83

PARKER, W. C., J. W. C. HAGSTRÖM and A. G. BEARN (1963) J. Exptl. Med. *118*, 975

PASTEUR, L. (1876) Etudes sur La Bière (Gauthiers-Villars, Paris)

PEARSE, A. G. E. (1961) Histochemistry–theoretical and applied. 2nd edn. (J. & A. Churchill Ltd., London)

PEETERS, A. and P. VUYLSTEKE (1960) In: H. Peeters (ed.) Protides of the biological fluids (Elsevier, Amsterdam) p. 31

PERLMANN, P., G. C. GOERINGER and U. LUNDKVIST (1964) In: H. Peeters (ed.) Protides of the biological fluids (Elsevier, Amsterdam) p. 232

PETERSON, E. A. (1969) This series of manuals to be published

PETRIE, G. F. (1932) Brit. J. Exptl. Path. *13*, 38

PETTE, D. and I. STUPP (1960) Klin. Wochschr. *1*, 109

PIGMAN, W., E. GRANLING and H. L. HOLLEY (1961) Biochim. Biophys. Acta *46*, 100

PITT-RIVERS, R. and J. R. TATA (1959) The thyroid hormones (Pergamon Press, London)

POLSON, A. (1958) Biochim. Biophys. Acta *29*, 426

PORTER, R. R. (1959) Biochem. J. *73*, 119

PORTER, R. R. (1967) Biochem. J. *105*, 417

POULIK, M. D. (1952) Can. J. Med. Sci. *30*, 417

POULIK, M. D. (1958) Federation Proc. *17*, 530

POULIK, M. D. (1964a) In: H. Peeters (ed.) Protides of the biological fluids. XI Colloquium, Bruges 1963 (Elsevier, Amsterdam)

POULIK, M. D. (1964b) Ann. N. Y. Med. Sci. *121*, 470

PRADER, A. (1966) Triangle. Sandoz J. Med. Sci. *7*, 200

PREER, J. R. (1956) J. Immunol. *77*, 52

PUTNAM, F. W., K. TITANI, M. WINKLER and T. SHINODA (1967) Cold Spring Harbor Symp. Quant. Biol. *32*, 9

PUTNAM, F. W., K. TOMINAGA, G. M. BERNIER and C. W. EASLEY (1964) Proc. IV. Internat. Symp. of R.E.S. Otsu and Kayato, Japan

RASKA, K. and K. COHEN (1968) Nature (Lond.) *217*, 720

RAUNIO, V. (1968) Acta Pathol. Microbiol. Scand. Suppl. *195* (thesis)

RESSLER, N. (1960a) Clin. Chim. Acta *5*, 359

RESSLER, N. (1960b) Clin. Chim. Acta *5*, 795

RITZMAN, S. E., R. H. THURM, W. E. TRUAUX and W. C. LEVIN (1960) Arch. Intern. Med. *105*, 939

ROBBINS, J. B., K. KENNY and E. SUTER (1965) J. Exptl. Med. *122*, 385

SCHÄFER, W. (1958) Behringwerk-Mitt. *35*, 33

SCHALCH, D. and M. PARKER (1964) Nature (Lond.) *203*, 1141

SCHEIDEGGER, J. J. (1955) Intern. Arch. Allergy Appl. Immunol. *7*, 103

SCHERAGA, N. A. (1963) In: H. Neurath (ed.) Intramolecular bonds in proteins. II (Academic Press Inc., N.Y.) p. 477

SCHLAMOWITZ, M. (1954) J. Biol. Chem. *206*, 368

SCHMID, K. and J. B. BENETTE (1961) Nature (Lond.) *19D*, 630

SCHULTZE, H. E. (1957) Scand. J. Clin. Lab. Invest. *10* (Suppl. 31) 135

SCHULTZE, H. E. (1961) Immunitätslehre. In: R. Cobet, K. Gutzeit and H. E. Bock (eds.) Klin. der Gegenwart. Handbuch der praktischen Med. (Verlag von Urban & Schwarzenberg, München-Berlin)

SCHULTZE, H. E. (1962) Zentr. Bakteriol. Parasitenk. *184*, 324

SCHULTZE, H. E., H. HAUPT, K. HEIDE and N. HEIMBURGER (1962) Clin. Chim. Acta *8*, 207

SCHULTZE, H. E. and J. F. HEREMANS (1966) Molecular biology of human proteins Vol. I (Elsevier, Amsterdam)

SCHULTZE, H. E. and G. SCHWICK (1957) Behringwerk-Mitt. *33*, 11

SCHUSTER, H., G. SCHRAMM and W. ZILLIG (1956) Z. Naturf. *11b*, 339

SCHWICK, G. (1967) Biochemie der Fibrinolyse. In: W. Künzer, G. Winckelmann and C. Walther (eds.) Verh. Deut. Arbeitsgemeinschaft, Butgerinnungsf. (Schattauer-Verlag, Stuttgart) p. 27

SCHWICK, H. G. and K. STÖRIKO (1965) Proc. 10th Europ. Soc. Haemat., Strasbourg (Karger Ltd., Basel) Part II p. 899

SELIGMAN, A. M. (1951) J. Biol. Chem. *7*, 190

SIA, R. H. P. and S. F. CHUNG (1932) Proc. Soc. Exptl. Biol. Med. *29*, 792

SINGER, S. J. and D. H. CAMPBELL (1952) J. Am. Chem. Soc. *74*, 1794

SINGER, S. J. and R. F. DOOLITTLE (1966) Science *153*, 13

SMITHIES, O. (1955) Biochem. J. *61*, 629

SMITHIES, O. (1959) Biochem. J. *71*, 585

STANWORTH, D. R., J. H. HUMPHREY, H. BENNICH and S. G. O. JOHANSSON (1967) Lancet *ii*, p. 330

STÖRIKO, K. (1965) Ärztl. Lab. *11*, 189

SÜLLMANN, H. (1964) Clin. Chim. Acta *10*, 569

SWEET, L. C., G. D. ABRAMS and A. G. JOHNSON (1965) J. Immunol. *94*, 105

TEILUM, G. (1956) Am. J. Path. *32*, 945

TENGERDY, R. P. and W. N. SMALL (1966) Nature (Lond.) *210*, 708

TILLET, W. S. and T. FRANCIS, Jr. (1930) J. Exptl. Med. *52*, 561

TIZELIUS, A. (1937) Trans. Faraday Soc. *33*, 524

TOMASI, T. B. and S. ZIGELBAUM (1963) J. Clin. Invest. *42*, 1552

URIEL, J. (1958) Clin. Lab. (Zaragoza) *65*, 87

URIEL, J. (1960, 1964) In: P. Grabar and P. Burtin, vide supra

URIEL, J. and S. AVRAMEAS (1961) Compt. Rend. *101*, 104

URIEL, J., S. AVRAMEAS and P. GRABAR (1964) In: H. Peeters (ed.) Protides of the biological fluids. XI Colloquium, Bruges 1963 (Elsevier, Amsterdam) p. 355

URIEL, J., H. GÖTZ and P. GRABAR (1957) Schweiz. Med. Wochschr. *87*, 231

URIEL, J. and P. GRABAR (1961) Anal. Biochem. *2*, 82

URIEL, J. and P. GRABAR (1956) Bull. Soc. Chim. Biol. *38*, 1253

VALENTINE, R. C. and N. M. GREEN (1967) J. Mol. Biol. *27*, 615

VAN ALTEN, J. and A. LaVELLE (1966) Exper. Neurol. *14*, 115

VAN DEN BERG, A. A. H. and P. MÜLLER (1916) Biochem. Z. *77*, 90

VAN FURTH, R., H. R. E. SCHUIT and W. HIJMANS (1966) Immunol. *11*, 1

VAN OSS, C. J. and Y. S. L. HECK (1961) Z. Immunitätsforsch. *122*, 44

VERGANI, C., R. STABILINI and A. AGOSTONI (1967) Immunochem. *4*, 233

WAXDAL, M. J., W. H. KONIGSBERG and G. M. EDELMAN (1967) Cold Spring Harbor Symp. Quant. Biol. *32*, 53

WEETALL, H. H. and J. BOZICEVICH (1967) Nature *215*, 1479

WHO (1964) Congress about nomenclature of immunoglobulins. Bull. World Health Organ. *30*, 447

WHO (1968) Bull. World Health Organ. (in press)

WIDE, L., R. AXÉN and J. PORATH (1967) Immunochemistry *4*, 381

WIDE, L. and J. PORATH (1966) Biochim Biophys. Acta *130*, 257

WIEME, R. J. (1957) Rev. Belge Pathol. Med. Exptl. *25*, 62

WIEME, R. J. (1959) Studies on agar gel electrophoresis (Arcia Uitgaven N.V., Brussels; and Elsevier, Amsterdam, 1965).

WILKINSON, J. H. (1965) Isoenzymes (Spon Ltd., London)

WILSON, A. T. (1964) J. Immunol. *92*, 431

WILSON, M. W. (1958) J. Immunol. *81*, 317

WOKER, G. (1914) Ber. *47*, 1024

WORK, E. (1967) Folia Microbiol. *12*, 220

WURMSER, R. and S. FILITTI-WURMSER (1957) Progr. Biophys. Chem. *7*, 88

YALOW, R. S. and S. A. BERSON (1960) Am. J. Med. *29*, 1

YALOW, R. S. and S. A. BERSON (1966) Trans. N. Y. Acad. Sci. *28*, 1033

Subject index